CW01218593

ORIENT-EXPRESS
HOTELS

VENICE
REVISITED

SANDRA HARRIS

DEDICATION

For Natale Rusconi,
without whom this book
would never have happened.

PICTURE CAPTIONS FOR FRONTMATTER
Cover picture: Doorway of Santa Maria Gloriosa dei Frari.
Endpapers: Reflections in the Grand Canal.
Page 1: The church of San Giorgio Maggiore at dawn.
Title page: The church of San Giorgio Maggiore in the evening as the sun sets.
Pages 6-7: Panoramic plan of Venice and the Islands.
Pages 8-9: A bird's eye view of Venice and the Lagoon.
Pages 12-13: On the Grand Canal at sunset looking towards Palazzo Grassi and the traghetto stop.

"IS THERE ANYONE BUT MUST REPRESS A SECRET THRILL, ON ARRIVING IN VENICE FOR THE FIRST TIME, OR RETURNING THITHER AFTER A LONG ABSENCE, AND STEPPING INTO A VENETIAN GONDOLA?"

THOMAS MANN, 'DEATH IN VENICE'

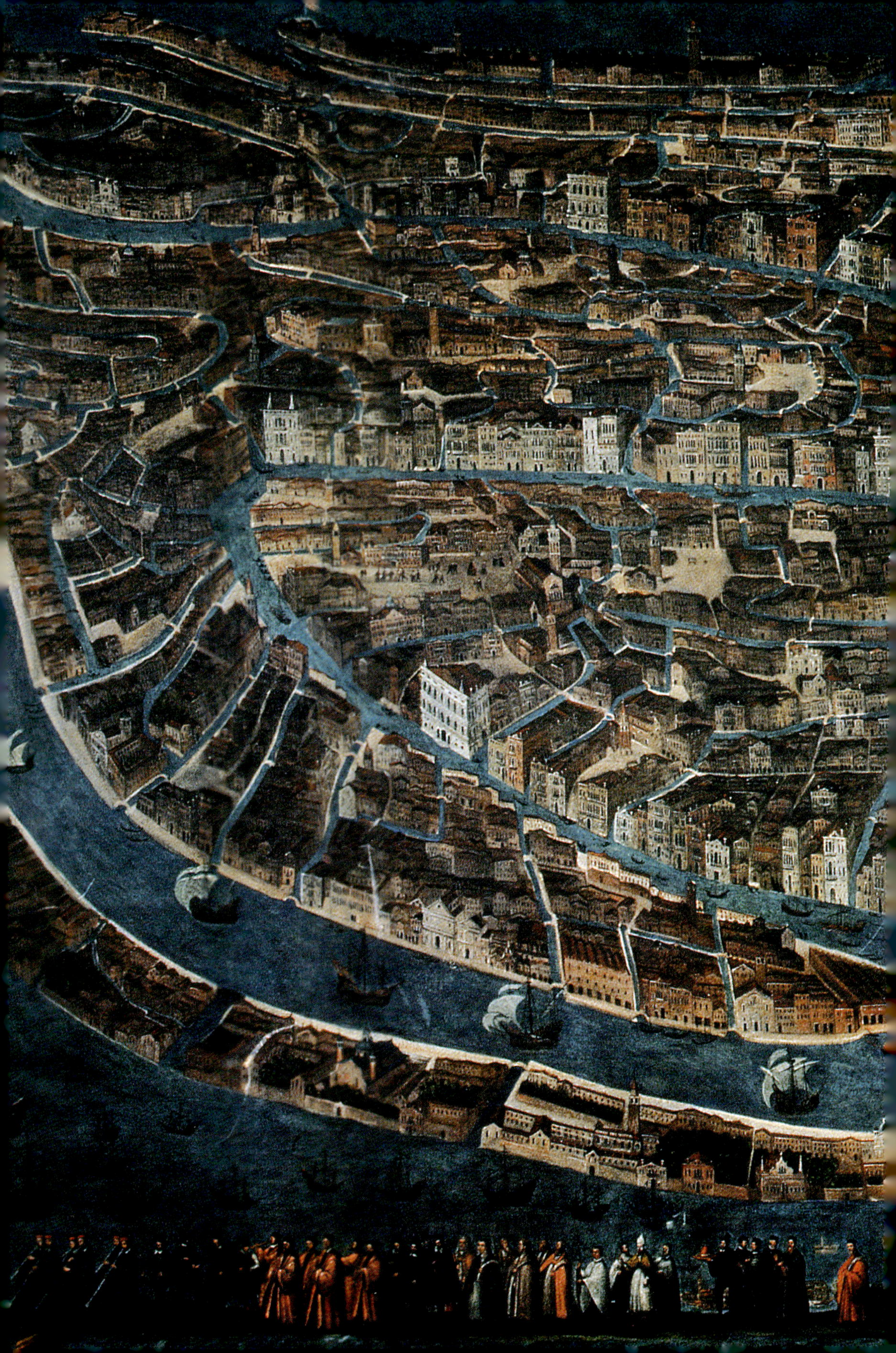

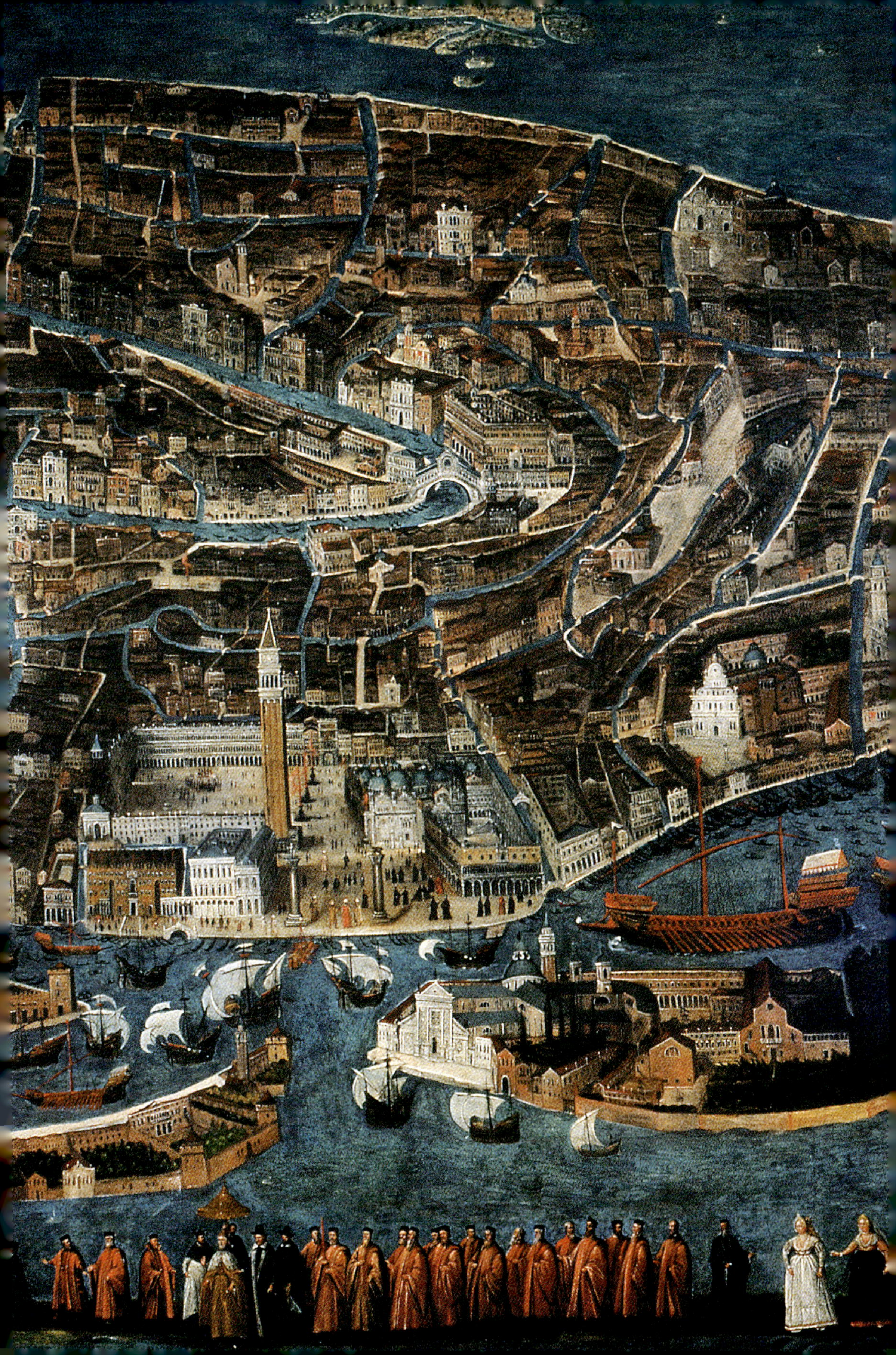

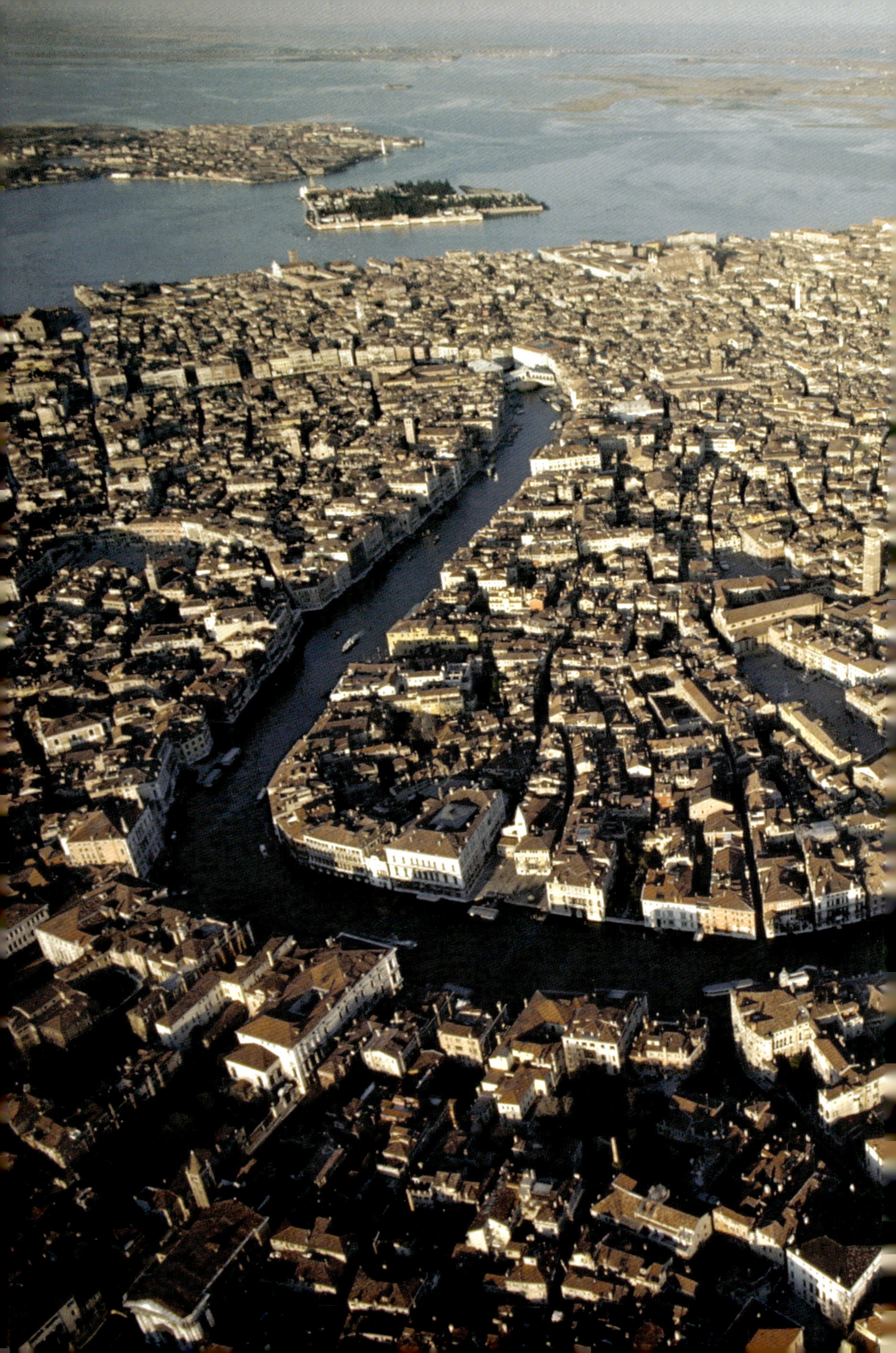

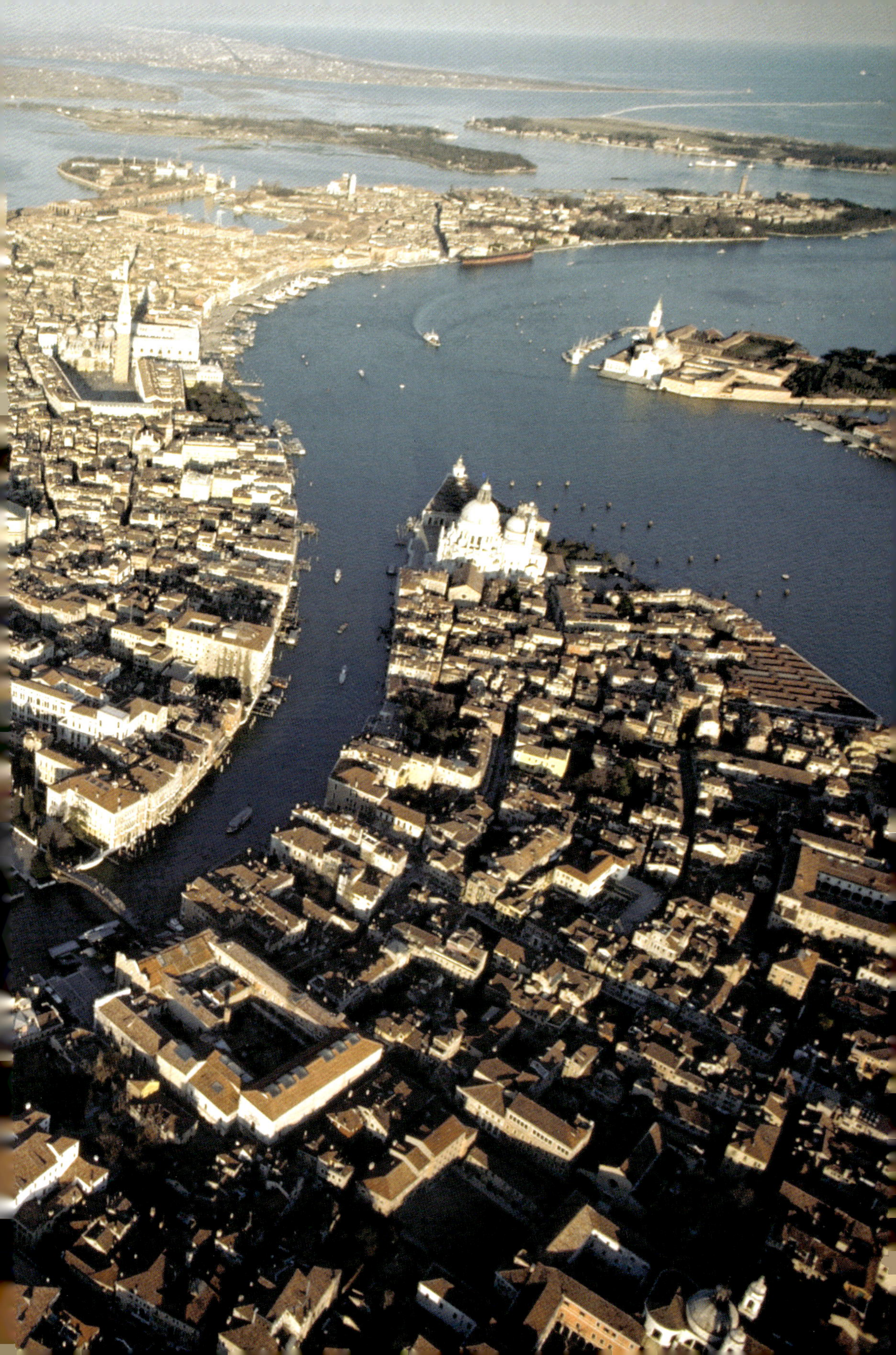

CONT

PREFACE 14
VENICE – LA SERENISSIMA 16
ONE: ARCHITECTURAL TREASURES 42
    IN PRAISE OF GOD AND BEAUTY 44
    BEHIND THE FAÇADES 46
    BRIDGES TO SIGH OVER 50
    CRUMBLING MAGNIFICENCE 52

TWO: CULTURAL DELIGHTS 86
    SAVOURING THE SUPERLATIVES 88
    LIVING ARTISTS, LIVING ART 90
    THE PERFORMING ARTS 92
    EASTERN MYSTIQUE 96

ENTS

THREE: RETAIL INDULGENCE 114
    FAMOUS LABELS 116
    THE ART OF VENETIAN GLASS 120
    SILKS, SATINS, BUTTONS, BOWS 122
    DISCOVERING THE UNUSUAL 124

FOUR: GOURMET PLEASURES 146
    OF MARKETS AND MANNERS 148
    CLASSIC RESTAURANTS 152
    OFF THE BEATEN TRACK 153
    ON THE BACARO TRAIL 154
    SWEET TEMPTATIONS 156

FIVE: THE HIGH LIFE 184
    MASQUERADE 188
    FESTIVAL TIME 192

SIX: AFTER DARK 216
    THE INTIMACY OF SILENCE 218
    A COCKTAIL LEGEND 222
    THE SOUND OF MUSIC – CLASSICAL 224
    THE SOUND OF MUSIC – JAZZ 226

SEVEN: COMING BACK 244
    COURSES IN VENICE 246
    A PERSONAL MASTERPIECE 250
    THE LAGOON 252

DIRECTORY 266
PICTURE CAPTIONS 280
ACKNOWLEDGEMENTS 288

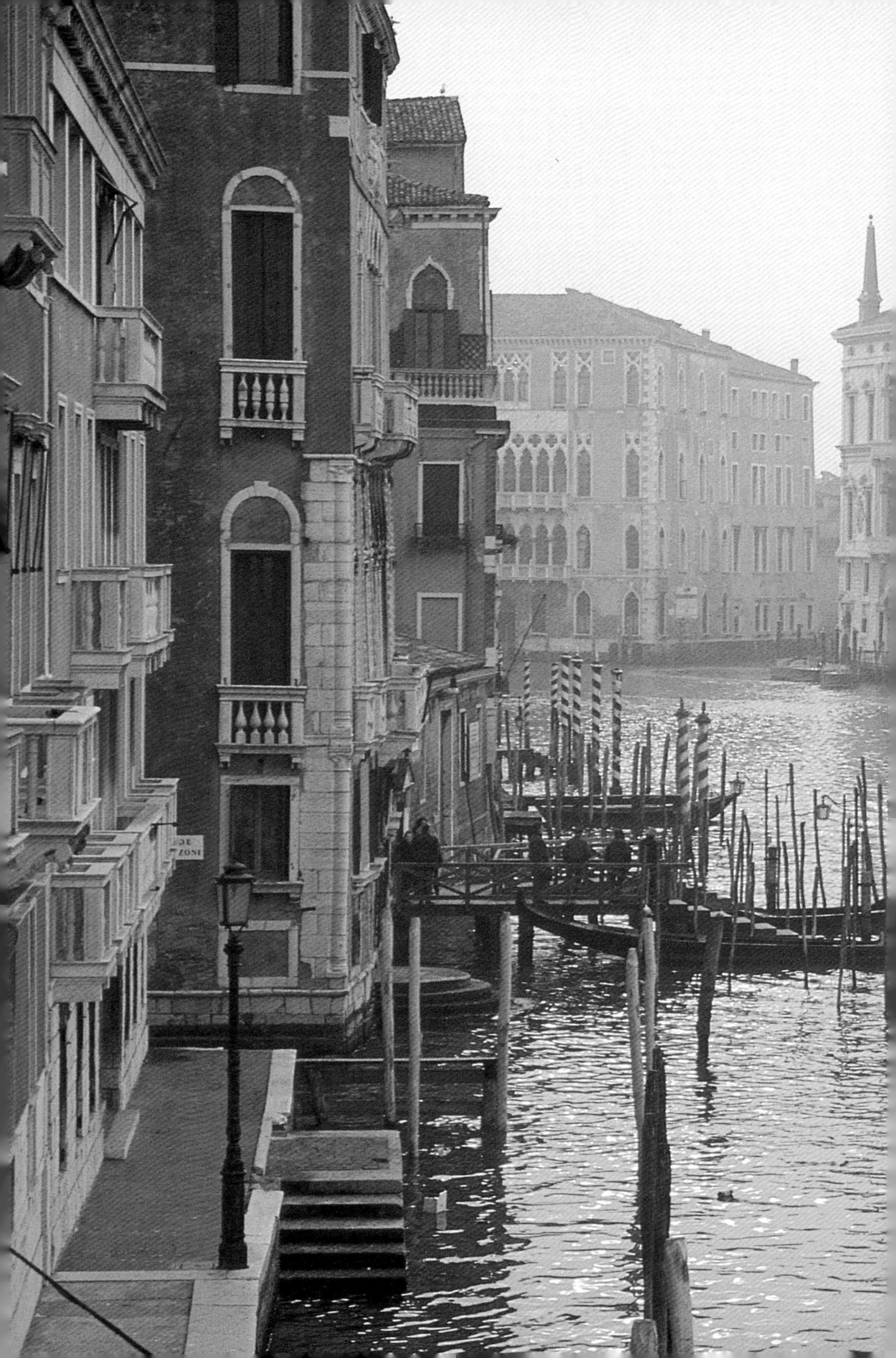

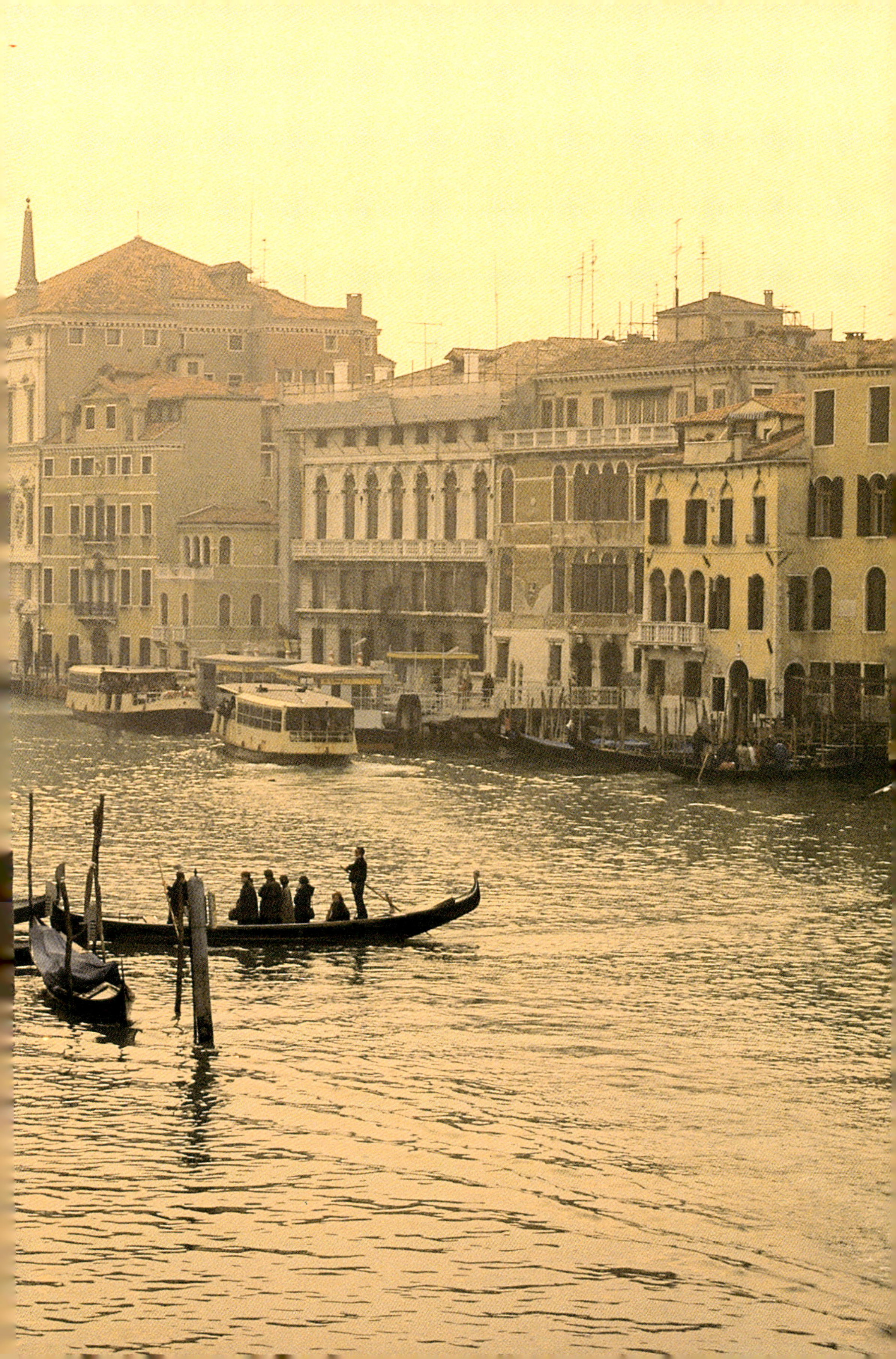

PREFA

At Orient-Express, our guests often ask us to share our secrets about the cities in which we live and work, or even just the ones we love. So when the opportunity arose to be involved with a series of books celebrating some of our favourite cities and their 'spirit of place' we were delighted to join in.

Such books can never be comprehensive; many places or experiences that are featured in every guidebook may well have been left out. But in their place are some insights, special glimpses that may not have been seen before. What we are talking about here is the joy of discovery which cities like Venice, Paris, London or Florence can still offer, if you know where to look, over and over and over again.

Venice is very much at the heart of Orient-Express, being the city where we purchased our first hotel, Hotel Cipriani, in 1976 and the home of the Venice Simplon-Orient-Express. It is also a vibrant, lively community, which lives and breathes behind the crumbling façades of the great *palazzi* of the Grand Canal. It is this beating heart of Venice that is celebrated in this book, which we applaud and heartily endorse.

In her own discovery of Venice, the author, Sandra Harris, made many stops on the way, all of which are listed in the back of the book, with the nearest thing you can get to an address in Venice, and opening times when they are applicable and not just a matter of whim. But getting lost is a prerequisite to getting under the skin of a city and coming to know it. We hope that you enjoy the experience.

SIMON SHERWOOD
President, Orient-Express Hotels

INTRODUCTION

VENICE ~ LA S

"What is there left to say about Venice? It has all

ERENISSIMA

been said." So wrote Canon Pietro Casola in 1494.

Centuries later, in the 1960s, Mary McCarthy noted much the same thing. "Nothing can be said here," she wrote, "including this statement, that has not been said before." But we don't listen, and for the past five hundred or so years legions of us, whole armies of writers and poets from Petrarch to Byron to Goethe to Proust to Jan Morris and John Julius Norwich, still insist on trying, just one more time, to capture the essence, the special, extraordinary quality that is Venice.

We write of the city's female quality, the way Venice can be daunting one moment and flirtatious the next, capturing hearts and minds with spectacular arrogance. Look at the purity of line, we exclaim, at the way she knows her best light and exploits it ruthlessly. But that is hardly new. Venice has a million lovers – the fact that she is mistress of both sexes and all nationalities is a celebrated part of her charm.

Then there is the theatricality of Venice. This is such an opera of a city, melodramatic in one light, tragic in another, comedic in a third which makes it a perfect setting for *Carnevale*. In the 18th century, as Maurice Andrieux observed in his book, *Daily Life in Venice During Casanova's Time*, life was just one endless round of pageants and pleasure-seeking. It started in October, winding down for Christmas then back again for the Feast of Epiphany leaving just a brief respite for Lent only to start again on Ascension Day. Such a mix and match of high and low brows, male and female, Grand Duchess and gondolier made for a heady cocktail of sensual revelry enjoyed by all. The use of masks was so popular that the makers had their own official artisan status, devising ever more elaborate and bizarre concoctions.

Wander now through the *calli* behind the Piazza San Marco and the Rialto and the selection of mask shops in Venice is rivalled only by smart restaurants and glass showrooms. Yet still we are fascinated by the extravagant disguises handmade by Venetian craftsmen. Still we love to hide ourselves behind the mask of the Faery Queen, The Devil or the Capitano with its beak nose and mischievous expression. When Pietro Casolo was writing guidebooks in the 15th century, the beak was stuffed with medicinal herbs and was used by physicians, intent upon protecting themselves from the plague. Today, the wearing of the Capitano mask, or any other flamboyant creation, may be just fun and games, but there is still an atmosphere that is not wholly European, that has more than a hint of the East about it.

After all it was in Venice that the cult of the Orient began. Marco Polo was a Venetian, and Venetian merchants of the 15th century, forever searching for the exquisite, the extraordinary, the amazing, travelled widely throughout Central Asia, intent on producing Oriental fineries never seen before. In her 15th century heyday, Venice was mistress of the eastern Mediterranean. Her wealth, which was stupendous, came from eastern commerce. "All the gold in Christendom," as one medieval chronicler accurately observed, "passes through the hands of the Venetians." Nor was she averse to finding something she admired and making it her own. The art of marbling paper, which became a Venetian speciality, originated in Japan around the year AD1000. The gorgeous silks, the exquisite tapestries, the exotic *objets d'art* we marvel at and long to copy were often picked up by wily Venetian traders.

As for her beauty, it is almost a cliché: Venice, glistening in a lilac-shaded mist on a winter's morning; Venice when the sun is setting and the wide waters of the Grand Canal are flushed with a rose-tinted light; Venice at night when the prettiest street lamps in the world, thoughtfully coloured green and pink, bathe her in a light that is the stuff of fairytales. No wonder American writer Mary McCarthy described the Piazza San Marco as "like a painted stage flat". "A fact," she wrote, "that everyone notices and which everybody thinks he has discovered for himself."

Yet isn't this the cleverest trick of all? That each morning as Venice wakes up and decides her mood for the day, sun splashed and girlish one morning, moody and grey on another, she convinces a whole new set of visitors that she is there for them alone? To come upon a shaded courtyard, empty of life except for a fastidious and well-fed Venetian cat polishing off a tangle of spaghetti thoughtfully left by a sympathetic citizen, is a once-only moment. To view a famous Madonna, only to see at her feet the kneeling figure of an old lady deep in prayer is another. To come across a gaggle of gondoliers in their favourite bistro tucking into a plate of pasta and a bottle or two of house red, in preparation for a hard afternoon's rowing up and down the canals, gives one yet another perspective on Venice. And the best of all, is finding a favourite view, possibly from the Accademia Bridge looking towards Madonna della Salute or on the terrace of Cip's Club on the island of the Giudecca looking towards San Marco, and coming back at different times of the day to watch the changes. Venice at night, Venice on a Tiepolo morning when the sun dances on the water, Venice on a lazy afternoon or on a misty evening; all present the city in different lights and different moods.

Henry James grumbled that "in Venice originality of attitude is utterly impossible". Yet the effect of Venice still surprises. A ruffle of Fortuny fabric, a splash of Titian red in a contemporary painting, shimmering reflections on a glass vase, elegant slices of golden polenta, a classic combination of champagne and peaches, are all Venice inspired. They are small things, moments, glimpses, but they heighten our senses and infiltrate our lives through art, through design, through the food we eat and the wine we drink.

The city behind the crumbling façades has an energy of its own that is ancient and modern at the same time. Visitors who arrive by train only have to step out of the station to step into a live Canaletto painting. The panorama in front of their eyes, the chatter, the hustle and the bustle, the living, breathing pulse of life on the Grand Canal would be instantly recognized by the artist 200 years ago. Yet it is a scene like no other, with the buildings of rose and terracotta, of vanilla and deep ochre, of Tiepolo blue and pistachio green, providing a backdrop for the countless craft that splash and criss-cross in front of them.

In Canaletto's day there were gondolas and flags and gossipy housewives arguing with fishermen and local merchants. Today there are grocery barges stacked with fat, red tomatoes and packets of cornflakes; there are boats carrying plump pigeons in cages and angry chickens in coops. Chugging *vaporetti* bounce carelessly against wet piers, sleek gondolas furnished with tasselled cushions slide by, while the busy little *traghetti*, a simple and unique ferry service with no seats, transport their passengers standing up.

If there is something called the real Venice it is to be found here, in its people and their determination to live in a city that is not merely a watery museum flavoured with expensive restaurants, some stylish bars and addictive shopping. Venice lives. People bring up their children, argue with their spouses, haggle over the price of fish, follow a football team and shrug their shoulders at the inevitability of us visitors falling helplessly in love with their hometown.

Stay a little longer than a few days and the rhythm of the city makes its mark. That most obvious observation, that this is a city where there are no cars, has a greater effect than we might realize. No cars does not only mean no cars in San Marco or the Rialto, it means no traffic jams anywhere in the city, no boiling frustrations, no big city stress. When we visitors agree to meet in Venice at a certain time, we say "depending on how many times I get lost", not "depending on the traffic". One is a delightful way of discovering parts of the city we somehow missed before; the other just gives us an ulcer.

Tourism, that cheerful business of people travelling in pursuit of their dreams and paying for the privilege, is the city's lifeblood. There are those who moan about it all, shake their heads and cluck their tongues at the crowds in the Piazza San Marco. "Sometimes", they say, "there are more people than pigeons." Five hundred years ago a medieval monk made the same observation. "The Piazza of Saint Mark's seems perpetually filled with Turks, Libyans, Parthians and other monsters of the sea," he sighed. Even earlier, in the 13th century, Venice had its own tourist police. While one of their jobs was to make sure hotels were clean and respectable, they rapidly developed the knack of directing lost visitors towards the shop, and preferably to one of the more expensive ones where their brother-in-law was in charge.

Today Venice is enjoying a vital, new renaissance. Instead of packing their bags and heading for Rome or Milan, young, ambitious Venetians are investing their vigour and their ideas into *La Serenissima*; instead of building ships for war, new Venice is building light, fibreglass pleasure craft for skimming across the canal on the way to a party. Behind the solid walls of the great *palazzi* are contemporary apartments, available and affordable to the visitor looking for another, more intimate view of the city. Young designers are creating contemporary fashion from traditional fabrics. Youthful sculptors, artists and architects are breathing new life into the old stones.

"OPEN MY HEART AND YOU WILL SEE, GRAVEN INSIDE IT, ITALY."
ROBERT BROWNING

This book is a celebration of the surprises Venice still has in store for us – a fairytale city that is reinventing itself for the 21st century. As a city of waterways it is unique, a superb mix of urban life where artisans are art connoisseurs, where ice cream-makers are opera buffs and where taxi drivers must have a canal licence. Travellers have always found Venice overwhelming, all-consuming, exasperating and fiendishly expensive – and still do. But we'll return again and again just to make sure.

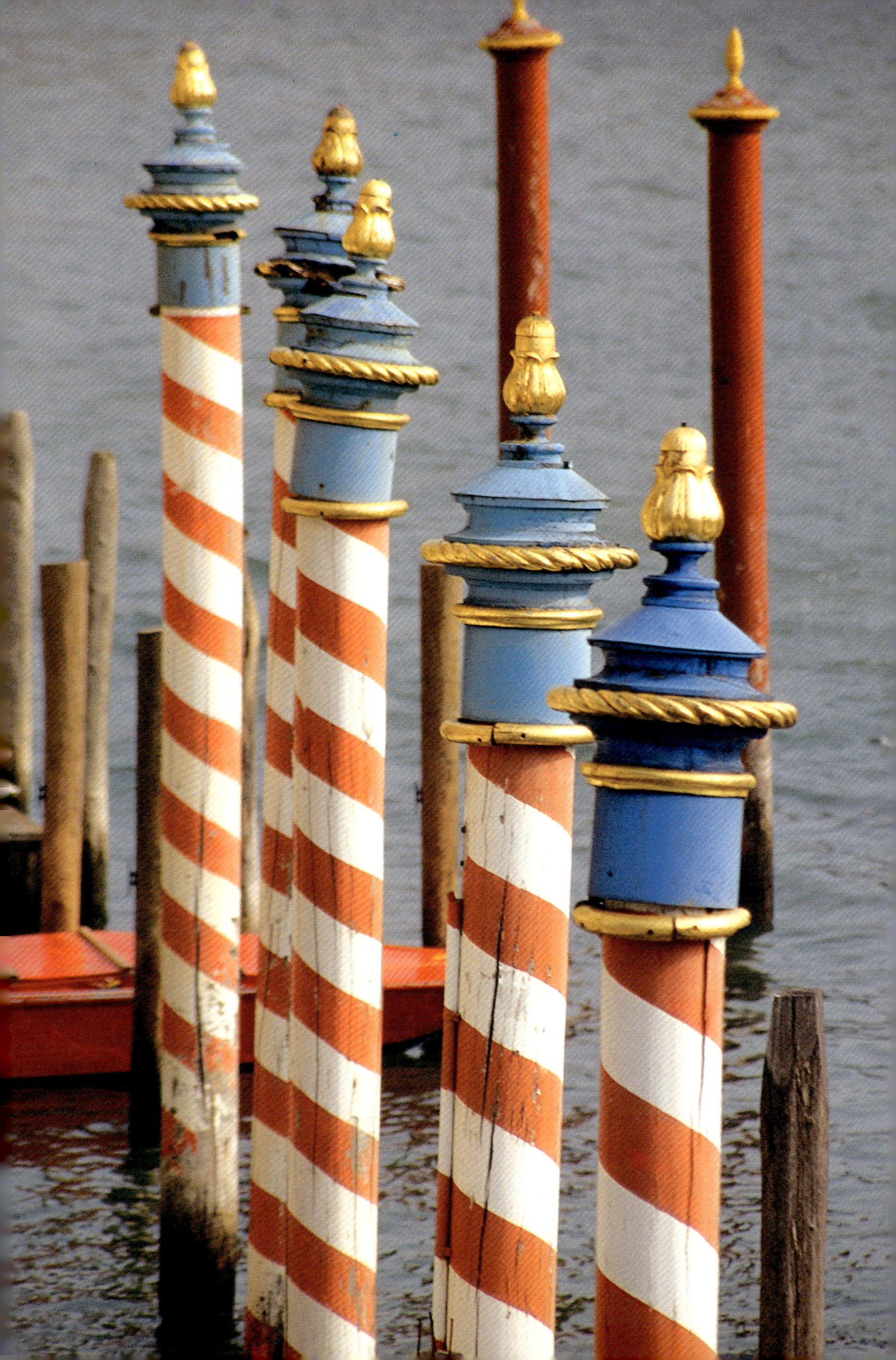

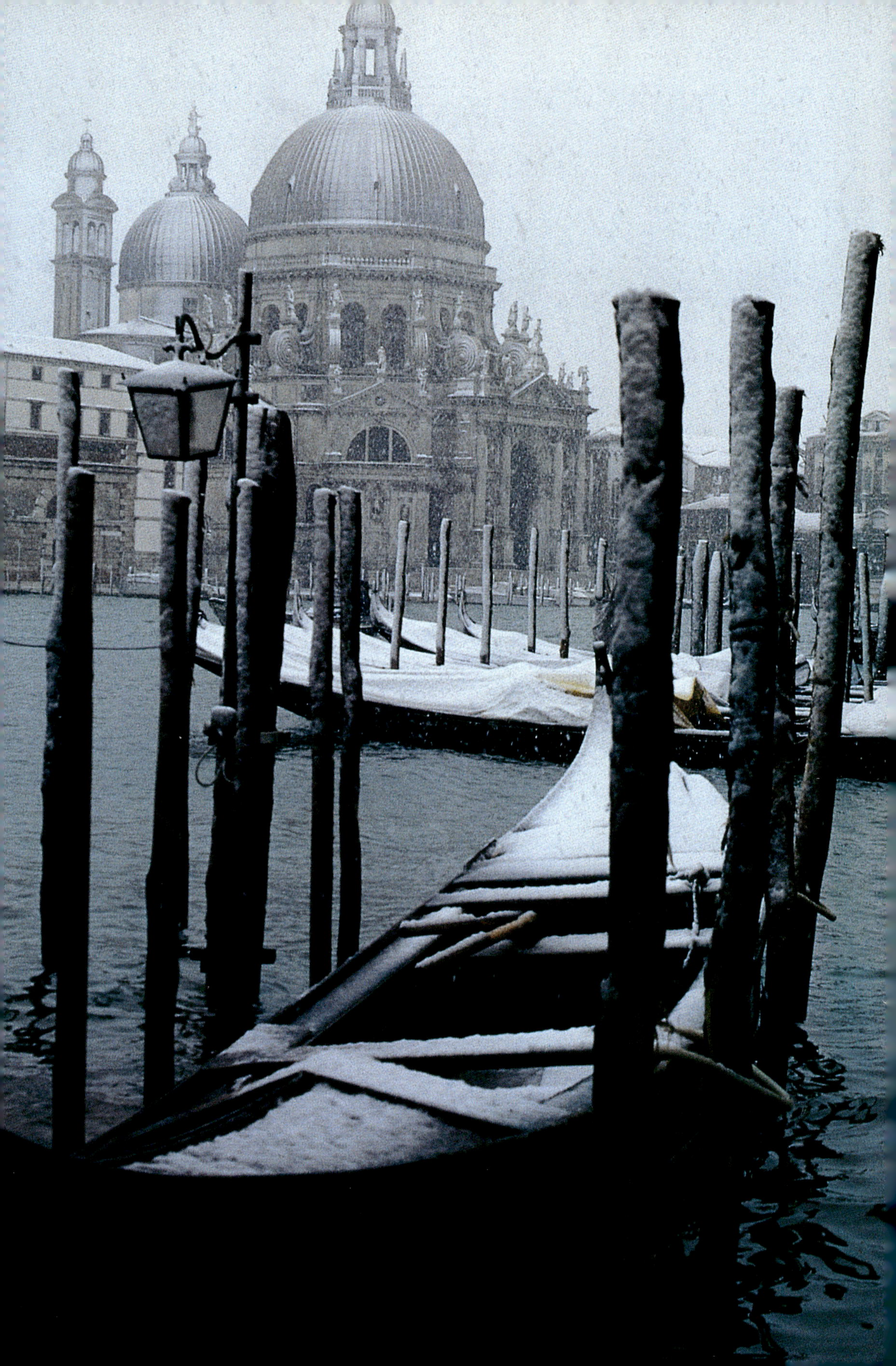

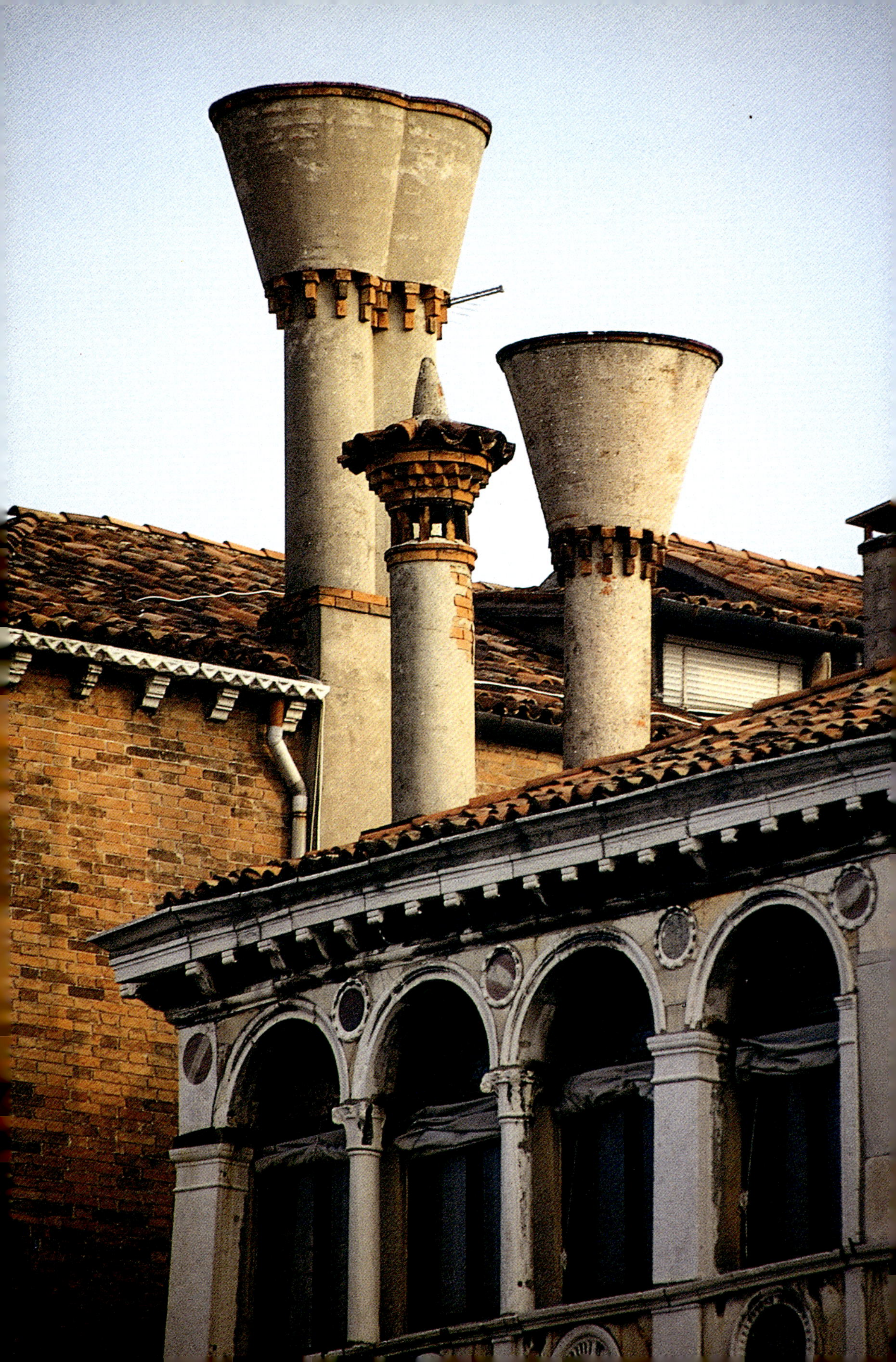

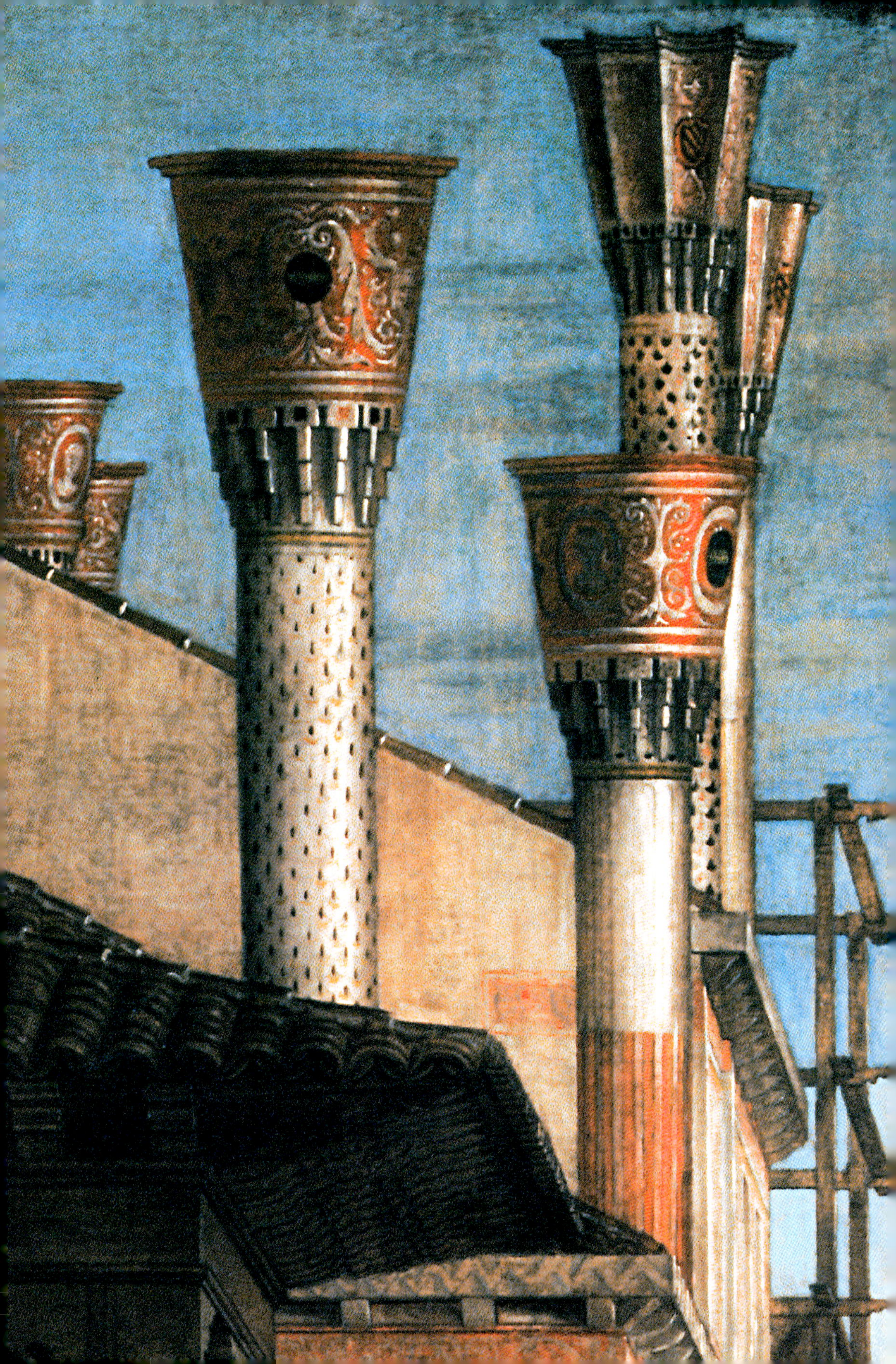

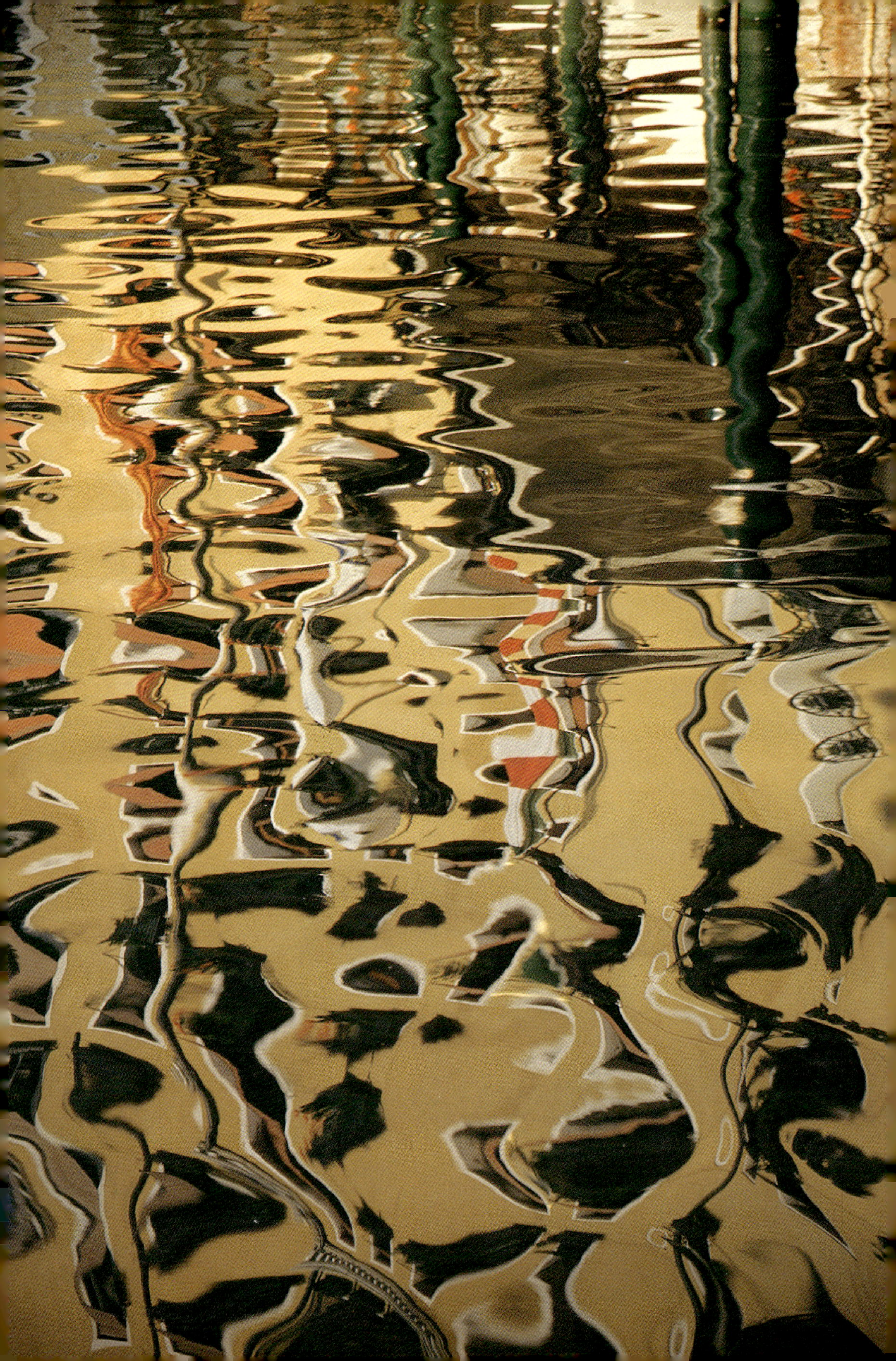

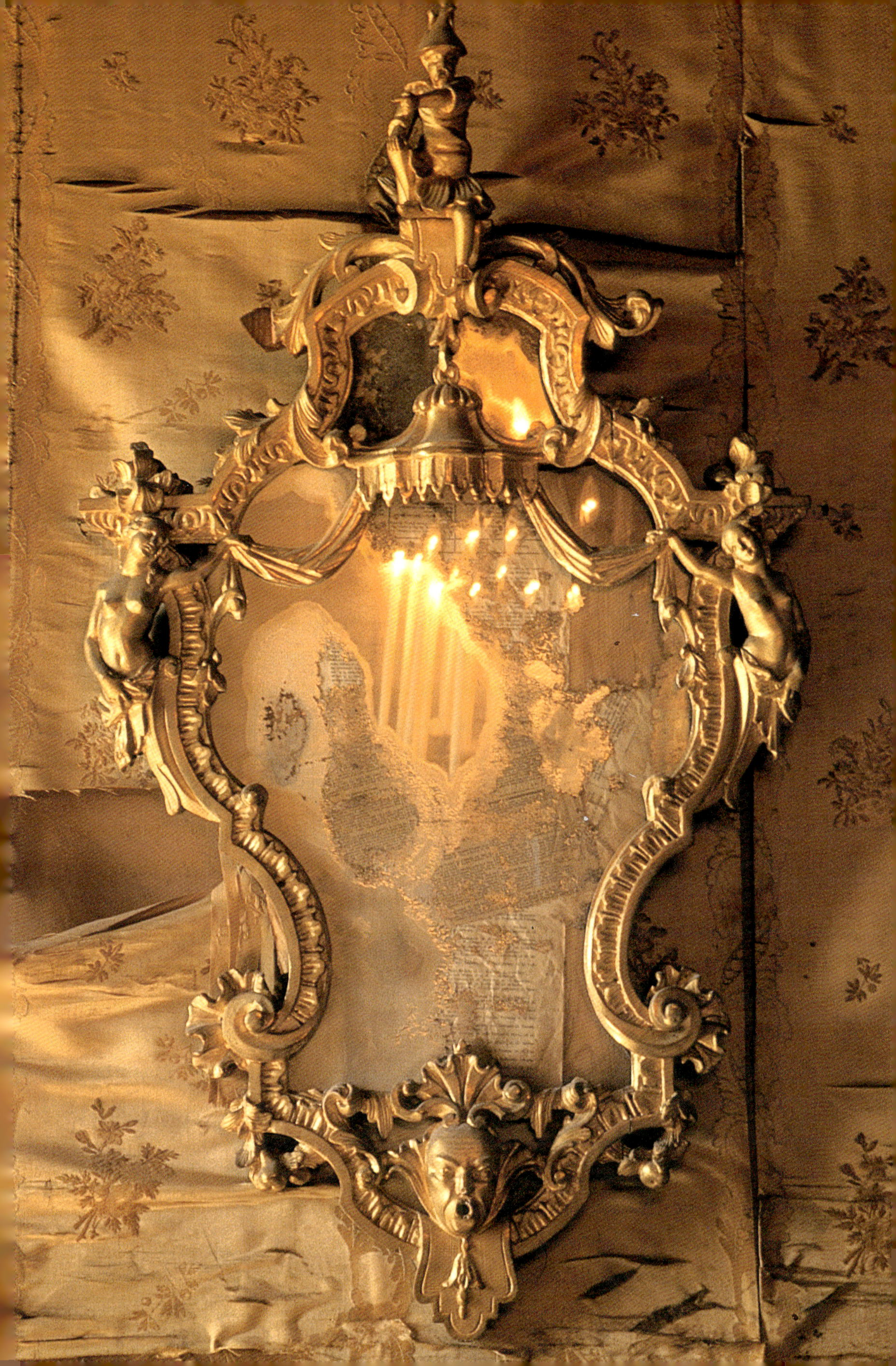

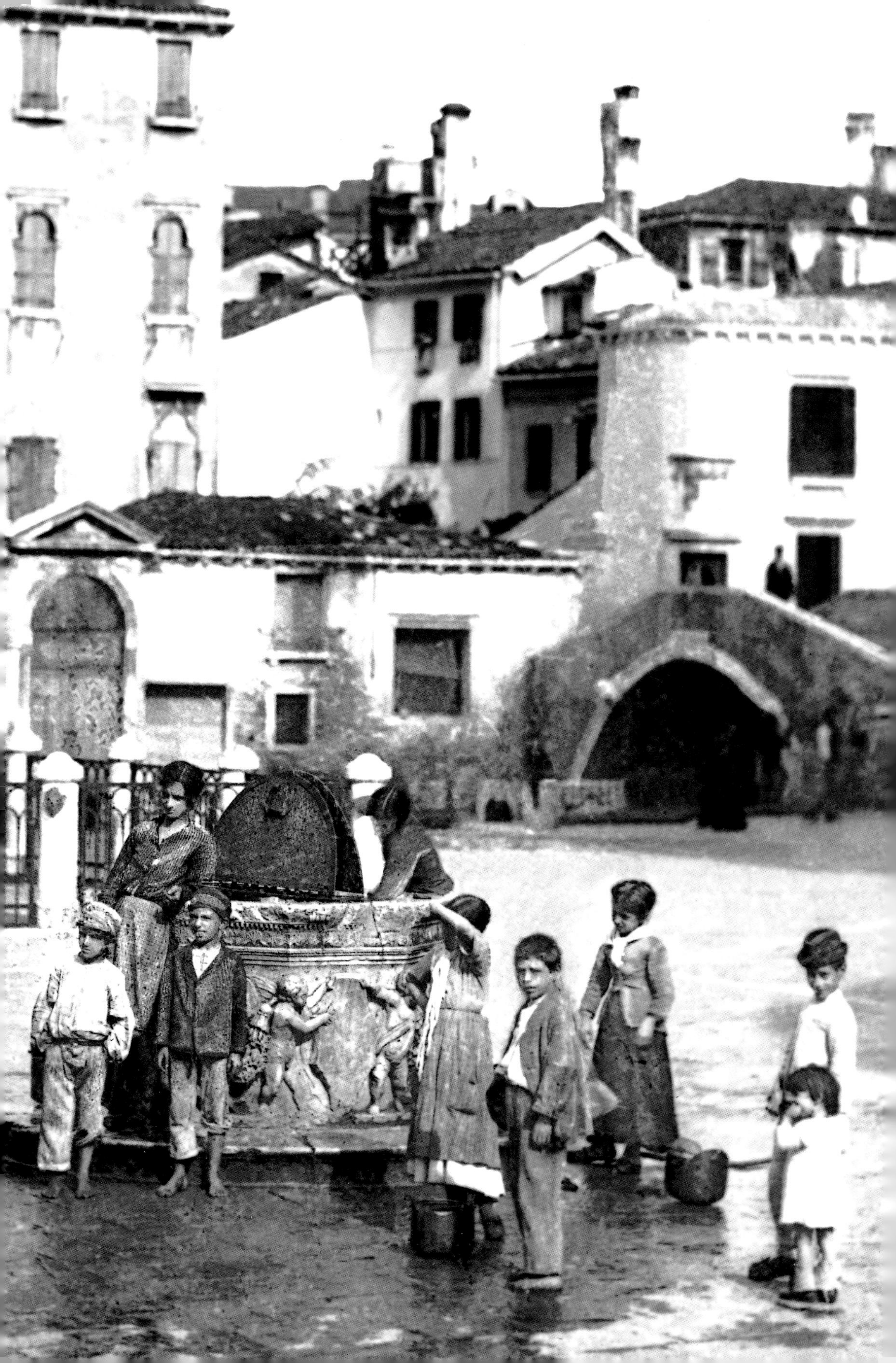

PONTE
STORTO

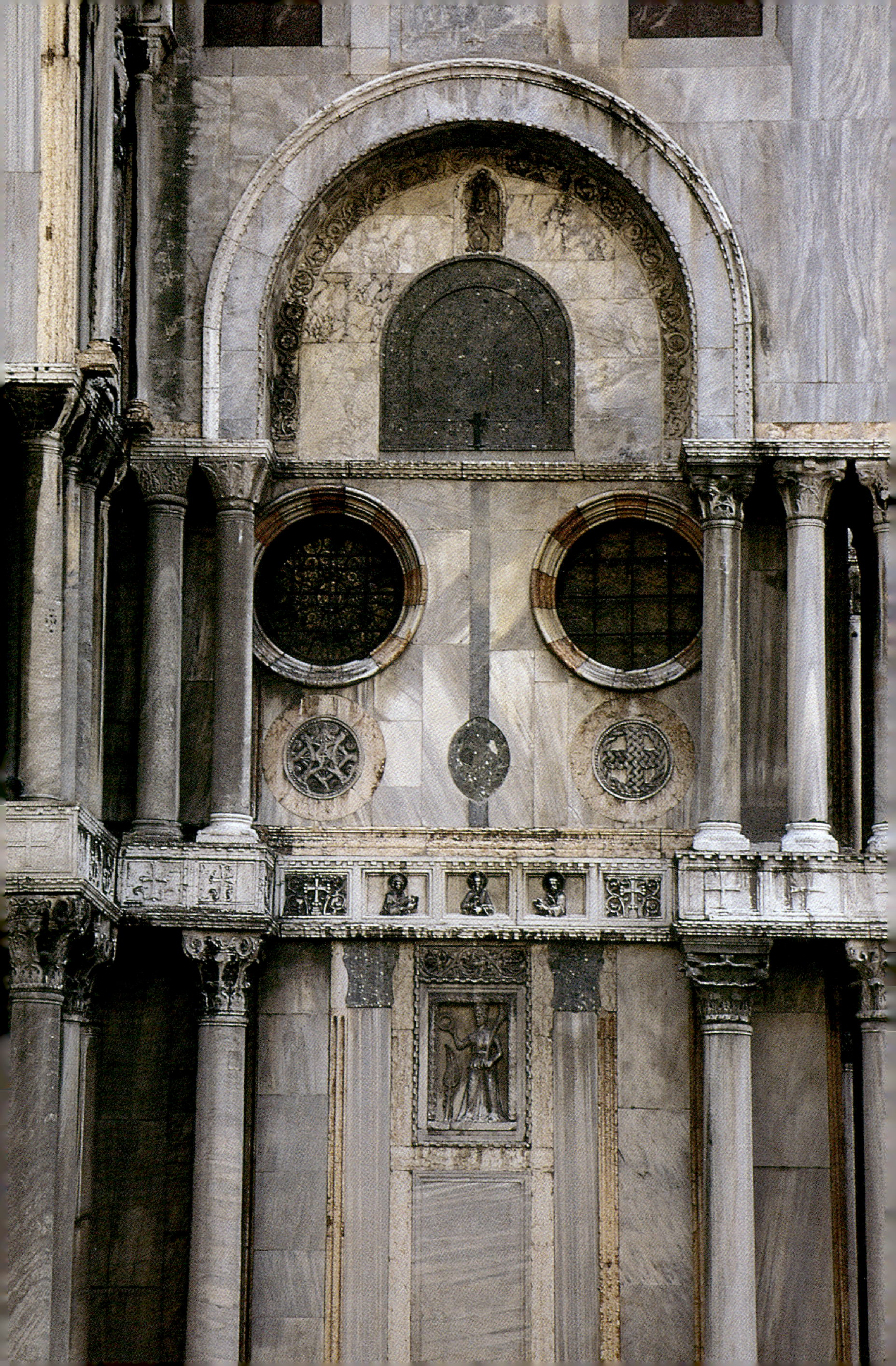

CORTE DEL
FONTEGO

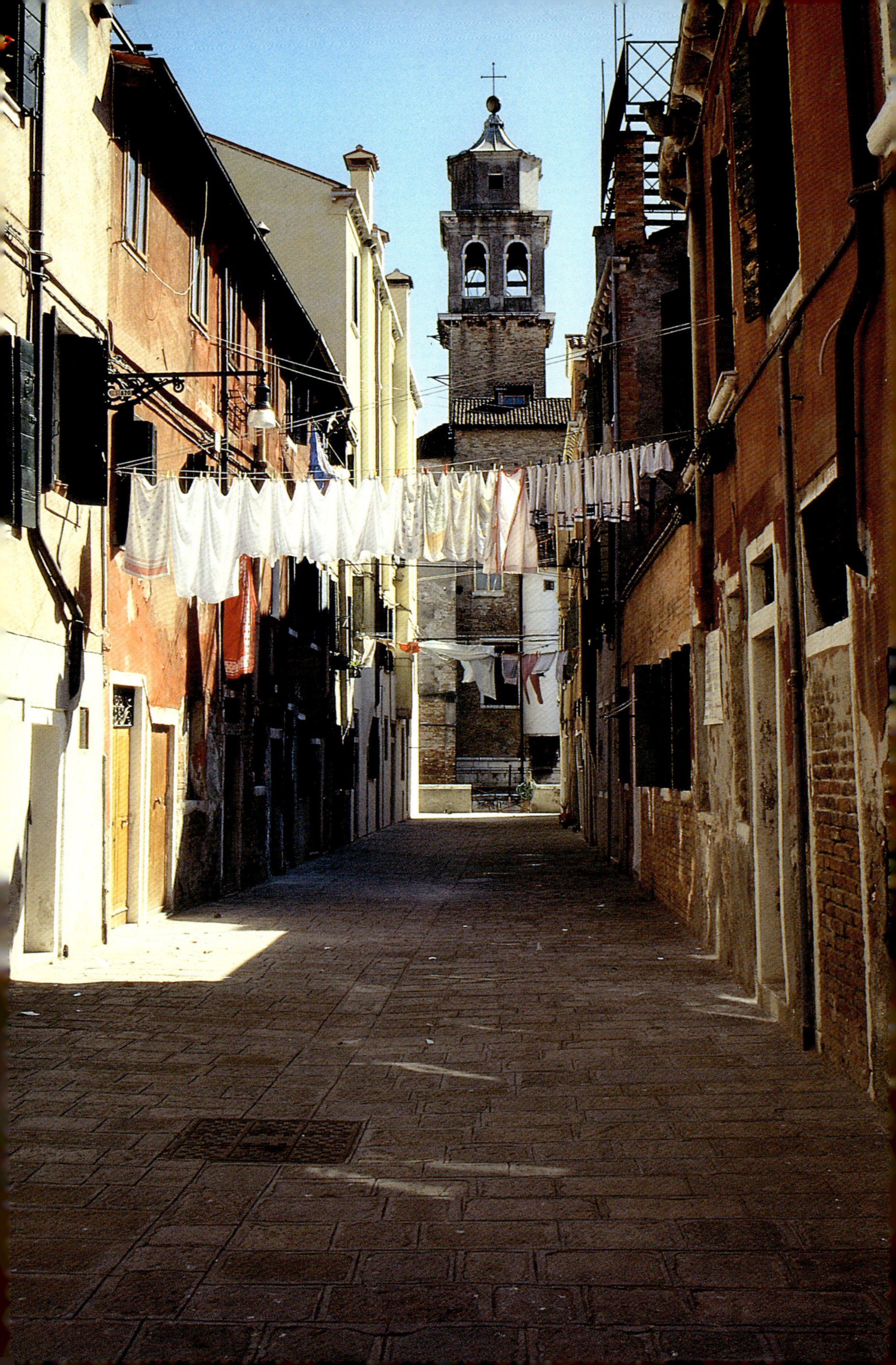

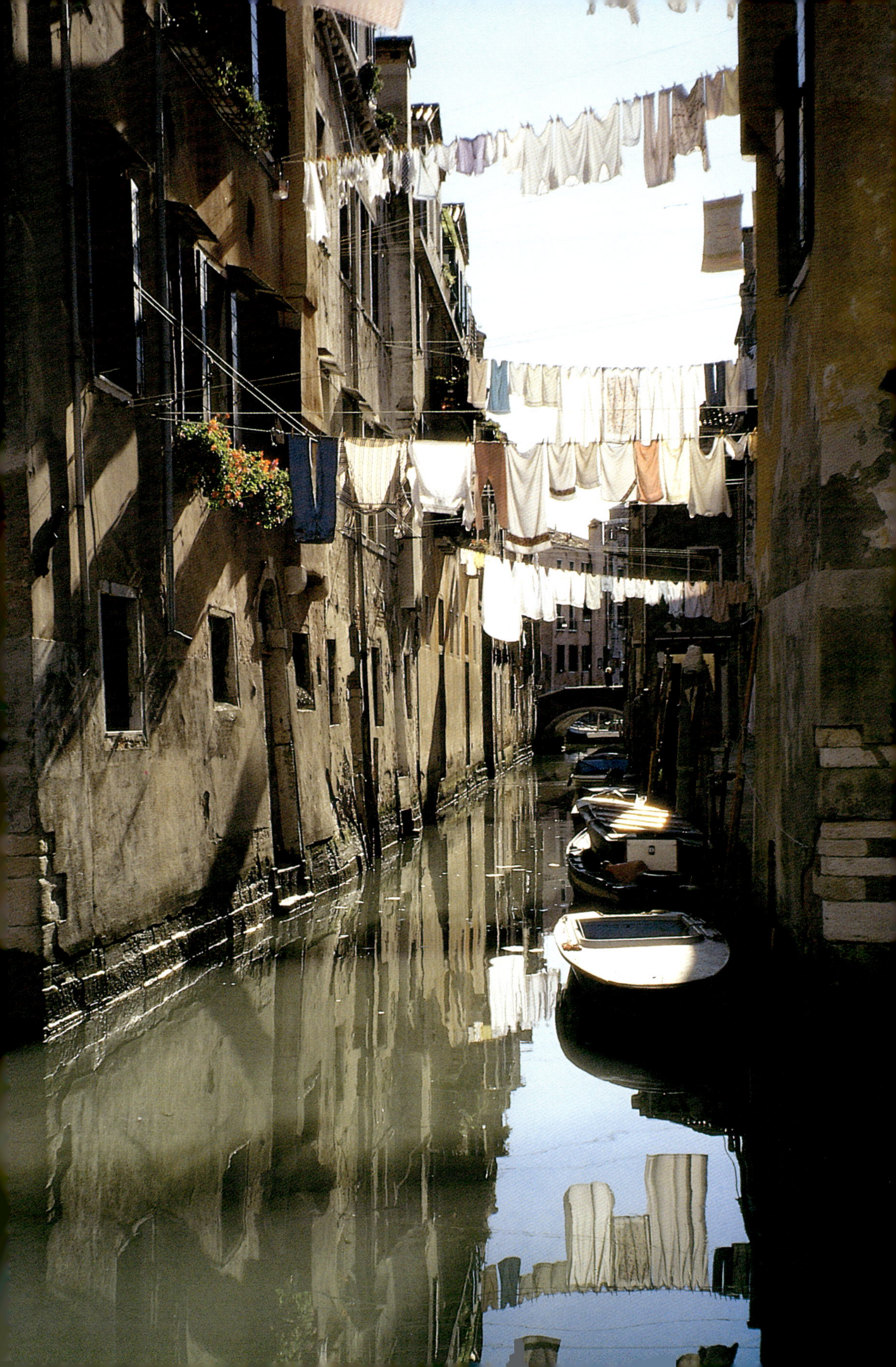

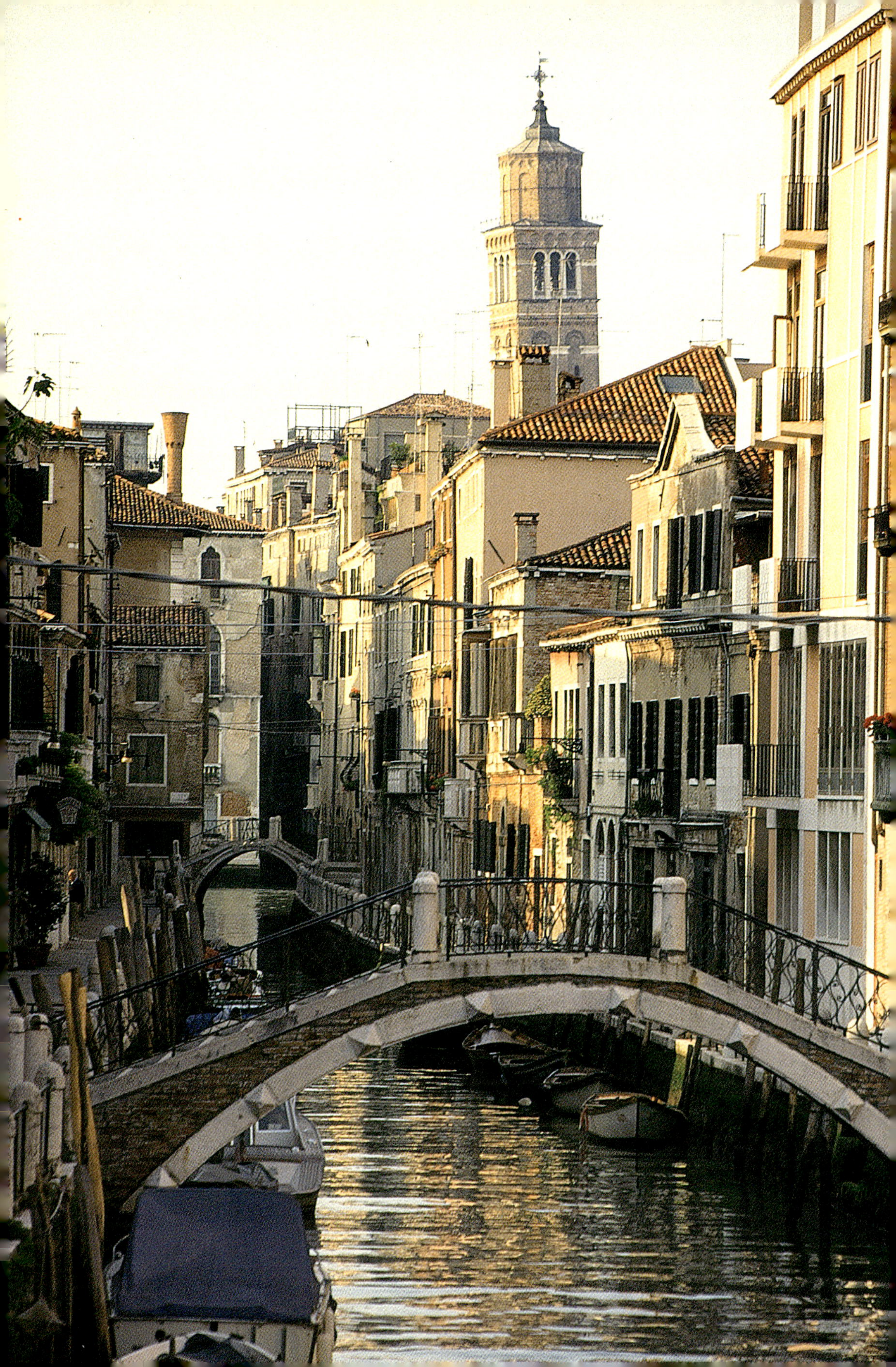

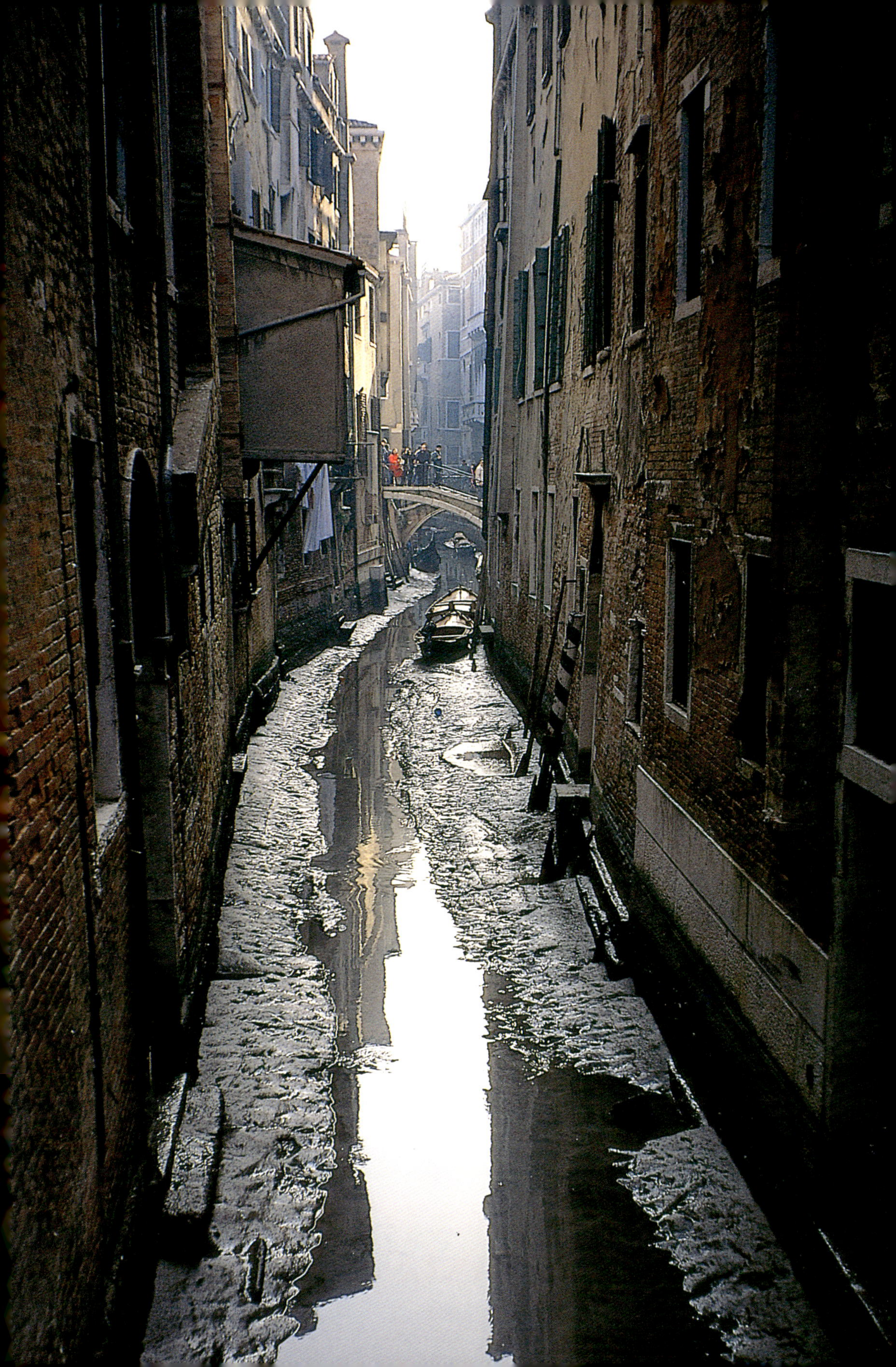

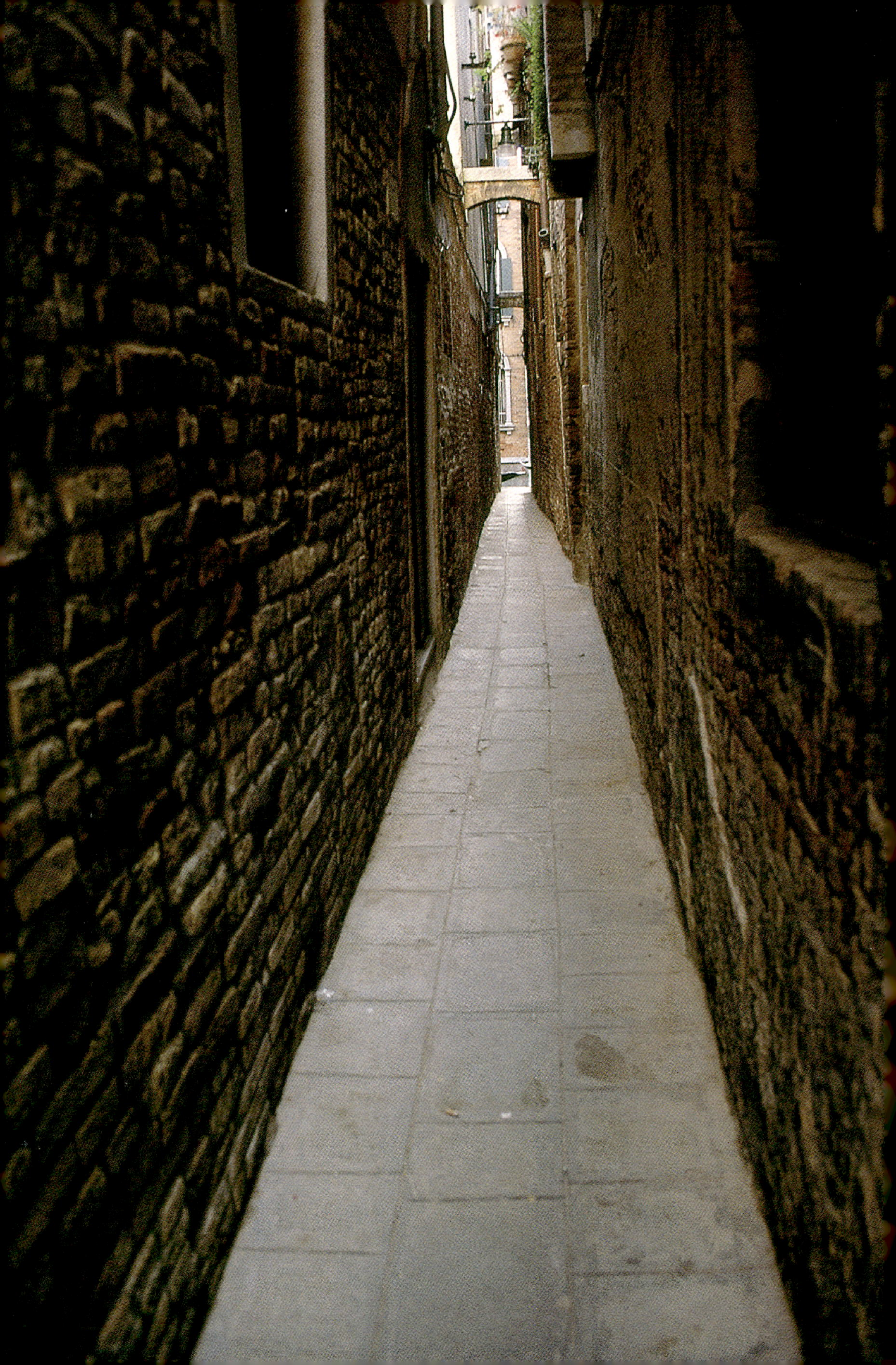

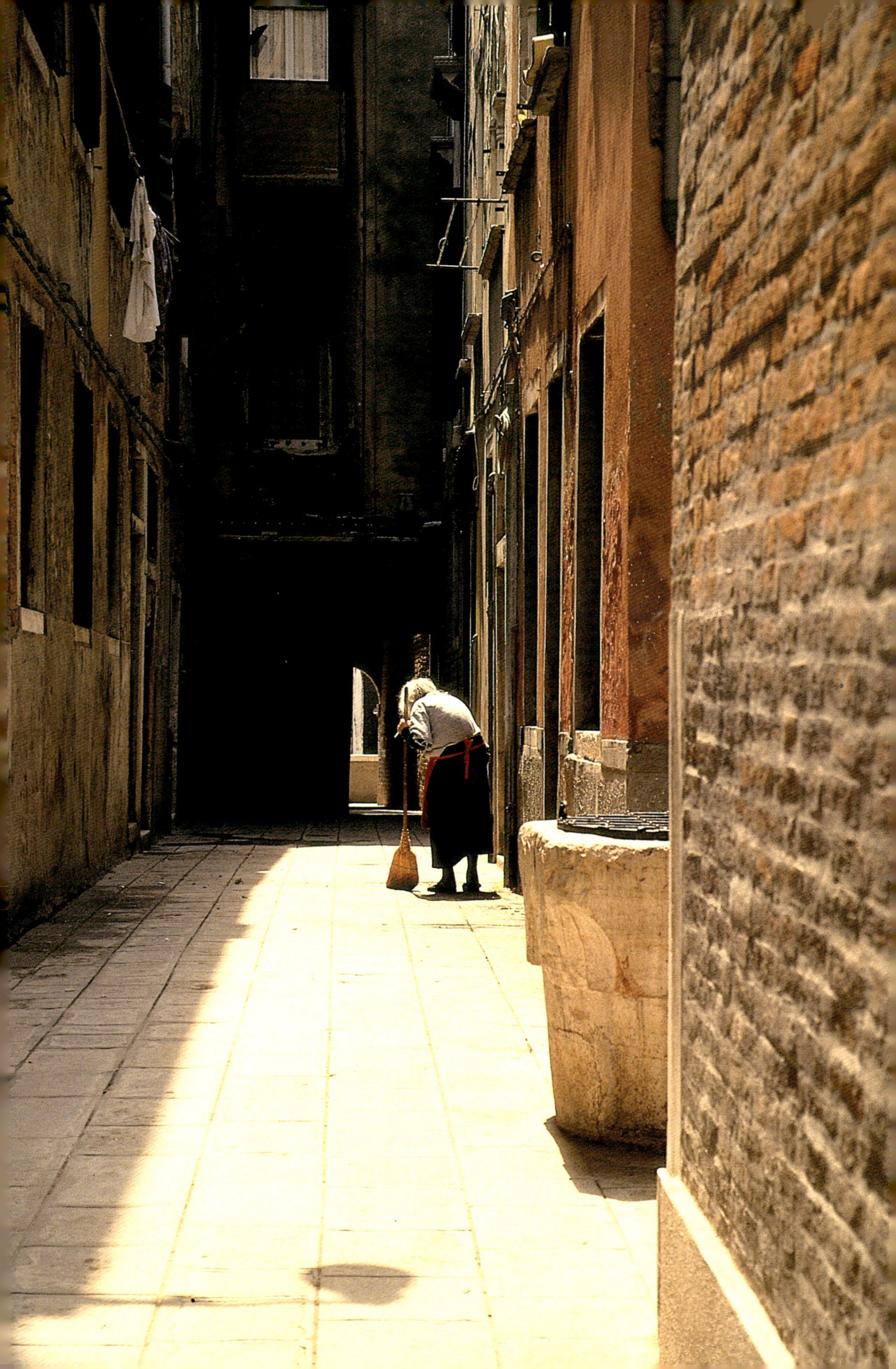

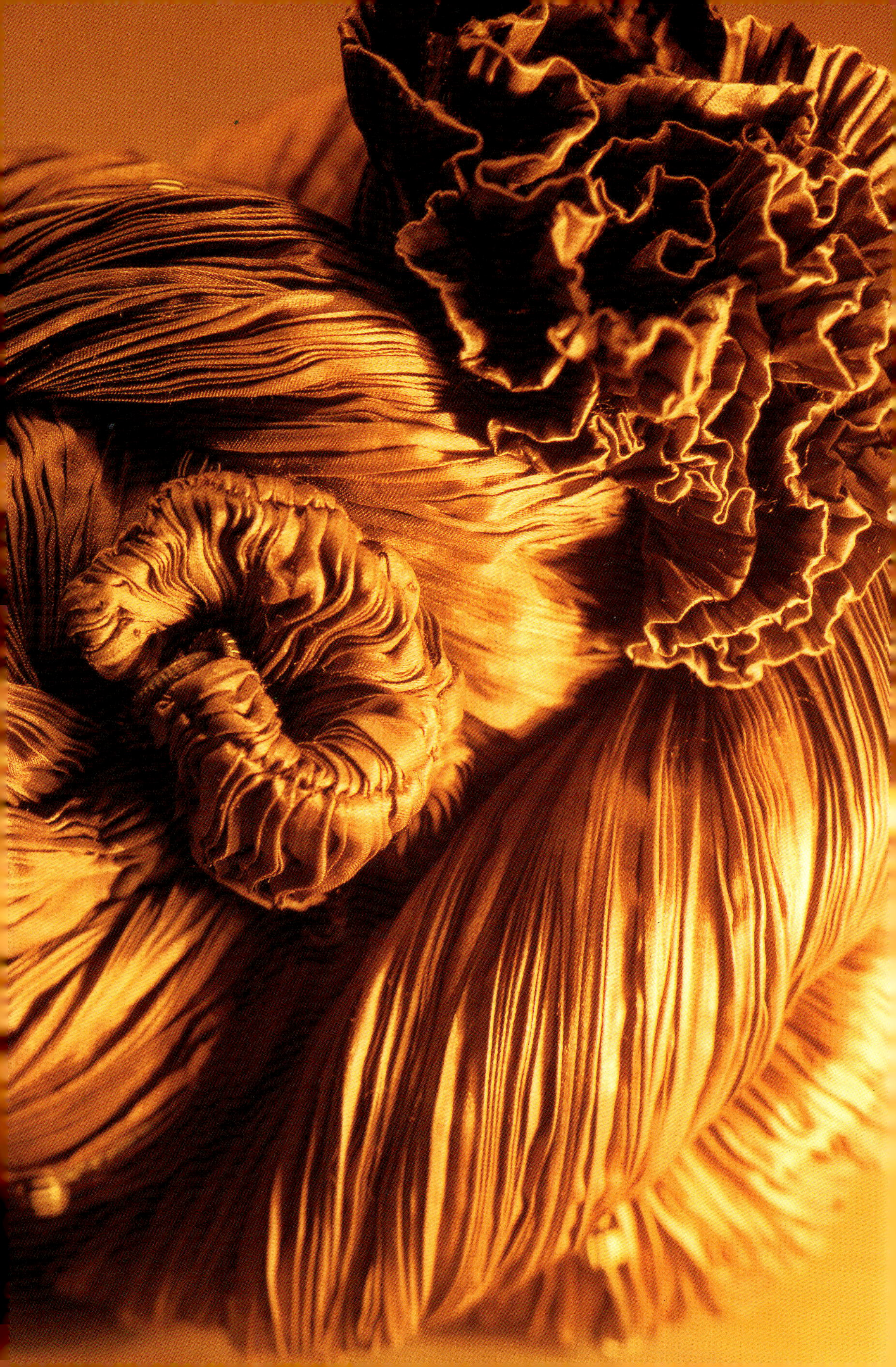

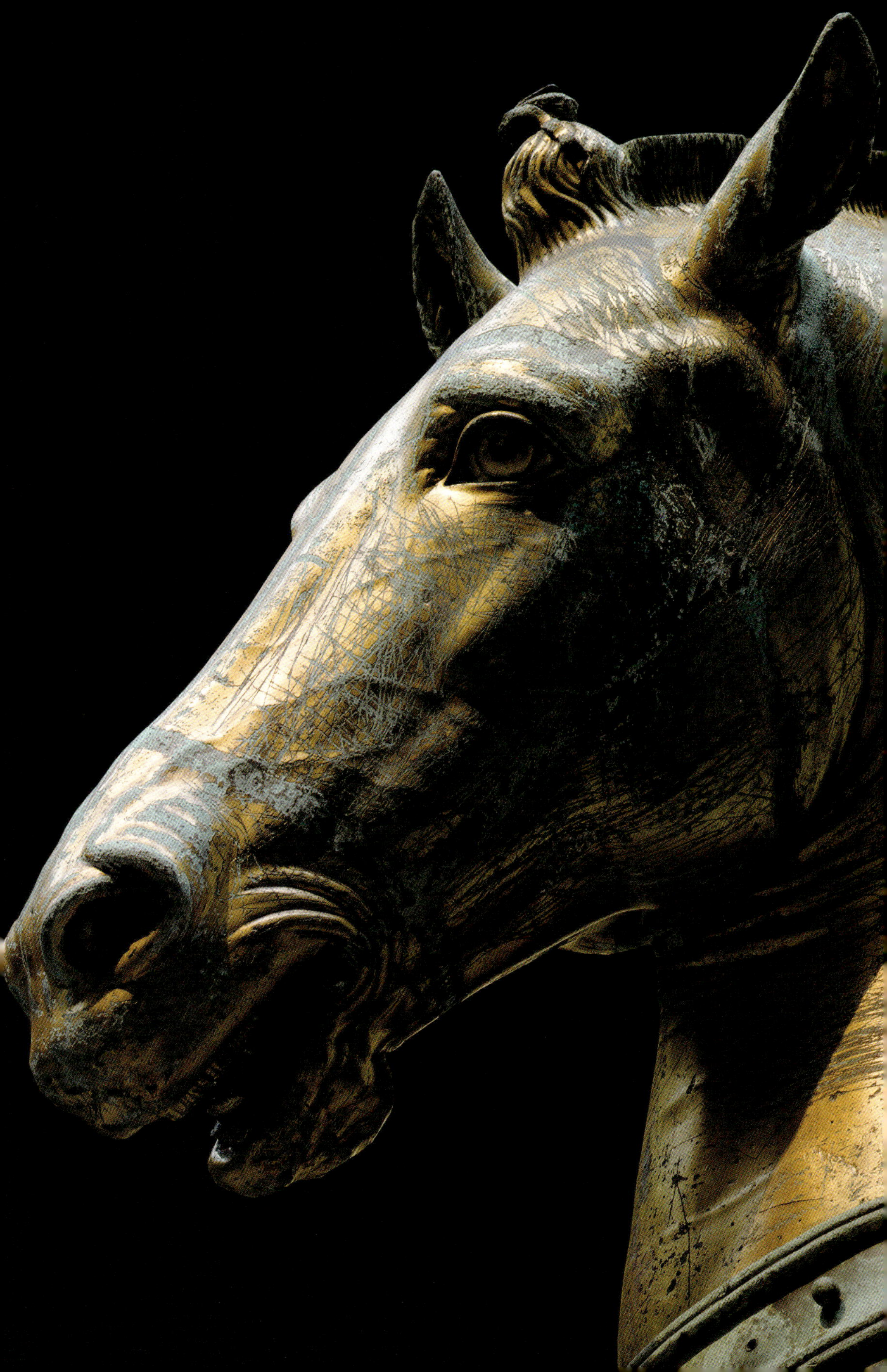

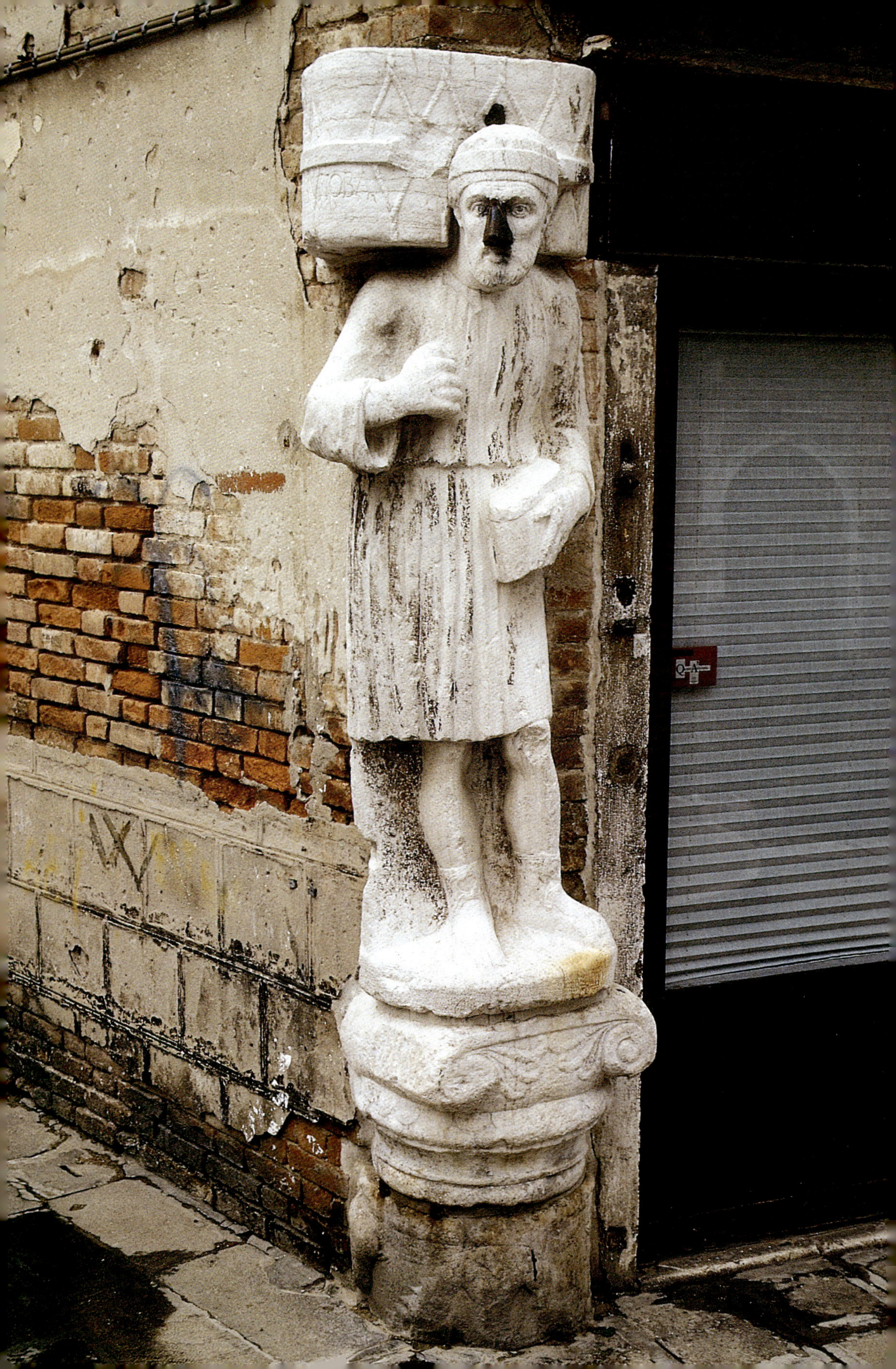

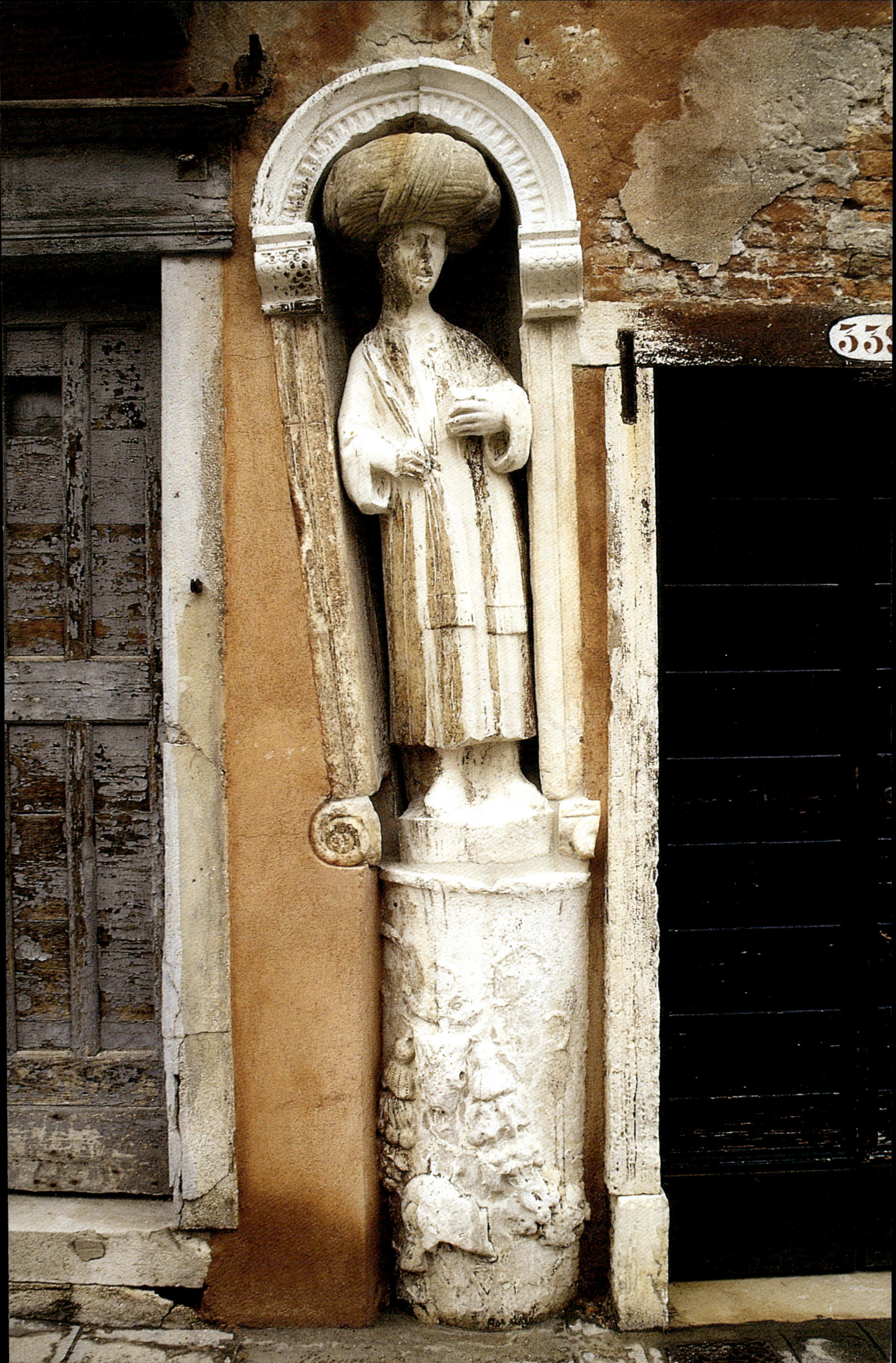
33

CHAPTER ONE

ARCHITECTUR

The many glories of Venetian architecture have

TREASURES

The cluster of palaces and churches that line the Grand Canal and decorate the *campi* and *calli* like precious gems are unique. The Basilica di San Marco, probably the most photographed church in the world, is a jumble of styles and centuries that has somehow come together in a perfect, awe-inspiring whole, most beautiful, some say, as a west side story, when the setting sun catches the mosaics in the façade and sets them aglow.

As for individual masters, there are those who insist that the greatest genius of all was Palladio. Look, they will say, across the water at the great church of San Giorgio Maggiore, so magnificent it has an island all to itself. Or what of the Redentore, built to celebrate Venice's deliverance from the plague of 1575-1577 and possibly the architect's most sublime creation?

AL entranced visitors for centuries.

Others may point to Sansovino, a Tuscan sculptor who was not really an architect at all. But he was a friend of Titian, who helped him secure the job as *proto* or resident architect of San Marco. Despite his lack of experience Sansovino produced some great Venetian landmarks, most particularly La Zecca, the state mint and the Bibliotheca Marciana, also known as the Libreria Sansoviniana. Pietro Lombardo, another great talent of the time, built that jewel-box of a church, Santa Maria dei Miracoli, and the lovely but lopsided Ca' Dario on the Grand Canal.

Then there is the Ca' Rezzonico, the museum of 18th-century Venice, actually designed in the 17th century by Baldassare Longhena. Newly restored and magnificent, it stares dismissively at its neighbour opposite, the Palazzo Grassi, taken in hand twenty years ago by Fiat and made into a showcase for fabulous exhibitions not only of Venetian treasures but of works of art from all over the world. And what of the Gothic masterpieces, most notably the Palazzo Ducale (or *Doges'* Palace) – how can anyone resist it, with its feminine pale pink exterior that effectively disguises the great machinery of power that operated beneath it? Picking out the Gothic windows, gradually identifying the pure Arabic style of the 13th and 14th centuries and the flamboyant Venetian overtones that came later, is a most rewarding game for Venice lovers to play.

But buildings are for people. Venetians have never doubted this; and still, today, the majority of *palazzi* along the Grand Canal and dotted throughout Venice are mysterious places, private homes where people lead 21st-century lives behind 15th- and 16th-century façades. Yet it is possible to venture behind some of those massive carved doors and see another, unique aspect of Venice. Equally, the churches of the city, beautiful and venerated, are not simply architectural gems or art galleries for the superb paintings they hold. When the bells of the *campanili* ring out they are calling the faithful to prayer and we visitors are able to join them or stand quietly and allow the real business of the church to continue. Looking behind the stones to discover a living city is the real excitement of Venice today.

It is a Saturday morning in October in the church of Santo Stefano, where a small huddle of us are gathered for a *battesimo*. The small Leonardo, first son of a fine Venetian family, is being baptized in the church where his parents were married, in front of assembled family, friends and a few silent visitors who happen to have dropped in to see the glory of a church and have found instead a slice of Venetian life.

IN PRAISE OF GOD AND BEAUTY

The moment the priest and Leonardo's proud mother conclude the wetting of the head the bells of the church ring out in celebration. Timing is, after all, one of God's talents; and if, in this case, the bells would have chimed anyway on the half hour, we enchanted visitors see it as an omen of good fortune: *buona fortuna* we whisper in our newly acquired Italian.

Santo Stefano is a fine Augustinian church and its façade features a splendid Gothic portal. It would not top most visitor's lists although it has many features of interest, such as a roof made from a ship's keel. But for Leonardo and his family it is "the church around the corner". There is a service each evening at 7pm and three at various times on Sundays. Over there in the corner Giorgio, who lovingly takes care of the church he has called his own for nearly 70 years, carefully replenishes candles or polishes the feet of the Madonna if they look dusty.

There are now some 150 churches in Venice, many of them still working for their living; celebrating communion, taking confession, listening to wedding vows, providing solace at funeral services and giving the ordinary church services that the small communities of Venice expect. Even in the great Basilica di San Marco confessions are still heard, often in many different languages. Priests in Venice, like traders, must also be linguists.

But these places of worship have become worshipped themselves – both for their splendour, which shines through despite crumbling façades and a certain fragility, and for their fearless *bravura* in the face of time and the elements.

Few are quite as they were when they were first built. In particular, several of their bell-towers, known as *campanili*, have developed their own quirks over the years. Santo Stefano,

Tiptoe into a church looking for a Tiepolo ceiling or a fine Bellini altarpiece and you may find unexpected flower arrangements: they have been donated by a happy bride after her wedding who leaves them and their perfume behind as a reminder of her and her most important day.

San Giorgio dei Greci, San Pietro di Castello all lean quite dramatically. Indeed, should you take a gondola ride in the tiny side canal called Marchini and look up at the *campanile* of Santo Stefano, it looms above you, slanting defiantly and undefeated.

The grandest of all, triumphantly rebuilt in the early 20th century after a deep sigh and total collapse ten years earlier, is the *campanile* of San Marco. Another of those moments of perfect timing made the inauguration on 25 April 1912 precisely 1,000 years after the day of its original foundation. Despite the millions of photographs and postcards the church has inspired it still must be viewed "live". Purists may criticize the confusion of its architectural style and forms. Yet no one, except perhaps Mark Twain, who likened it to "a vast and warty hog taking a meditative walk", can deny it has presence. We admire the Byzantine frescoes, compare them with the opulence of the mosaics and look out for the sculptures and the Romanesque arches that inspired Ruskin to break into purple prose: "The crests of the arches break into marble foam," he wrote, "and toss themselves far into the blue sky in flashes and wreaths of sculpted spray."

Then there are the bronze horses. No one is quite sure whether they are Greek or Roman or even precisely how old they are; but they do make the heart sing. Those outside, pounding their hoofs and tossing their manes are replicas. The originals, which have travelled back and forth from Venice, trophies of war and icons of Venetian pride, have now been relegated to a small room inside the basilica, far away from the pollution of the 21st century. Only the smallest possible sign leads the way to the windowless cocoon where they are now confined after all their years of adventure. *Cavalli* it says, and there they are, flaring nostrils, eyes wild, staring contemptuously at us mere mortals.

Other musts include the intriguing Gothic church of the Madonna dell'Orto in Cannaregio, also known as the Tintoretto church, which has an exterior of such warm hues it glows like a Persian carpet. San Sebastiano, cooler on the outside, houses one of the most colourful interiors in Venice, by Paolo Veronese. Timekeeping is quixotic; so check before venturing forth. And be wary as you wander in; there may well be a wedding or baptism going on.

Any guide will point to other well-known Venetian masterpieces which they will say are unmissable, and they are right. But lesser-known buildings have their charm: I Gesuati, whose real name is Santa Maria di Rosario, in Dorsoduro, soars in a most satisfactory way over the Fondamenta Zattere. It combines the restraint of Palladio's greatest creation, the Redentore church on the island of Giudecca opposite, with engaging 18th-century flamboyance. And San Trovaso, which contains five Tintorettos by various family members, is another underestimated church.

What is it about the grand houses and *palazzi* of Venice that makes our hearts beat a little faster? Is it the purity of the stones that so excited Ruskin; or the way the Gothic windows and their pointed cusps sit so perfectly proportioned side by side? Is it their magnificent and noble rooms that excite our imagination with their columns and friezes and splendid decoration? Or do the shadows of those who lived within the walls provide a colour and humanity that other, lesser buildings cannot hope to have?

BEHIND THE FAÇADES

The beauty of Ca' Rezzonico, one of the most stately *palazzi* lining the Grand Canal, becomes even more entrancing when we discover that Robert Browning died here, that Pope Clement XIII lived here, that the last Holy Roman Emperor, Francis II, stayed here, as did Whistler and Cole Porter. Might Browning have found here an elusive line he was searching for, could Cole Porter have tinkled on some Venetian ivories, did Whistler miss his mother as he wandered from room to room?

Ca' Rezzonico is now the Museum of 18th-Century Art and each room is filled with lavish and delightful paintings, especially the pastels by Rosealba Carriera and a Tiepolo ceiling in the Sala del Trono that has such mischievous charm that one forgets the crick in the neck to stand and stare. But it is the life that has been here that sets a visit to this beautiful place in another dimension.

Other grand *palazzi* open to the public include the Palazzo Pisani-Gritti, otherwise known as the Gritti Palace Hotel, the Palazzo Grassi, and, the most famous of all, the Palazzo Ducale. Other *palazzi*, like the elegant Palazzo Papafava overlooking the Misericordia Canal can be discreetly hired for special occasions, as can the dazzling Palazzo Pisano Moretta overlooking the Grand Canal, which provides the setting for some of the great balls during *Carnevale*. All have fascinating architectural features to be spotted and admired. But how much more interesting are those that remain in private hands, that might permit the occasional visitor, but only under special circumstances?

The public museum in the lovely Palazzo Mocenigo in Santa Croce is filled with the kind of 18th-century furniture and fittings that a stylish family might have required. But the same family's private *palazzo* on the Grand Canal is where the poet Byron lived, breaking hearts and swimming records. He once swam the full length of the Grand Canal starting from the Lido. It took him around four and a half hours and he was only slightly out of breath when he appeared, dripping wet, at the *palazzo*'s back door. Chiarastella Cattana, daughter-in-law of the present owners, the Asta family, uses the same entrance. It's up a small *calle*, through a leafy garden and into a *palazzo* that feels like home. The proportions are noble but not overwhelming, the furnishings are beautiful, but cosy and inviting, and the room Byron used as his bedroom is now a family room where Chiarastella shows her wares to private clients. She has also just opened a shop in Salizada San Samuele. This young Venetian is a fabric and textile designer whose beautifully woven bedspreads, window drapes, tablecloths and napkins are designed to incorporate the crests and architectural detail of Venice. She is one of a new breed of Venetians who are breathing fresh life into the city's commercial scene, producing original but firmly Venetian artefacts that have less to do with tourism than with preserving artistic traditions.

On the other side of the city, enjoying a history that goes back nearly 400 years, is the Palazzo Donà delle Rosa. When the great carved doors are firmly shut it appears impenetrable and slightly forbidding. But inside, the present members of the family, their walls lined with ancestral portraits that have art historians going weak at the knees, play with their small daughter, mix extra garlic into their pasta sauce and concoct 20th-century marketing ideas for their soft furnishings design company. In a workroom on the first floor Gaia Imperiali, *née* Gaia Donà delle Rosa, designs exquisite fabrics using her surroundings and the art of Venice as inspiration for her own label, Donatus. Her customers, like those of Chiarastella, come to the *palazzo* by private appointment.

Another private *palazzo* on the Grand Canal, on the San Polo side just before the Accademia Bridge, is the Palazzo Loredan, now owned by the Gaggia family. The grand façade is in fine Veneto-Byzantine style. Inside, alongside the family accommodation, Filippo Gaggia has created smaller, cosy apartments for those travellers who want to experience living in Venice rather than merely visiting. He has 40 apartments throughout the city and other up-and-coming entrepreneurs are doing the same thing.

Byron was a superb swimmer, despite his lameness. Frequently, after dining at the Palazzo Albrizzi he would dive, in full evening-dress, into the Grand Canal and swim home. At other times when he felt like a swim a servant used to follow in a gondola with his dry clothes.

Architect Michael Carapetian creates exciting, contemporary living spaces within the ancient walls of Venetian *palazzi*. While he draws inspiration from Venice and the masters that created her, Carapetian designs for people of today. Which, if you think of it, like so much in Venice, is nothing new. Palladio was doing the same in 1570.

"A VILLA SHOULD CONSERVE OF AND RESTORE SPIRIT THE AGITATION TO PEACE AND

HELP

THE STRENGTH

ITS INHABITANTS,

RE THEIR

S, WORN OUT BY

N OF CITY LIFE,

TRANQUILITY."

ANDREA PALLADIO, VENICE, 1570

You can see them any time in Venice ... Earnest sightseers, map in hand, scurrying across the bridges of Venice, scouring the landscape for the important view. That *campanile* to the left, the wondrous dome on the right or the façade of that church – all must be seen and admired. Of course their efforts will be rewarded: Venice is stuffed with fascinating sights; but stay, pause for a moment – you might be crossing one at this very moment. The bridges of Venice, as the 17th-century diarist John Evelyn observed, "tack the city together", and they have their own history and their own charm. There are 450 of them, more, it is said, than anywhere else on earth. Many are so low and dark that a gondolier can lose his jaunty straw hat, if not his head, if he doesn't remember to duck. Luckily, he has been entertaining his passengers for over 30 years with this little trick and dips down just in time.

BRIDGES TO SIGH OVER

Venice's bridges can be large and practical, like the Accademia Bridge, or tiny and totally perfect, like the private bridge leading to the Palazzo Tiepolo. They can be inappropriately named, like the eponymous Bridge of Sighs (the Ponte dei Sospiri), built between 1595 and 1600, and so called because of the "lamentations" of the prisoners of the Serene Republic as they crossed the canal to face their inquisitors: to describe their quaking terror as "sighing" seems rather an understatement.

> An average of ten people were probably killed during these skirmishes. If not bludgeoned with clubs or worn out by fisticuffs, they would fall into the canal and get stuck in the mud – possibly underneath a deluge of household bric-à-brac chucked in after them by an over-excited crowd.

Or they can be aptly named, like the Bridge of Fists (the Ponte dei Pugni), near San Sebastiano. This appears to be a perfectly harmless bridge, joining the Campo San Trovaso to San Barnaba. But look down. Those footprints in the white marble were the starting point for boxing matches, dating back to the time when two rival gangs, the Nicoletti and the Castellani, fought out their grievances before interested spectators. It was not the only venue: the Ponte della Guerra, literally the Bridge of War, was another, as were the nearby bridges of Carmini, Fosca and San Marzial. This jolly sport continued for a several hundred years and was only banned, after an especially nasty free-for-all, in 1705.

The Rialto Bridge, a favourite landmark and photo opportunity, also has a chequered history. While the present construction, which a duchess once remarked was shaped just like her favourite tiara, seems as if it has been there forever, it is in fact the sixth bridge on the site. The first was a bridge of boats in the late 13th century; the next shaky structure collapsed during the Tiepolo revolution of 1310 when Boemondo Tiepolo led a failed conspiracy to restore democratic government. The version that followed buckled and sank, rather embarrassingly, during a wedding procession in 1440; and the fifth had a drawbridge in the middle, but was never built to last and consequently didn't.

The building of the sixth and final bridge (to date), known as the Rialto di quà ("this side") and Rialto di là ("that side") was a result of a competition in which all sorts of illustrious artists and architects competed, including Palladio and Michaelangelo. The job went to a little-known architect who was lucky enough to have the name Antonio dal Ponte (Antonio of the Bridge). How could he lose? It took three years to build, from 1588-91, and while it was not much admired by Venetians at the time – too big, too ordinary, not ordinary enough and, finally, when shops were built on it, too messy – it is much loved by visitors today. Structurally it has been as sound as a bell: not only robust under the feet of literally millions of visitors every year, but when they fired a cannon from its steps in 1797 to quell some pesky rioters there was not so much as a shudder from it.

The only two other bridges to cross the Grand Canal are both modern, originally built in the 1930s. The Ponte Scalzi, near Santa Lucia train station, is an imposing stone structure, but has never been popular with the Venetians. Whereas the Accademia, made of wood and so rickety it was replaced in 1984, has captured our hearts. The vista has much to do with it. Its view of Venice, to be checked on at various times during the day, is unsurpassed. But the bridge itself? How much more exciting if it were made of glass! This is not just a wild idea, but a brilliant and imaginative venture which has been proposed by one of Italy's leading sculptors in glass, Luciano Vistosi. His table-top model, made to scale, is not only beautiful, but also practical. Glass, properly treated, is as hard as nails and could withstand daily life in Venice, even with the ten million plus visitors a year the city attracts. Will we ever see Vistosi's vision tacking the *sestiere* (districts) of San Marco on one side of the Grand Canal and Dorsoduro onto the other? In Venice you can never be sure.

An ideal bridge for poignant thoughts is the Ponte di Sacca, overlooking the northern lagoon and the tranquil island of the dead, San Michele. Viewed at dusk, the clean lines of the cemetery walls look like an embroidered canopy.

Think of the colours of Venice and the theme is soft and faded. It wasn't always so. One of the favourite *palazzo* museums is the Ca' d'Oro, literally the House of Gold. We love it, not despite the fact that the colour has faded and the water, lapping gently but relentlessly, is nibbling at its very foundations, but because of it. Had we swept along the Grand Canal in our gondola in 1431, when wealthy merchant Marin Contrarini was inviting all his friends to admire his newest residence, we would have happened upon a positively psychedelic sight. Those lovely pastel-shaded walls were originally Mediterranean blue and deep burgundy with splashes of 24-carat gold to brighten them up. Even today, after time has kindly toned down its excesses and blurred its garish edges, Ca' d'Oro is still the most flamboyant example, after the *Doges* Palace, of ornate Venetian Gothic style.

CRUMBLING MAGNIFICENCE

"Poverty," someone said, "is picturesque." It was a cruel, but nevertheless accurate observation of how we like to view our ancient civilizations. Would Rome look quite as romantic with all its columns intact? Would the Parthenon appear such a graceful and serene construction without the grasses and weeds that grow beneath its broken feet? Venice, at the height of her glory, was a place of overwhelming magnificence. No one had seen anything like it, and even great kings and emperors were struck dumb when they beheld *La Serenissima*. But modern admirers, dismissive of gold by the yard, prefer a Venice that has ever so slightly let herself go, exposing a vulnerable side. This way she is still beautiful, still haunting, but with the air of a great courtesan who knows that her past is always going to be more interesting than her present. Naturally, this does not stop us agonizing over the future of Venice; and we are right to do so.

Since 1966 no storm has ever quite reached the epic proportions of the floods of that year, which very nearly engulfed the city and took it back into the sea from whence it came. But in recent years Venice has been lashed by high tides, by torrential rains and by the insistent change in world weather patterns that we call global warming. As soon as the wooden platforms are stacked up ready in the Piazza San Marco, gumboots suddenly appear in shops that shrugged their shoulders at the very existence of

> "I have oftentimes observed many strangers, men wise and learned, who arriving newly at Venice and beholding the beautie and magnificence thereof were stricken with so great an admiration and amazement that they woulde, and that with open mouth, confesse never anything which before time they had seene, to be thereunto comparable."
> English tourist of the 16th century, (Anon.)

such mundane items a month before. Venetians are pragmatic, and while they mutter to each other that the Piazza has been under water more often than ever recently, they also reveal a history of always presenting a stoic resilience to bad weather.

For some years places in Venice that used to be at ground level have now been well below it. Doorways that once needed a step or two to cross now appear flat; columns that appeared to be constructed on solid ground can be sitting in a puddle at the first sign of rain. San Marco is always one of the first *piazzas* to fill with water, as it is several notches lower than most others in the city. Yet, not even in this modern dilemma are we original. The peeling façades, that sense of inevitable decay that we might have thought belongs to the 20th century, is not new at all. Neither is the concern. Whereas today it is groups like "Save Venice" and "Venice In Peril" that scratch our consciences and insist that we save Venice, not just from sinking but from itself, so it was the English poets who lamented the decline of the Most Serene Republic. In 1817 Byron wrote:
"In Venice Tasso's echoes are no more.
And silent rows the songless gondolier;
Her palaces are crumbling to the shore and music meets not always now the ear:
Those days are gone – but Beauty still is here."

Venice is built on soggy mudbanks but the subsoil is in layers, like a lasagne. First comes the soft mud, and then several feet of firm clay, followed by a layer of peat mixed with sandy, watery clay. It is said that the ongoing firming up of the clay has been gradually forcing the water upwards and causing the subsidence. So we are no longer speaking of Venice sinking, but water rising, or *alta aqua* as it is now discussed daily in the city.

As for the construction itself, Venice is resting on a forest of wooden stakes. No one knows how many, although it is said that the church of Madonna della Salute is balanced on over one billion. How anyone thought that this was a good idea back in the 5th century defeats logic. But then Venice is not about logic. It is about beauty and glory and the power of a people who came out of a lagoon, pioneers who built the most fantastical city in the world.

Those who cannot possibly imagine how the lagoon first appeared to those early Venetians might take a trip to the island of Torcello and look at the view from the *campanile*. The surrounding marshes, sliding masses of slippery, wet mud, must have appeared precisely the same here 1,600 years ago.

As the early pioneers said to any who dared challenge them, "This Venice, which we have raised in the lagoons, is our mighty habitation and no power of Emperor or Prince can touch us." We who believe in the miracle of Venice can only agree.

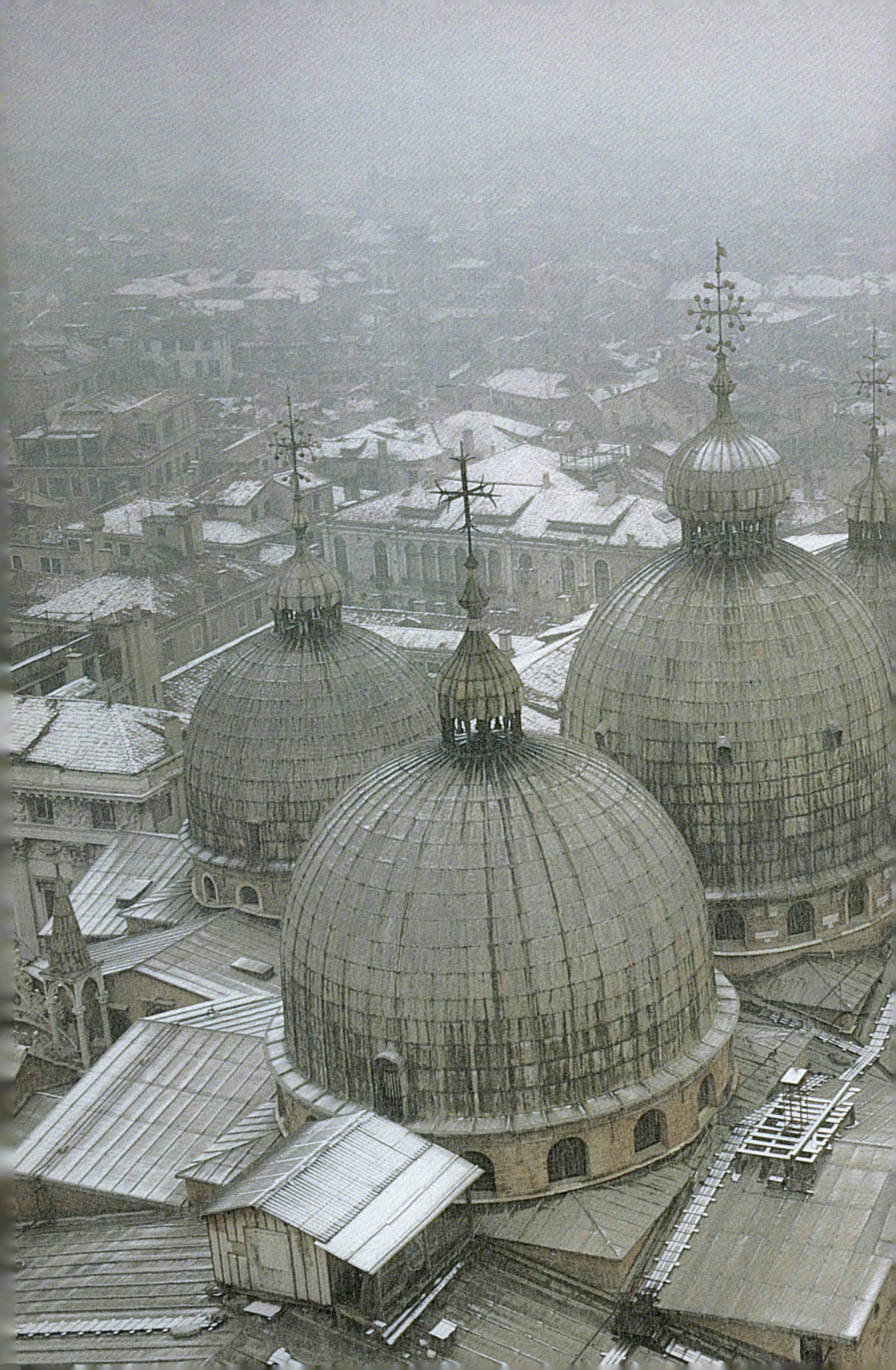

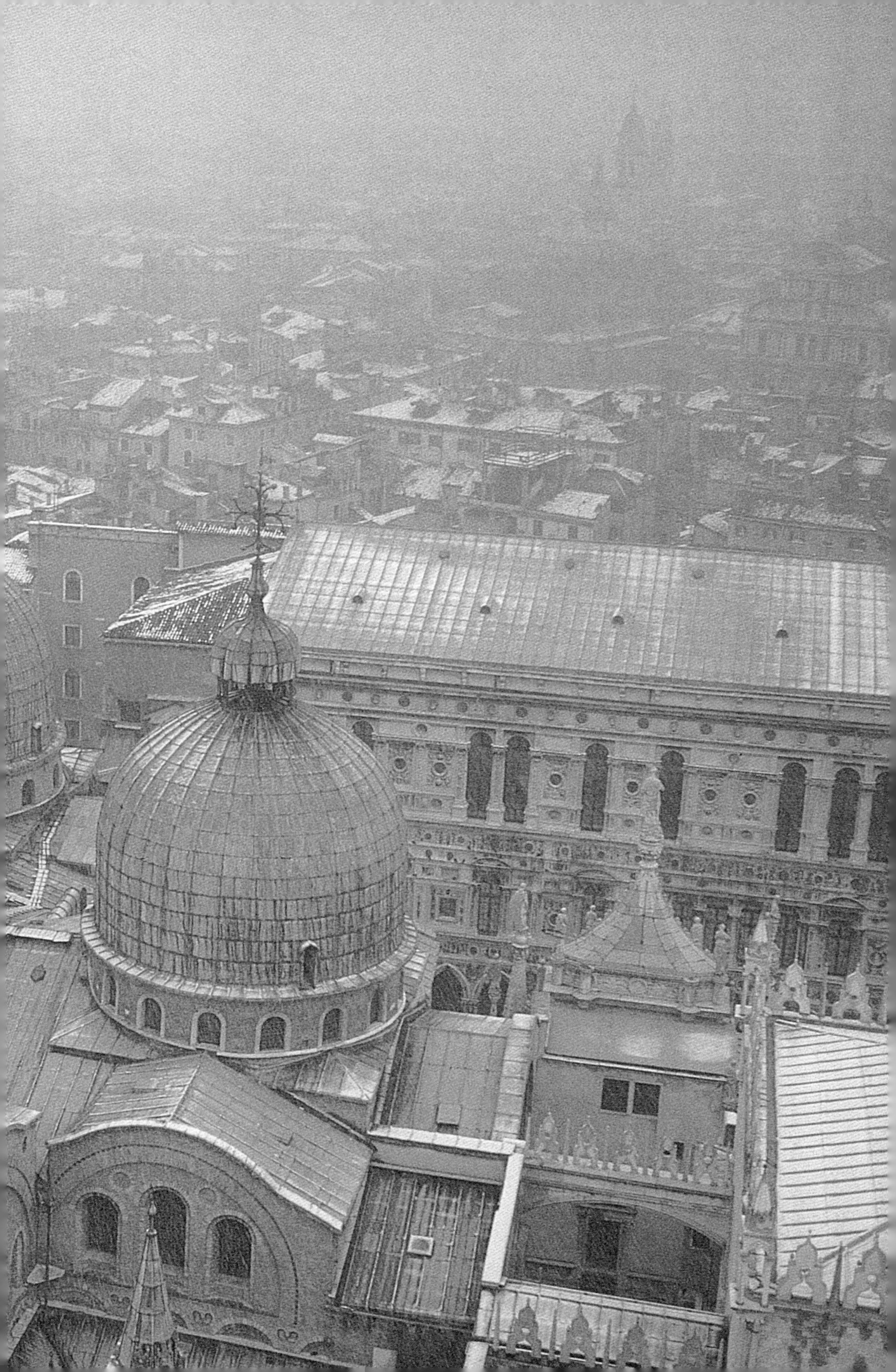

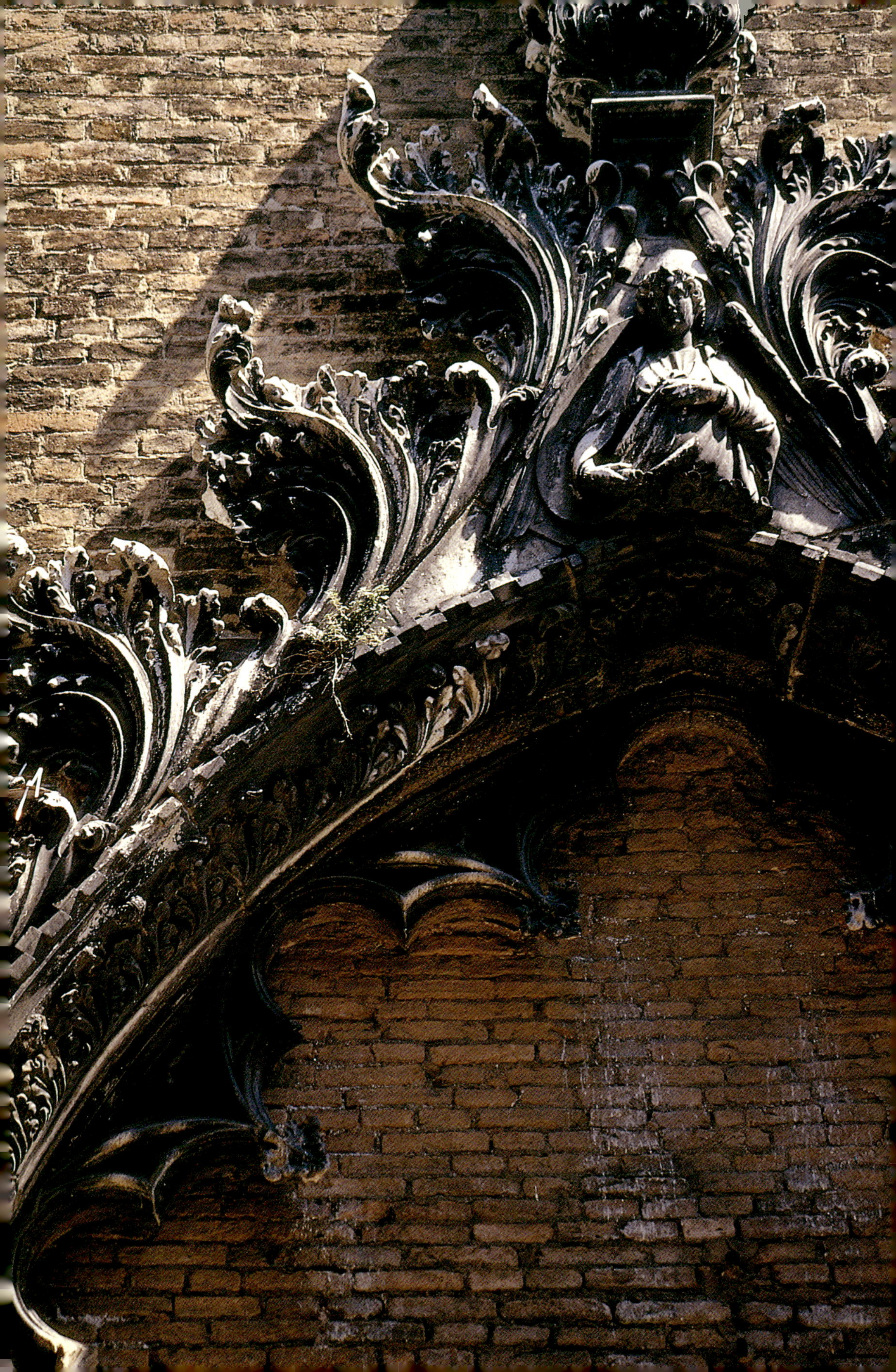

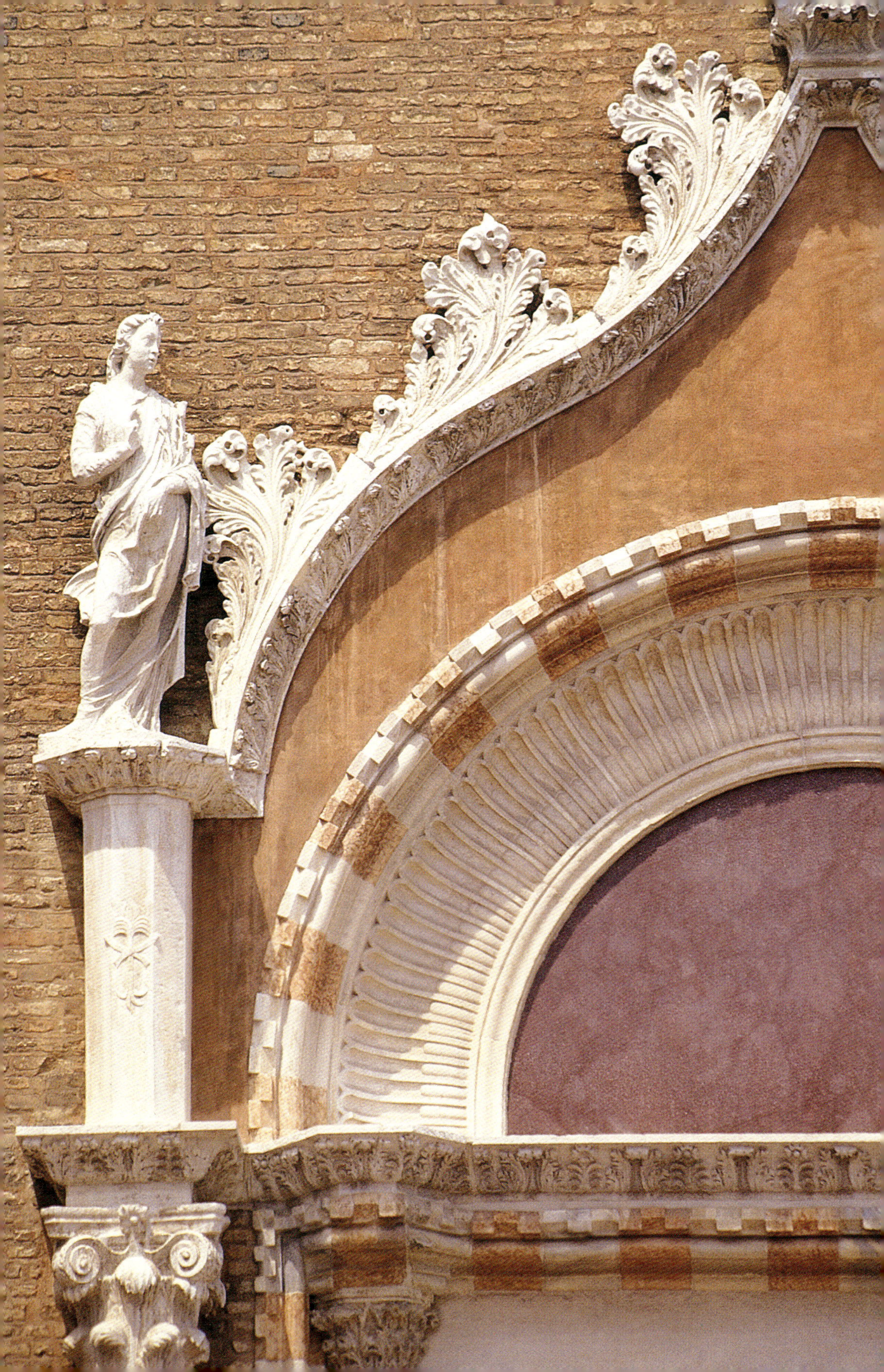

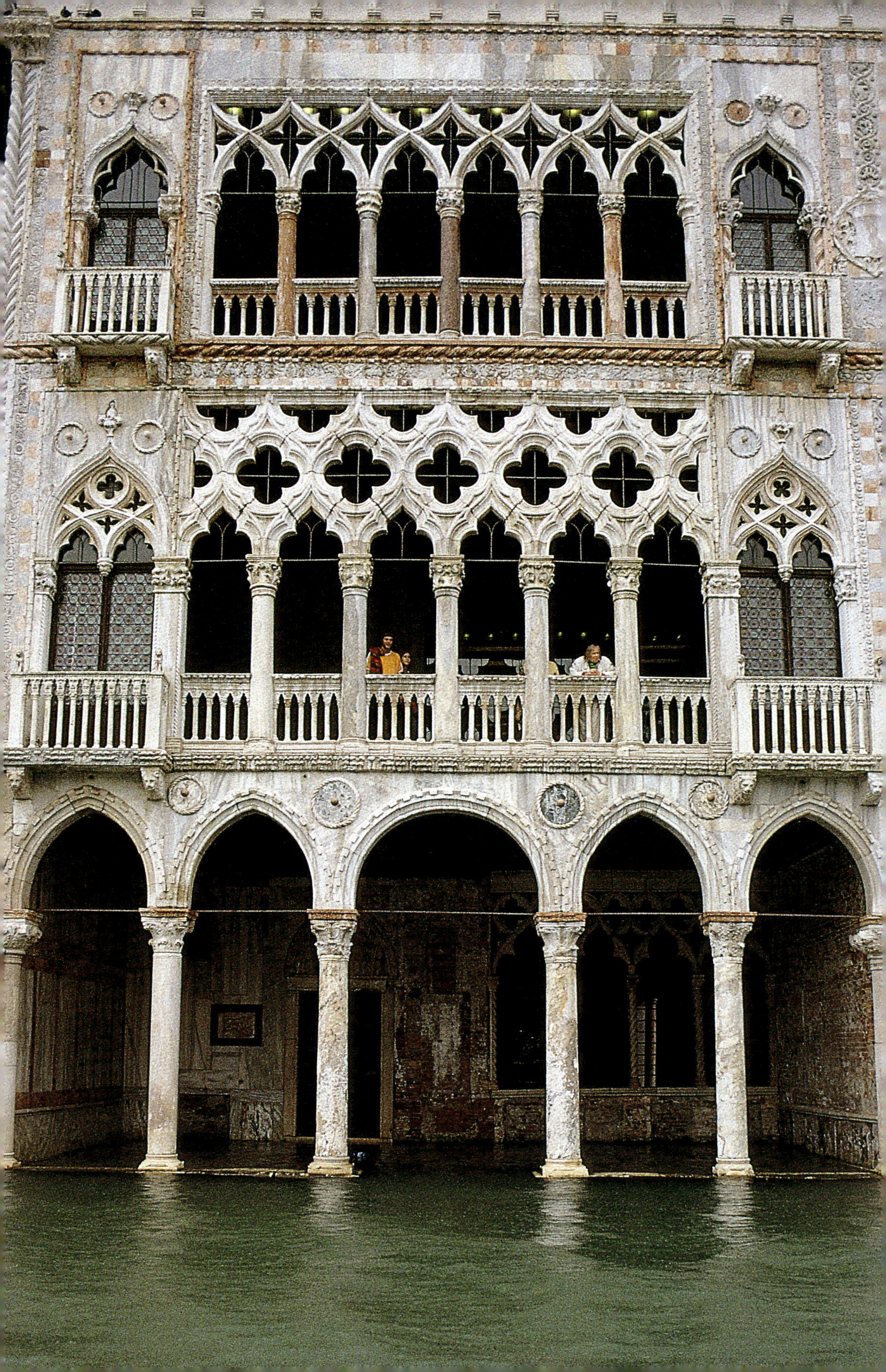

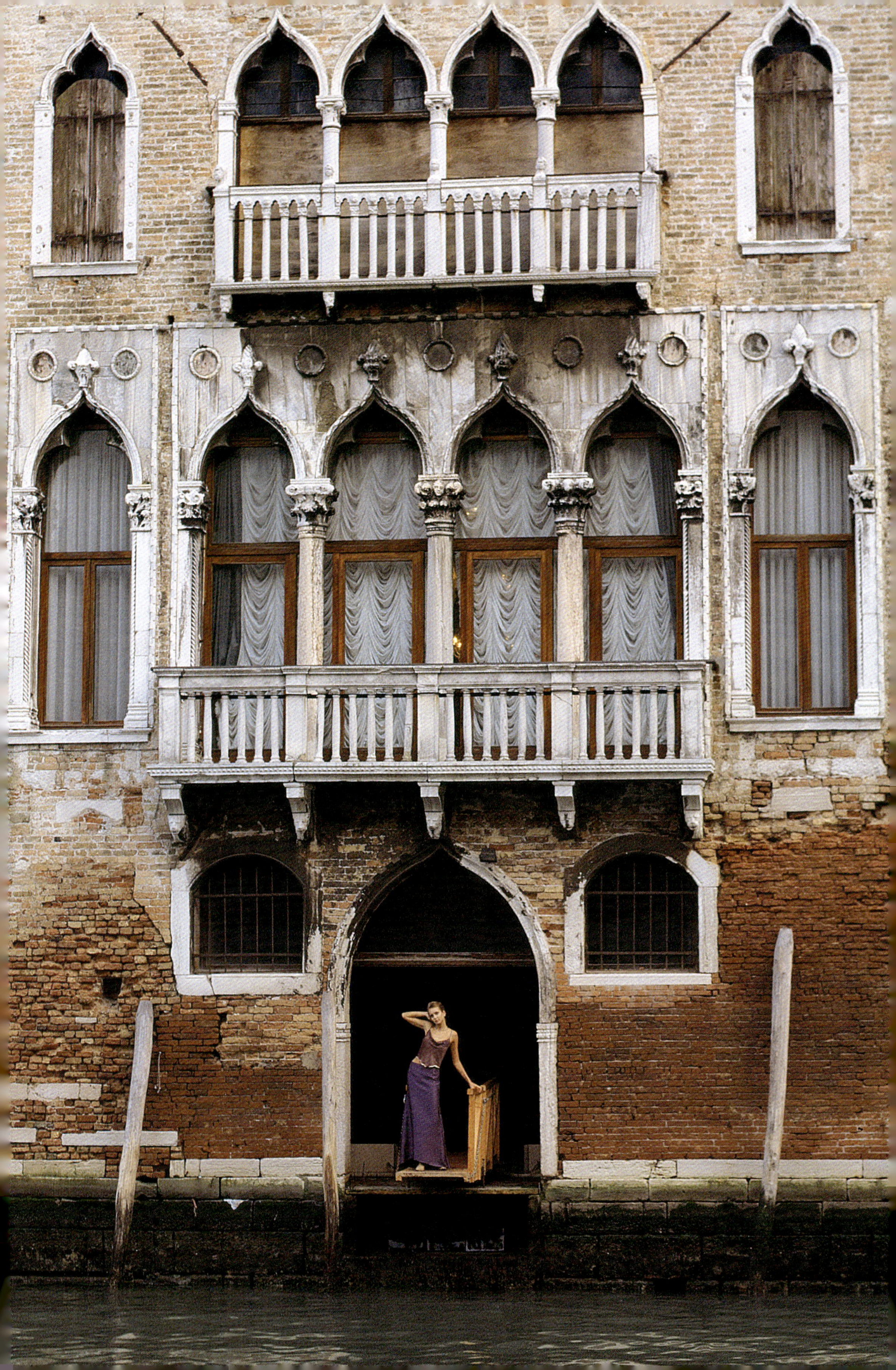

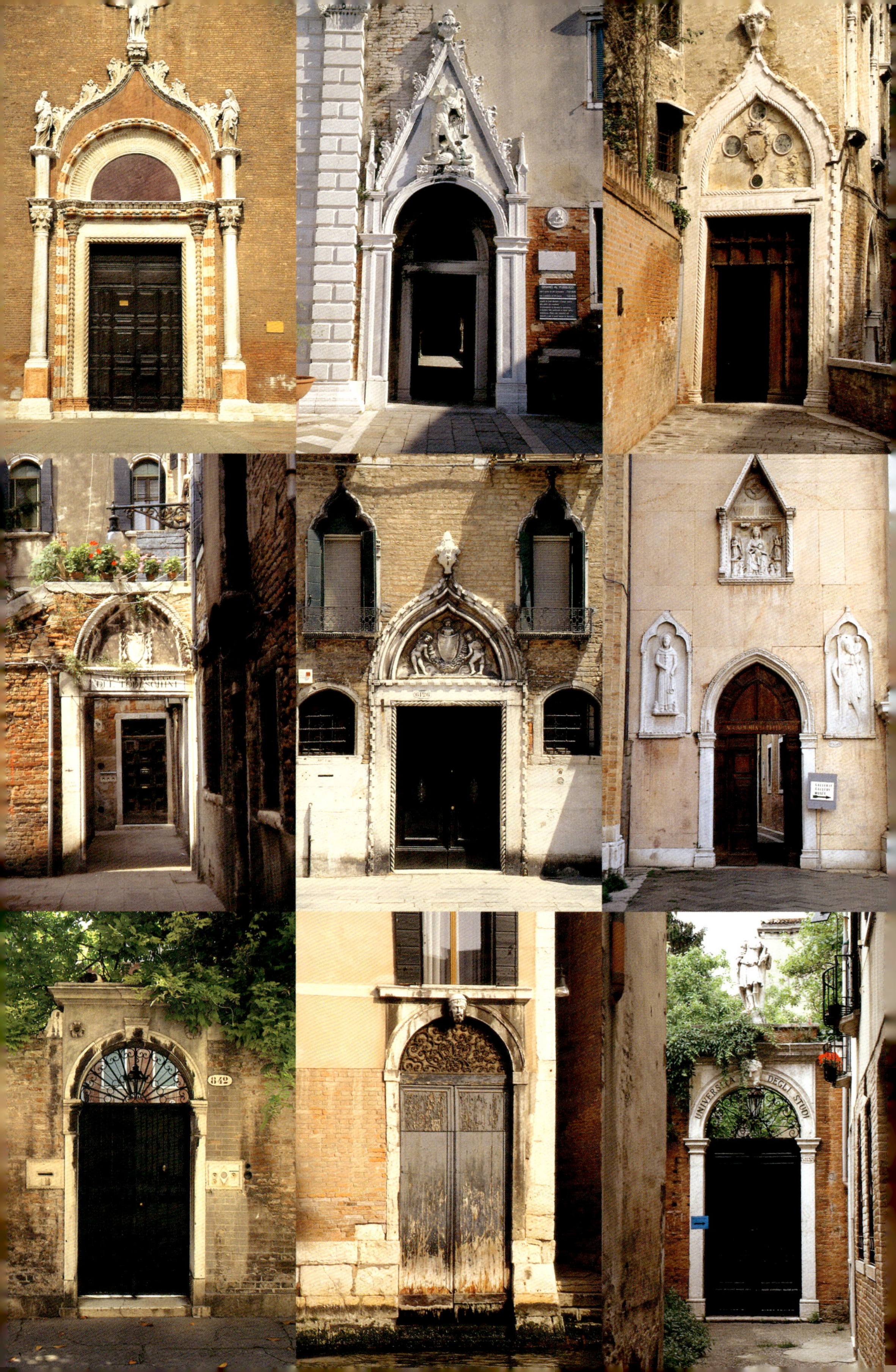
6126
842
UNIVERSITA DEGLI STUDI

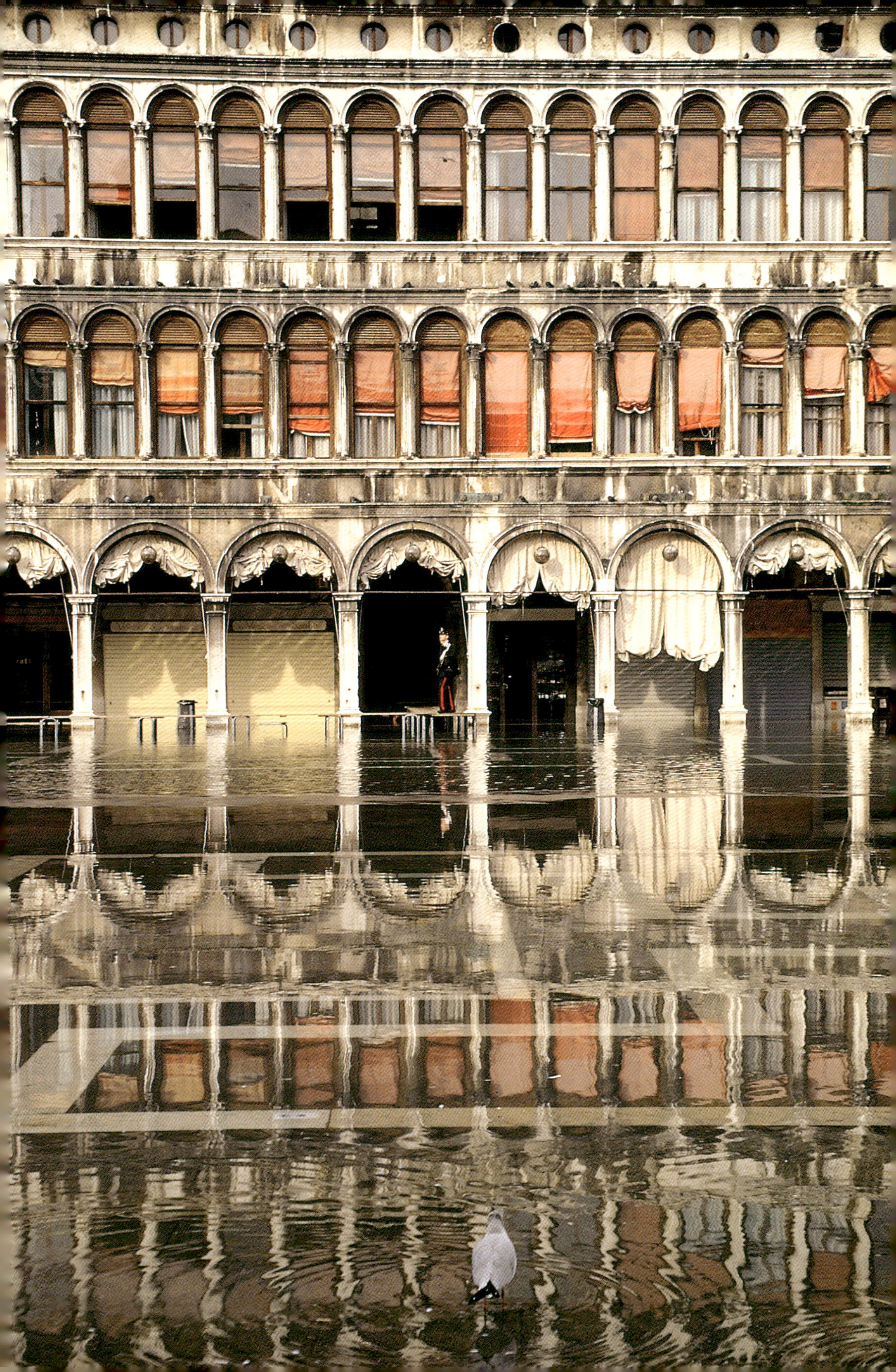

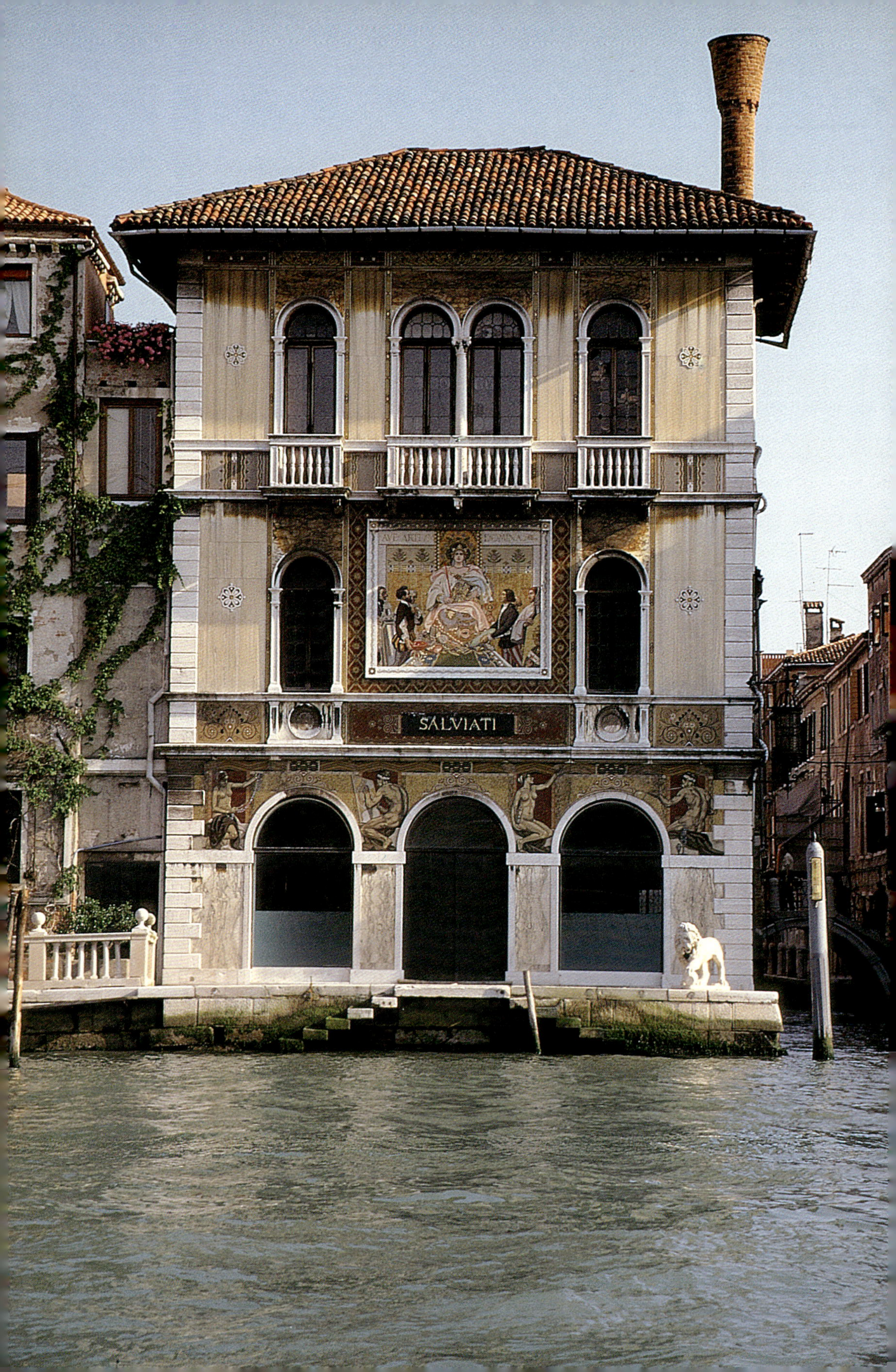
SALVIATI

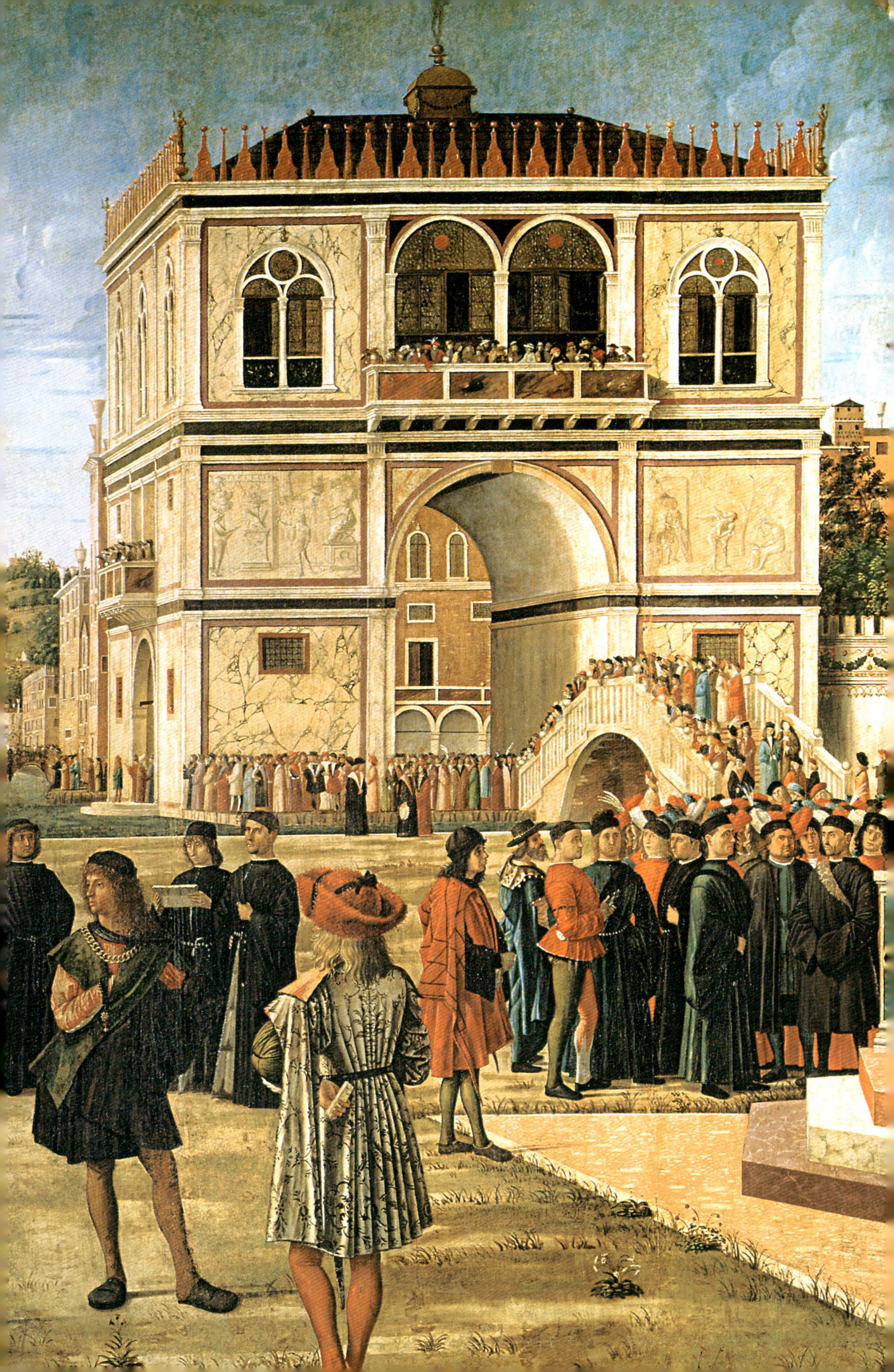

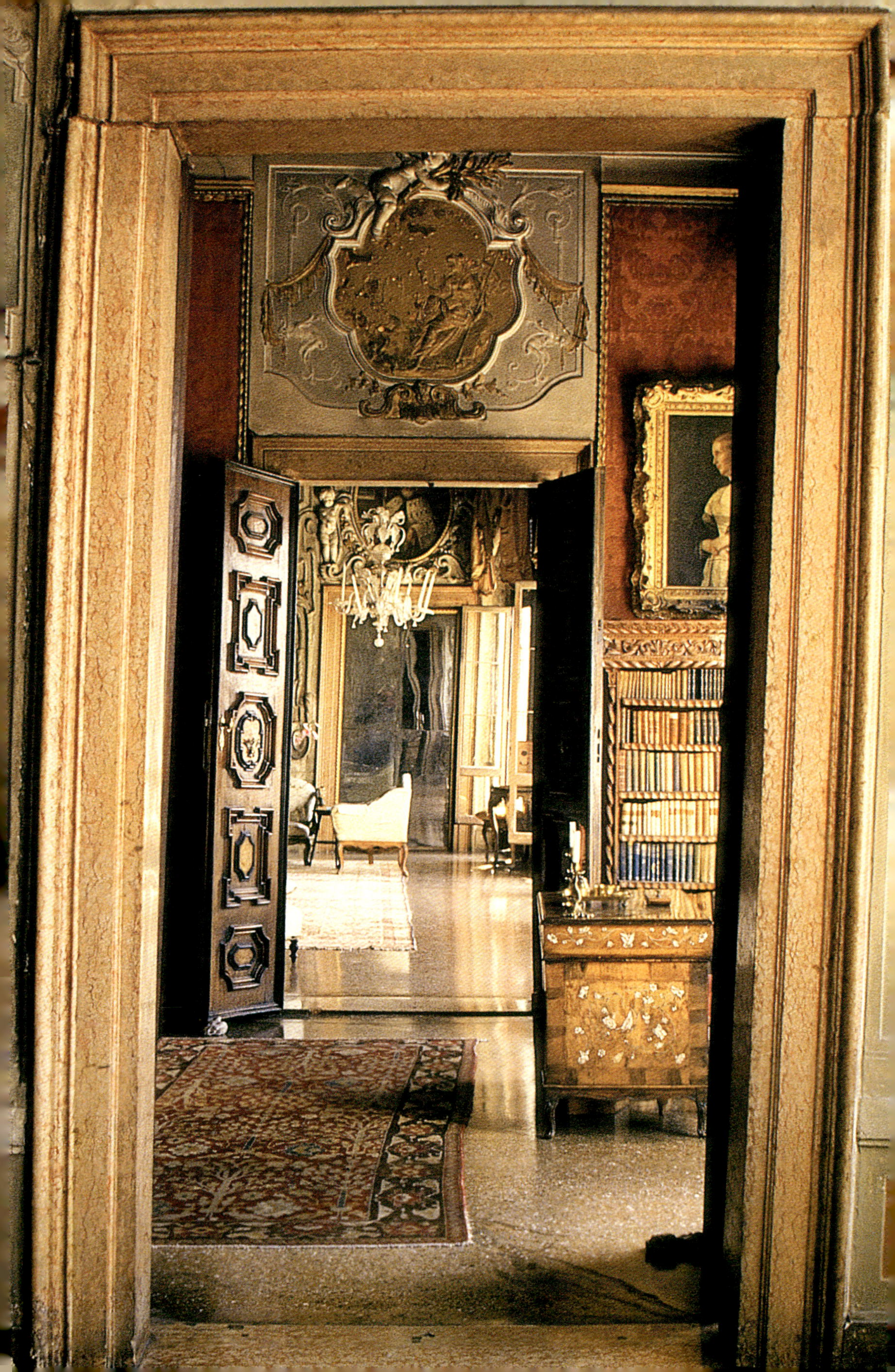

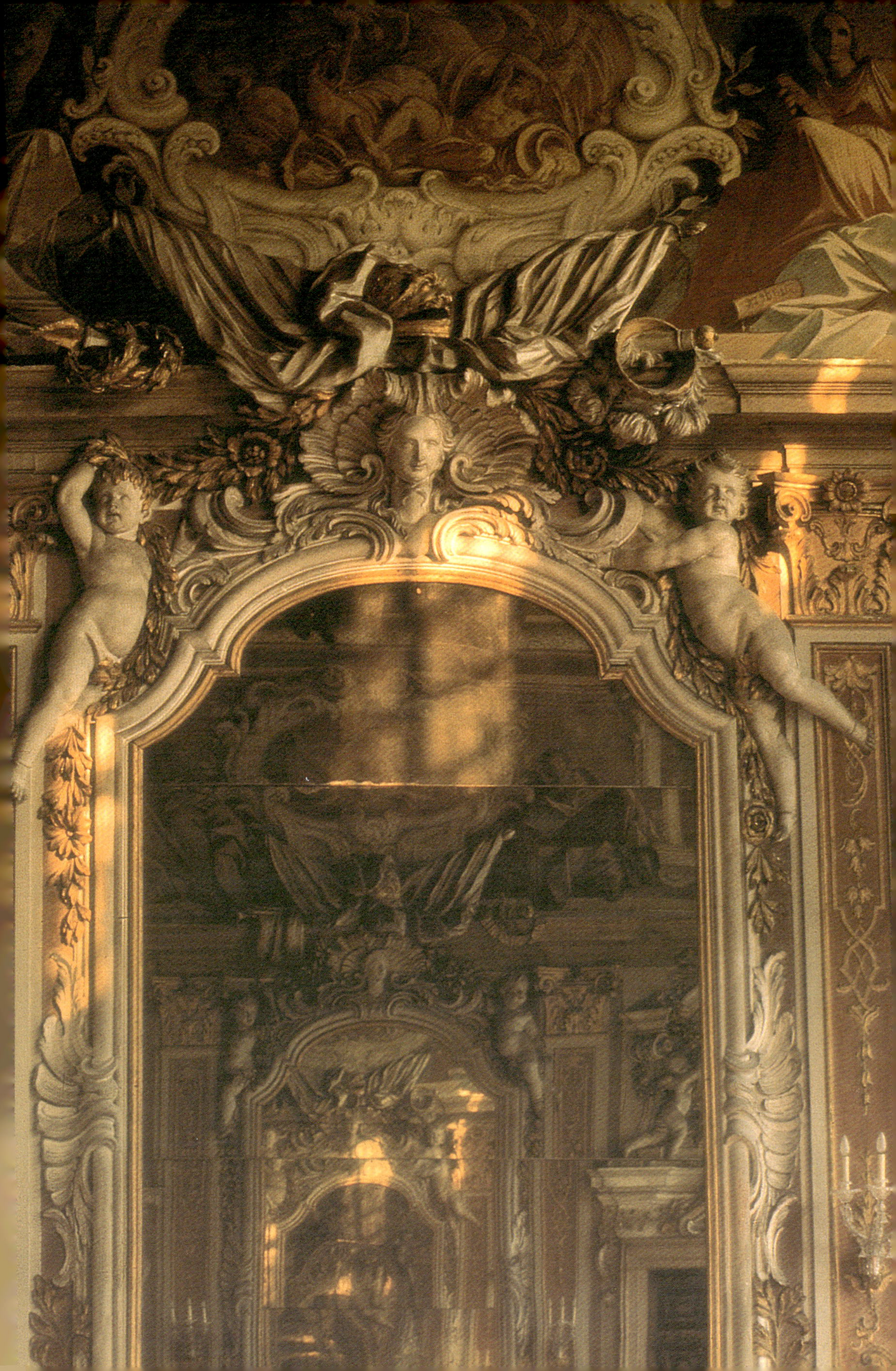

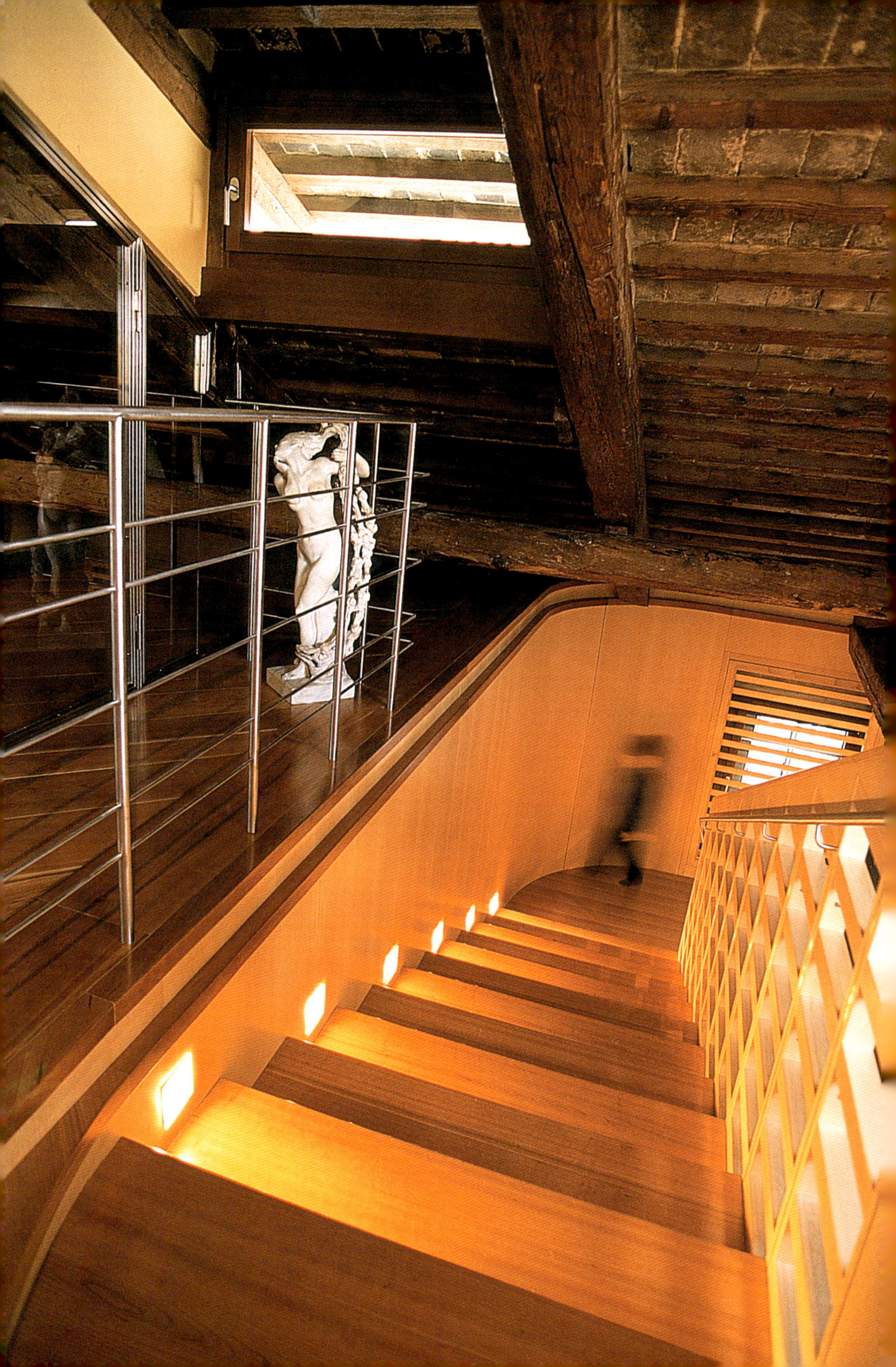

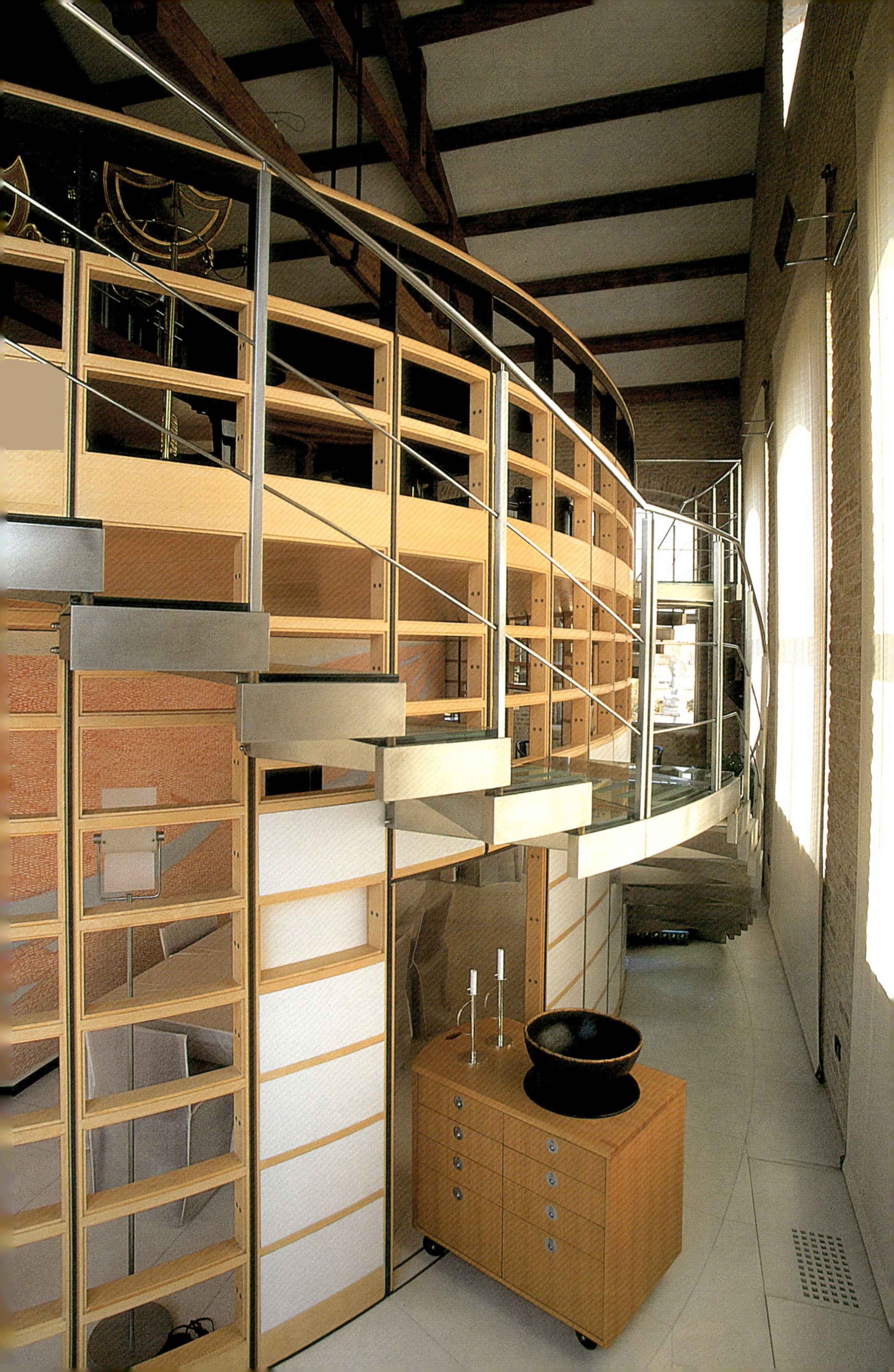

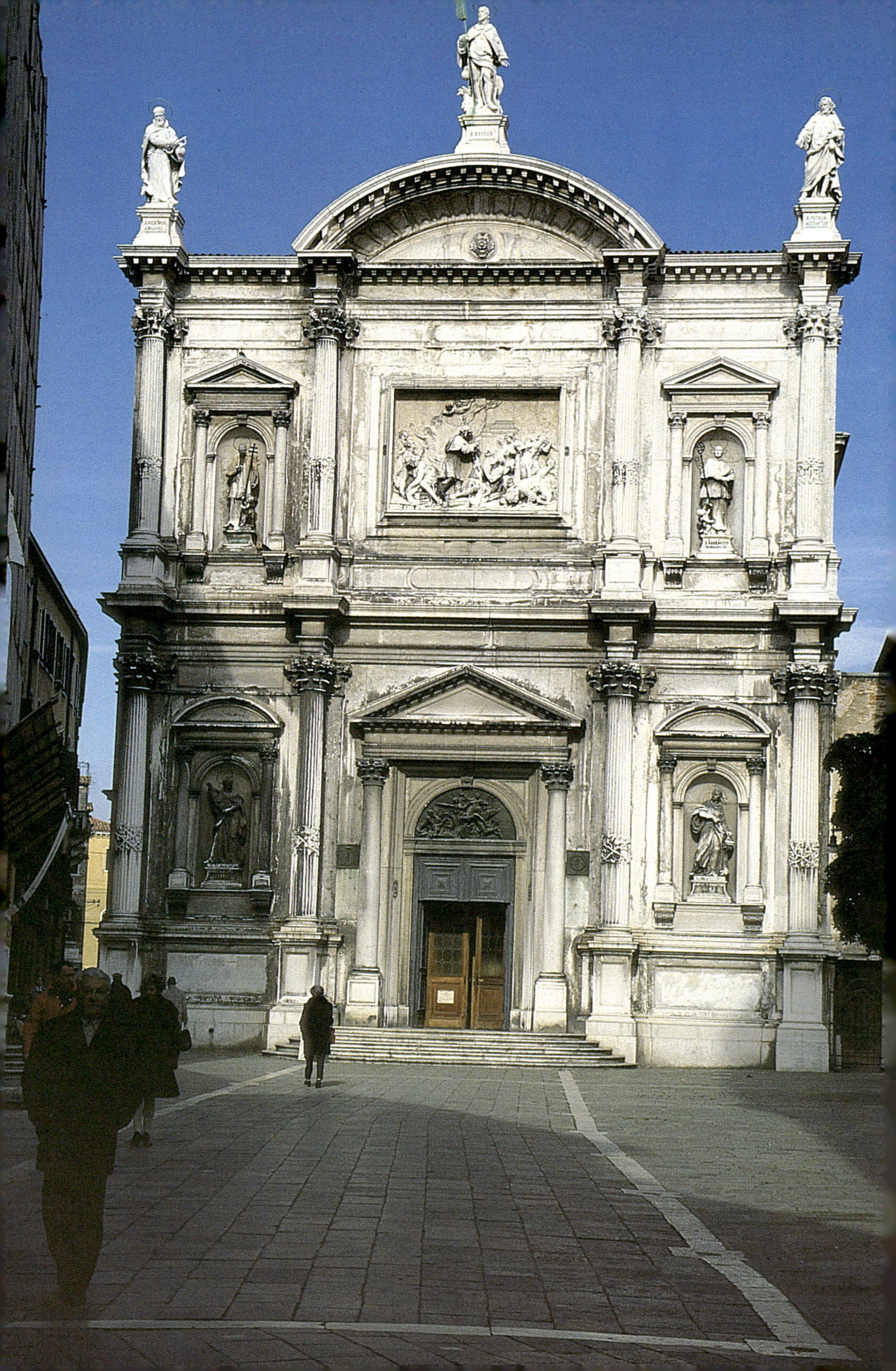

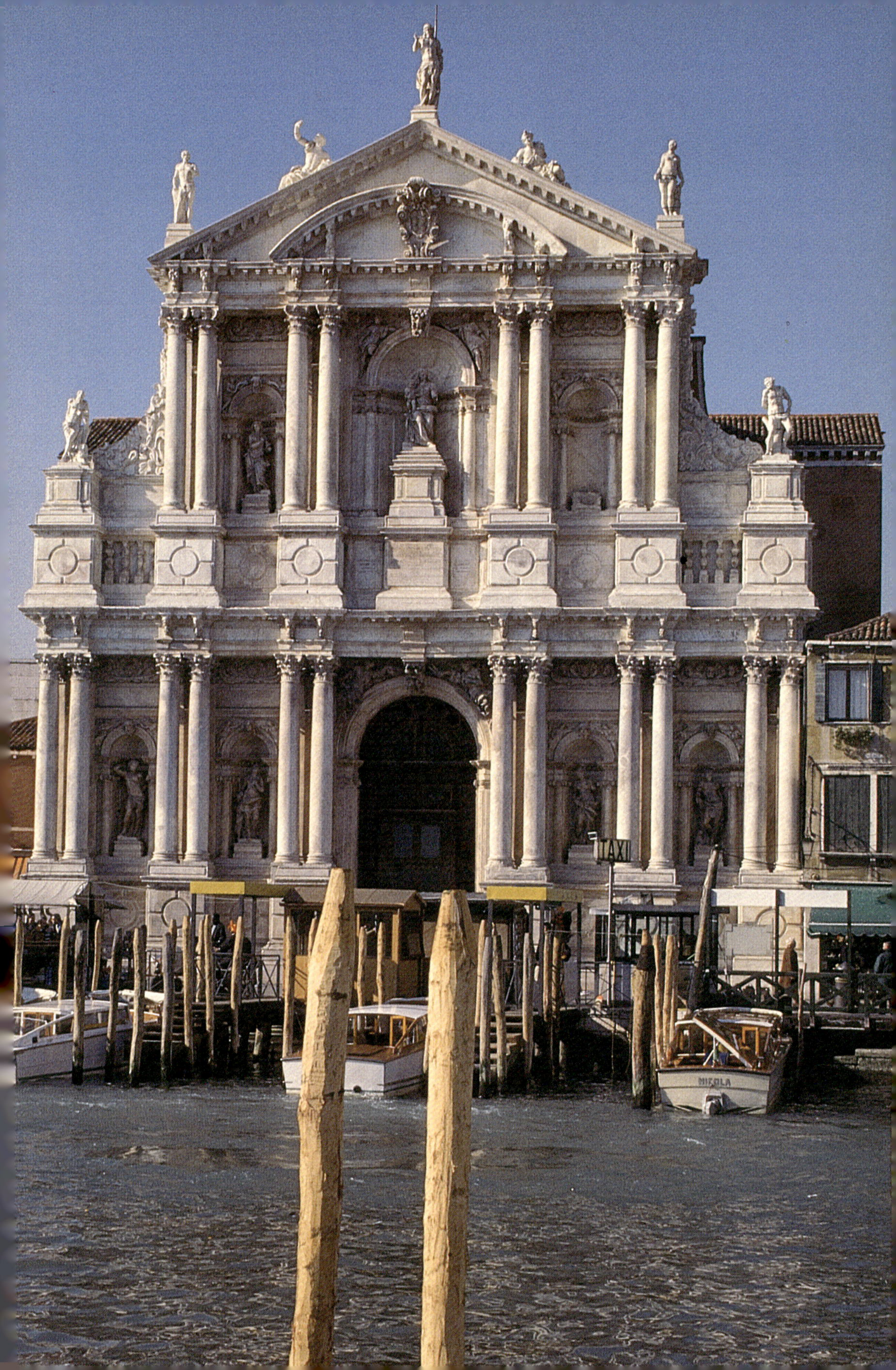
TAXI

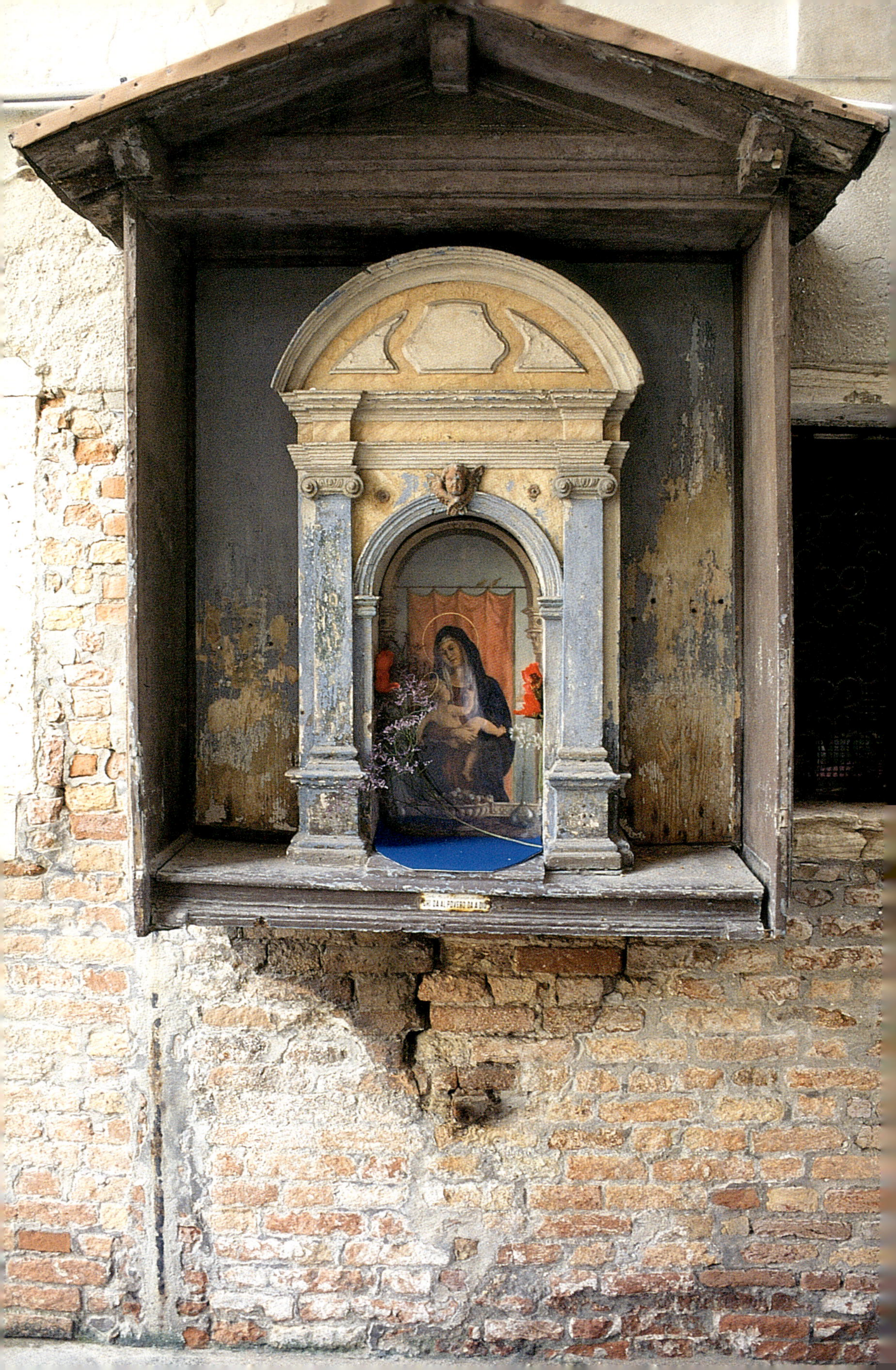

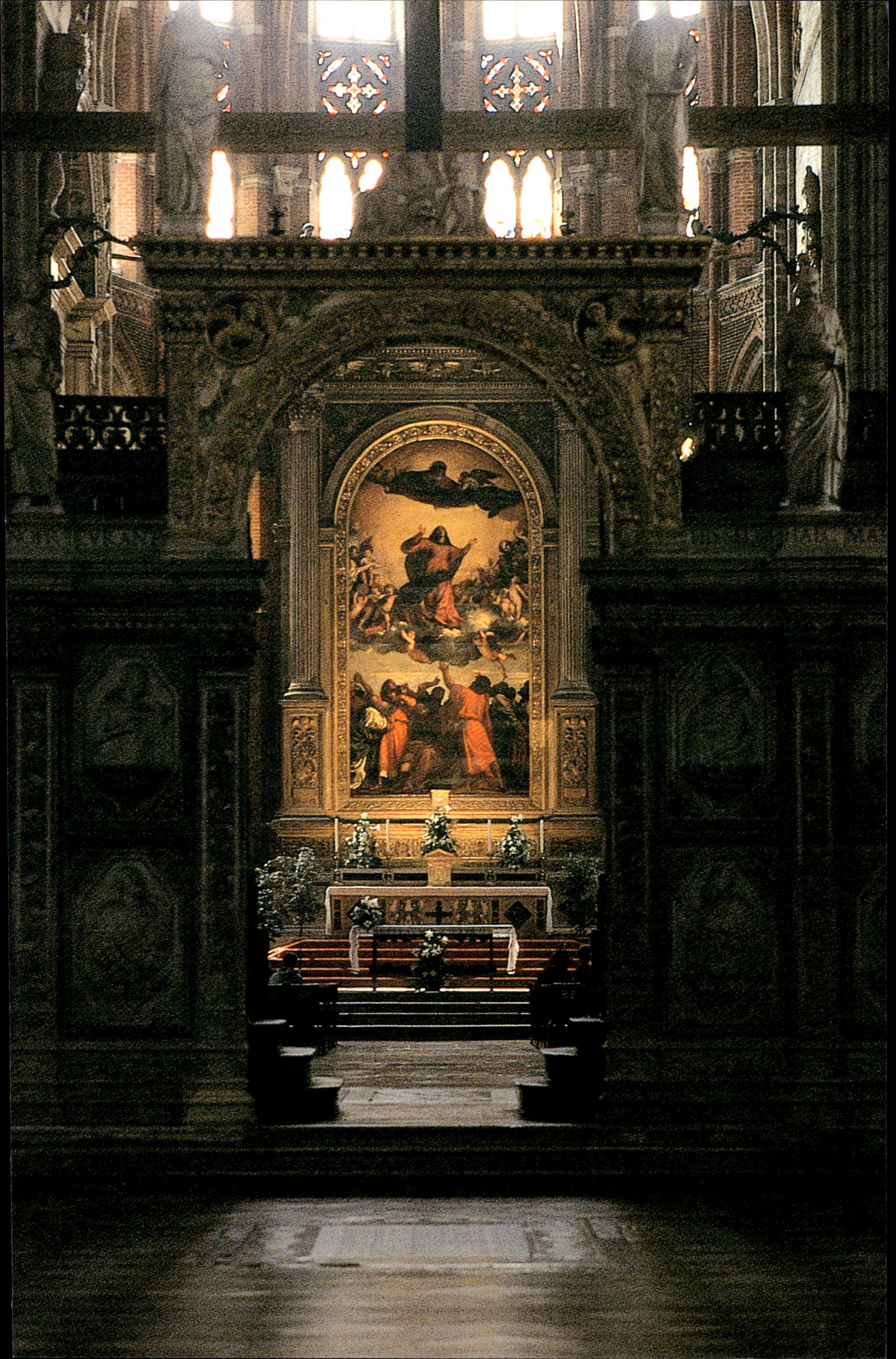

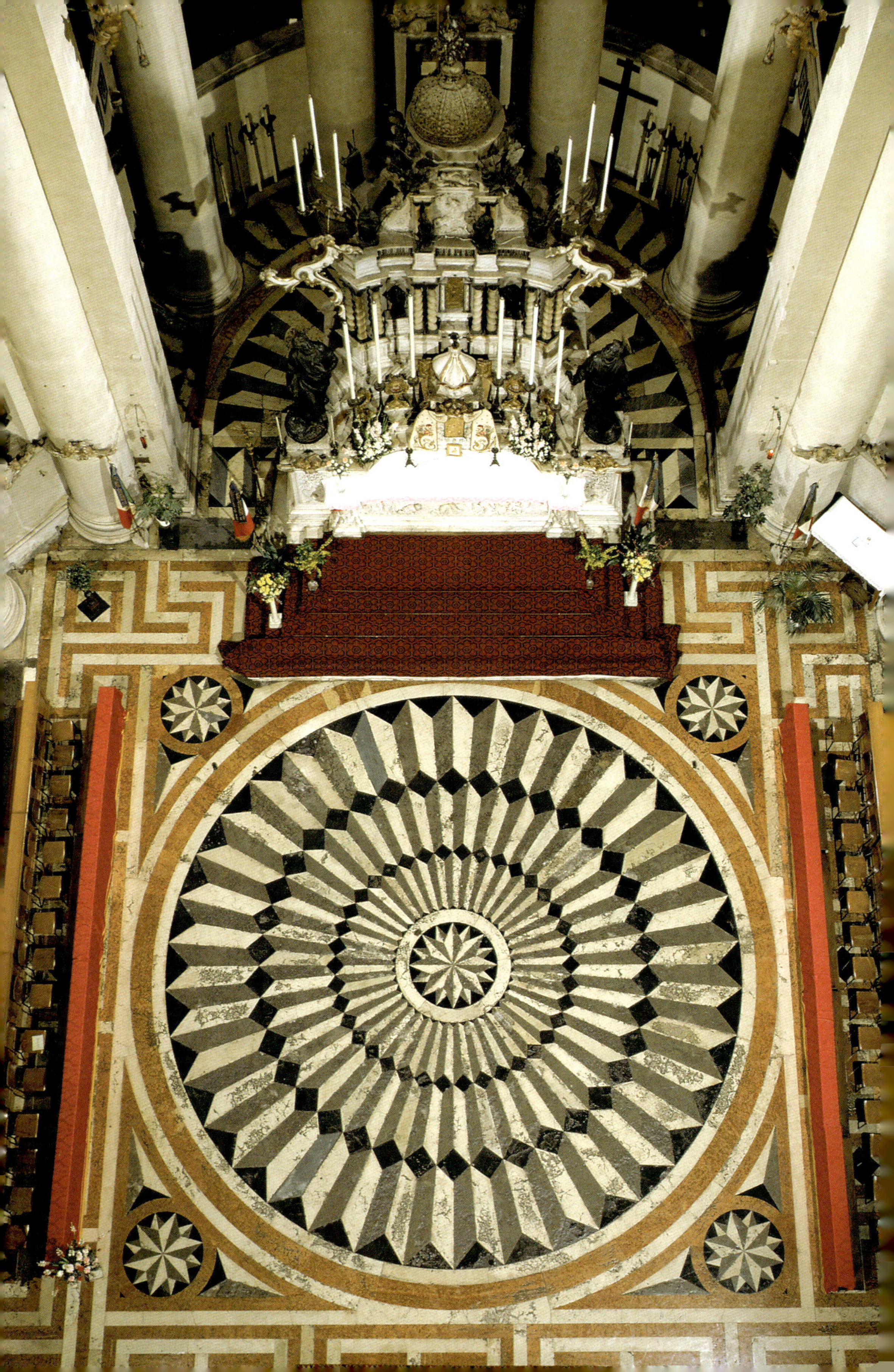

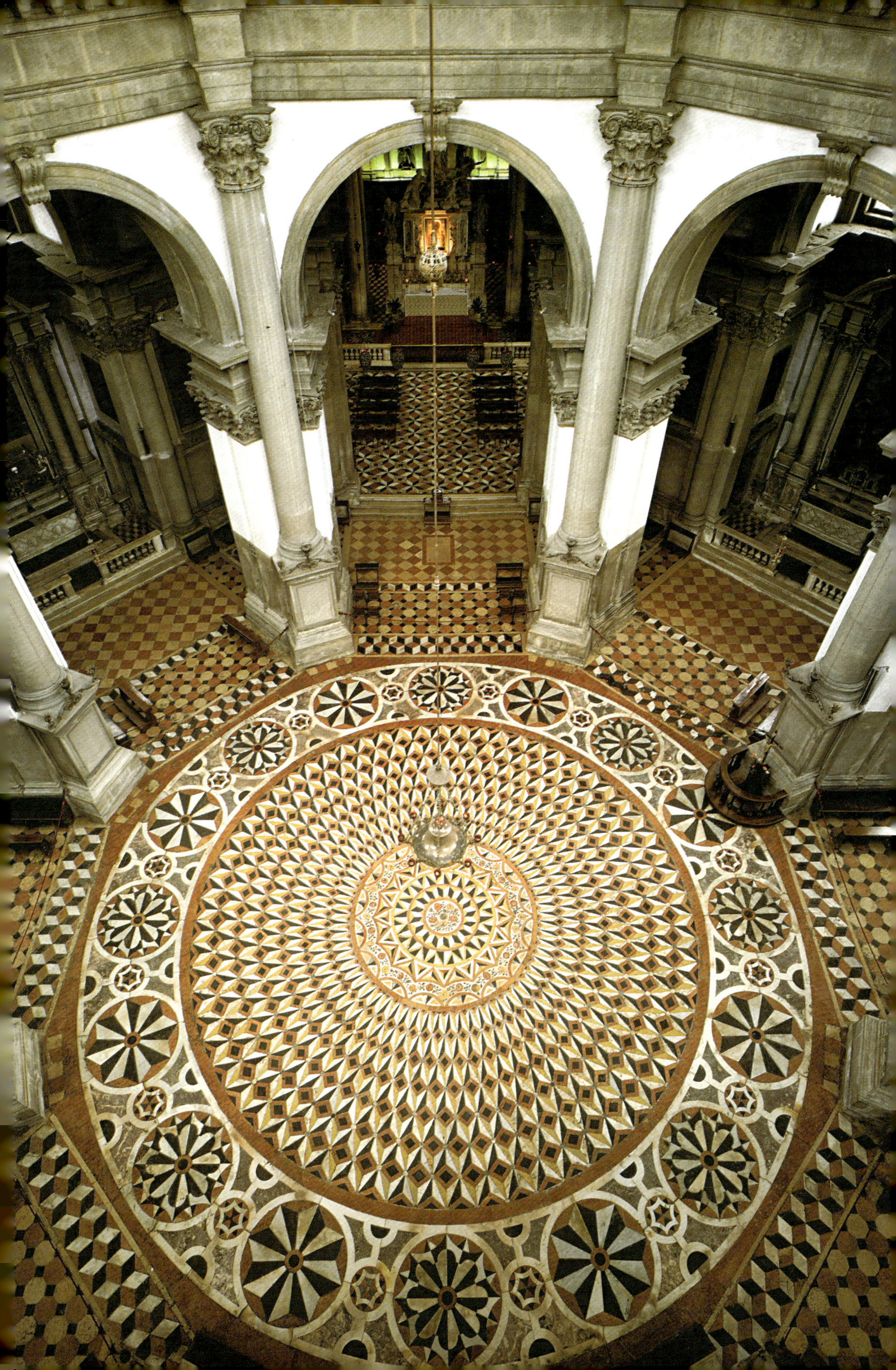

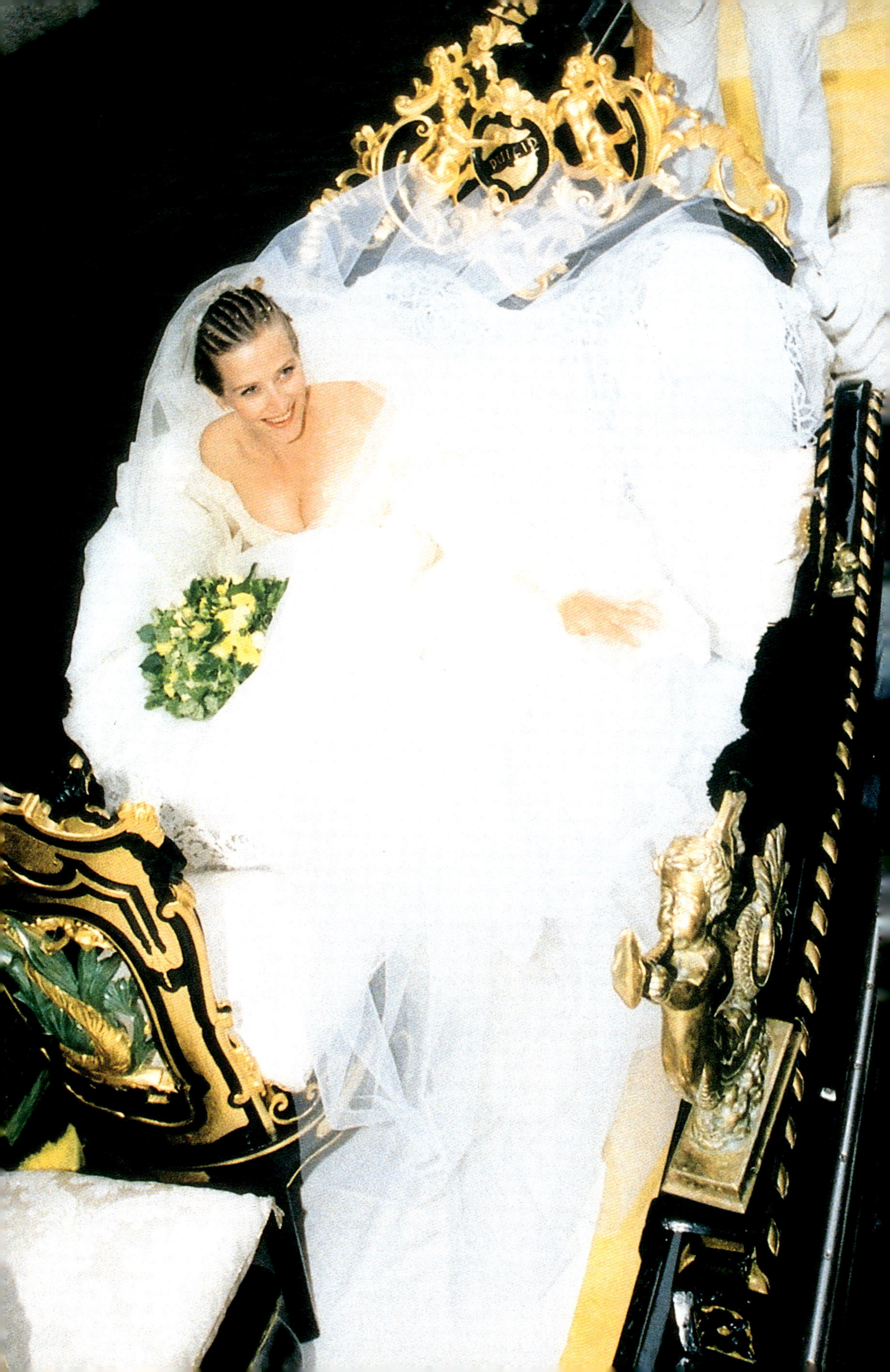

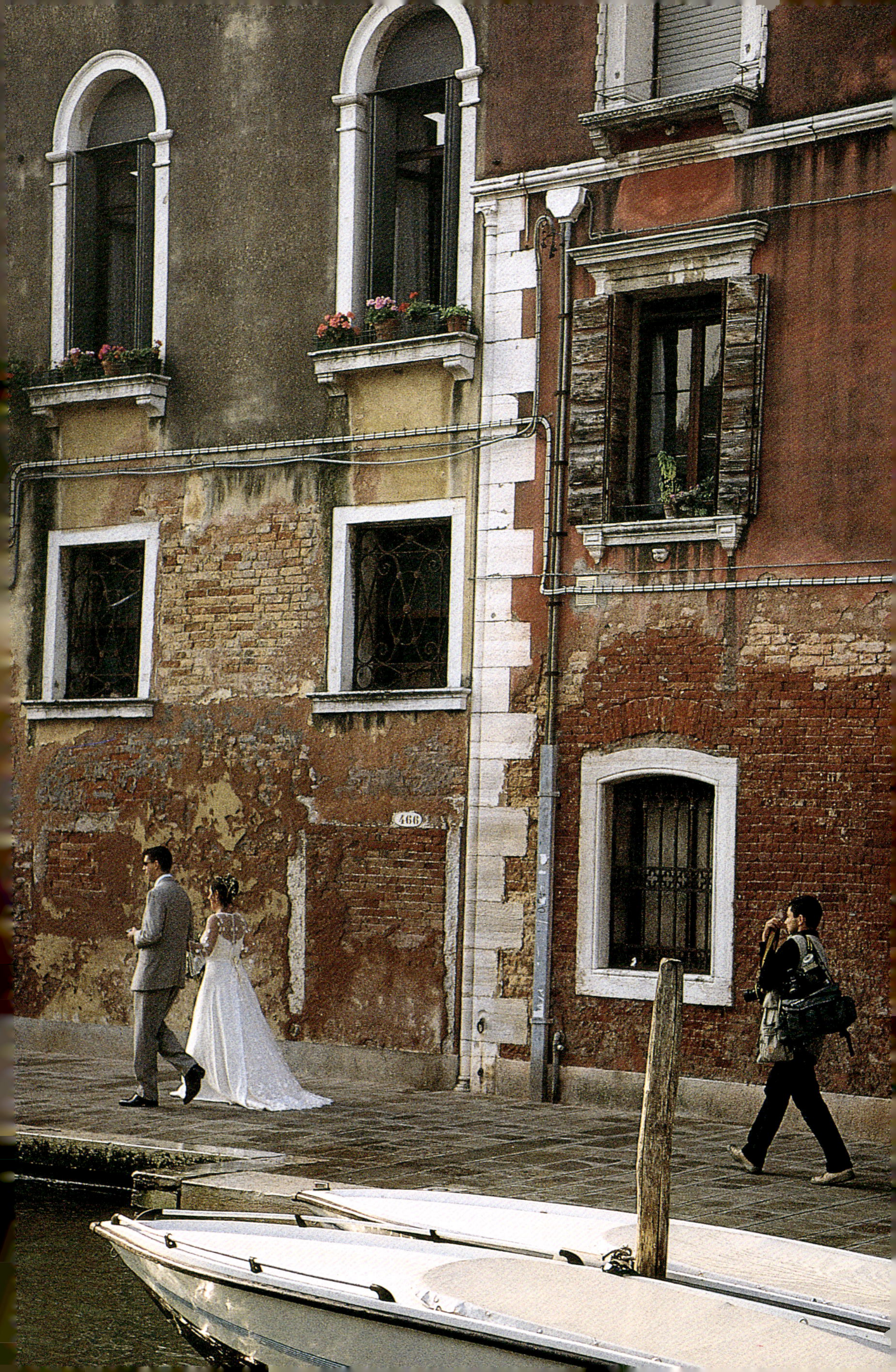
466

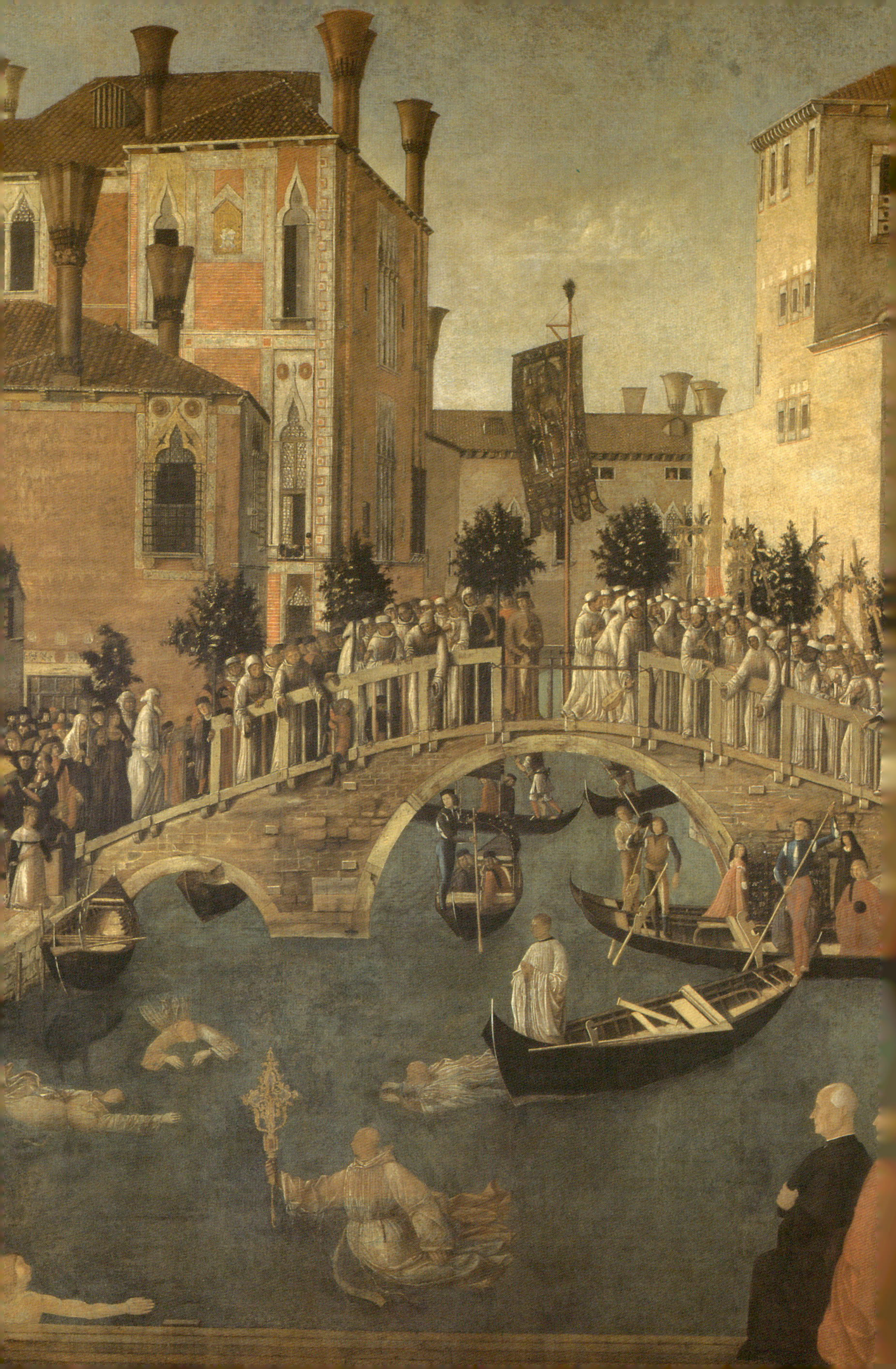

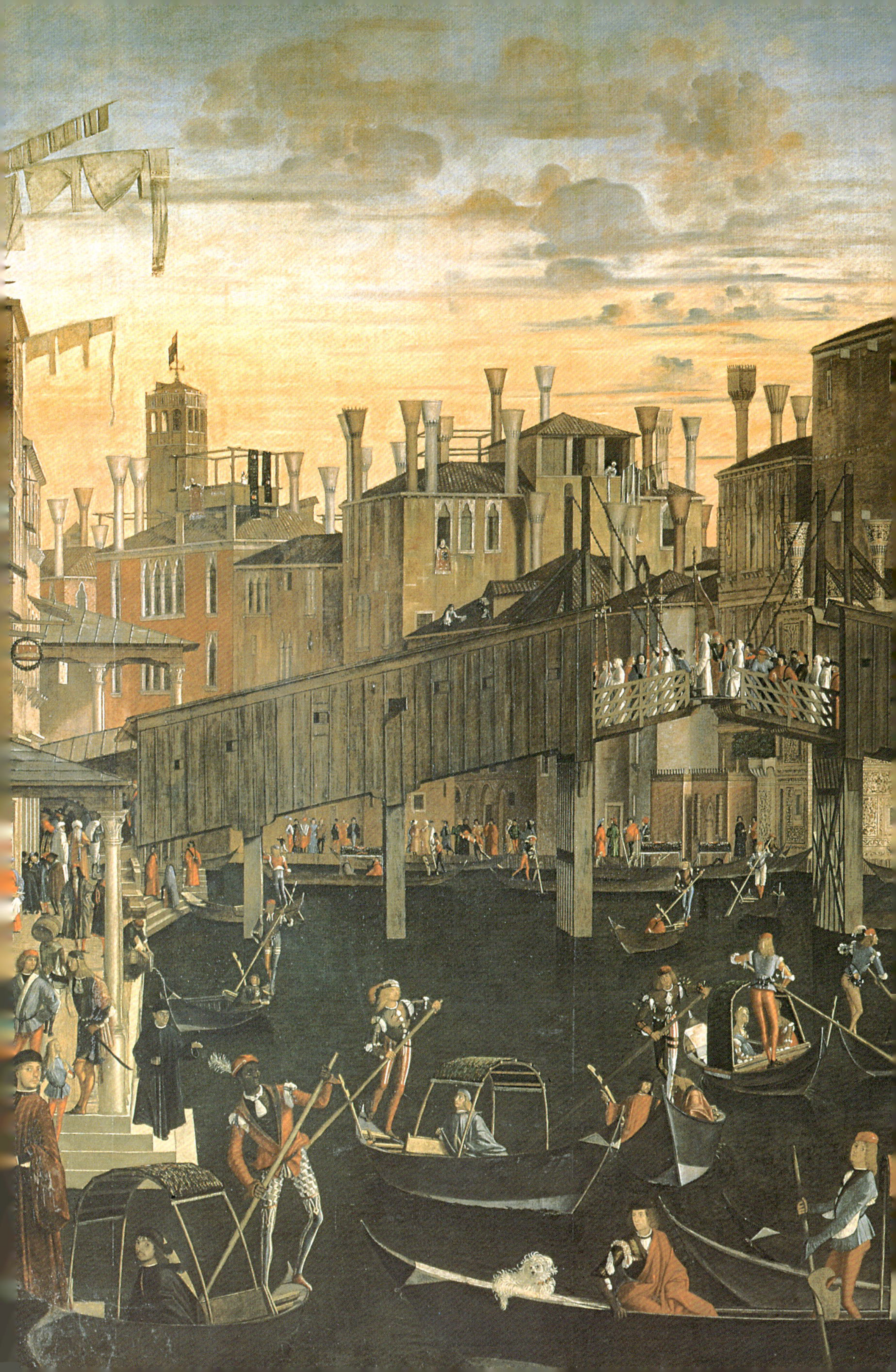

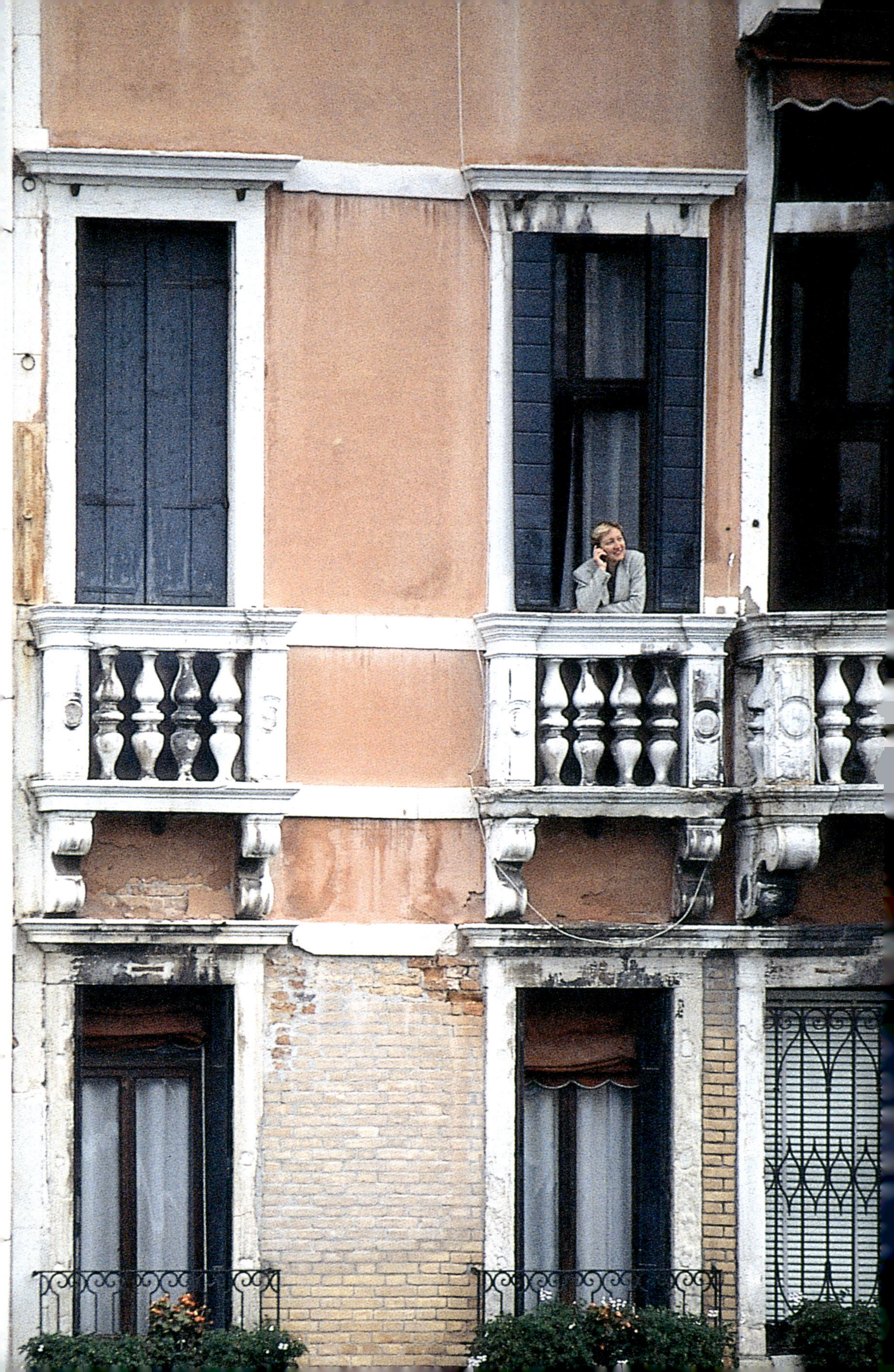

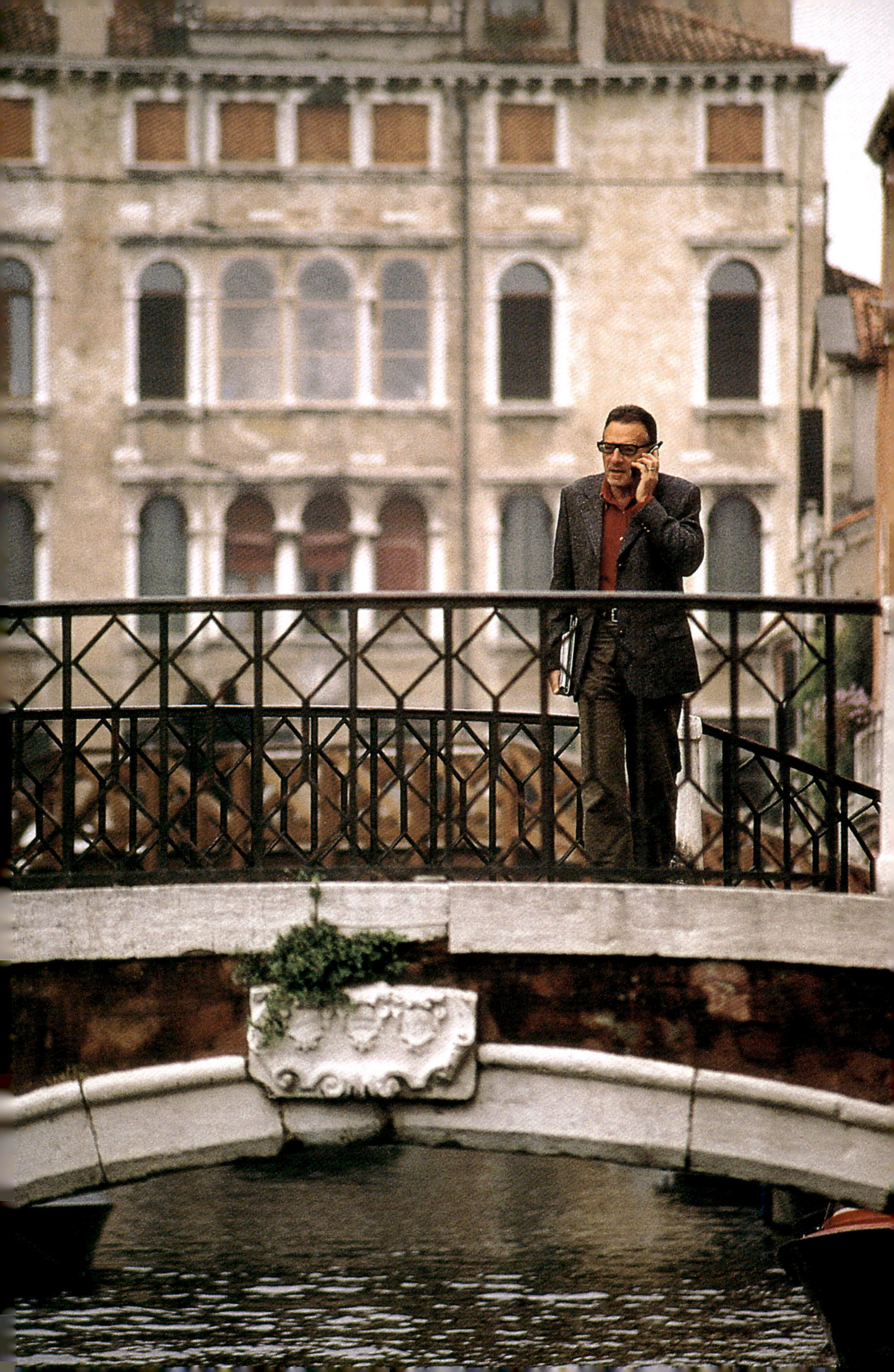

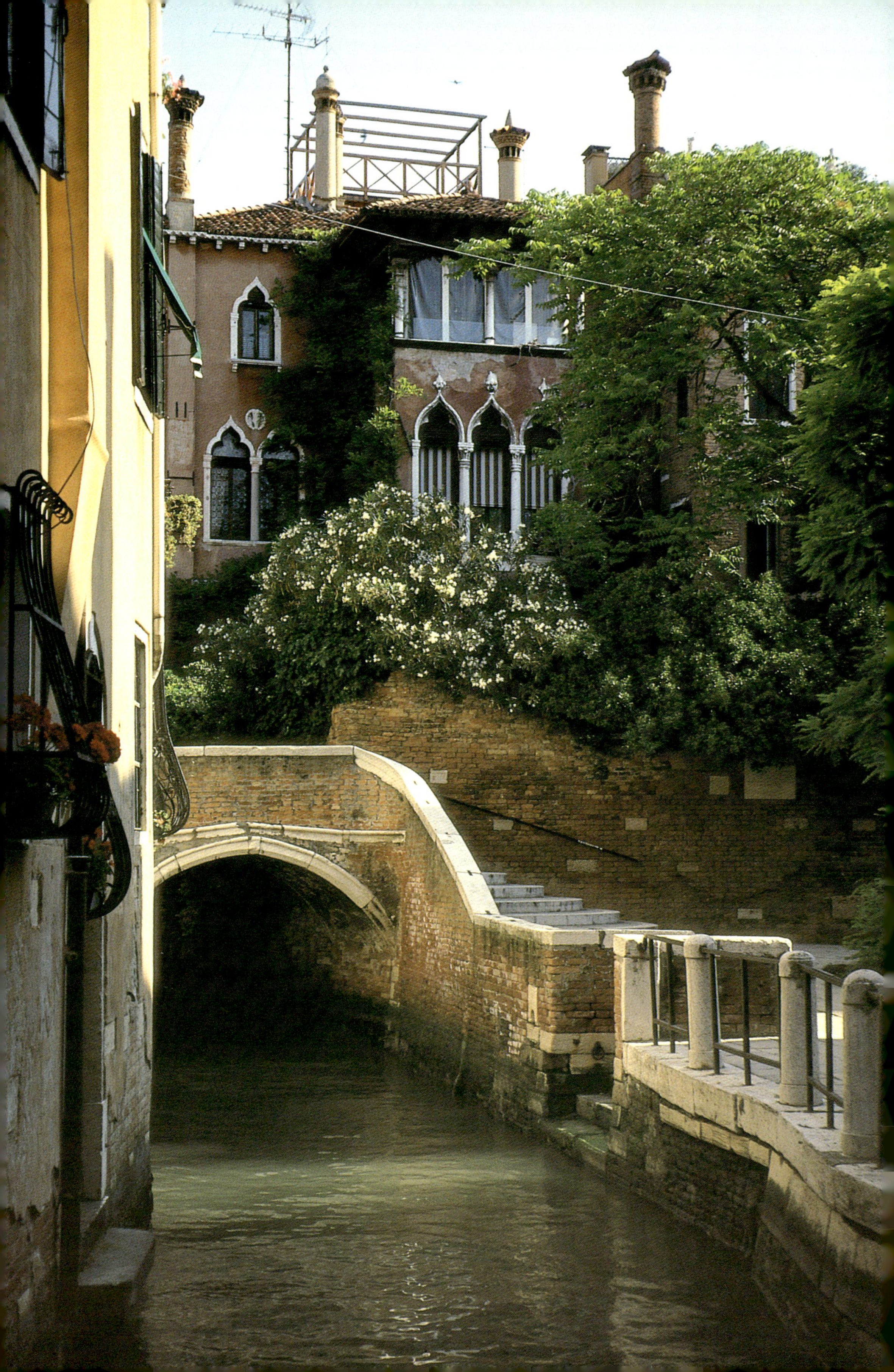

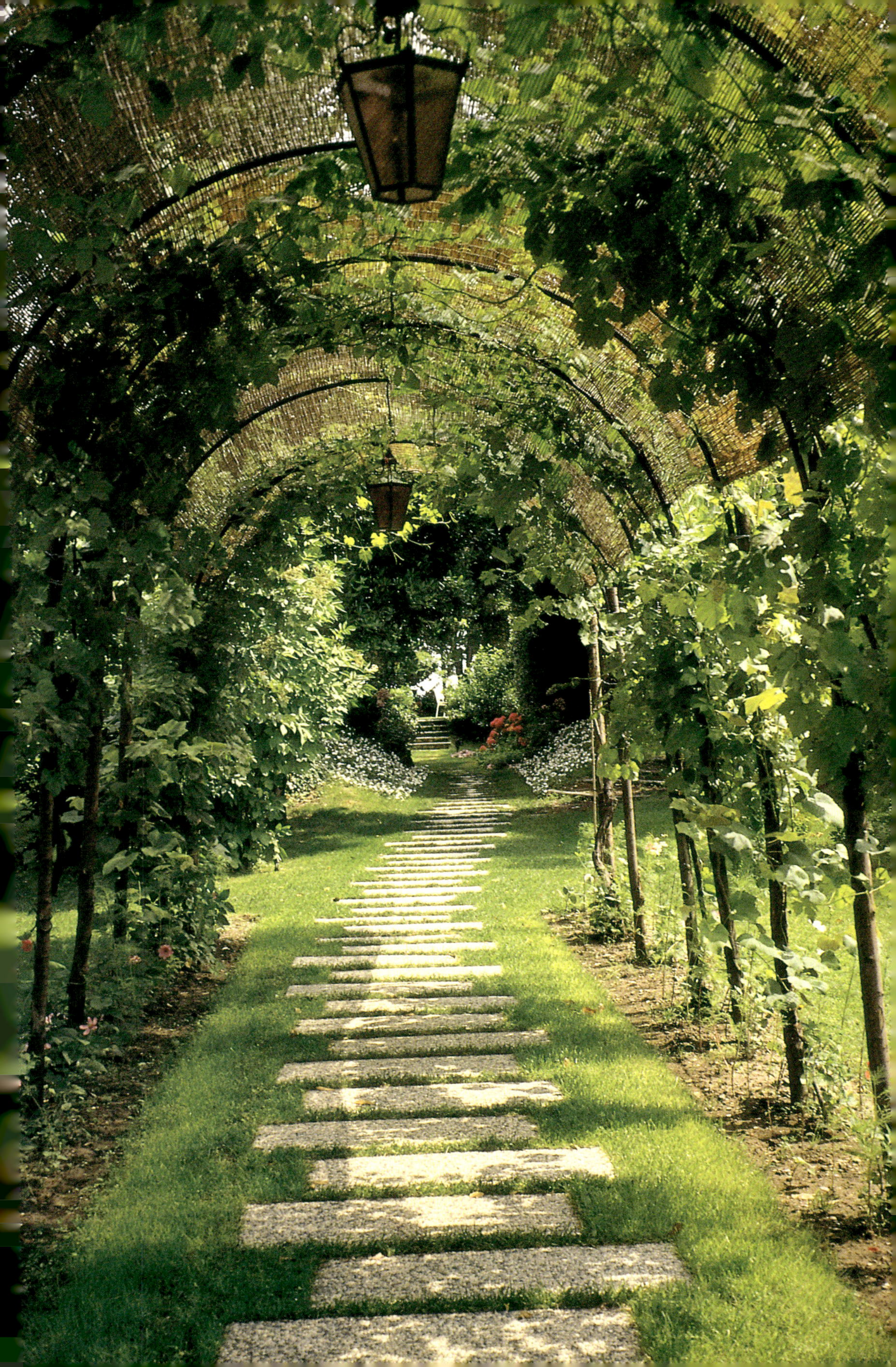

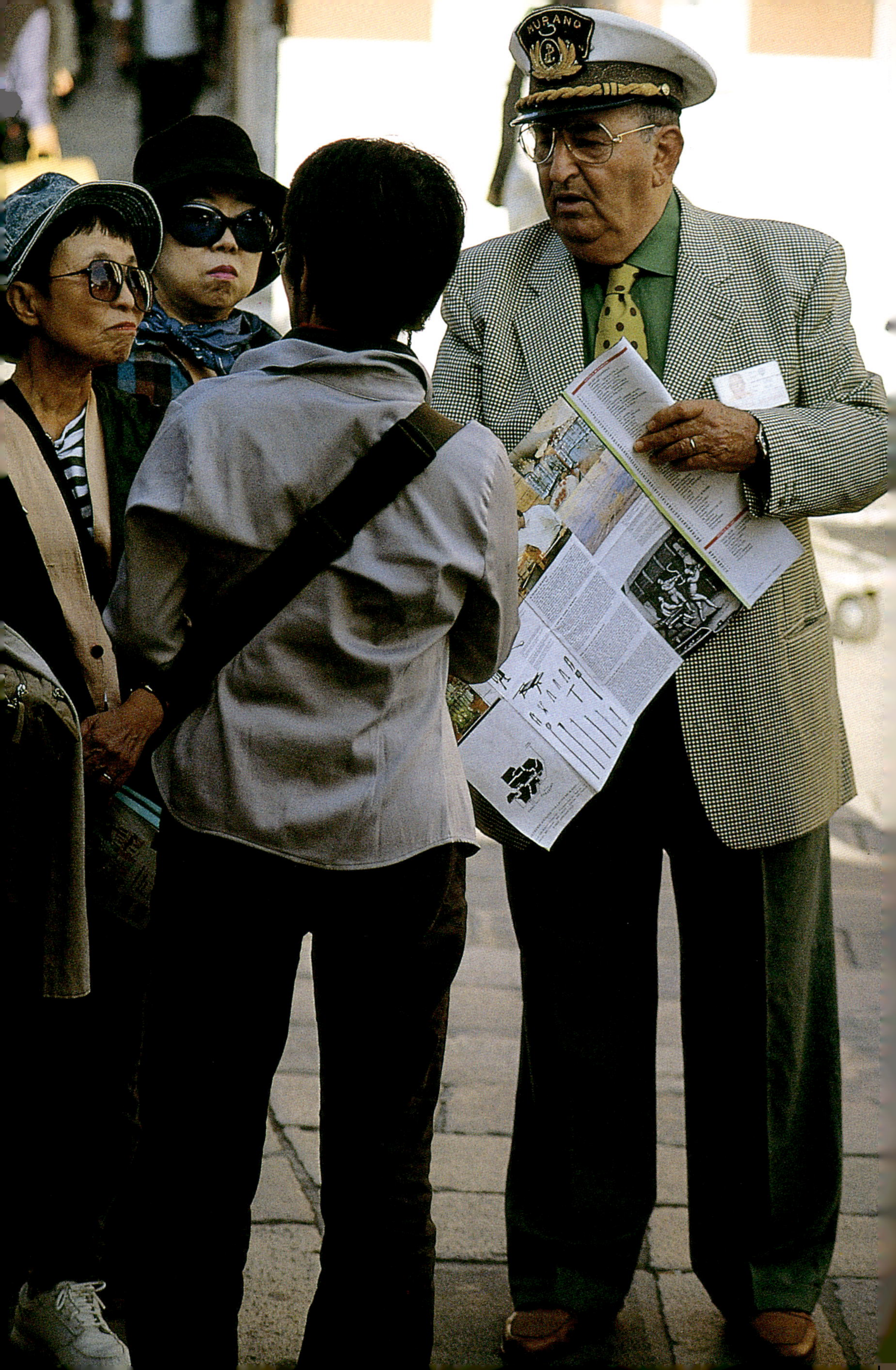
MURANO

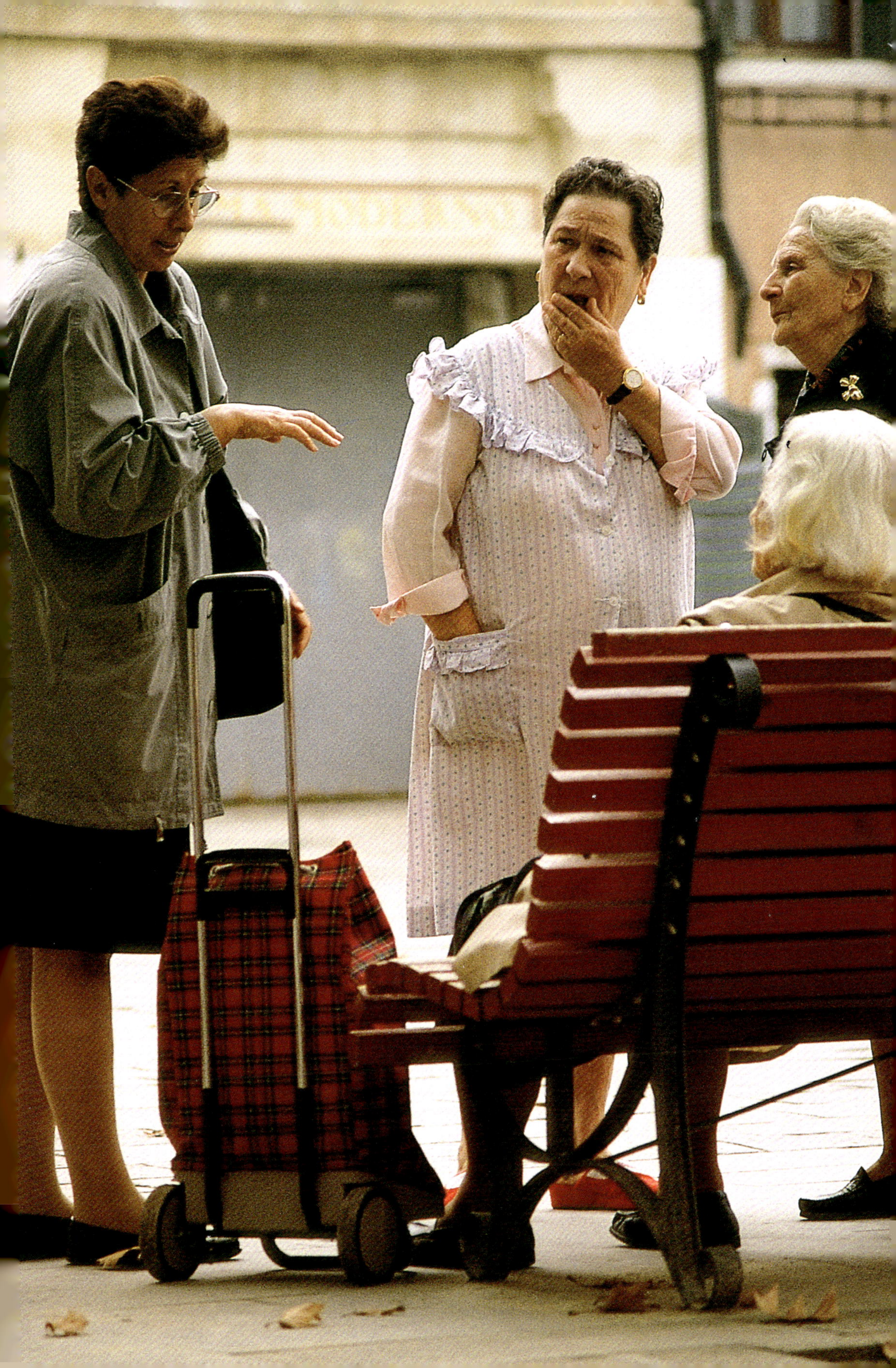

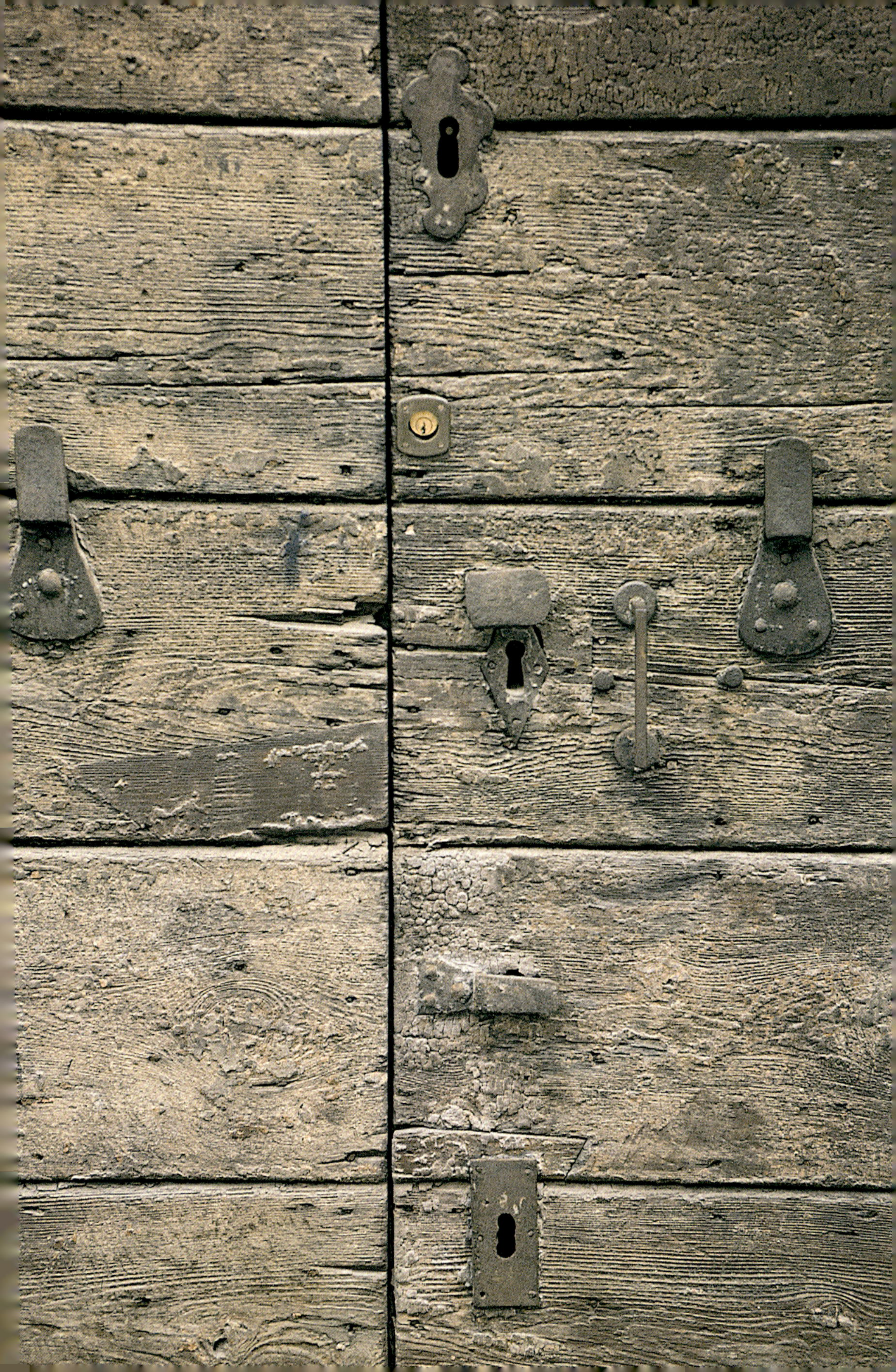

CHAPTER TWO

CULTURAL DELIGHTS

You could spend a year in Venice and still not see

But when we speak of the culture of Venice what do we mean exactly? The abundance of great works of art dazzles and overwhelms us. We can visit galleries and churches every day, awestruck by masters such as Carpaccio, Bellini, Titian or Tiepolo. The musical heritage of Venice is equally vibrant. Composers like Vivaldi, Monteverdi and Gabrieli were once every bit as well known as visual artists such as Giorgione, Veronese or Canaletto. Similarly, the wealth of sculpture is astounding. The talent seems to have run in families, with the brilliant Pietro Lombardo and his sons, who created the church of Santa Maria dei Miracoli, and the delle Masagne family, helped along by their Bellini in-laws, who were responsible for the central window of the Palazzo Ducale.

everything the city has to offer.

Sansovino, a Florentine by birth, became a son of Venice, spending the last 40 or so years of his life here. Alessandro Vittoria was another fine sculptor whose talent shone with a light that was purely Venetian. This ability to turn their hand to anything and then do it superbly well is, John Julius Norwich has noted on occasions, "one of the most astonishing and, it must be said, the most irritating aspects of the people of Venice".

But the culture of Venice is in its very being: the fact that every day the entire population of Venice walks to work or travels on the water gives the city a shape like no other. No one has to get their car started, no one has to remember to fill it up with petrol, no one gets stuck in traffic. Regulars on the *vaporetti*, huddled in their coats in the winter, fanning themselves in the summer, have their own personal rapport with the culture of their city. So do those who stride out to their place of work each day.

The light and shade of Venice, the way these alternate, dancing on the underside of a bridge or against a wall, reflect another unique aspect of the city. A Venetian may pass this way all his life, yet still, on some days, a flickering reflection will catch his eye and give him pleasure. It is part of the culture of his city. The culture of the gondola, of a skyline pierced with 30 different varieties of *campanile*, of Venetian Gothic windows and of carved lions, all add their particular something to our perception of Venice.

They can't be ignored any longer; the pictures so glorious they defy description, the glowing examples of such enormous talent that those who see them are rendered speechless have to be seen. Venice demands it.

SAVOURING THE SUPERLATIVES

Titian's gigantic masterpiece, *The Assumption of the Virgin*, dominating the high altar of the Frari church and the largest panel painting in the world, has a force and dynamism that is something to behold. No wonder it put the Frari monks in a state of turmoil when it first appeared. This superlative Gothic church, huge and meditative, especially at night when its corners and alcoves glow in the light of candles lit by the faithful, is full of wonders, including an exquisite altarpiece by Bellini. Another splendid Titian in the same church is *The Pesaro Madonna*, in which the Pesaro family are grouped around the Madonna and St Peter.

Just around the corner from the Frari is the Scuola di San Rocco with a collection of sacred paintings by Tintoretto that are quite overwhelming in their impact. Too grandiose and gloomy for some, Tintoretto's *Crucifixion* has yet been known to move strong men to tears.

Then there is the Accademia, not only an enchanting gallery with a warmth and friendliness missing from many of its ilk but a distillation of Venetian cultural treasures. Many pictures by great Venetian painters are, in fact, elsewhere, carefully and lovingly exhibited in galleries and museums dotted across the world. Look for a favourite Canaletto or an adored Guardi and you possibly won't find them here. Canaletto, especially, was such a popular artist that visiting 18th-century collectors carried him off by the armful. Guardi was almost as covetable. The place to see both these artists' best work is probably London.

But the joy of wandering through the halls of the Accademia is that everything you are seeing, relishing, marvelling at, was inspired by the tiny city outside, hardly the size of any regional town, which you can traverse on foot from one side to the other in half an hour. What an inspiration Venice provided for its wealth of artists! Of the earliest, Paolo Veneziano is probably

Those who have come to Venice prepared for ceiling-gazing will be well rewarded by a most spectacular ceiling by Giannantonio Fumiani in the unassuming church of San Pantalon. It might be worth comparing his painting with that of Paolo Veronese in the nearby church of San Sebastiano, and then, later, the superb Tiepolo ceiling frescoes in the Gesuati church on the Zattere.

the best known, and his splendid *Coronation of the Virgin* is here, as is Paolo Veronese's famous *Feast of The House of Levi*.

The Titian *Pietà* can also be found here. This was his final work, intended for his tomb. The ageing artist's Madonna has a careworn face, with eyes tired and resigned: it is a painting to break your heart.

The magnificent Bellinis are well represented at the Accademia: one can find Gentile Bellini's *Procession in Piazza San Marco* and Giovanni's (Gentile's younger brother) *Madonna and Child*. Of course the great Giovanni Bellini became even more famous after his death, not merely because of the sizeable output of work but because he was the inspiration for Venice's best-known cocktail.

The most famous and unmissable painting of Vittore Carpaccio is his *Miracle of the Relic of The True Cross*, a charming picture depicting the muddle of daily Venetian life. Also important is his *St Ursula* cycle here in the Accademia, while his collection of masterpieces, *St George* and *St Jerome* cover all four walls of the delightful Scuola di San Giorgio degli Schiavoni. This is the smallest of galleries or *scuole*: it can't be much bigger than a small back bedroom, but it has such charm, mostly because of the work of Carpaccio, who reveals a subtle sense of humour. His dragons writhe, his damsels look suitably distressed, as well they might with various limbs missing, and St Jerome sits in a corner, the picture of perfect manly calm in the centre of chaos.

Tintoretto, who rose to fame in 1540, had a fine sense of business and marketing and was known to offer three pictures for the price of two and excellent discounts when times were hard. He was a practical man by nature, especially when composing his epic masterpieces. Various members of his family were called upon to act as models. Tintoretto's daughter sits at the feet of St Christopher in his mighty *Paradise at the Palazzo Ducale*, and both he and his wife are in his *Calf of Gold* painting in the church of Madonna dell'Orto. Unlike the works of many other Venetian artists there are dozens of Tintorettos to be discovered in Venice, especially in the church of Madonna dell'Orto, which became his shrine: the artist, who died penniless despite his knock-down prices policy, is buried there.

The Feast of the House of Levi by Veronese was actually a painting of *The Last Supper*, but the figures of "buffoons, drunkards, Germans, dwarfs" so upset the church committee in 1573 that they commanded that he change his painting. With commendable lateral thinking Veronese didn't even pick up his paint-brush but merely altered the painting's title, which has been admired ever since.

To get to the Palazzo Tiepolo one must take the *traghetto*, walk down several small *calli* and cross a tiny private bridge, through a garden and there it is: Palazzo Tiepolo, as beautiful and harmonious as any in Venice. Neither the *palazzo* nor its furnishings are included in any guidebook, which is just as well for those of a conservative nature. The present owners, Pietro and Silvana Maindarnis, are collectors of Pop Art, and the *palazzo*, beautifully restored and presented in the Venetian tradition, is also a showcase for their favourite pieces. Beside a splendid 18th-century painting of a revered ancestor is a pink plastic animal with a wide grin on its face. In a perfectly proportioned circular room with silk-lined walls, and lit by candelabra that only the best artisans in Murano can provide, is an enormous sculpture of a dinosaur.

LIVING ARTISTS, LIVING ART

Silvana Mainardis is a woman of great energy and passion. She has two art galleries in Venice, called Venice Design. Both are dynamic spaces, exhibiting art with all the edge and the attitude of the contemporary scene in London, New York or Paris. To Silvana, Venice is the natural home for young artists making a name for themselves. Titian created a furore in his time, and so did Veronese. The style they created led the way for Italian art into the 17th century. Why should the 21st century be any different?

> "When I see Mrs. Guggenheim sunbathing on the roof", remarked Peggy's neighbour, the Prefect of Police, "I know that spring has come."

Peggy Guggenheim thought in much the same way 50 years earlier. One of the greatest art collectors of the 20th century, Peggy Guggenheim started with four nudes by Cocteau, which she bought in Paris in the '20s, long before modern art was taken seriously. She then went on to amass a formidable collection, buying at a rate that astounded critics who hadn't quite got around to understanding what was going on. Whether she was as compulsive in her obsession with picking up Kandinskys and Picassos as she was about husbands (often other people's) is the subject of several biographies, the latest of which is Anton Gill's *Peggy Guggenheim: The Life of An Art Addict*. But the value of her collection and the way it spans the most exciting and innovative growth of contemporary art is there for all of us to see in the Palazzo Venier dei Leoni, which used to be her home. In the old days we used to go along the Calle dei Leoni and ring the bell. Today the *palazzo* is the Guggenheim Museum. We can wander about its gardens, greener and more lush than most in Venice, sip a coffee in the café, and in a museum that still feels like a home we can feel the spirit of Peggy and her continual and restless search for The Next Best Thing.

Another energetic patron of living art in Venice is a lively American called Holly Snapp. Holly arrived in Venice 14 years ago on a fellowship, to work on her PhD from New College, Oxford. These days her life is divided between teaching English Literature at the University of Venice and running one of the most exciting galleries in the city. Gallery Holly Snapp celebrates living impressionist art. Not for Holly the short, sharp shock: she shows artists with a soft, glowing style often using watercolours, sometimes oils, that capture the spirit of Venice today. Geoffrey Humphries, English resident of Venice for the past 35 years, whose cabaret-based works are vibrant and luminous, is just one of her artists. His powerful images of Venice and fabulous nudes, in pencil, oil, and watercolour, are highly collectable.

Australian John Orlando Birt, a greatly acclaimed industrial designer and watercolourist, captures Venice in a way that makes your heart stop, drenched with light and echoing with reflections. Birt has an annual exhibition at Holly's gallery. Visitors bewildered by the rows of artists, busy with palettes and canvases lined up outside the Piazza San Marco or the Accademia Bridge, would do well to visit Holly Snapp first.

Especially this is true for those who might be enticed by the work of a particular artist who can be seen every day at his spot on the Dorsoduro side of the Accademia Bridge, sitting with his back resolutely to the view he is supposed to be capturing. Has he seen it all once too often? Is he not allowing fact to get in the way of a good picture? Or has he, which is most likely, mapped in the outline years ago, copied it many hundreds of times, and is now filling in the colours and lines as he remembers them? Even Venice has its jaded sophisticates.

Canny art lovers make the studio of Geoffrey Humphries on the Giudecca their first port of call. He has portrayed literally hundreds of visiting celebrities from David Bowie to Alexandra Sitwell. Not only is he one of Venice's great living artists, but his parties are also legendary, two excellent reasons why many consider a visit to Venice incomplete without a sitting for Geoffrey Humphries.

THE PERFORMING ARTS

Venice has always had a thriving theatrical life, but most of it takes place in nearby Mestre, which, most unromantically, can be reached by bus.

It was a typical January afternoon. Clouds were gathering over the city and *vaporetto* commuters hurried home, hoping to miss the inevitable storm. The rain never came, but a fire that was to change the face of Venice took its place. On 29 January 1996 the Gran Teatro Fenice, the oldest and largest theatre in Venice, was burned to the ground. Unfortunately, the canal that provided access to the city was being dredged at the time and the emergency services just couldn't get there to save it. When the massive blaze was finally extinguished only a charred shell of one of the prettiest opera houses in Italy was left behind.

What made it all worse was that the orchestra of La Fenice is one of the best in Italy, offering at least two concert seasons a year. To have an orchestra of that calibre with no home in which to settle and develop has been disastrous. La Fenice now performs at Palafenice, a large tent near the multi-story carpark on the island of Tronchetta. It has been a brave move, and, even though the opera house could only squeeze in around 900 music lovers, whereas the tent can take 1,200, it was hardly the ideal venue for such an orchestra.

Fenice means "phoenix" in Italian, which makes the theatre's continual rising from the ashes even more poignant. At the time of the last fire, the Mayor of Venice, Dottore Massimo Cacciari, like his predecessors pledged instant commitment: "The Fenice will be rebuilt where it was, as it was." After seven years of waiting that promise has been fulfilled.

However, Venetians have never allowed a little thing like fire to get them down. The city was ravaged so disastrously by fires in the 13th century that all furnaces were removed by decree to the island of Murano – hence its status as the glass-blowing centre of Venice, well out of harm's way.

But fire continued to be a hazard in Venice. In the case of the Fenice it was a regular occurence. The original Fenice was burnt to the ground, in 1774, just four years after it was constructed. There was no question but that it must be rebuilt, and it was, only to suffer the same fate in 1836, when again a huge bonfire was seen from across the lagoon as flames consumed the pink and gilt auditorium, demolished the cherubs and destroyed the delicate charm of a theatre in which performances varied, but the décor never disappointed. An enthusiastic workforce rebuilt it once more, and within 12 months the theatre opened yet again, with only the slightest alterations, and, if anything, more cherubs and gilding than ever. Modern theatre-goers have had longer to wait. But now, at last, thanks to the determination of a group of Venetian art and music lovers, the *'commissione de salva guardia'*, the Fenice theatre is once again set to take its place as the *'Gran Teatro'* of Venice. December 2003 will see the curtain rise once more on one of the prettiest theatres in Europe.

Musical events also take place in the *scuole* of the city. Vivaldi's church, La Pietà, and the Scuola Grande di San Rocco are both beautiful and glorious venues with excellent acoustics. Other churches that stage musical events with great aplomb are Dei Frari and the churches of San Samuele, Gesuati and Santo Stefano.

While Venetian music and theatre lovers patiently waited for their beloved Fenice theatre to rise again, an unheralded understudy stepped into the breach in true theatrical fashion to save the day. The Malibran theatre, for years an off-and-on affair, was restored and emerged as the new centre of theatrical and musical life in Venice. Reopened in May 2001, the Malibran has become a fixture to be reckoned with in the cultural calendar of the city; and it couldn't have happened to a nicer theatre.

Once just a local concern in the Rialto, it was saved from certain extinction by actress Maria Malibran in 1835. She came to Venice to sing the role of Desdemona in Rossini's *Otello* at the Felice, but hearing that the small local theatre was in trouble she offered to sing for nothing. Everyone was enormously grateful, but it was not what you would call a full house, and ticket sales were not enough to save the theatre from going dark. Signorina Malibran, who had a large heart, decided to throw in her fee from the Felice as well, and saved the building. The owners were so grateful they named the theatre after their generous angel.

The other true theatre of Venice, also in the Rialto, is The Goldoni. Carlo Goldoni (1707-1793) was the city's most famous playwright, producing no less than 136 plays. That Goldoni should have his own theatre is only right and proper. He was a true son of the Republic, with a dedication to pleasure only equalled by his friend, Casanova. As for his theatre, it's here where visitors might find something familiar. I once saw *un marito ideale* or 'An Ideal Husband' at The Goldoni. Oscar Wilde, translated into Italian works very well, especially in Venice. Intrigue and mystery flow throw the city as surely as the canals.

To translate *scuole* into "schools" will only confuse. The *scuole* of Venice were much more complex than this. Originally they were religious and charitable institutions reserved strictly for lay people. Rather like the livery companies of The City of London, their members practised a common craft: boat building, shoemaking, painting, baking and so on, but while officially politically impotent they were hugely wealthy and wielded great power. The *scuole* provided food and shelter for the poor and also offered training for artisans and apprentices. In times of war they provided ships and men, and in peacetime were benevolent supporters of the arts. Today both the *scuole grandi* (San Rocco, San Giovanni, Misericordia, San Marco, I Carmini, Caritá, San Teodoro and San Giorgio) and the smaller *scuole*, of which there are many, are mostly museums and a joy to behold.

"AFTER DINNER, I
INTO THE HEART OF THE
WHERE I FOUND
STRANGE REGIONS
'THE ARABIAN NIGHTS'
THAT I DID NOT IN THE
WANDERINGS HIT UP
SPACIOUS PIAZZA OF
NO TOURIST HAD EV

"WENT OUT BY MYSELF,
ENCHANTED CITY
MYSELF WANDERING IN
LIKE A CHARACTER IN
IT WAS VERY SELDOM
COURSE OF MY
ON SOME STRANGE AND
WHICH NO GUIDEBOOK,
ER TOLD ME..." MARCEL PROUST, 1900

What creeps into the consciousness when struggling to capture the culture of the city is a growing awareness of the eastern underbelly of Venice. Its oriental flavour can be sensed not just in the atmosphere along the small, dark *calli*, just wide enough to catch a passing whisper and too narrow for a couple to walk hand in hand, but also in the secret grills on its windows, in the pouting ironwork of its balconies, in its love of the heavily scented ritual of pageants and Saints' Days.

EASTERN MYSTIQUE

A *Doge* of Venice, dressed in magnificent robes, painted by the greatest artists of his time and waited on by sycophantic servants would appear all-powerful, yet he was as much a gilded prisoner in his palace cage as a concubine in an oriental harem. Although the *Doge* was seen to be a supreme head of state, the equivalent of a king or emperor, all decisions went through the Greater Council and over the centuries the *Doge* was reduced to not much more than a bejewelled caricature. He was forbidden to speak to strangers, unable to accept gifts except possibly flowers and herbs and discouraged from writing letters, which in any case would be censored ... even those to his wife. There were 120 *Doges* in Venice over eleven centuries from 697-1797. Few lived to a ripe old age, but honour was all – to serve The Serene Republic was enough for any Venetian aristocrat.

Only the wily Enrico Dandolo (1192-1205) showed real spark. At the age of 88 and completely blind he led the Fourth Crusade into sacking the noble city of Constantinople, looting its most precious treasures and removing the Byzantine Emperor, who as a man of oriental cunning had nothing on Doge Dandolo.

The role of the Jews of Venice, most poignantly portrayed by Shakespeare's Shylock, has contributed in no small way to the eastern atmosphere of Venice. It was during the 16th and 17th centuries that the community thrived, trading mainly with Jews of the Levant, mixing the Arabic and Hebrew languages and sharing the same taste for glistening fabrics and sumptuous jewellery. None of this could be displayed outwardly. Visit the Jewish ghetto today and one finds a dark, secretive place where the streets converge in a labyrinth of alleys and where the synagogues, deceptively simple from the outside so as not to

High under the eaves of the Palazzo Ducale and along its dark corridors and lonely passages one can get an inkling of what life must have been like for the Doges and the civil servants who ran their lives. The Itinerari Segreti, the secret tour, is well worth following to begin to understand the murky history of La Serenissma.

draw attention to themselves, are splendidly elaborate and decorated to the glory of the One God inside.

And what of the gondola? Sleek, black, unique, with a sexuality of its own, made to glide, to slip in where it is least expected, the gondola has an inscrutability far better suited to an eastern personality. Its unique design was actually devised by carpenters who knew nothing about the sea, in the mountain towns of Cortina and Zoldo. As the Venetians knew nothing about wood but everything about the sea, putting these two traditions together was a masterstroke.

The modern craft with its carved metal beak had emerged by the mid-18th century (as paintings by Canaletto and Guardi show), when it was firmly established as part of the culture of the city. As for its origins, why go further than an old Venetian narrative poem that tells the tale of how the crescent moon dropped out of the sky to shelter a pair of young lovers? As a vessel of love the gondola has no equal. Naturally the amoral Venetians of the 18th century took this characteristic way beyond the limits. The *felze* was not a cabin but a boudoir, and only the cleverest gondolier, with great balance and expertise could control the violent rocking that ensued from time to time!

Gondoliers became important cultural icons in Venetian society. The city's most prolific playwright, Carlo Goldoni, used to arrange house seats for them at his shows, recognizing that a favourable review from a gondolier could make the difference between success and failure. They also played the part of go-between in affairs of the heart, knowing which delightful young lady lived where and precisely where her secret landing stage may be.

The gondolas, lined up alongside the steps of Piazza San Marco, jostling for position, their prows prodding each other to catch the eye of the willing tourist, are an expensive cliché, and their role is now a touristic one, but they are no less important for that. Venice thrives on tourism. In the latter years of the 18th century, as the last frantic days of gaiety heralded the end of the Serene Republic, the death of a *Doge* was kept secret for two weeks in case it upset the tourist season. The fusion of beauty, practicality, pragmatism and commerce has always been the Venetian way – this is the culture of Venice.

Today the gondola garage, a charming edifice looking like a Swiss chalet along the Zattere end of the Canal di San Trovaso, is as busy as ever, scraping hulls, repainting and occasionally making new gondolas from scratch. Another, lesser-known gondola workshop is on the island of Giudecca, past Il Redentore church. Here Roberto Rossi is as skilled an artisan as his fore-fathers, putting together 280 pieces of eight different kinds of wood to make the asymmetric wonder that is the gondola.

In the 15th century the gondolas of Venice were used mainly by the elite, whose *felzi*, or cabins, were very colourful, in vibrant shades and often painted with the family crest. When the city was in mourning after the devastating plague of 1570 the magistrate declared that in respect for the dead all gondolas should be black; and they have been so every since.

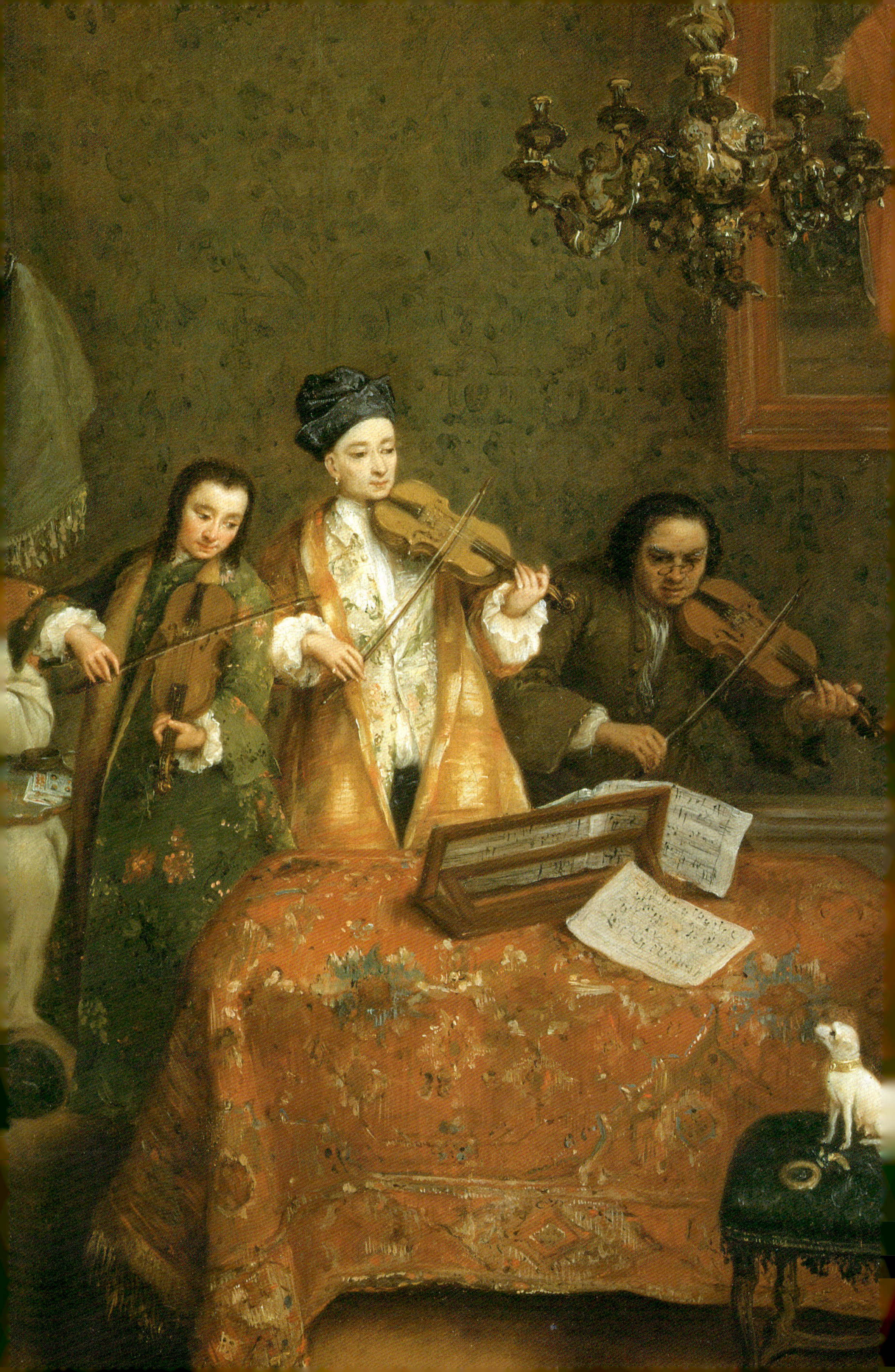

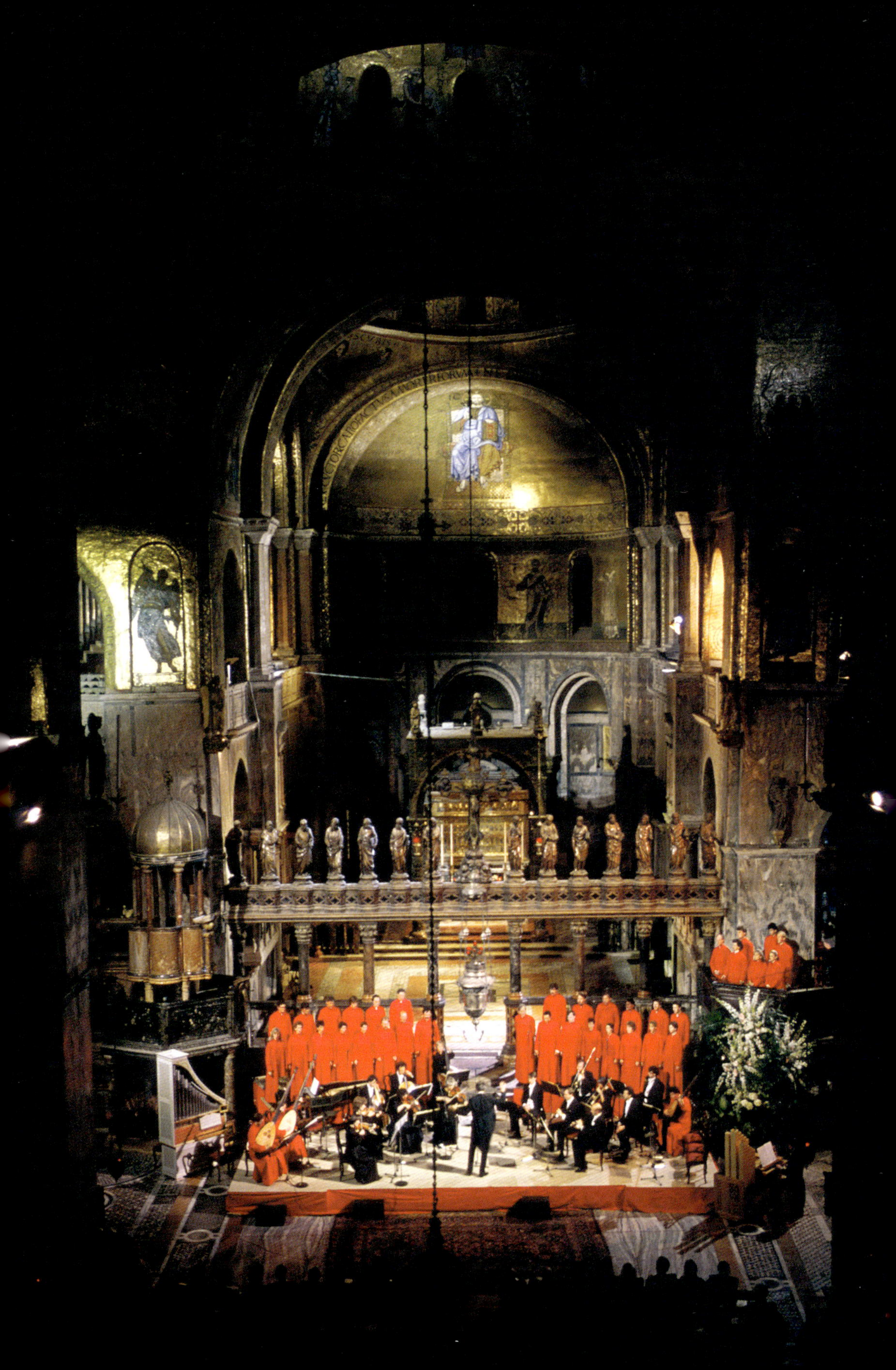

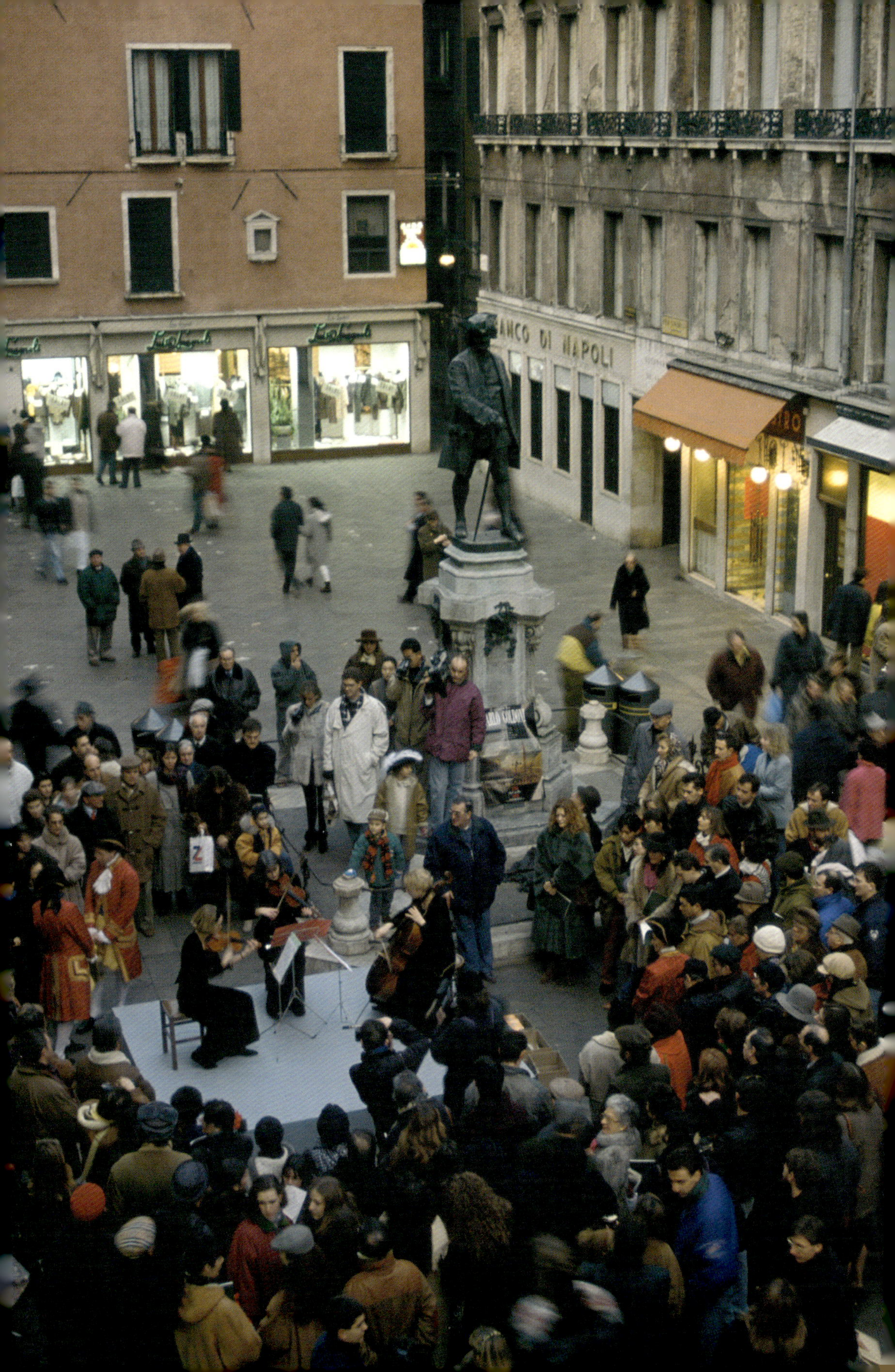
ANCO DI NAPOLI

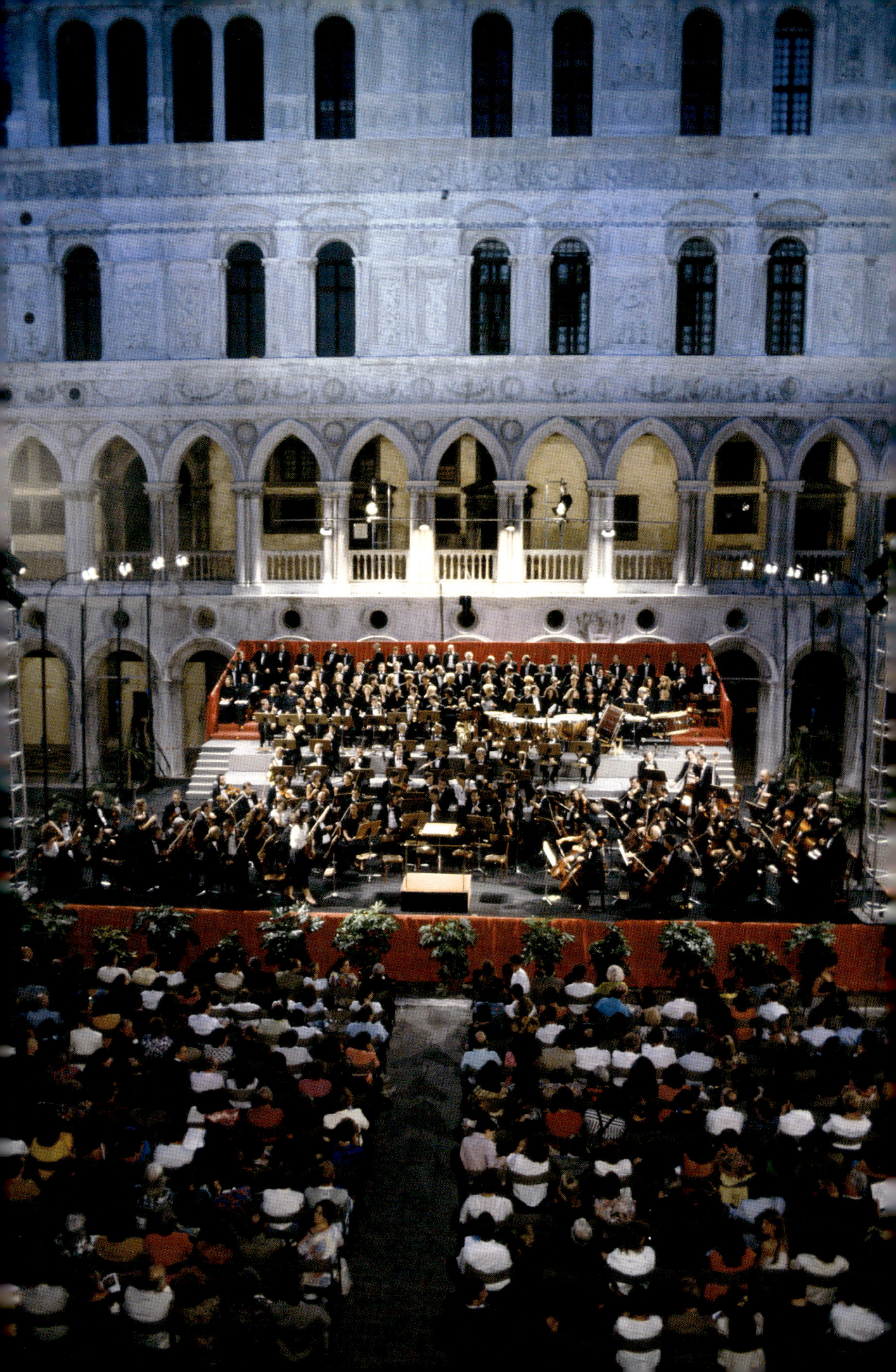

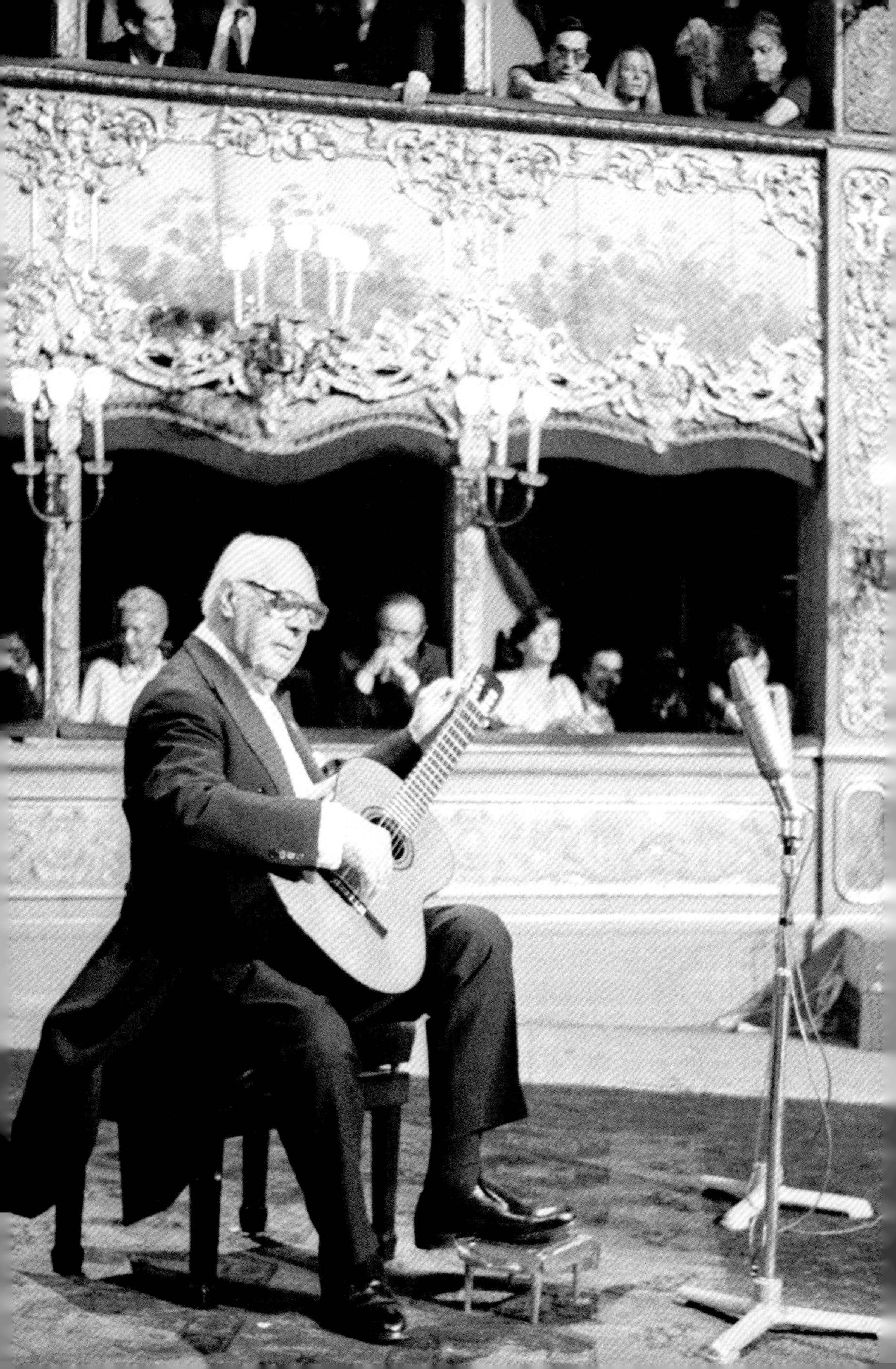

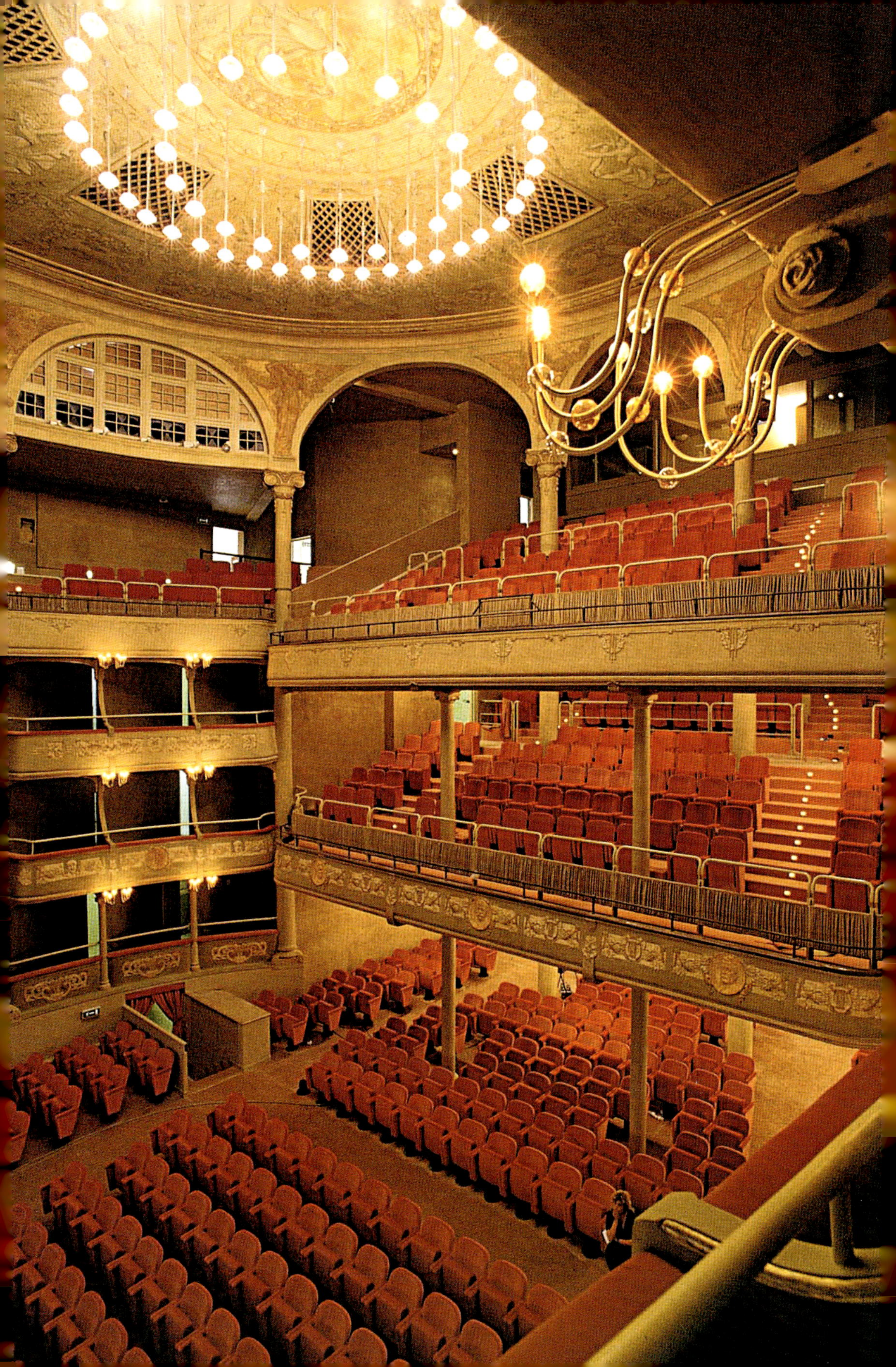

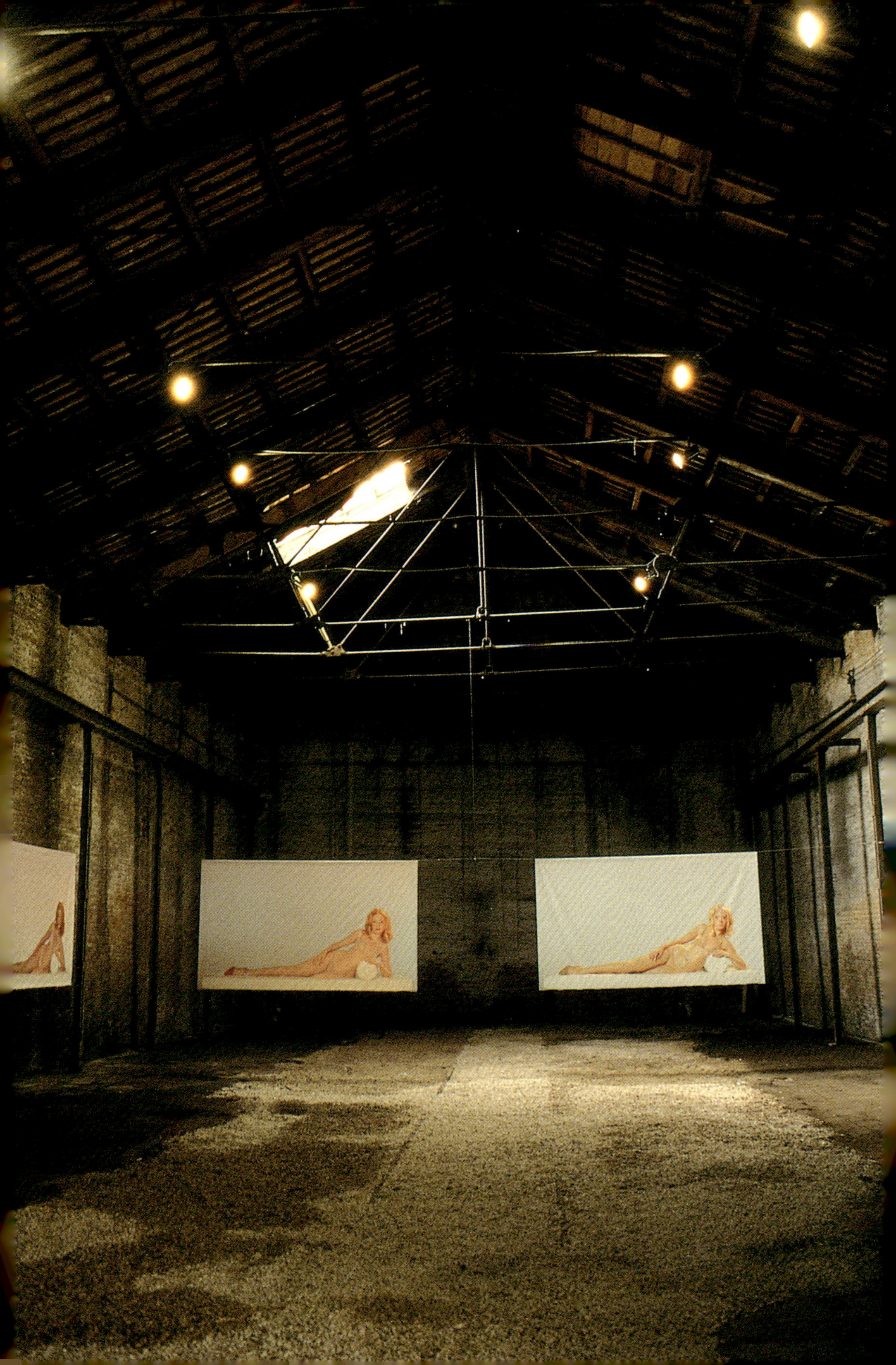

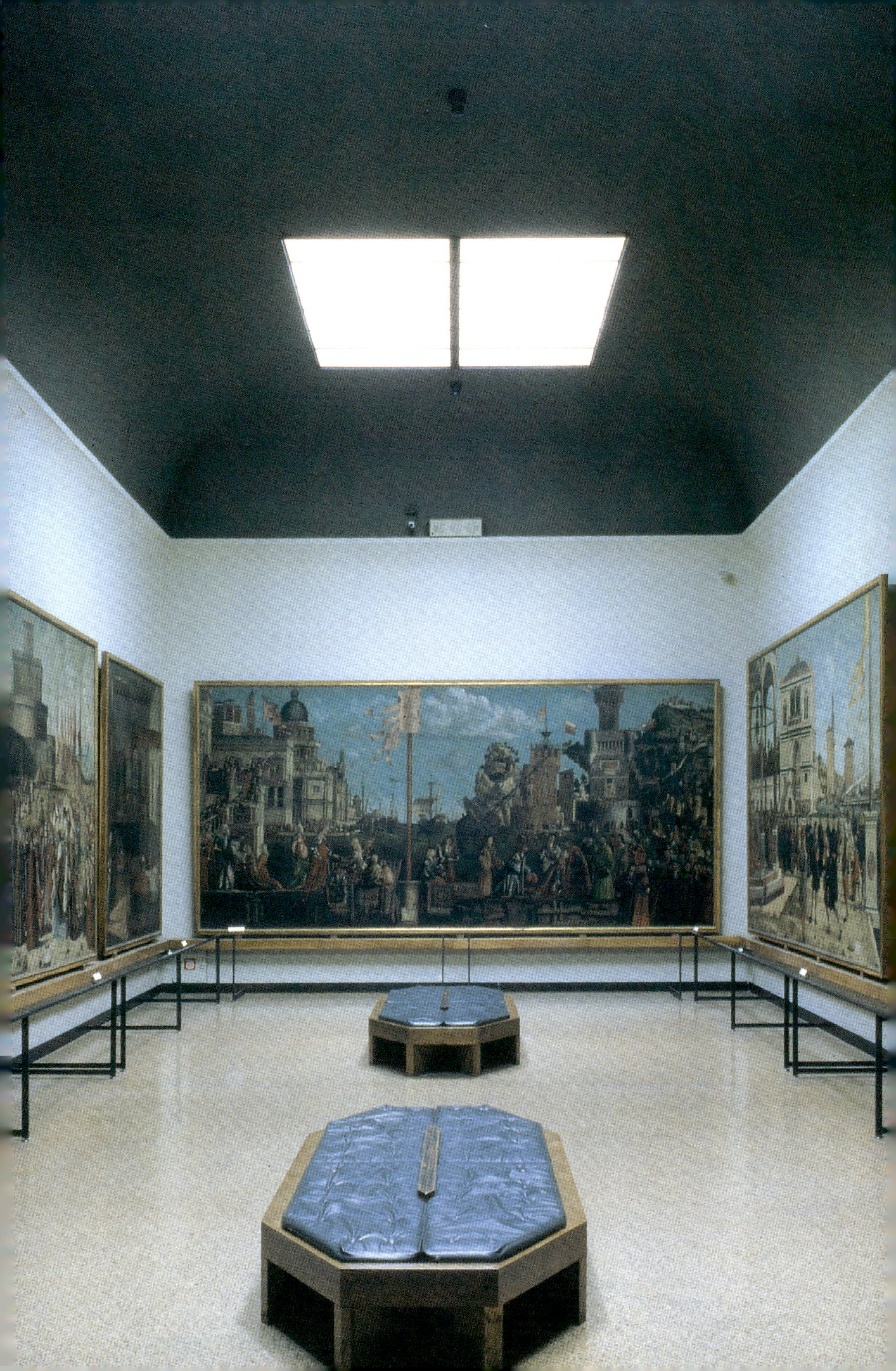

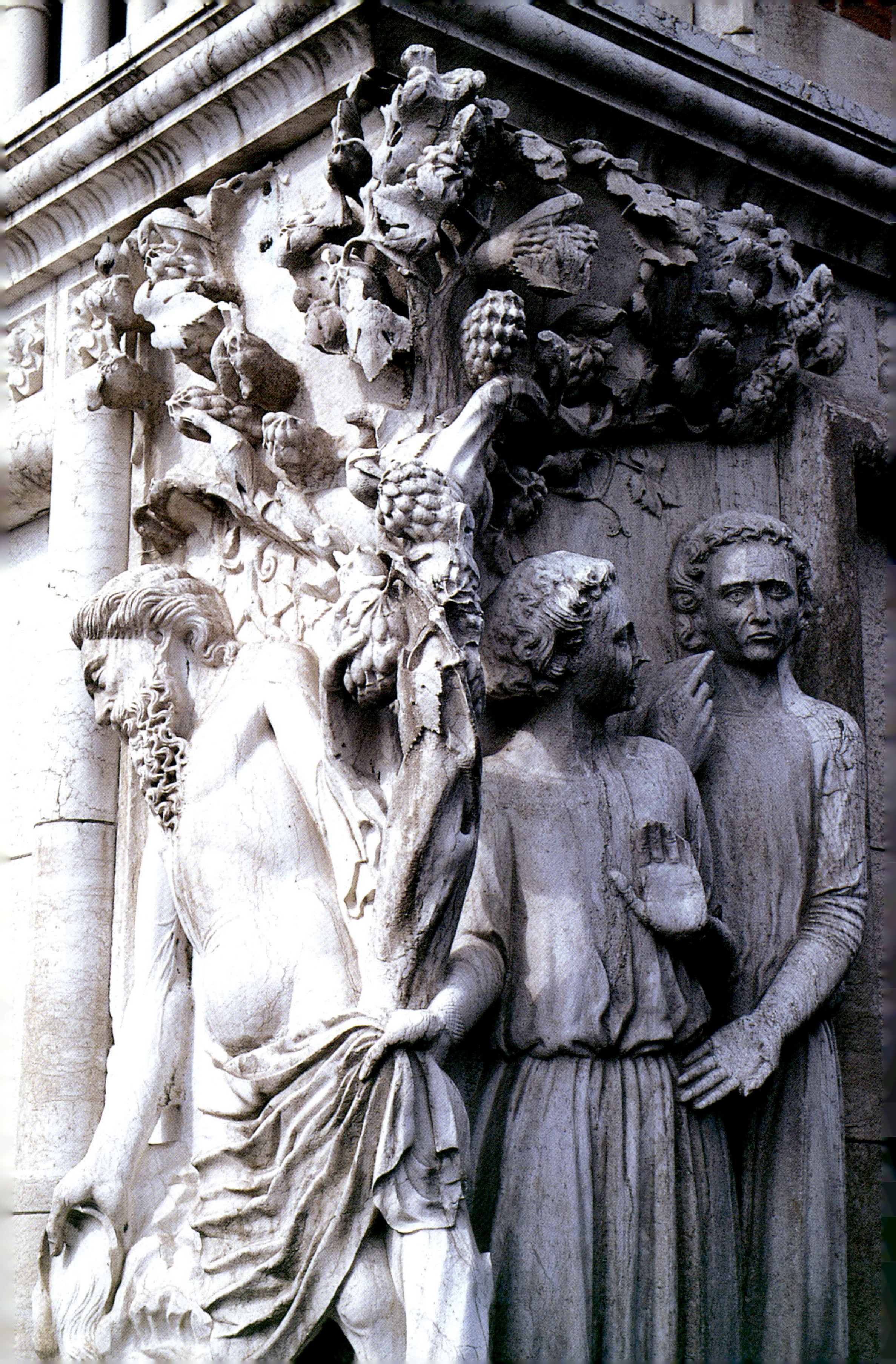

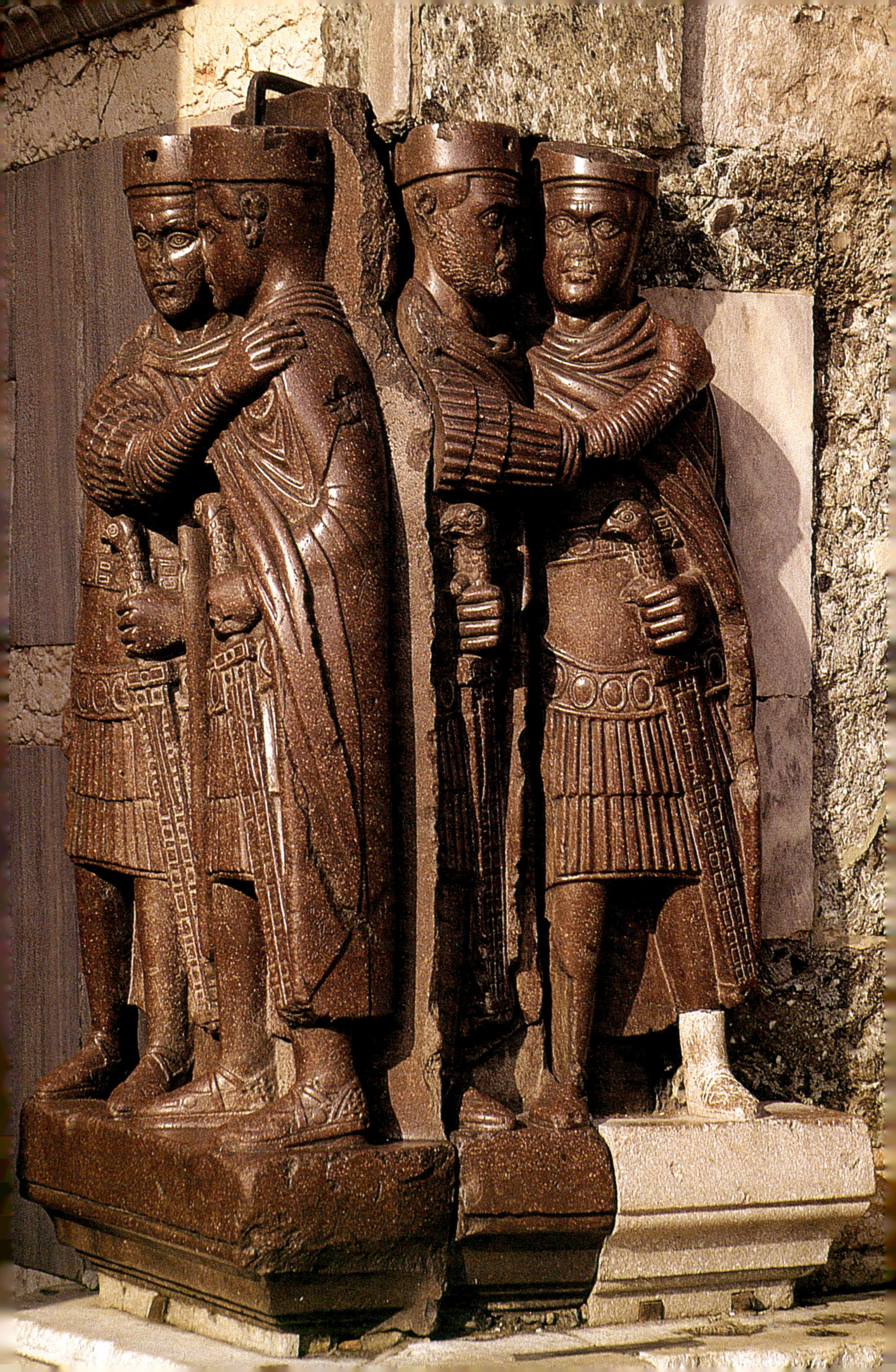

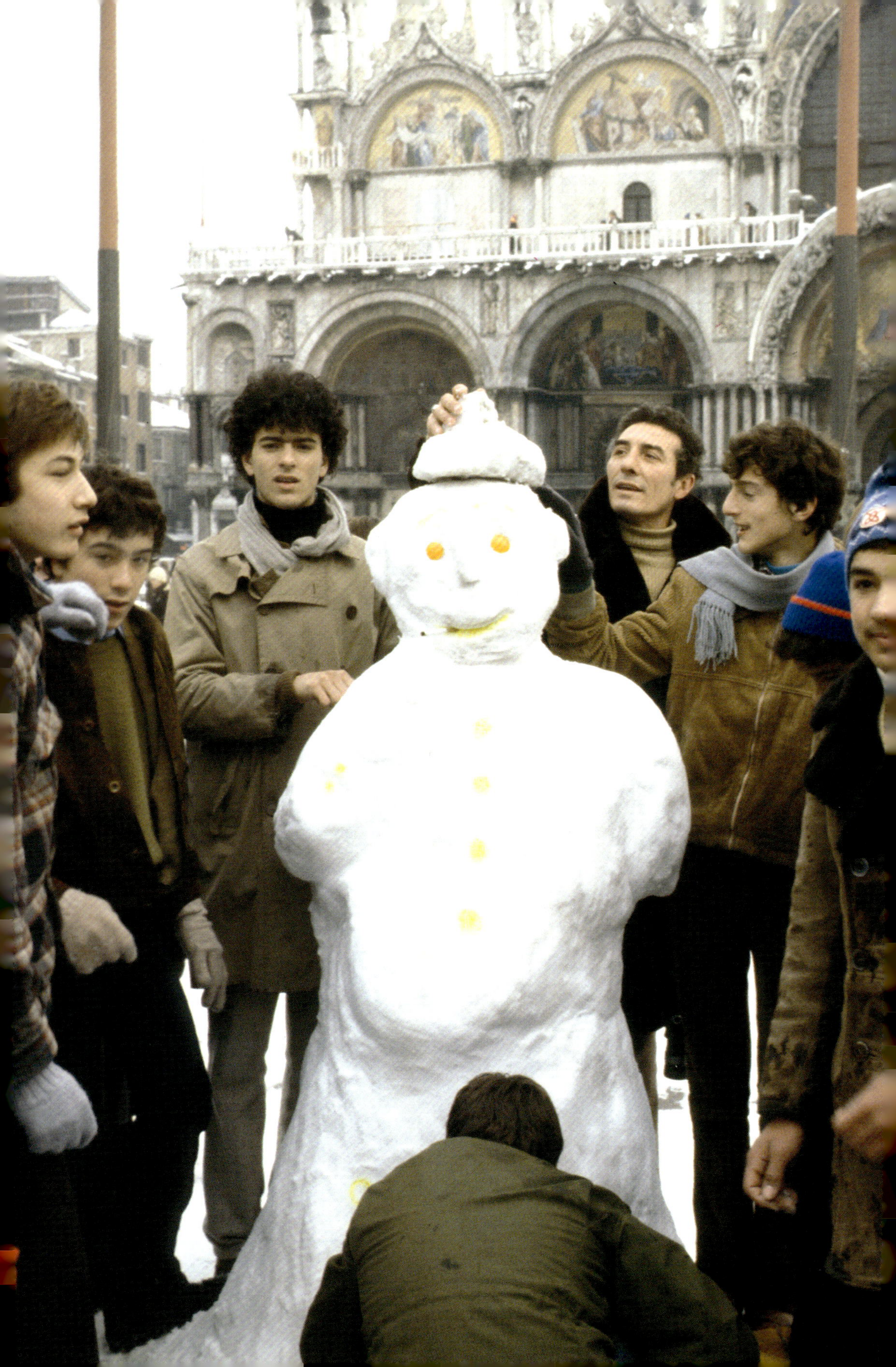

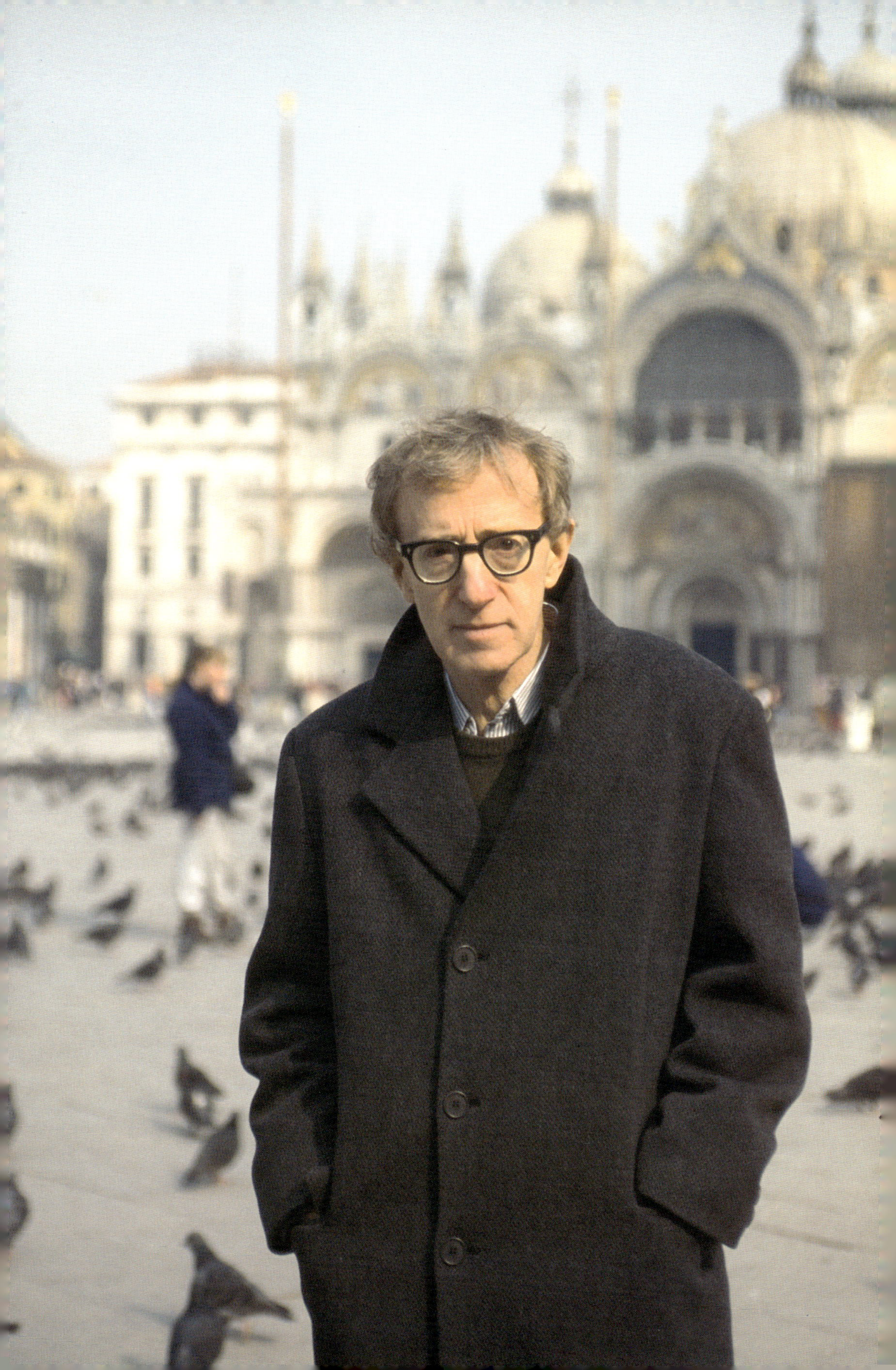

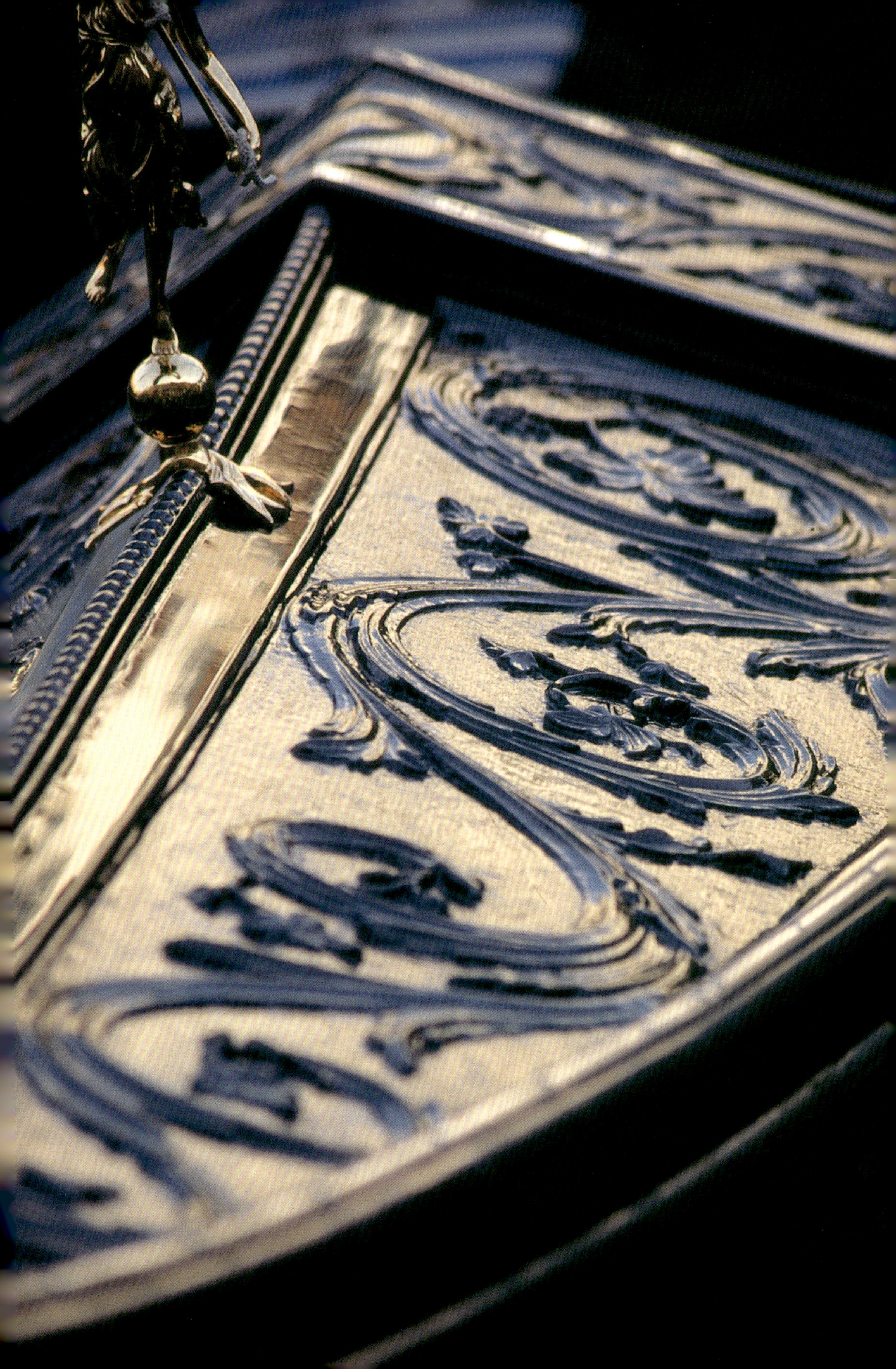

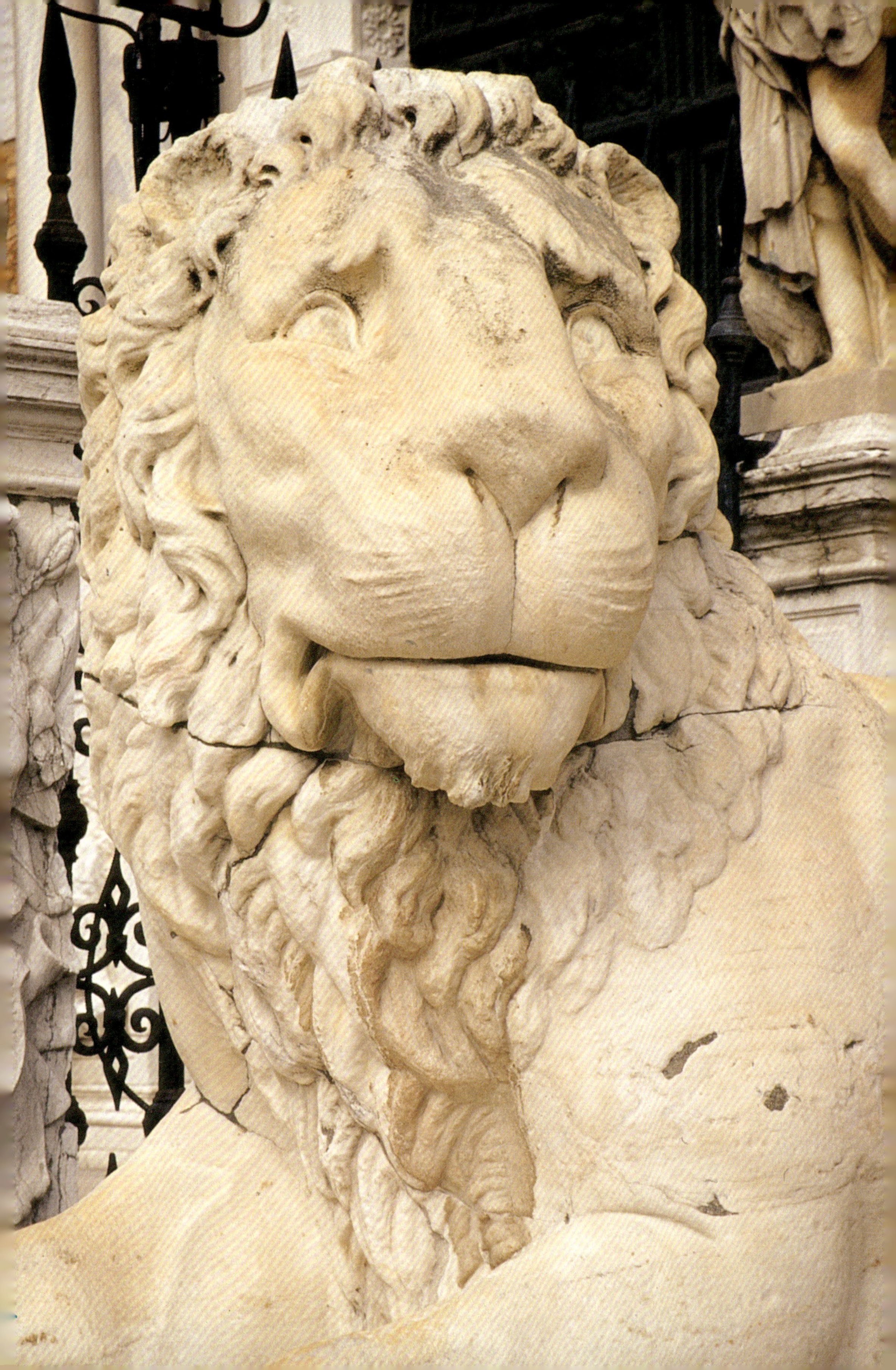

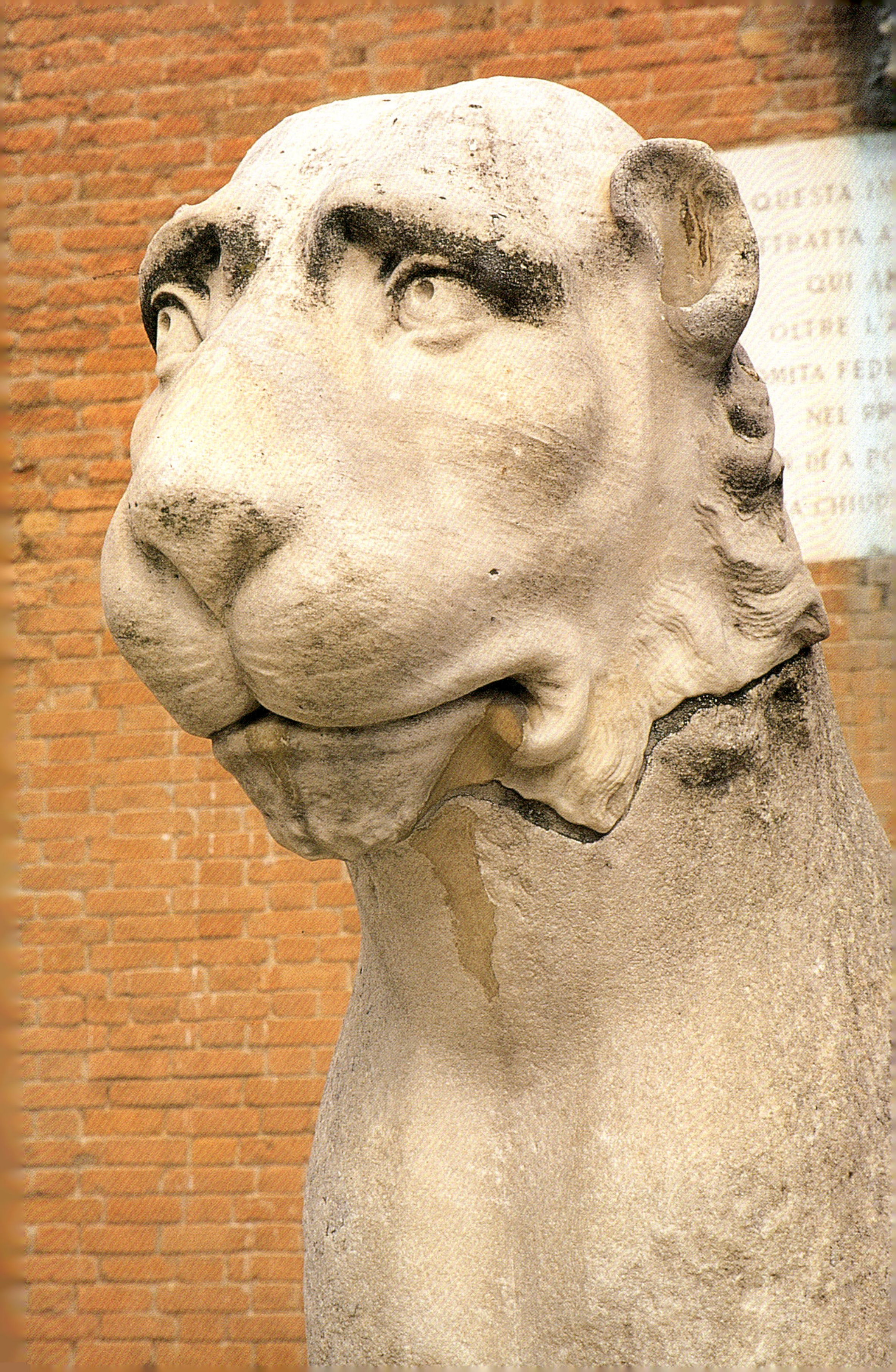

CHAPTER THREE

RETAIL
INDULGEN

There comes a time when a discerning Venice lover

Possibly it is after a reviving cappuccino and a tasty brioche, when a visitor is filled to the brim with the beauty of the art and the churches. The frivolity we speak of is shopping, that delightful occupation that lightens the wallet, but brightens the spirit. This is especially so in Venice where narrow streets illuminated by the shining lights of commerce entice us into shops filled with so many "must-haves" that we need several gold cards to cope.

Venice has always understood the pleasures of retail indulgence. "The most triumphant citie I ever set eyes on", historian Philippe de Commynes wrote in 1495, and so she was.

longs to indulge in something a little more frivolous.

Bedecked in all the precious gems of Arabia, India, Byzantium and China, from silk and velvet to cloth of gold, and emeralds and rubies, Venice was the kind of mistress who saw something she liked and demanded it, instantly, for herself. How well she must understand those happy shoppers today, as they leave one of the great designer stores behind Piazza San Marco, laden down with famous name carrier bags, stopping only briefly to sip an energizing *ombra* (a glass of wine) before striding out, once more, to do the same thing all over again. Getting delightfully lost in the maze of the bustling, crowded, narrow alleyways that make up the Mercerie, which run between the Piazza San Marco and the Rialto, discovering just how many shoe shops there are in the jumble of winding streets that make up the Frezzeria, and wandering around Calle Larga XXII, where all the big names from Prada and Fendi to Versace and Valentino have set out their extravagant stalls, provides another view of Venice – possibly not as spiritual as gazing at a perfect Tintoretto or Palladio creation, but joyful and exciting nevertheless.

But while shopping in Venice can be eye-wateringly expensive it is just as possible to find something special, even unique, that is not about price but about quality and inventiveness. Craftsmen and women not only exist, they thrive in Venice, and their works of art can be sought out by the diligent shopper who is prepared to venture a little further and dig a little deeper. The city is alive with a young and vigorous Venetian design culture that works in much the same way as the great artisans of the city used to do in times gone by. Finding them is half the pleasure…

We are in Malo, one of the many glamorous clothing shops of great prestige in the Mercerie. A male shopper has admired a particular jacket. It is fashioned in the softest cashmere, coloured in the palest shades of cream and blue, and would not only caress the body of its wearer but would also provide solace for the soul. Cashmere has that effect on people.

FAMOUS LABELS

Unfortunately its price tag takes the breath away: cashmere of this quality is not for the faint-hearted. But this is Venice and a canny Venetian sales lady doesn't give up this easily. "Ah," she explains, "but this cashmere was gathered along the high, arid plains of Mongolia and China. In tufts." The drama of this revelation does not go unnoticed. The whole shop stops to listen as the cashmere expert, earnest, beautiful and probably aged 21 or maybe 22, continues: "Only some of it in tufts," she says, "the rest comes from the Kashmir goats' beards. They are combed." She explains by miming beard-combing on her own chin, "and from their bellies." More miming.

As we watch, transfixed, we learn that a little scarf takes one Kashmir goat one year to produce. She tosses one such example, light as air, on the counter to demonstrate. A sweater, nowhere near as nice as the jacket in question, requires the efforts of three goats. A coat? Phoof! With all the tell-tale cashmere softness and natural sheen, something like that would need at least 24 goats producing more tufts than we could possibly imagine.

Chinese goatherds, we are told, have been gathering wool from the Kashmiri goat in this fashion for some 700 years, and Venetian merchants have been bringing such treasures into Venice for about the same time. The jacket, once just a garment on a rail, has become the subject of a romantic tale of historical importance and daring-do. No matter what outrageous figure is scribbled on its price tag, it must be bought. And so it is, by a customer happy, contented and inspired with a little Venetian magic.

The pleasure of buying famous labels in Venice is not just about finding a garment spied in the pages of *Vogue*; nor is it about investing in the highest quality. These are not mere shops. They are mini-theatres. Every morning as Malo or Ferré or Versace open their shutters and polish their windows, they are preparing for another performance. The cast, led by our cashmere expert, must be carefully chosen, not only for their training, experience and enthusiasm, but also for their looks. Sales women are likely to be beautiful, simply but elegantly dressed and have that confident air that comes of being Venetian. The men might be youthful and lanky or comfortable and discreet. All could appear in an Italian movie and not look out of place.

Then there is the set design, which must be perfect. Bright and cheerful enough to entice the customer in, discreet and flattering enough in the changing-rooms to keep him or her there long enough to make the purchase. No wonder the great labels have not neglected Venice.

Most can be found along Calle Largo XXII Marzo, which is Venice's answer to Fifth Avenue or Bond Street or Avenue Montaigne. Ferré is here, as is Versace, nudging up against delicious shoe shops and accessory shops filled with brooches made from Murano glass pearls or delicate hair clips made of spectacular feathers.

Ferragamo has set up a superstore, so has Gucci – both in Calle Largo XXII Marzo. Armani, Prada and Bulgari are also in Venice, clustered like all the other great names, either in Calle Largo XXII Marzo, the Mercerie or in Calle Valleresso, with Harry's Bar on the corner for a reviving Bellini after some serious retail therapy. Cartier is in the Mercerie while Valentino, Fendi, Louis Vuitton and Magli are two minutes' walk from Piazza San Marco near the Hotel Bauer-Grunwald. Missoni is in Calle Valleresso and so is Dolce e Gabbana.

Another Italian designer which has found its way into Venice is Ermenegildo Zegna. Zegna is the label you'll find in those effortlessly elegant garments worn by stylish Italian males. Fabrics are soft and understated, they don't crush but neither are they too smooth, and everything fits. Their shop, open-planned and as chic as the clothes displayed, is just footsteps away from the Piazza San Marco towards Calle Largo XXII Marzo.

Heartening news for non-EU citizens is that if you keep your receipt, and Italian law says you must, you could claim a rebate of sales tax on any item over 155 euros. Shopping in the designer boutiques suddenly seems not just desirable but sensible.

During the high season, from June to October, and also Easter for *Carnevale*, and the four weeks before Christmas, most major boutiques stay open all day, from 10 or 10.30am to 6 or 7pm. Some stay open later, and even on Sundays. In the off-season it is wise to check. The siesta habit has not disappeared.

BOTT
WERE
ALIVE T
WORKING

"IF BOTICELLI

TODAY

HE WOULD BE

FOR 'VOGUE'."

PETER USTINOV

Once upon a time the Venetian artisans of Murano were the only people in Europe who knew how to make a mirror. Up to the 14th century, stately palaces and great mansions had to make do with steel mirrors, which looked impressive but were sadly lacking as looking-glasses. So, when the Venetians' glass foundries were removed from the city to Murano in 1292, supposedly because of the furious fires that ravaged Venice during the 13th century, the island became the principal glass manufacturing area of Europe, turning out real mirrors, great chandeliers and any manner of vases, doorstops and glass menageries.

THE ART OF VENETIAN GLASS

So impressed was Henry III by the glass-blowing techniques displayed during that legendary party of 1574, that he ennobled the guild of glass-blowers when he visited them on his way back to France.

The mysteries of their art came from Syria where glass and glass paintings had been spied during the Crusades. The Venetians, already used to borrowing ideas from the East, adapted and refined the techniques, turning the craft of glass-making into a professional skill so valuable that the government offered special protection to glass-blowers and gave them gentlemanly status.

By the mid-15th century, with the invention of crystal, great glass-making families established themselves on the island and, amazingly, the descendants of some of those families are still active on Murano, producing extraordinary glass in the oldest and most prestigious glass foundries of the western world.

Holy Roman Emperor Frederick III (1419-1493) was offered a very elaborate glass service by the Venetians during a state visit, but he hated it so much he instructed his court jester to be over-bumptious in his tumbling routine and bump into the display. It broke, they say, into thousands of pieces.

Visitors looking for an example of Murano glass to take home today need to remain strong in the face of unscrupulous vendors and their representatives who can be found, milling in with the throng around the quayside of San Marco, offering "free" tickets to Murano. As there is no such thing as a free lunch, a free boat-ride is just as unlikely. In fact, its sponsor will be one of the big showrooms on Murano that is only interested in a one-way trip. How you get back, especially if you have failed to buy, is up to you.

Much better to explore Murano independently, either by *vaporetto* from Fondamenta Nuova (number 41 or 42, first stop after San Michele) or take a water taxi straight to Fondamenta Vetrai which is stuffed with glass showrooms. An ideal place to start could well be Barovier & Toso. There have been Baroviers making glass in Venice since the 13th century, which makes the present showroom positively modern – it is housed in a 17th-century *palazzo*. There is a contemporary room, but antique collectors should go to the third floor for the historical pieces. Another great showroom is Venini, which was only founded in the 1920s but whose expertise is in design. Carlo Scarpa and Ettore Sottsass, two of Europe's finest designers, have produced pieces for Venini, as did Gianni Versace just before his death. Another exciting name to look out for, both on Murano and in Venice itself, is Berengo Fine Arts, whose works display Venetian glass-making in its finest form, conceived and created by great painters and sculptors and executed by a Murano-glass maestro.

Browsing through the great showrooms often filled with glass so garishly coloured you need sunglasses is interesting, but the fun is to be had out at the back where the glass-blowers are working at their furnaces. Most of the showrooms are happy to welcome visitors who wish to watch a master glass-maker at work, quietly self-assured as he raises a long pipe to his lips only to give it the gentlest blow to produce a bubble of glass, as effortlessly as if he were chewing gum. He then gives it a twist, a tiny flick; great long-handled pliers are used to nip the neck of his bubble just so and *èccola*! There is a wineglass or a bird or an ornament. It is all show business, but of the best kind.

Gaining access to the factories as opposed to the showrooms is much more difficult but, while not as theatrical, is even more interesting. Some will allow visiting tourists, and when they do, in limited numbers, the lucky few can not only see how it is done, but buy at factory door prices.

Venetian glass is not to all tastes. Often it is too loud, too violent, or too ostentatious for modern interiors. But things are changing: the innovations of new, young designers who initiate conceptual works which are then produced by a master artisan have resulted in a modern Murano glass with all the heritage and tradition of Venetian Renaissance glass.

But watch out. A trip to the glass museum on Fondamenta Giustinian can tickle a curious interest into the beginning of a real obsession, to which there will be no end. Yet another aspect of Venice which has become addictive.

Fun as it is to visit Murano, the best of Venetian glass and glass design can be found in galleries and boutiques in Venice itself. Look out for Galleria Rosella Junck, Genninger Studio, Berenger Fine Arts and Galleria Marina Barovier.

Fratelli Barbini specializes in mirror-making and turns out some of the most attractive and original designs in Murano. Elite Murano is another address that is worth noting, producing the best quality Venetian goblets and beautifully executed reproductions of antique glass.

Right at the end of Calle Larga XXII Marzo is Venetia Studium, where the most gorgeous silk velvets in every jewel colour imaginable can be found. Finely pleated Fortuny scarves and evening bags finished off with delicious tassels and flirtatious detail are here. So are those lampshades most of us first see in the Hotel Cipriani and long for ever after. Shaped like hanging goblets and made of pinky-beige silk traced in chocolate, they seem to be the essence of Venice. This is yet another of her tricks: the silk that Venice has made her own came from China, where it was discovered before the Serene Republic was even thought of.

SILKS, SATINS, BUTTONS, BOWS

Once having laid eyes upon Chinese silk Venetians had to have as much as the traders could find them, and both fine ladies and glamorous courtesans wrapped themselves in silks, satins and velvets. They tied their hair with embroidered ribbons, added silken bows to their shoes and velvet buttons on their bodices. Much later, in the 19th century, a Spanish designer, Mariano Fortuny, made Venice his home, and his inspiration created finely pleated silks and velvets that have become synonymous with Venetian style. The only shop in Venice where you can buy original Fortuny fabrics is at Trois and at considerably less than you would spend anywhere else in Europe or the United States. Of course this doesn't make them cheap, but they are unique to Fortuny.

A much more recent designer and leader of the renaissance in Venetian design is Emma Gaggio, whose boutique Gaggio is in a charming street, Calle delle Botteghe, filled with all sorts of fascinating shops. Emma specializes in hand-painted velvet, not only in home furnishings, especially drapes and cushions, but evening jackets suitable for both sexes. The male of the species, for hundreds of years the peacock sex, has had a tedious time of it in the 20th century. Now, at last, the ubiquitous men's suit, delivered in various shades of dull for the past 80 or so years, is being brightened up. Why not consider a Gaggio velvet jacket? Or a matching smoking hat set at a raffish angle with a tassel?

Renaissance courtesans were women of great taste and refinement, both in their clothes and their manners. Bedecked in silks and velvets they spoke of love, of life and of politics with wit and considerable knowledge. So respected were they that the name "courtesan" was considered impolite and they became known as donne del buon tempo, which, translated literally, becomes "good time girl".

Another tiny shop crammed to its ears with luxurious fabrics is the Rubelli Boutique, first opened in 1918, presenting all the luxurious fabrics designed by Lorenzo Rubelli. This is the place for designers, decorators and those who are passionate about beautiful things. The pleasure is in the richness of the silks and velvets, but clients can also refer to the extensive collection of historical documents and designs to help them create their own unique patterns and motifs. Many of the recently renovated *palazzi* in Venice have used the services of the Rubelli Boutique, most notably the newly restored grand apartments of the Palazzo Ducale.

As for the fine lace that Venice is also famous for, the best-known shop and the one that visitors head for in their droves is Jesurum, with its main boutique in the Piazza San Marco. It has all the quiet confidence of a business that has been providing handmade lace for over 100 years and will probably go on doing precisely the same for years to come. Prices seem steep, but only compared to the open-air stalls on the island of Burano, or lesser establishments in town, where pretty tablecloths, hand towels and lacy goods appear cheap because they are not only machine-made but probably made in Taiwan.

Other establishments you can trust include Martinuzzi, also in the Piazza San Marco and even older than Jesurum. Here you can find exclusive designs for bobbin lace goods like placemats, tablecloths and linens. Annelie in Dorsoduro is run by a charming lady who specializes in lace-embroidered baby clothes, which is unusual in Venice – surprisingly so because Venetians adore babies and pushchairs are always given right of way on the bridges.

La Fenice Atelier is another genuine lace shop, not quite as expensive as Jesurum, possibly because it is the other side of town. The embroidered nightgowns are exquisite, and there is also a catalogue of made-to-order goodies.

Venice may not have discovered silk, nor lace, satin and velvet, but if ever a city invented sumptuousness this is it. Somehow these luxurious fabrics have added cachet when found and lovingly purchased here. It is part of the Venice effect.

Venetian shopkeepers have an interesting marketing technique. Quite often the older establishments don't display the name of the shop at all. The only way you can find where you've been is to read your receipt. There is a number above every doorway: it refers not to a street number but to where the house or establishment is in the neighbourhood. In fact, business cards only occasionally mention a street name. We have bucked the trend in our listings at the back of this book and have attempted to make finding our favoured shops relatively easy. But as getting lost is part of the Venice experience we can only shrug our shoulders at that inevitability.

Wandering into the Campo Santa Margherita two visitors spy a pair of soft, suede shoes in a small shop window. Everything about them is perfect: their pale honey colour, the patina of the suede, the elegant, understated style. It is only when the excited shoppers press their noses to the window to take a closer look that all is revealed ... the shoes are carved in wood.

DISCOVERING THE UNUSUAL

Loris Marazzi is 26-years-old and a sculptor of extraordinary talent. That pair of shoes is carved in intricate detail, down to the label inside. There is a crumpled overnight bag, complete with zips and buckles. A line of washing, so typical of Venice, is strung across his shop window, all made of wood. Be prepared to breathe in the sawdust of his workshop and recognize his talent.

The Campo Santa Margherita is also the home of another young designer, Gualti, who has been experimenting with soft resin decoration for shoes, scarves and handbags. His designs, inspired by the lagoon, are unique, often in coral or aqua shades. They can look quite spiky, like sea urchins or anemones, but are soft, and they bend, so even when embellishing the highest heels or the sleekest handbag they are delightfully practical.

Ten minutes away, in the Palazzo Falier overlooking the Grand Canal, Servane Giol is painstakingly fastening tiny Murano glass pearls to the stylish sandals and chic little evening bags she creates under her own design label Ve'nina. Her workroom is the family living-room, and Servane's small daughter Ambra "helps" by choosing the prettiest pearls. Servane's sandals and purses, most of them one-offs, are sold in the boutique of the Cipriani hotel and in Vogini, a lovely shop in Salizzada San Moisé, just near Harry's Bar. Clients who'd like a more personal service can contact Servane at the Palazzo Falier near Campo Santo Stefano for a private viewing of the collection.

Only a short walk away is Campo Manin where Patrizia Fiorenza and her sister Samanta have set up Godi Fiorenza, a most exciting young fashion label. The girls, half English, half Venetian are both designers, Samanta working in jewellery and Patrizia in women's wear. Patrizia's contemporary touch combined with a superb tailoring skill has already made her clothes eminently collectable. Her speciality seems to be creating fluid, feminine

Serious art collectors should look out for Cornici Trevisanello in Dorsoduro which sells beautiful gilded frames for those with pictures that deserve them. All are hand-made on the premises and have been for many years. Cornici Trevisanello is at least as Venetian as a Bellini.

Dorador, also in Dorsoduro, is another must with a window filled to over-flowing with angels, plump and personal but with divine expressions. They might look too fragile to take home, but are easily snuggled into a suitcase, wrapped in something soft and silky from Venetia Studium or from Norelene, a shop specializing in hand painted silk and velvet.

gowns in the finest silks finished with exquisite hand-embroidery. Samanta designs delicious jewellery to complement the look.

Light years away in style, but 20 minutes by foot, is a charming shop near Campo San Polo called Gilberto Penzo. Gilberto's speciality is gondola model kits. Or, for the more adventurous, kits for the lesser-known boats like the *sandolo* or the *toppo*. The simplest can be picked up for next to nothing, although you do need to recall all those sticky evenings with balsawood and glue to put them together. If the finished effect is what you're looking for, Gilberto's reproductions are astonishing.

And what about those traditional marvels that Venice is famous for, souvenirs that you long to buy – but only the genuine article, not some highly priced copy? For handcrafted marbled papers seek out the shop of Linda Maria Gonzalez, where you can watch young artisans using the ancient techniques and producing beautiful cards and writing-paper. You'll also find beautiful leatherbound books, marbled paper, hand-made pens and stationery at La Ricerca, minutes from Piazza San Marco at Ponte della Ostreghe. It's a delightful family business – very Venetian, very charming.

Then there is that most famous souvenir, the mask. Nothing says Venice quite as convincingly as a mask, hand-made and painted in one of the tiny workshops that are hidden in the back streets. Venetians have a love-hate relationship with masks. On the one hand they understand their fascination. On the other they lament another butcher or delicatessen closing down to make way for another mask shop. Most guidebooks will point you towards Mondo Novo (Stanley Kubrick used their services for *Eyes Wide Shut*). The masks are excellent, but if you prefer a warm welcome take yourself to Rialto and La Bottega dei Sogni. Franco and his sister are superb; their masks are unique, made in leather, and the family is warmer and friendlier than the artisans of Mondo Novo. Their other shop is near San Marco on Calle Fiubera and just a walk away. Other good mask shops include La Bottega dell'Arte in Campo San Barnaba in Dorsoduro; Ca' Macana also in Dorsoduro; La Venexiana Atelier at Ponte Canonica in Castello, and also in the Frezzeria just beyond Piazza San Marco; Il Canovaccio, also in Castello; and El Sole e La Luna in the Frezzeria.

The longer you stay in Venice the more you want to take home something really special to keep the memories alive. It may be a mask, a handcrafted card, a tiny wooden angel from Campo Trovaso, or a cloth of hand-made lace to display with a glass vase from Murano. You could go to Codognato in Calle dell'Asscensione for some delicious contemporary jewellery with more than a touch of American designer, Ken Lane about it. You'll see swirling snakes with jewels for eyes, chunky bracelets of jet and emeralds and cascading pearls mixed with turquoise and coral. Jackie O shopped here ... why not you?

If this book inspires you to find others, try Libreria Editrice Filippi in Castello for a heady selection of beautiful books on Venice from every aspect; art, history, culture, secrets. Whatever you choose it should speak of Venice, and who could ask for more than that?

"OUR SILKS ARE THE PUREST AN[D] WE CAN FIND AND SHOT W[ITH] LIGHT ON T[HE] OU[R] WONDERFULLY AND OUR EMBROIDERY I[S] THE GLASS OF THE ISLAND O[F] SO I THINK YOU COUL[D] WE REFLE[CT]

D FINEST
TH COLOUR LIKE THE
E CANALS.
VELVETS ARE SLEEK AND
INDULGENT
DONE BY HAND USING
PEARLS
F MURANO,
AY
CT VENICE."

PATRIZIA FIORENZA, FASHION DESIGNER

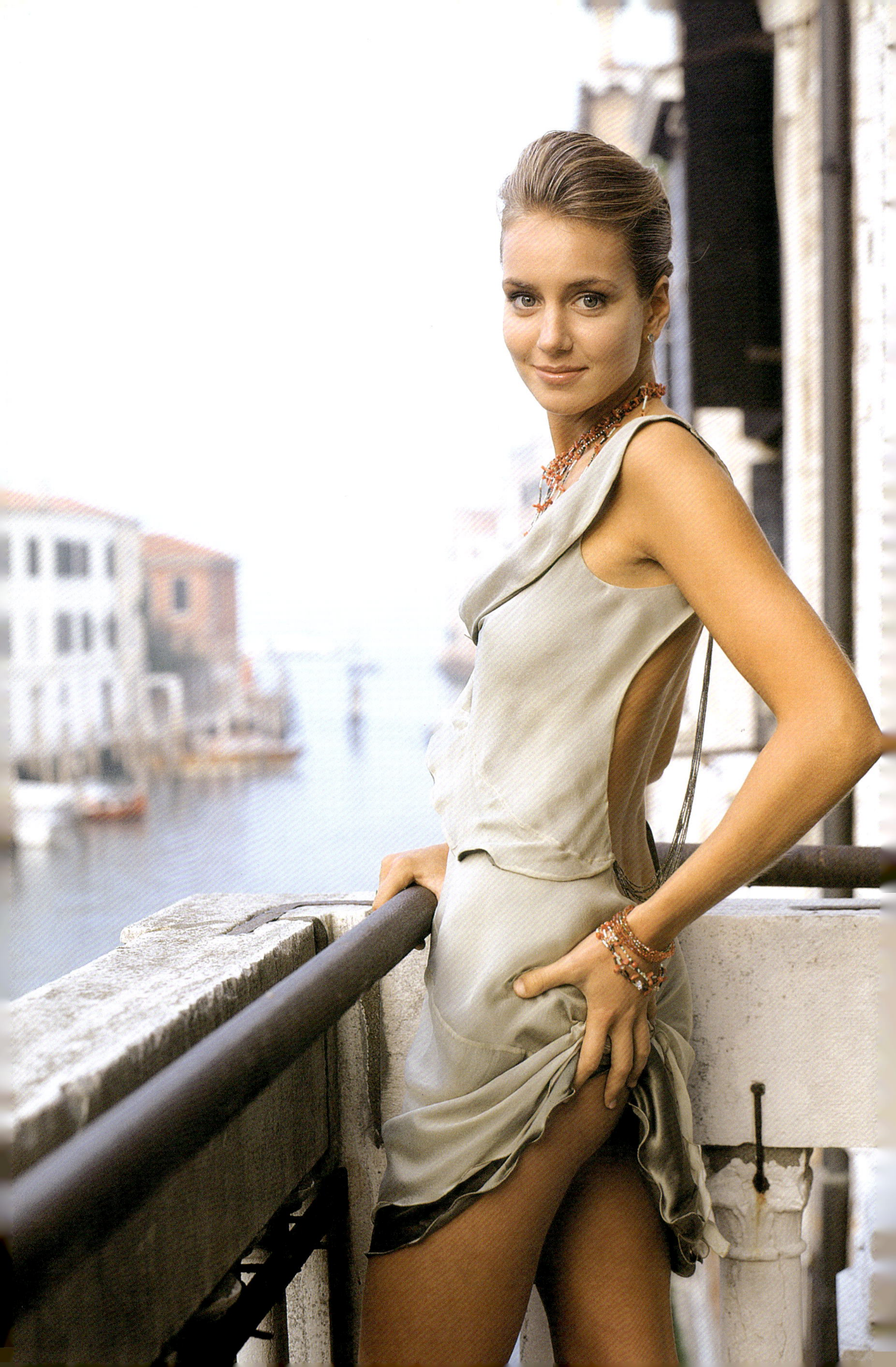

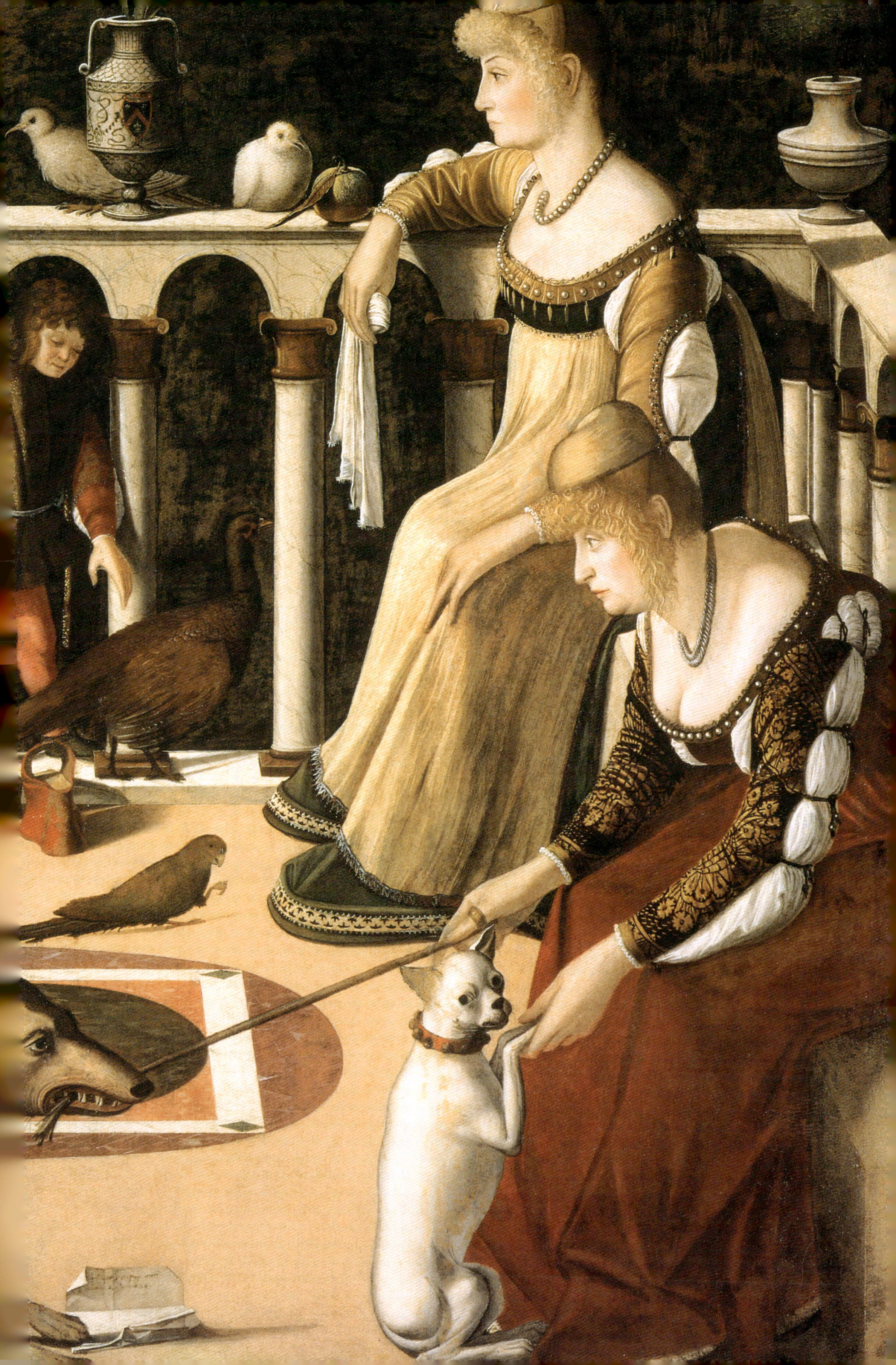

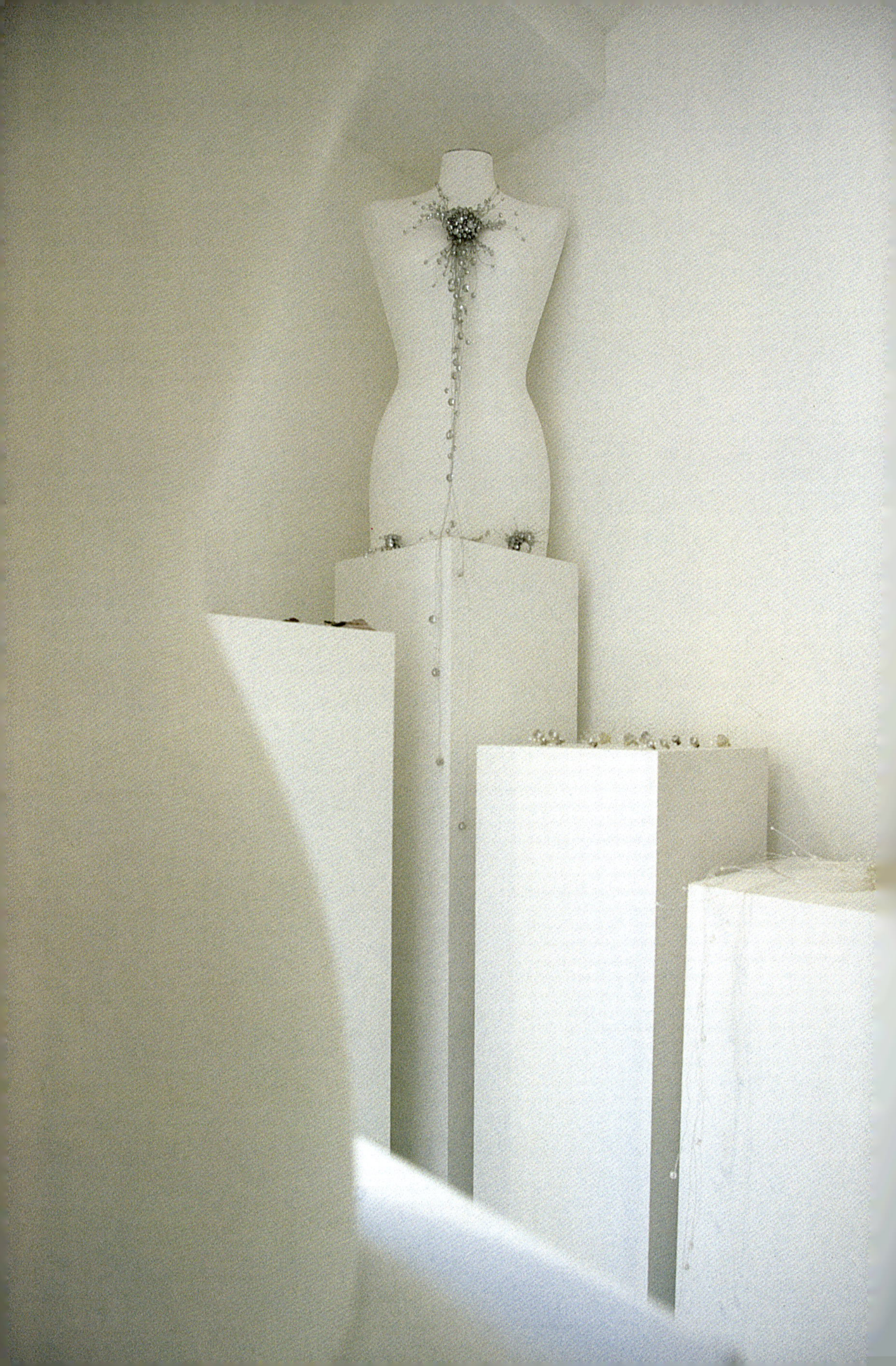

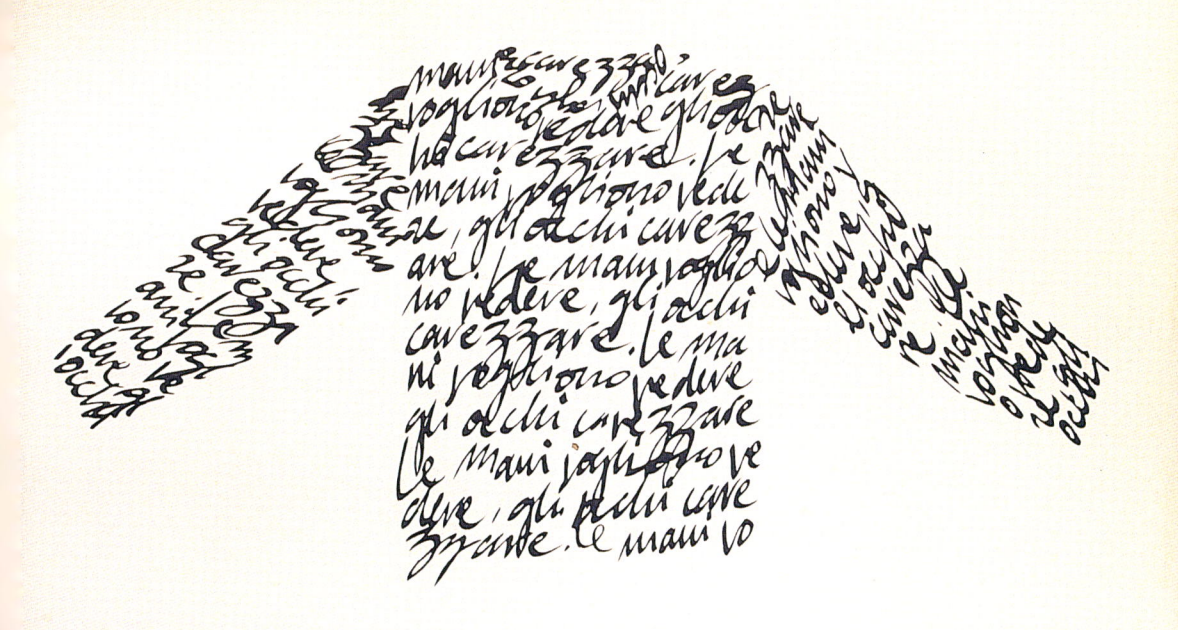

LE MANI VOGLIONO VEDERE, GLI OCCHI CAREZZARE

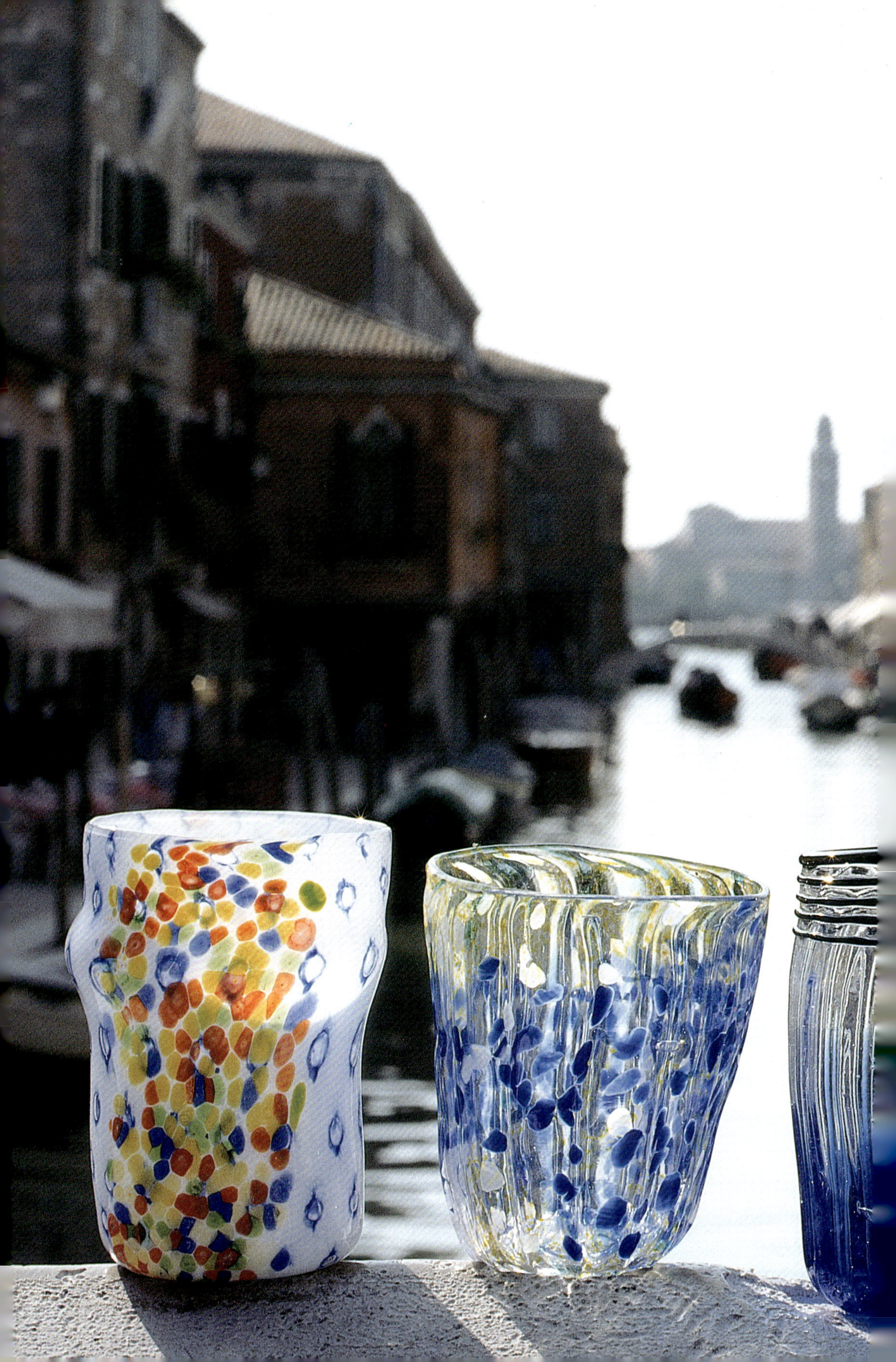

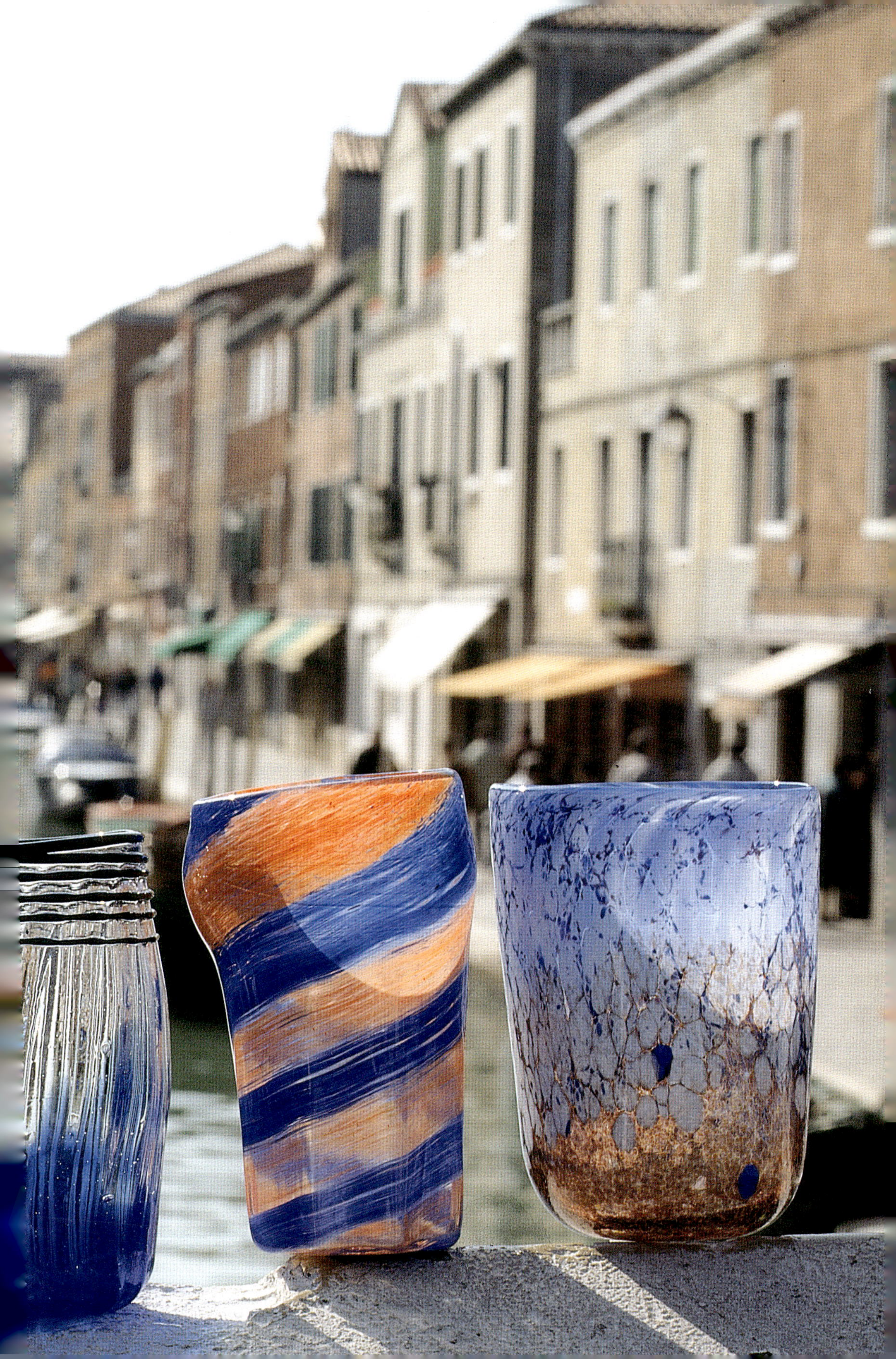

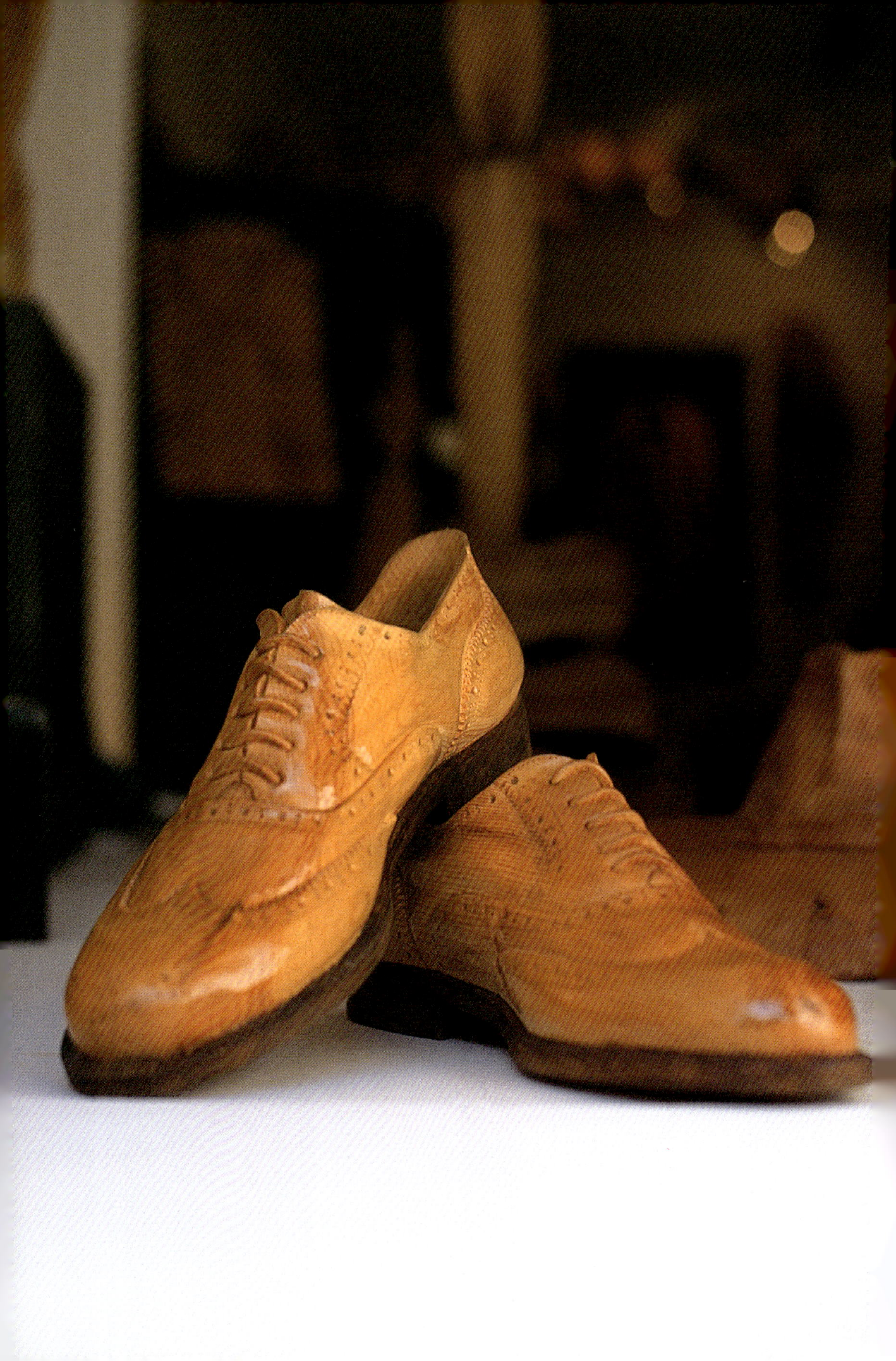

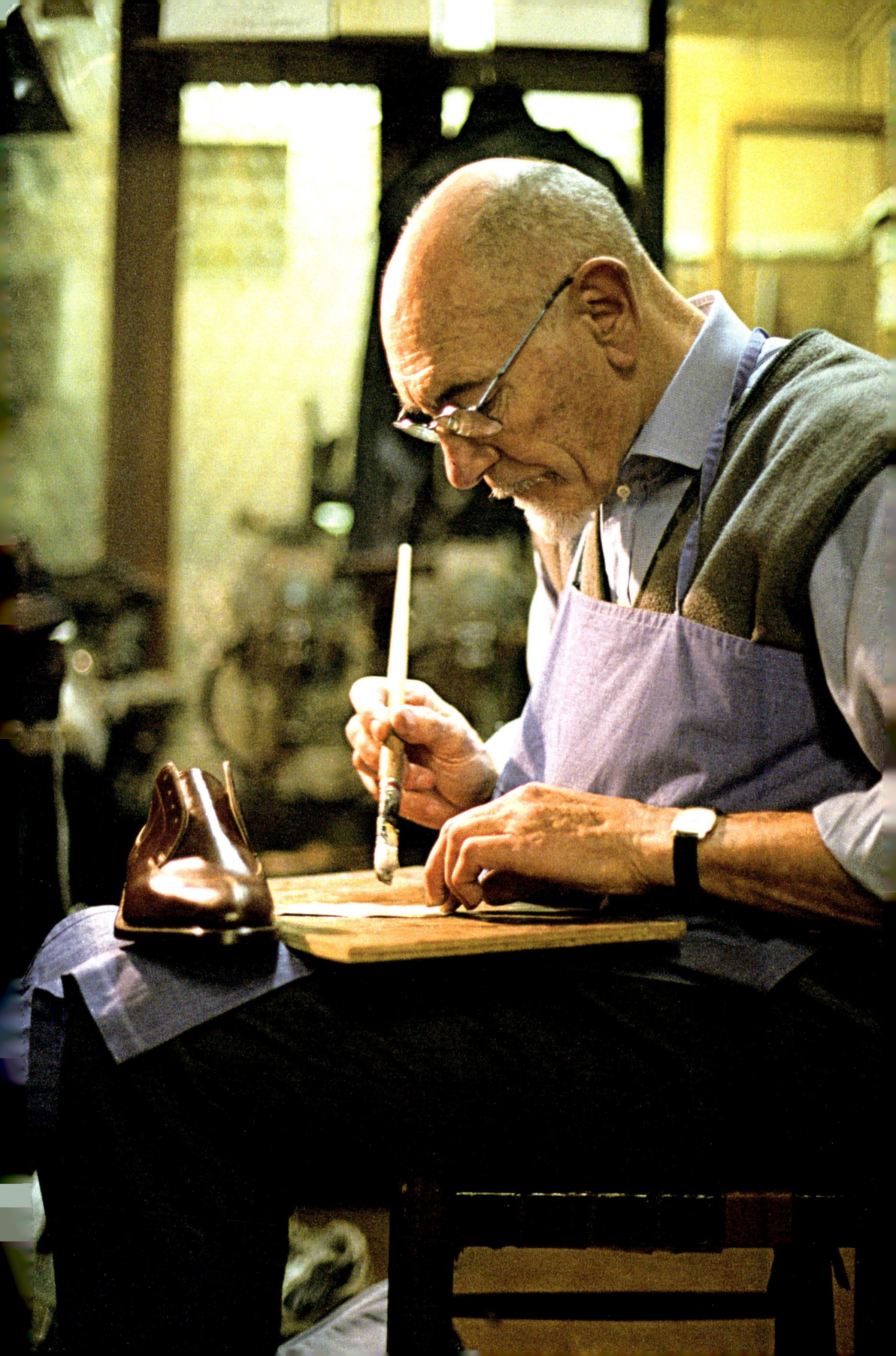

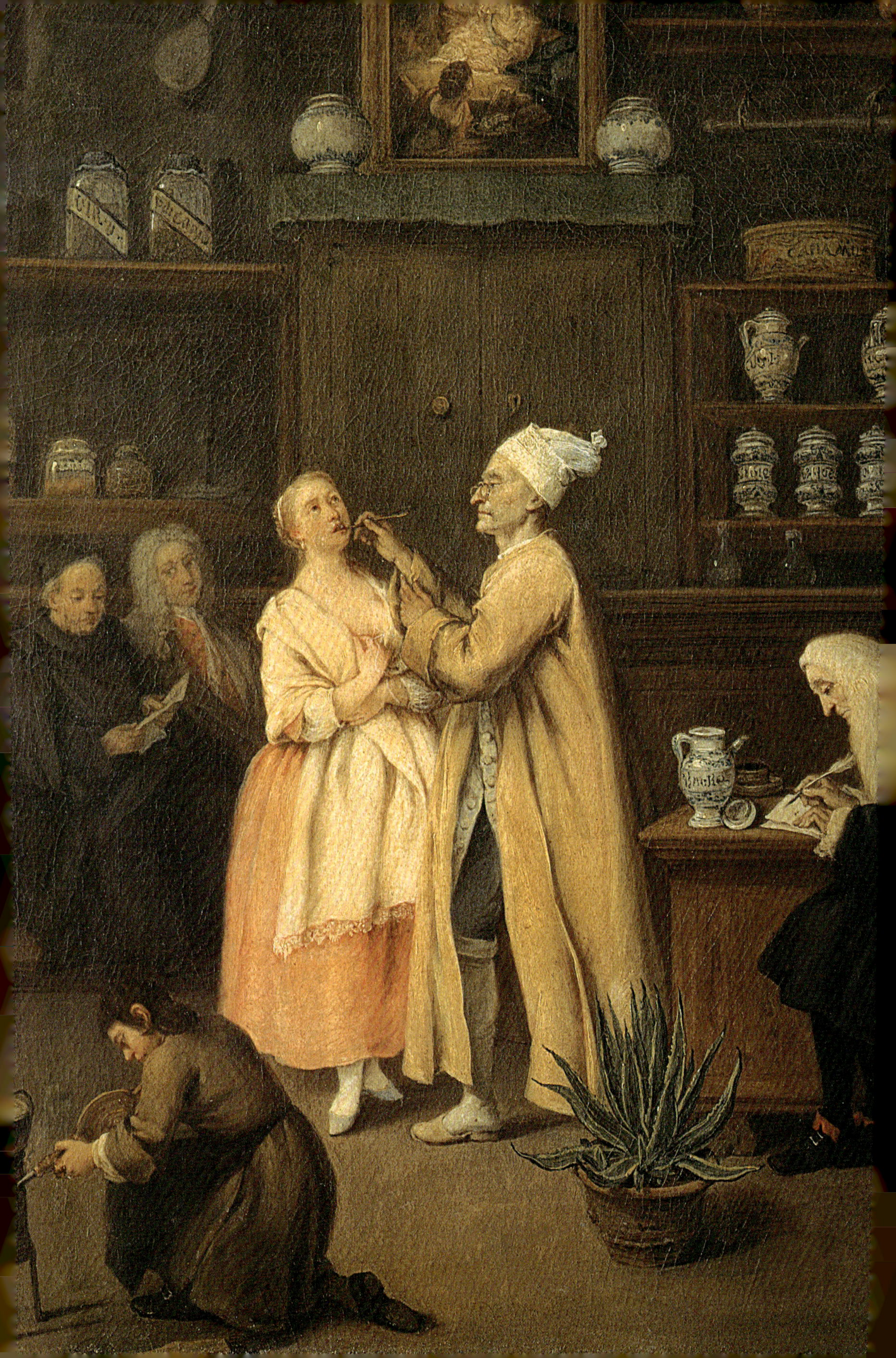

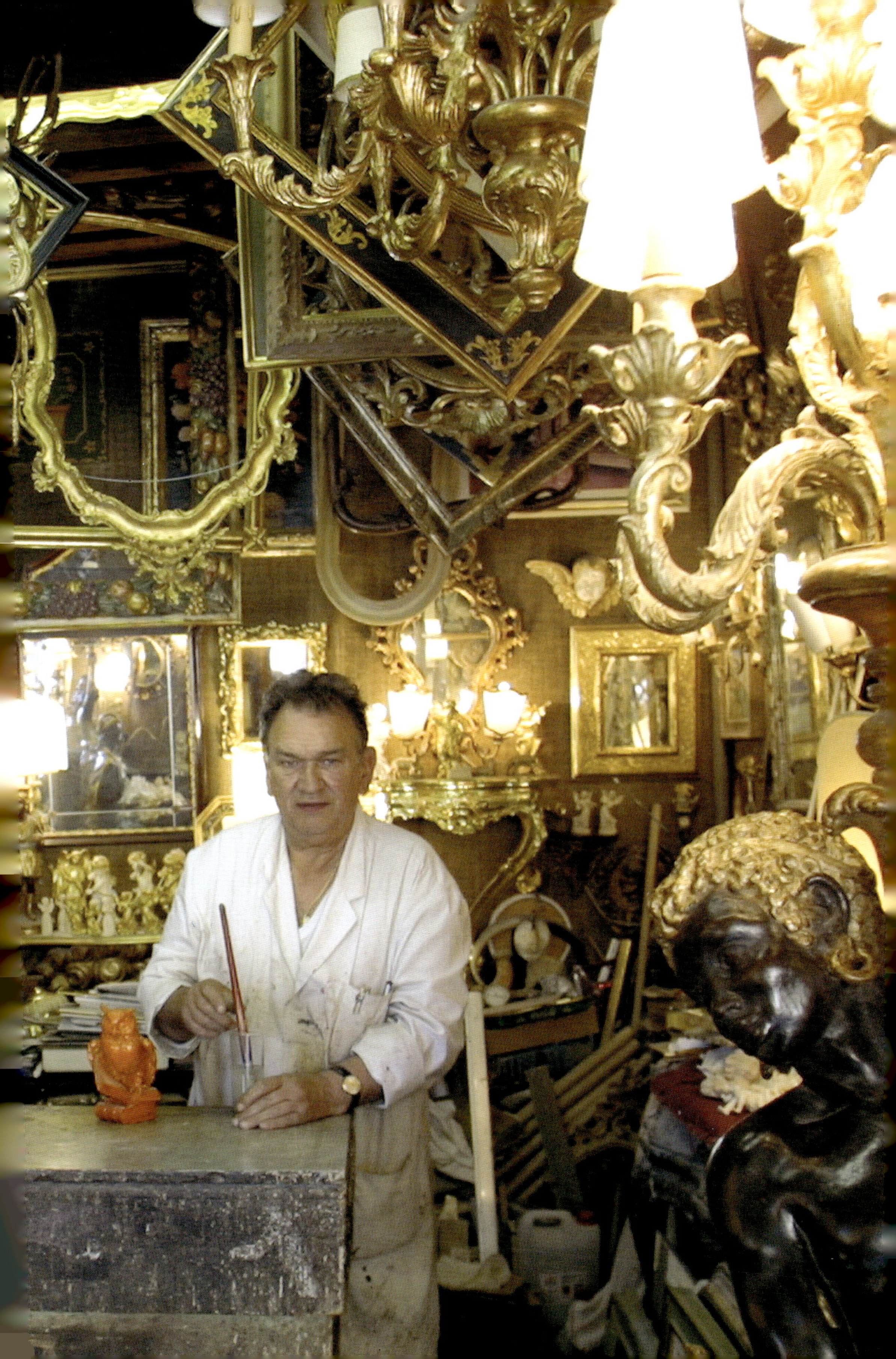

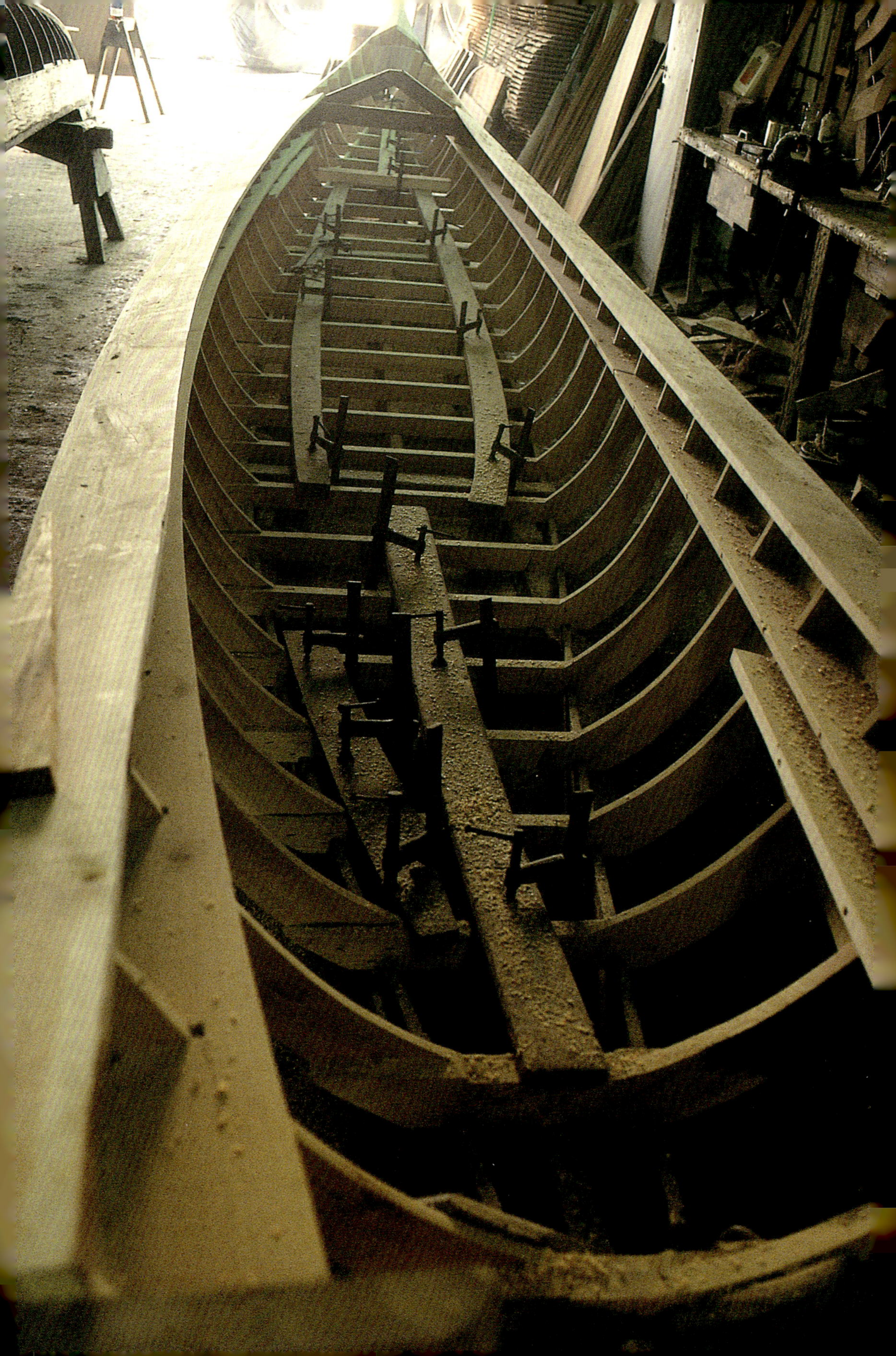

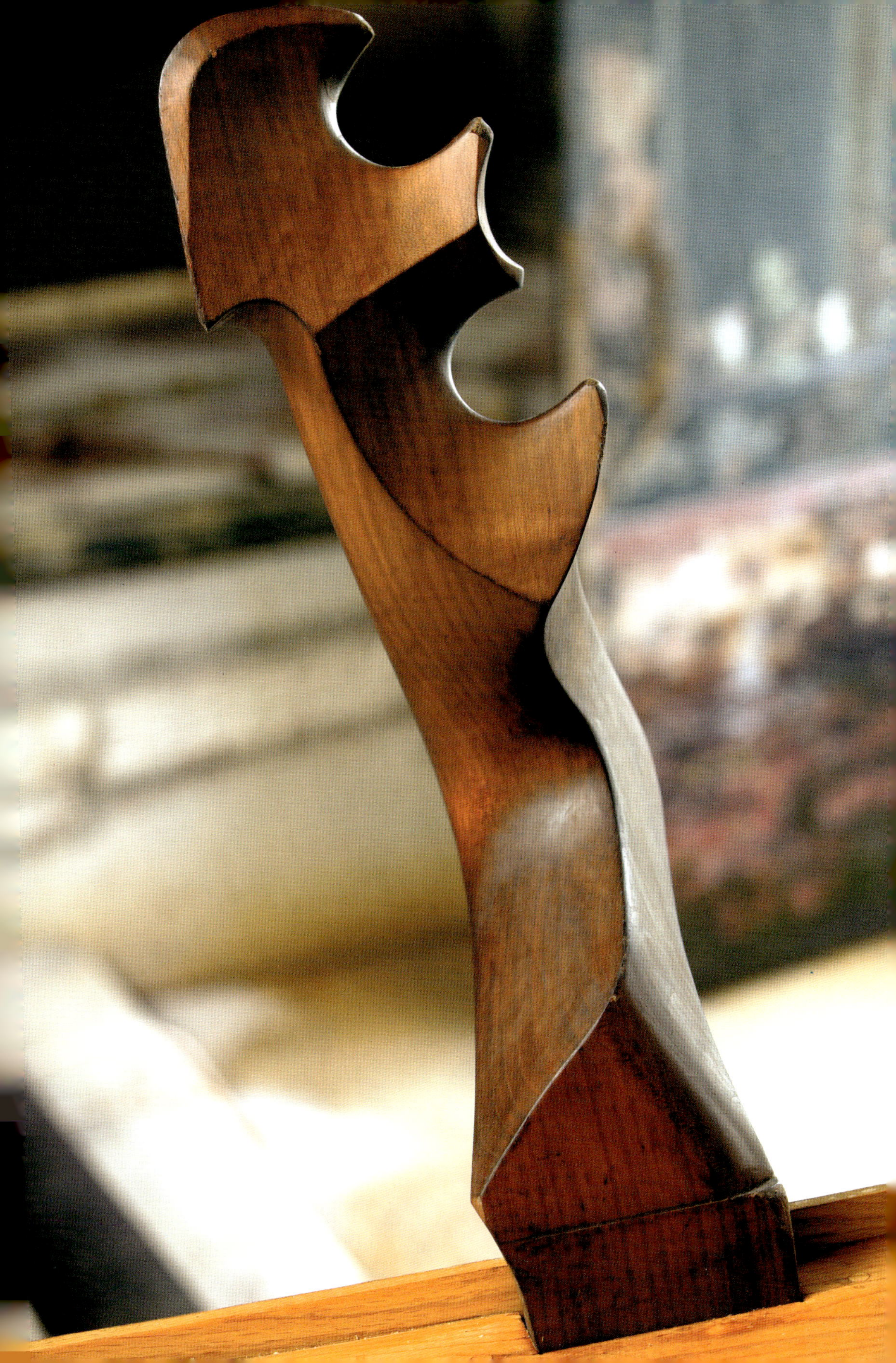

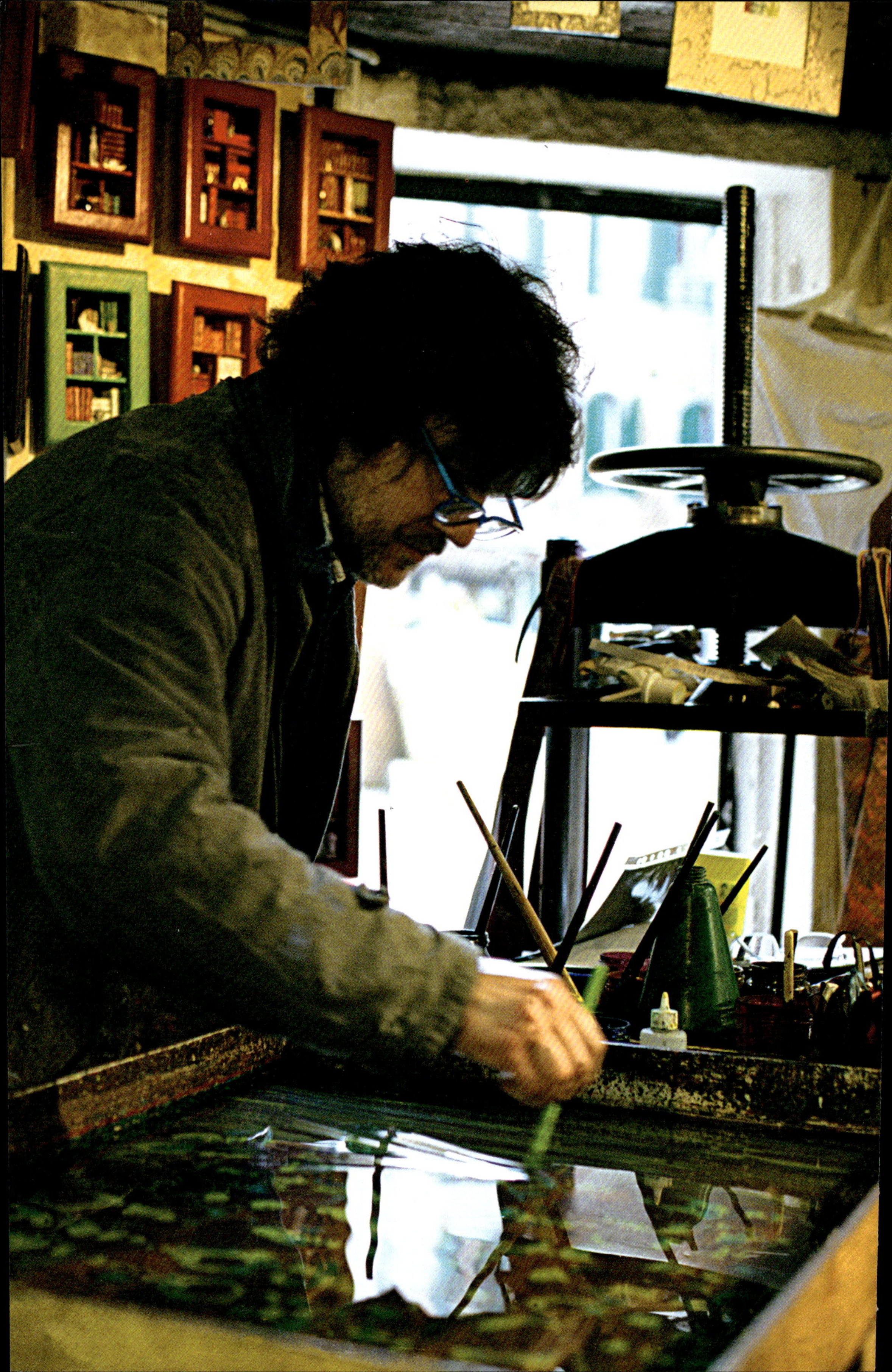

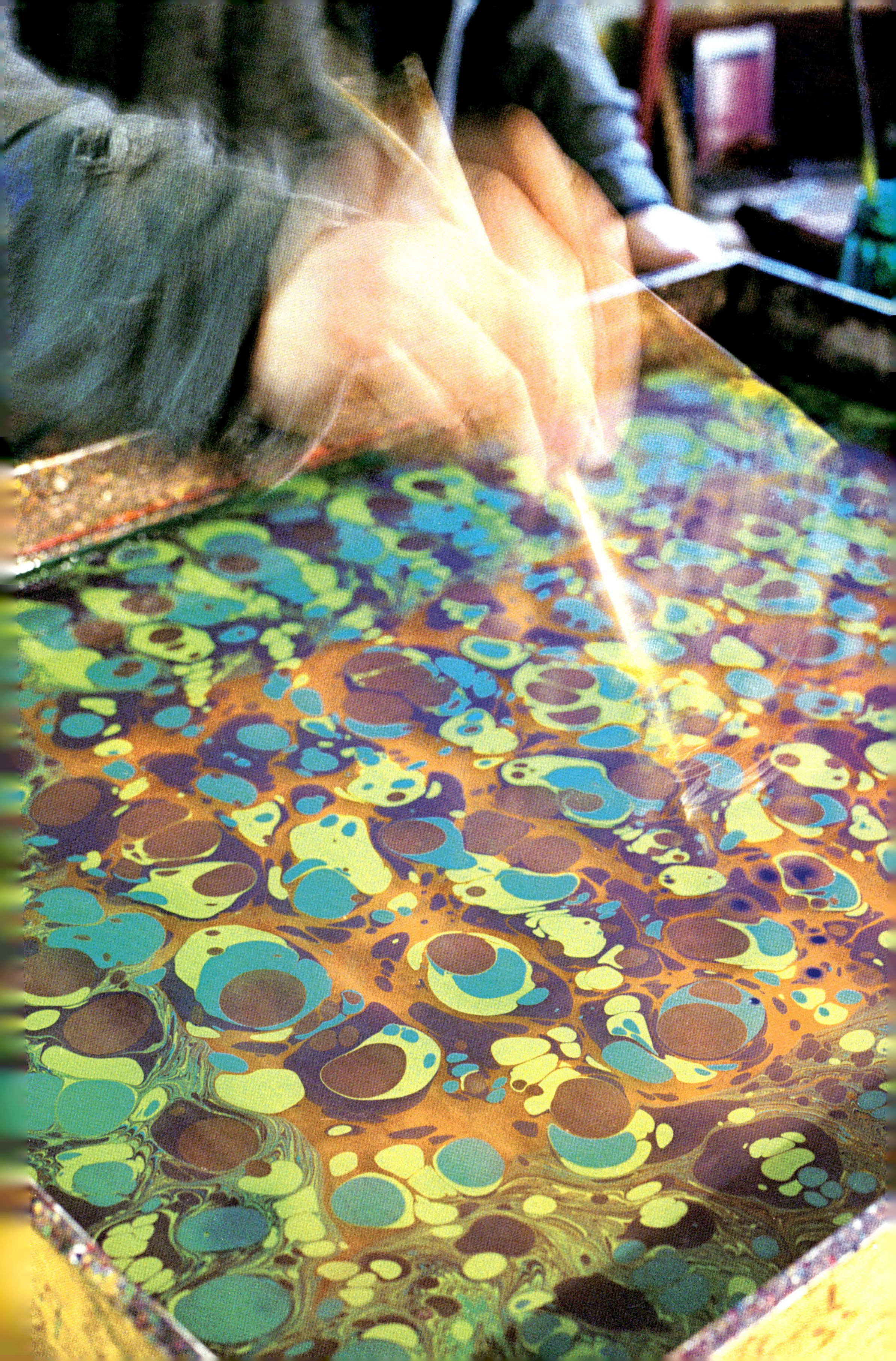

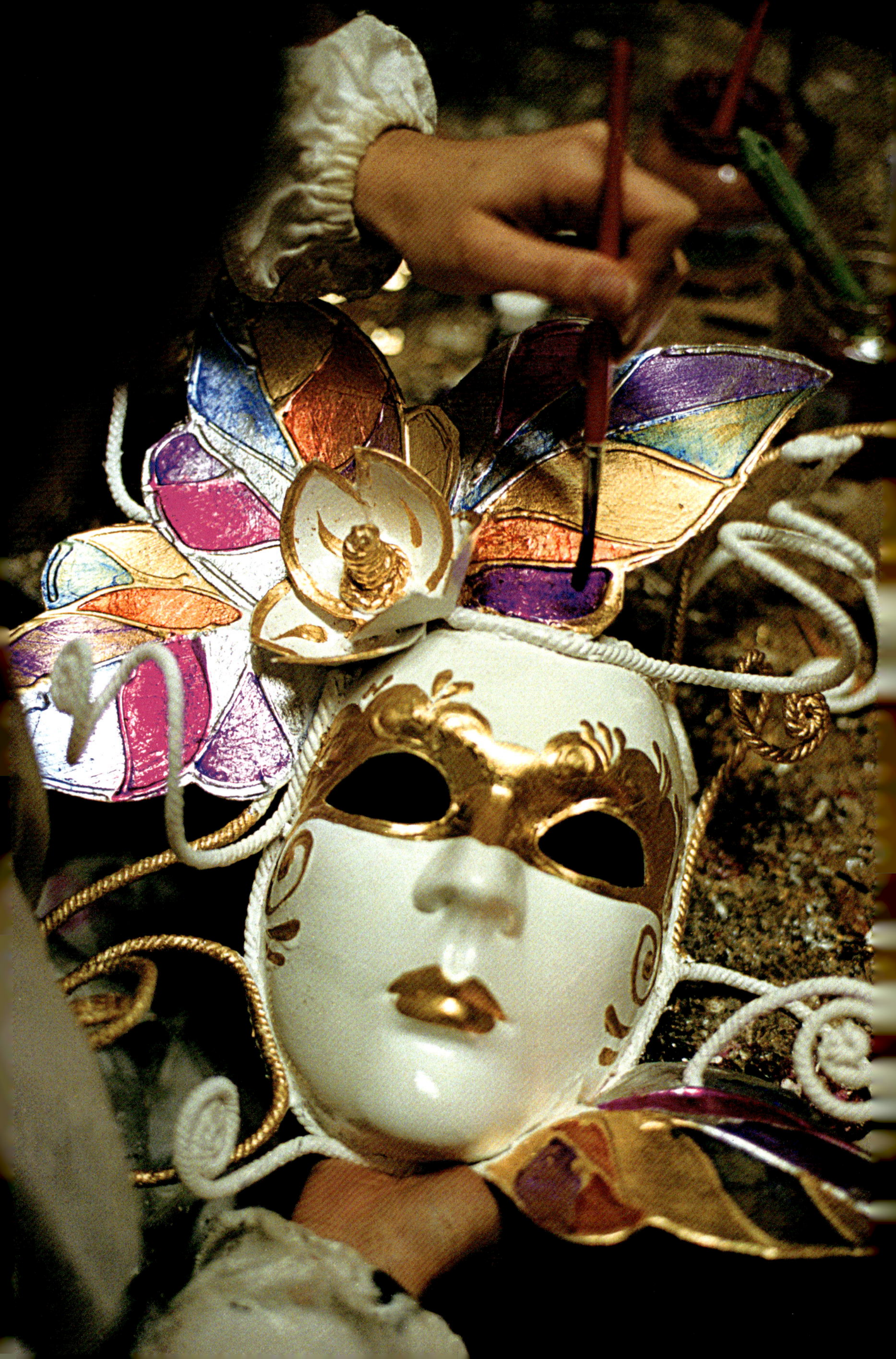

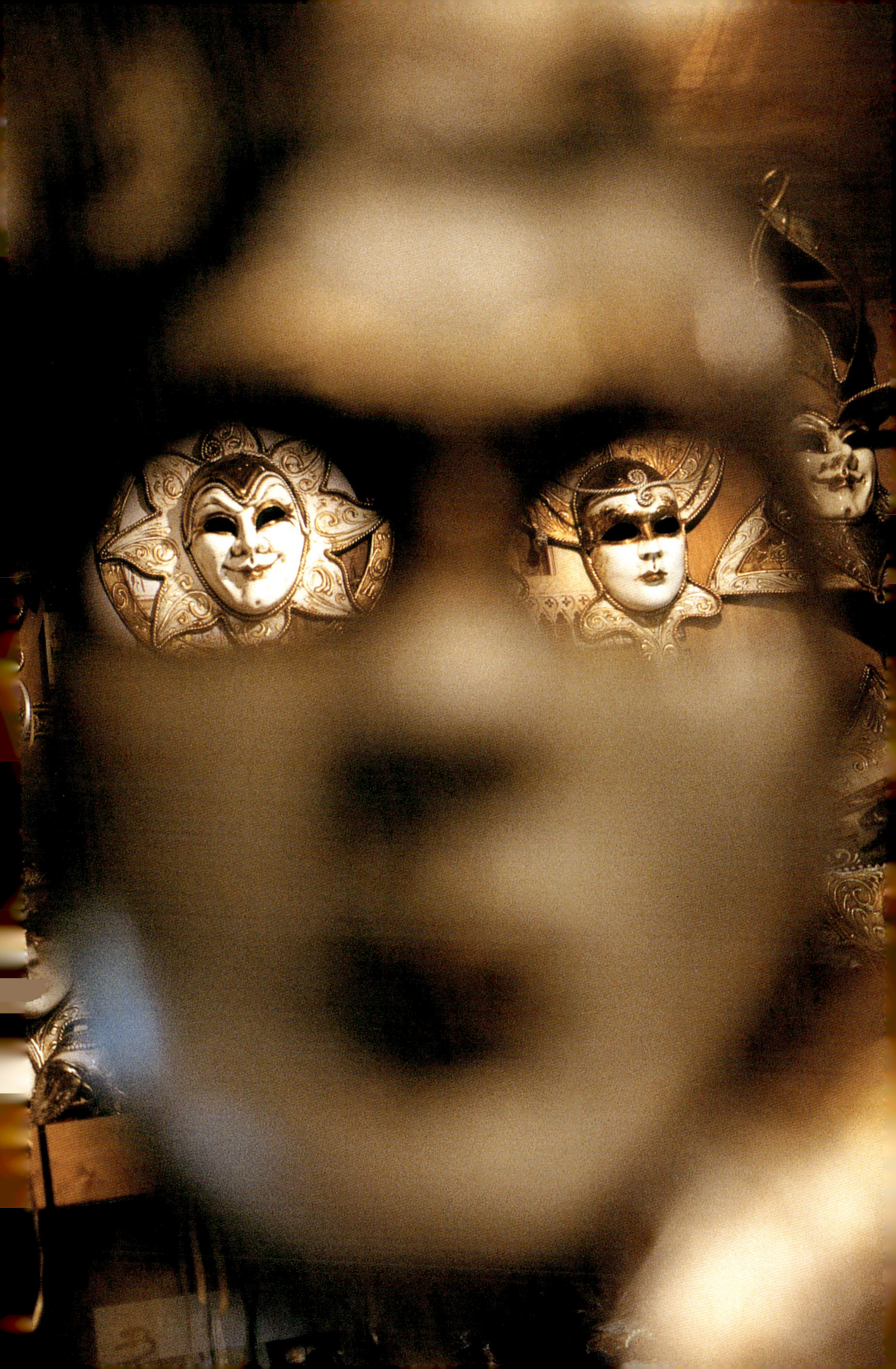

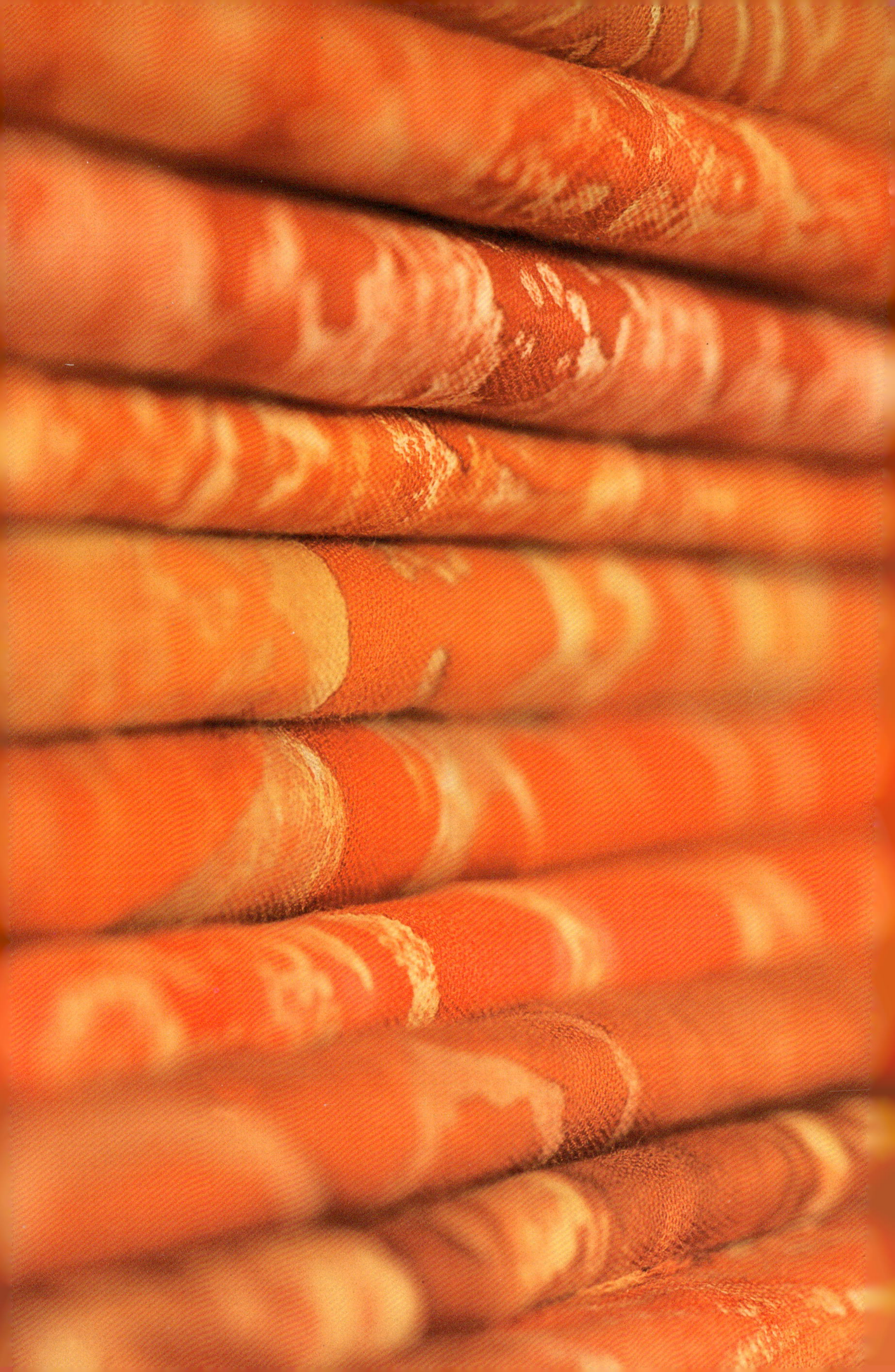

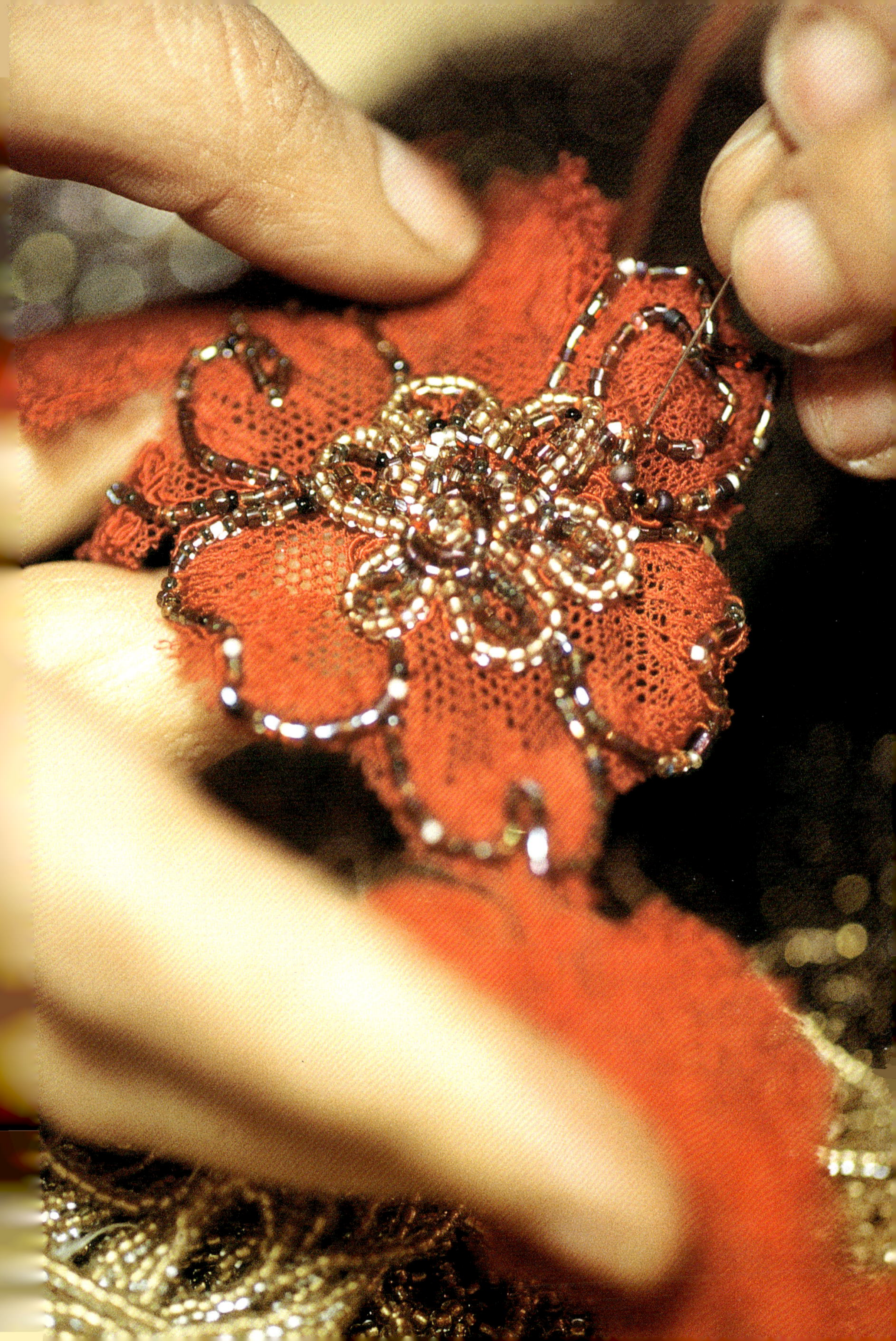

CHAPTER FOUR

GOURMET PLEASURES

The food on Venetian tables is more famed for its

Think classic fish or seafood with a scattering of parsley and a drizzle of olive oil. Think risotto, bursting with porcini or speared with asparagus. Venice's command of the spice routes is the stuff of legend, but look for evidence of eastern history in her cuisine and you may be disappointed. You may well find that you have to search for the pepper and salt on your table. Quite often waiters simply forget to add them, convinced that the chef will make the food quite tasty enough without. Le Bistrot is different. Here the menu comprises dishes from 15th-century recipes, coloured bright with saffron and flavoured with any number of exotic spices, from cumin and cardomon to cinnamon and chilli. But this is an exception.

Vegetables, fresh and tasty from the Veneto area appear on most menus, yet there is no restaurant designed specifically for vegetarians. Venetians don't really understand the concept. Not when the lagoon, even today, is still full of fish and the Adriatic continues to yield favourites such as *branzoni* (sea bass) and the deliciously versatile eel, or, to give it its more appealing Italian name, *anguilla*. A plate of tasty little baby squid cooked in their own ink may look black and exotic but again is based on simple principles. Why invent sauces when the fish has its own? Venetians are nothing if not practical.

simplicity than for the city's spicy past.

Only one restaurant in the entire city concentrates on meat dishes. You won't find any fish on the menu at L'Incontro, but then the chef is Sardinian and his concoctions, tasty, saucy and delicious, taste of that island in the sun. In Venice, the quintessential dish is risotto from rice grown in the Po Valley, and of every type, from fish varieties, such as *risotto di mare* or *risotto dei pescatori* to countless vegetable dishes. All are inventive and delicious when cooked by an imaginative chef from ingredients chosen from the market that very morning.

As for sweet dishes, the Venetians can't live without them. From ice cream and sugary delights through to cakes and biscuits, and squashy cream-cakes from Harry's Dolci to the most glamorous desserts taken on the terrace at the Cipriani Hotel, the selection rivals the best in Europe, or possibly *is* the best in Europe.

But it is the restaurants that are the opinion-makers and there are so many to choose from. Of course you can't go wrong when you choose one of the *grandes dames* of the genre. But dining in great style and, it must be said, at considerable expense is not for every day. Neighbourhood restaurants, bistros, *osterias* and *hostarias* are around every corner and down every *calle*. We have listed some particular favourites, but discovering one's own special place adds a unique pleasure to a trip to Venice. Mistakes can be made, but if you avoid anywhere that features a *menu turistico*, are not enticed into an establishment by an over-enthusiastic *maître d'* trying to pluck customers off the street, and trust your nose as it sniffs some delicious aromas, you could discover a real gem.

It's 7am. The sun is already climbing out of the mist over the Lagoon, and under the Rialto Bridge the market is coming to life.

OF MARKETS AND MANNERS

The real activity is in Venice's superb fish market, a glorious, wet, succulent place, into which fleets of barges bring the day's supply of seafoods. Each of the stalls is lined with greenery, damp and cool, onto which expert stall holders slap writhing, slippery eels, fine red mullet, shiny silver anchovies, undefeated crabs and piles of skate, flatfish and wriggling squid.

A few yards away, along a passageway is the Erberia, the fruit and vegetable market, jolly and ribald. There are luscious peaches, strings of pink and brown onions, untidy piles of parsley and fennel, sweet oranges from Sicily and purple aubergines. Tomatoes of a deep, even red are piled in pyramids, while green jagged leaves of dandelion and arugola are hanging out of their boxes. Grapes come in all different colours, shapes, tastes and colours. *Muscata* is the familiar muscatel. Beside them are *pizzutella*, that crunchy variety we call lady fingers. Then there is a small, blackberry looking variety called *fragola*. Why? They don't taste of strawberries. Or perhaps they do, just a little. Figs in September are sweeter than honey, small and green or purple – buy them piled high in a plastic punnet with handles. Mushrooms in October come in bunches with caps like small brown flowers, or languid and lily-like in pale beige and cream. Pears are small and exquisitely formed, with just a blush colouring and a firm cheek, and plums are golden or purple and fit to burst with ripeness.

In Casanova's day, when the coffee houses and casinos finally closed at the break of dawn, late night revellers and gamblers went to join the hustle and bustle of the Erberia. There the victims of recklessness or ill fortune, as Casanova relates, "enjoyed a soothing stroll, in company with everyone else who needed to recover from a night's career or perhaps to draw a defiant breath of morning air".

The marketplace is the true heart of Venice. Venetians are passionate about food and wine and it is here where everything begins. Stall holders are at least as knowledgeable as their customers. Those scampi are so fresh, they'll say, they barely need cooking at all. This *branzoni* will make a perfect *carpaccio* with just a drizzle of oil and maybe a touch of hot, spicy pimento. A familiar figure, relishing the advice, is chef Renato Piccolotto of the Cipriani Hotel. Are the aubergines good enough for a subtle risotto? Those crabs, still trying to scuttle their way to freedom, would be tender and sweet with *tagliolini* flavoured and coloured with squid ink; while the glistening squid, the plump, grey prawns and all those various molluscs are perfect for *fritto misto*.

Out on the canal, barges are being loaded up with ragged lettuces, crates of tomatoes, hessian sacks of bananas and a neat construction of cornflakes packets. Another vessel is being stacked with boxes of slithering fish and buckets of scurrying molluscs, reprieved for at least half an hour until their journey's end. Until witnessing this scene one doesn't stop to wonder how all the smaller, local markets throughout the city are able to display fresh produce each day. Anywhere else in the world lumbering lorries appear, belching fumes and effectively bringing the street, if not the whole area, to a frustrated halt. In Venice a purposeful fruit barge, squat and nearly as wide as some of the canals it carefully circuits, can do the same thing if it wants to. Yet traffic jams rarely ruffle the waters in *La Serenissima*.

Unconcerned drivers, one bare foot on the tiller, navigate their way around the city. Sometimes a woman is at the helm, her face as weather-beaten as any man's, expertly keeping her vessel on an even course with just inches to spare on either side. Occasionally her only companion is a dog, standing poised at the prow, ears back, nose to the wind, the fitting, living, breathing figurehead for such a practical craft. Their final destination could be the Campo Santa Margherita where there is a lively daily fish market and no less than three fruit and vegetable stalls for locals who consider the ten-minute walk to the Rialto a market too far. Driver and dog, having hoisted the last crate of tomatoes onto its nearest canalside stand, will pause and may well head for one of the cafés in the area. In Campo Santa Margherita it might be the Bistrot ai do Draghi where a quick *grappa* is tossed back alongside a tiny cup of sweet espresso – or possibly the friendlier Bar Rossi, tucked around a back alley and always packed with students taking a break between lectures.

You do not need a driving licence in Venice, but you do need a canal licence. There are few traffic signals, although they do exist, and a commercial vehicle's engine must be registered and taxed if it generates more than three horsepower.

Just minutes away is one of the few remaining vegetable barge emporia, permanently moored under the bridge of San Barnaba outside the Campo San Trovaso. Too small to take all the produce, there is a fruit stall opposite, piled to the ceiling with apples, pears and careless bunches of grapes. Here the driver is the shopkeeper and is never known to desert his post. Only in the early evening when any decent housewife has chosen her family's supper will he cover his boat with its tarpaulin canopy and let it rest till the dawn call tomorrow.

"IF THE EYES LOOK AT ME FROM THE FISH ENOUGH FOR THE

BACK THE SLAB, THEN I KNOW IS FRESH

CIPRIANI KITCHEN."

CHEF RENATO PICCOLOTTO

CLASSIC RESTAURANTS

The stuff of legends, famous, expensive and rightly so, these great restaurants are part of the Venice experience.

Quadri

For romance, it is difficult to beat the atmosphere at Quadri. The restaurant above the historic Caffè Quadri not only serves delicious food but the music from the *piazza* below wafts up, the décor is palatial and the view is of San Marco – but only if you have a corner table, of which there are only four. Reserve one well in advance and infer that you or your guests are rather famous. At *Carnevale*, afternoon or evening, the view down over the *piazza* of masked revellers is unique.

Da Fiore

For 15 years this restaurant has set the gourmet standard in Venice, and it is not difficult to see why. Maurizio Martino is the finest host, his wife Mara concocts magic in the kitchen and their son, Damiano, helps out front of house. Especially outstanding is the risotto, but then so are all the main courses, while the desserts are too delicious to ignore. Prepare to wander down a hidden side street into a restaurant of understated elegance and impeccable service.

Hotel Cipriani

Maurizio's greatest rival is Renato Piccolotto at the Hotel Cipriani. The only reason that the two are not jostling for supremacy is that the Cipriani is a hotel-restaurant. But the location, style and, most importantly, the food are all outstanding. The *antipasti* at lunch beside the pool must be amongst the best in Italy, with each lobster beautifully presented and every arugola leaf perfectly arranged. In the evening, to dine on the hotel terrace as the moon drifts over the dome of San Giorgio Maggiore is unforgettable. Diners are invited to use the complimentary hotel motorboat from San Marco which has you arriving in style and in five minutes.

Do Forni

A top favourite with VIPs, with the Italian President topping the list, Do Forni is a Venetian institution. Warm and friendly without being overbearing, the food is good but the décor even better, being a wood-panelled replica of a dining car on the Orient-Express train. It is also easy to find, behind the Piazza San Marco.

La Cusina

Another hotel-restaurant with style and a good chef. Situated on the terrace of the Europa e Regina Hotel on the Grand Canal, at lunch you are treated to the passing parade of Venice life, while in the evening you have the dazzling views of the illuminated San Giorgio Maggiore and Madonna della Salute.

Fiaschetteria Toscana

Don't expect platters of Tuscan food here. The name refers to the time when the building was a depot for Tuscan oil and Chianti wine. Today, it is a traditional Venetian restaurant, run by the same family for 40 years with *mama* making the desserts, which are heavenly. The wine list is also excellent. In the summer it is a delight to sit out in the garden.

OFF THE BEATEN TRACK

A handful of local restaurants not yet featured in all the guidebooks will provide some happy and delicious memories. It is always a good idea to arm yourself with a fistful of Euros when venturing off the beaten track. Only highly sophisticated restaurants accept credit cards.

Osteria enoteca San Marco

When Luca Dei Rossi, a waiter at Harry's Bar, decided to open his own place in 2002 with three equally professional friends it was bound to be a success. And so it is. Simple, modern, but warm and welcoming, Osterie San Marco is a winner. I ate the best pasta in Venice here. The menu changes every two months according to season.

Taverna La Fenice

Now that the Fenice theatre has risen again, so has the *taverna* that bears its name. First opened in 1907, *'tutto Venezia'* went to the Taverna Fenice until, like so many others, it lost favour. Now it is back, brought to life in 2003 by restauranteur Lucio Zanon. Both the food and the décor are deliciously old-fashioned Venetian. A new jewel in *La Serenissima*'s crown.

Osteria di Santa Marina

There are more than a few Gallic touches to this restaurant, including the hosts, Danilo and Agostino in their long, French aprons. The menu though is classic Venetian with enough of an innovative twist to make it interesting. The venue is stunning – the interior has a restrained Parisian feel about it, while the outside is pure Italian, with twisting vines overhead and chairs that are, for once, wooden and not ghastly plastic. The reds on the wine list are especially good.

Il Sole sulla Vechia Cavana

A stylish neighbourhood restaurant, warm and friendly, with terracotta walls and attractive, wooden floors. The cooking is superb, the wine list is one of the best, especially the whites, but what adds that special touch is the angel who waits on table. Aptly named, Angela knows both her food and her wine, and her enthusiasm turns a simple meal into a happy occasion.

Al Mascaron

Once a *bacaro*, now a funky, lively restaurant with an atmosphere like none other, Al Mascaron is an experience. This is where *La Serenissima* lifts her skirts, lets down her hair and enjoys the superb *piatti di giorni*. The bar groans with fresh seafood, visitors battle with locals to grab a table and it is all good fun. Book well in advance or come very early or very late.

Il Nuovo Galeon

There are those who consider Via Garibaldi near the Arsenale just too far, but not Queen Paola of Belgium, who not only wandered here but discovered Il Nuovo Galeon. This is a charming little place, very neighbourhood and informal, but the food is delicious. Marinated fish, fresh and succulent, some classic Venetian dishes and the best black pasta flavoured with squid ink in Venice. Queen Paola's letter of appreciation is on the wall. This is mine.

A glass of wine is called an *ombra*, meaning "shadow". This dates back to when the wine was kept in the shade of the *campanile* to keep it cool. As the sun shifted across the sky, so the glasses were moved to remain in the shadow.

On the English language menu of Le Bistrot is a delicacy called "toothpicks". Le Bistrot, as already noted, is not a celebration of French cuisine as the name implies but a restaurant specializing in the cuisine of 15th-century Venice; and no, Patron Sergio Fragiacomo is not suggesting that Marco Polo and his contemporaries were concerned with etiquette and carefully cleaned their teeth after dinner. "Toothpicks" in this instance means *cicheti*, which can probably be more accurately translated as toothsome nibbles, or Italian tapas. But, let's face it, "toothpicks" is the name we are going to remember…

ON THE BACARO TRAIL

Restaurants like Le Bistrot provide *cicheti* because little snacks of stuffed olives and marinated fish and meat were part of life in old Venice, and the dishes Sergio and his chef Ivano Frezza have recreated are from genuine, ancient Venetian recipes. But those hoping to catch a lively glimpse of life behind the Venetian façades will find any number of "toothpicks" in the *bacari* of the city. These are traditional wine bars where locals and others can drop in for an *ombra* and something to munch on.

Drinks for a Romantic Moment:

Bellini – made with purée of peaches and *prosecco*

Canaletto – raspberries and *prosecco*

Rossini – fresh strawberry juice and *prosecco*

Puccini – fresh mandarin juice and *prosecco*

Tiziano – fresh *fragola* grape juice and *prosecco*

Tintoretto – fresh pomegranate juice and *prosecco*

A good *bacaro* is warm, cheerful, certainly not expensive, and the variety of "toothpicks" can range from a hunk of cheese and some crisp biscuits to plump scampi wrapped in tissue-fine seaweed and served Asian style on a palm leaf. Sometimes the "toothpicks" are displayed along the counter, arranged in cheerful piles to tempt the customer; or they might be more substantial and kept in simmering pots at the back of the shop. This is when the *bacaro* is the front of house, so to speak, with a proper restaurant available for hungrier customers upstairs.

One such establishment is Bancogiro, located under the portico of the old Banco di Giro firmly in the heart of Venice, which, according to chef Elena Dainese, is the Rialto fish market. Wines are from the Veneto and Friuli regions, and "toothpicks" can be a delicious paste of aubergine and ricotta on a sliver of toast, or *lardo* (a smoky bacon spread with sliced olives and capers), which tastes much better than it sounds, or there are chopped eggs mixed with pimento.

Just moments away is one of the oldest and best known of the *bacari*, Cantina Do Mori, which claims to have been around since 1462. Here the local red wine, Raboso, is especially good. So is a Tuscan wine called Dogajolo. Just make sure you pronounce it carefully. Gudrun Kosmos, whose handbook *Venice Outdoors* is a foodies' Bible, points out that the similar sounding *donnaiolo* means a man who chases women. Ask for the wrong thing and you could end up with more than you bargained for! "Toothpicks" include *baccalà alle erbe*, a tasty mix of fish, peppers and onions in spicy oil, and *crostini al porcini* or "mushrooms on toast".

Not too far away is the Osteria alla Botte in Campo San Bartolmeo, one of Venice's liveliest meeting places, especially for the young and trendy. The wine bar is tiny, the buzz turns into a roar around 9pm, and the wine is on the cheap and cheerful side. But for people-watching there is nowhere better.

The best possible *cicheti* (you really can't call these creations "toothpicks") are at La Cantina in Cannaregio, and therefore off the main tourist trail: it is a good ten minutes' walk away from the Rialto, but is worth finding and staying there. Wines are excellent, a choice of both local and national, but the *cicheti* are outstanding. Tasty crabs, dressed in their shell and garnished with a little arugula and served with a drizzle of pimento oil seems out of place in these traditional Venetian surroundings, but both owners, Andrea and Francesco, have imagination coming out of their finger-tips, and it shows.

Other *bacari* to discover include Vini da Gigio, more a stylish bistro than a *bacaro*; the wonderfully named Sacro e Profano hiding under the arches of the Rialto Bridge; La Columbina, a new addition to Venice on the Strada Nuova, with an excellent selection of wines and an impressive cheeseboard to go with them; and Enoteca do Colonne in Cannaregio, another neighbourhood bar with some fine, well priced wines, and delightful local specialties including *museto*, a cheesy sausage served with mustard.

While *bacari* are officially wine bars it is not worth asking for a classic Bellini at any of them. The Bellini, created by the great Guiseppe Cipriani, is a glamour drink and not for the rough and tumble of everyday life. For a Bellini go to Harry's Bar, or to Walter Bolzonella at the Hotel Cipriani; but even here, don't expect a Bellini from Walter unless it is the season for peaches. The Hotel Cipriani wouldn't entertain the idea of using a substitute, so when that time has passed, usually around mid-October, ask for a Canaletto. A tempting combination of raspberry juice and prosecco, the Canaletto was invented by Walter when he was required to produce something interesting for a group of VIPs. The Canaletto, along with the Bellini, the Tintoretto, the Tiziano, the Rossini and the Puccini, remains in the Cipriani repetoire. But don't ask for one in a *bacaro*. They'll direct you to the nearest art gallery.

Arguments can get heated in Venice, especially about ice cream. Some people swear that only Da Nico on the Zattere knows how to mix a *gelato cioccolato* to the perfect chocolatey, rich consistency, while others swear that Il Doge in Campo Santa Margherita is a world-beater not only with its fruity *fragola* sorbet but for its luscious coconut ice cream. Then there is that place with no discernable name, like so many Venetian establishments, near the gondola garage in Campo San Trovaso, which nearby students maintain beats both. Of course one can sit outside and people-watch at Da Nico, and you can only lick a cone from Santa Margherita or San Trovaso, but it is that moment when tongue meets cold, creamy ice cream that soothes the fervent sightseer and sets us striding forth to view another Tiepolo ceiling.

SWEET TEMPTATIONS

Gelaterie are not alone in providing sweet temptations. Standing at the bar in the busy Pasticceria Balarin on the way to the Rialto market, sipping a warm cappuccino and biting into a soft, freshly made brioche scattered with icing sugar and filled with a little vanilla cream is a very satisfying way to start the day. In the window are pyramids of candied orange and lemon dipped in chocolate, nougat in pistachio icing, and *gondole* – feather-light biscuits, crescent-shaped and almond-scattered. Too much for just now perhaps, but later there comes a time, perhaps around 5pm, when further visions of cakes and pastries float into one's head – maybe soft golden cakes topped with marzipan, or a creamy *meringata*, crumbly on the outside and satisfyingly chewy in the middle, or perhaps just a classic *tórta cioccolata* as seductive and rich as Venice itself. These are cakes that need a strong, black espresso beside them, properly bitter to contrast with the wonderful sweetness.

Mandorle, or almonds, are everywhere in Venice. Few cakes or biscuits seem complete without a smattering of *mandorle*, adding an extra chewy crunch. Most popular are *pan dei Dogi*, which are not, as might appear, slightly circumspect bread-sticks, but muffins, usually chocolate and studded with whole almonds.

If it were *Carnevale* one would look for *frittelle*, round doughy sugar cakes rather like doughnuts, or *crostoli*, similar to pancakes dusted with icing sugar but made from pastry. *Baicoli*, a deliciously light and crumbly biscuit named after the Venetian fish it is cut to resemble, is also found only at *Carnevale* time, whereas in November, on the 2nd to be precise, brightly coloured marzipan balls called *fave* are made for All Saints' Day.

Available all year round are golden wonders called *zaleti*, made with cornmeal and flavoured with lemon and raisins, and the ubiquitous *pan dei Dogi* appear in all the *pasticcheria* windows. *Strudel mele*, or common or garden apple strudel, is another enticement, but hardly Italian one would have thought. *Apfel Strudel* must have come with the Austrians. But even nicer, and more Venetian, is *cestone de mandorle* – almond tarts with *amoretto* cake nestling underneath.

One of the great names in *pasticcherie* is Antico Caffè Rosa Salva in Campo San Lucca. Locals say that Rosa Salva must have special cake-scented sprays blown into the street to catch unwary tourists. Long before you hit the Campo you can smell the wares: a hint of almond, a dash of cherry, the seductive aroma of baked apple mixed with cinnamon or the thick, rich tang of the best dark chocolate lead us helplessly into one of the most famous *pasticcherie* in Venice.

If you have managed to sniff, savour and not buy there is always Florian's, where you could sit at Goethe's or Byron's or Rita Hayworth's table and toy with a cake you saw in one of the city's *pasticcherie*, but at three times the price. This is only to be expected of course. Caffè Florian is nearly as famous as Piazza San Marco itself, and, with its shaded terraces and intimate corners has been a prime player in many a romance.

Opposite is its arch-rival Gran Caffè Quadri. Fifty years younger than Florian's, Quadri's great claim is that it invented the espresso. Famous admirers include Stendahl, Balzac and Woody Allen, while Proust used to scurry from table to table in the winter to escape the draughts. There are some, possibly the café owners, who insist that when Proust said of Venice "I turned my dream into my address", he meant Quadri's.

Harry's Dolci, an offshoot of Harry's Bar but across the lagoon on Guidecca, just up from the Hotel Cipriani, is another mouth-watering experience – as are the scrumptious desserts and cakes at the Hotel Cipriani itself. A *Tiramisu* comes with its own little chocolate gondola on the Hotel Cipriani terrace and ice cream flavours vary daily, according to the season – figs and honey, pistachio and almond – who knows, who could possibly guess?

Apfel Strudel is but one memory left by the Austrians. In 1849 they put down a heroic Venetian uprising led by Danieli Manin and only managed to recapture the city under the leadership of Marshal Radetsky, who was the kind of indefatigable aristocrat Casanova might have admired. He sired his last illegitimate child when he was 81, and had a rather jolly march, composed by Johann Strauss I, named after him.

Tiramisu, now on so many Italian menus, is, in fact, a 20th-century invention, and means, literally, "pick me up", which it does when made by a master dessert-maker.

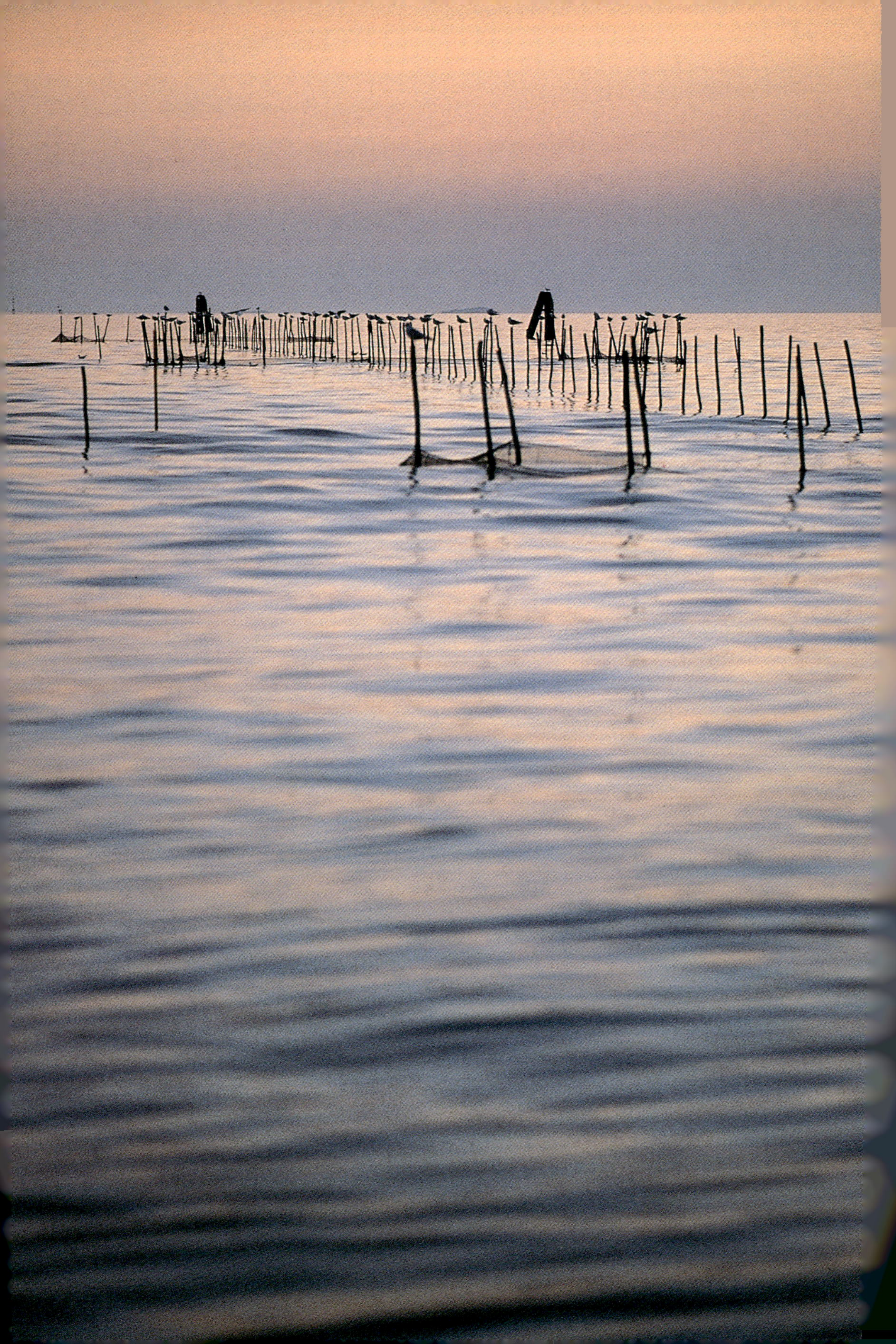

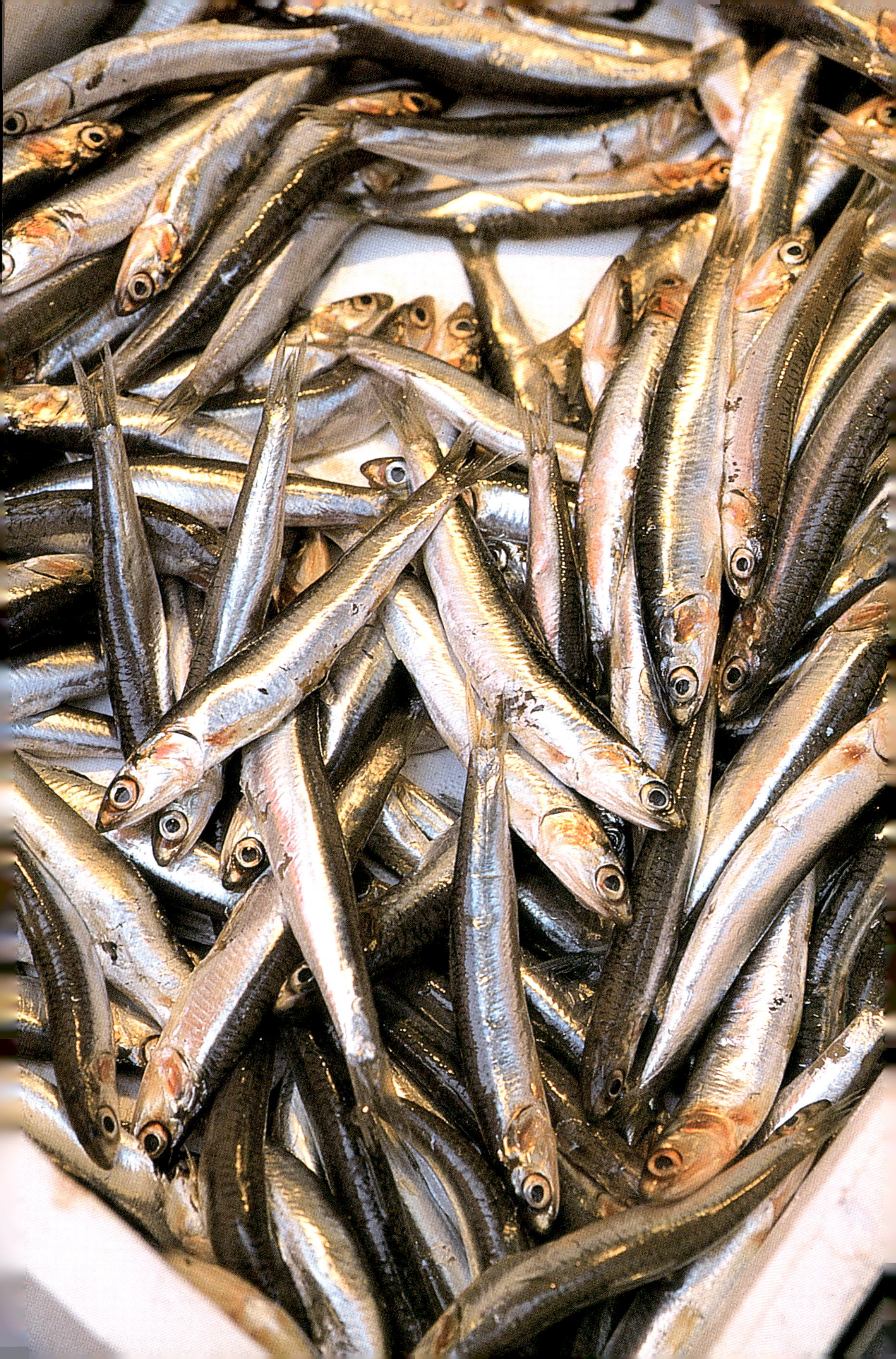

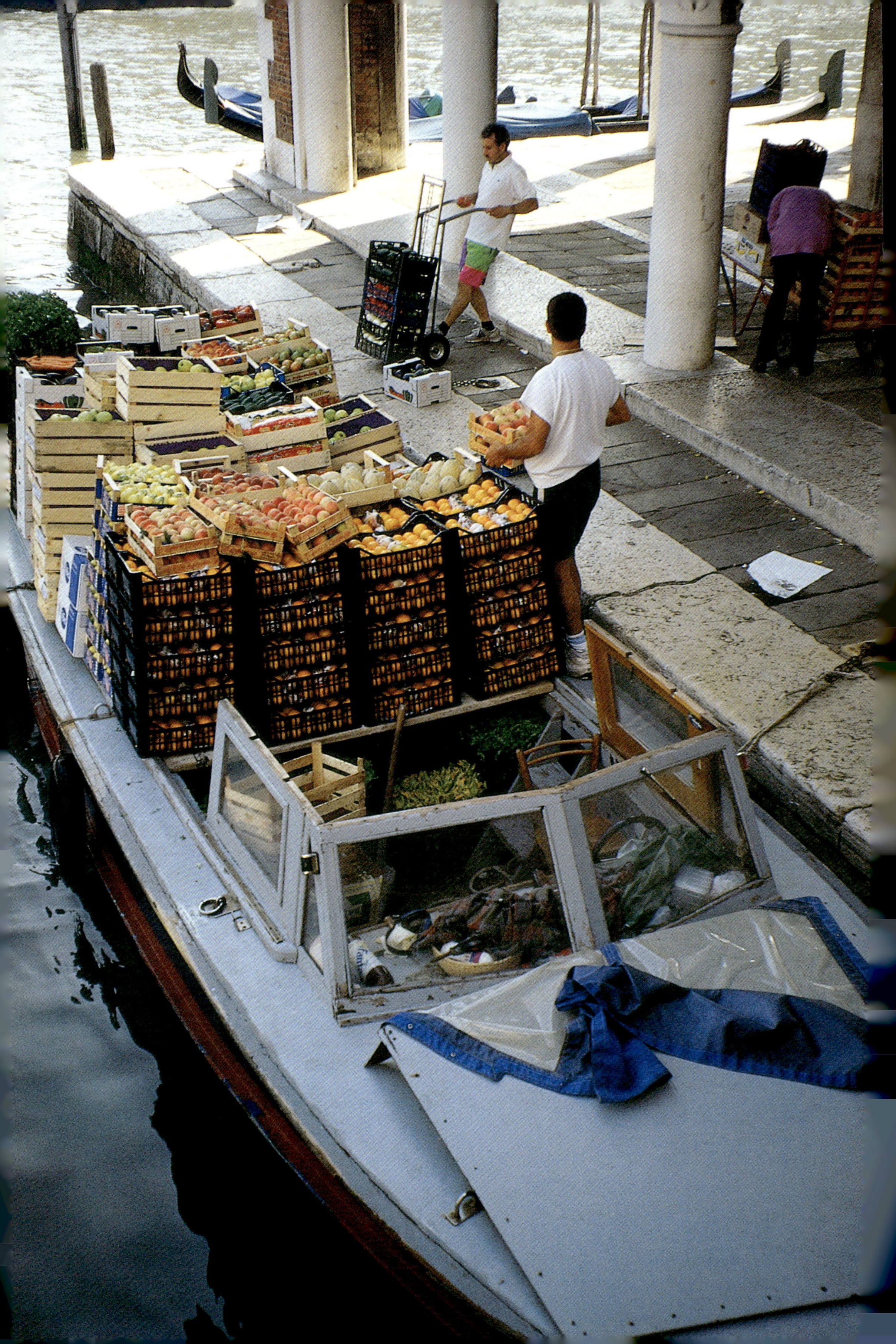

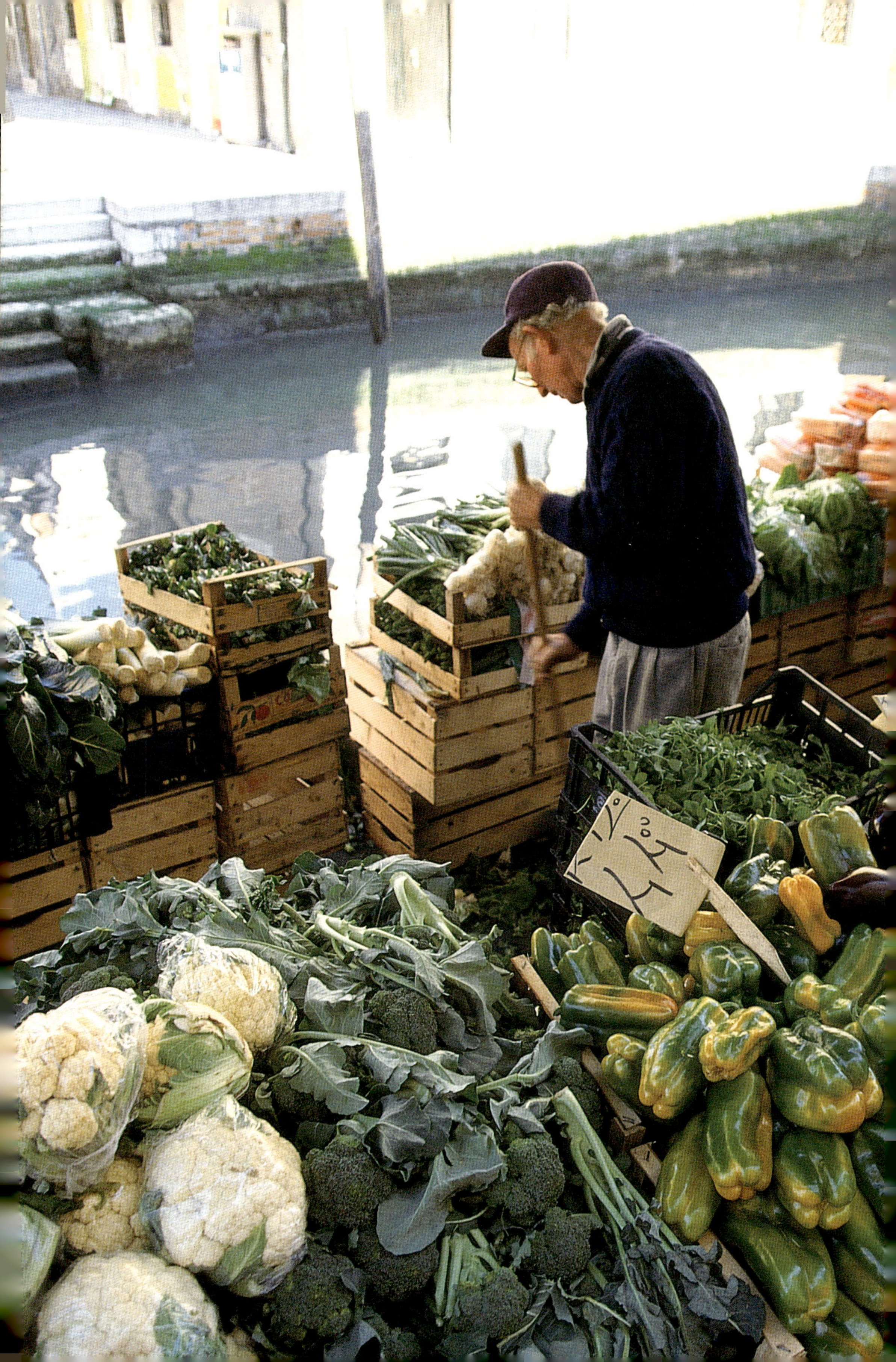

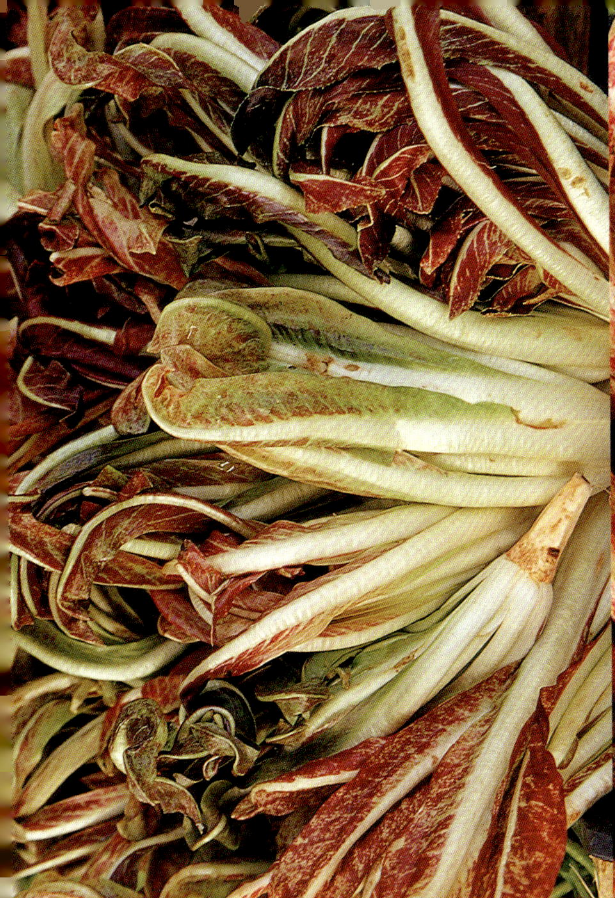
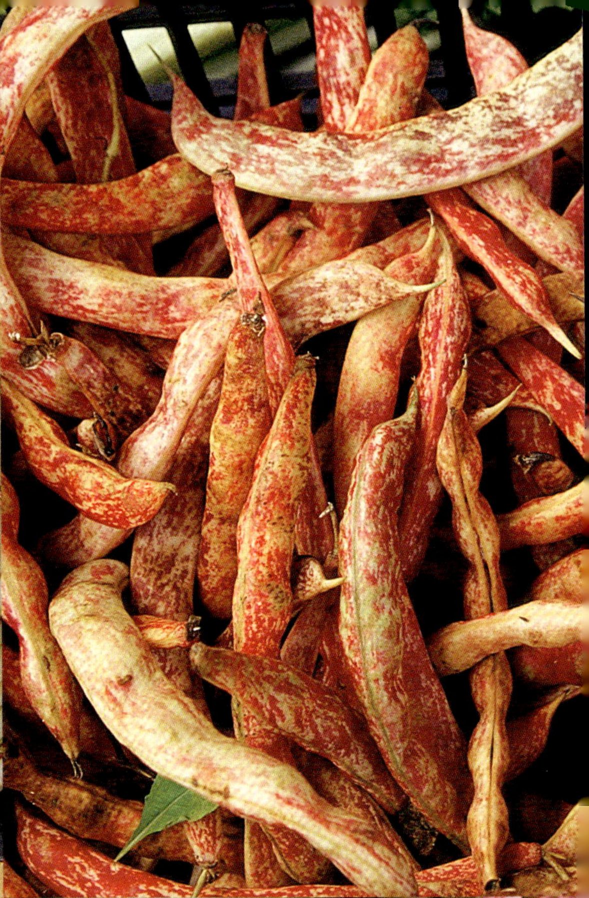
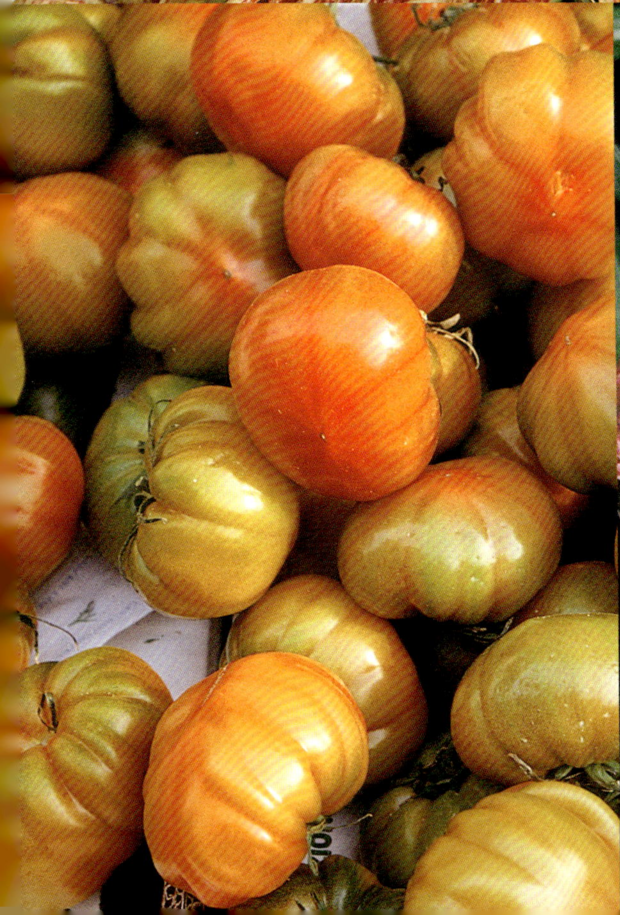
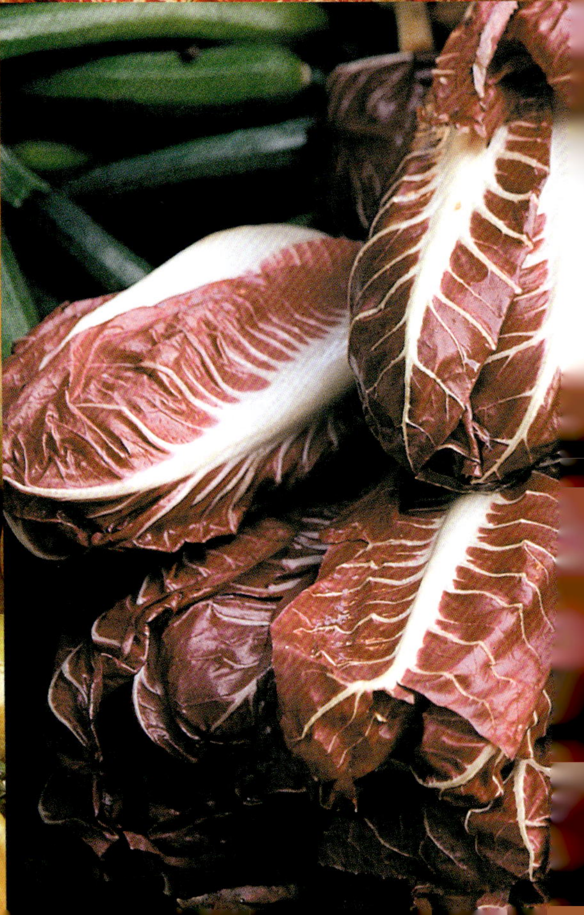

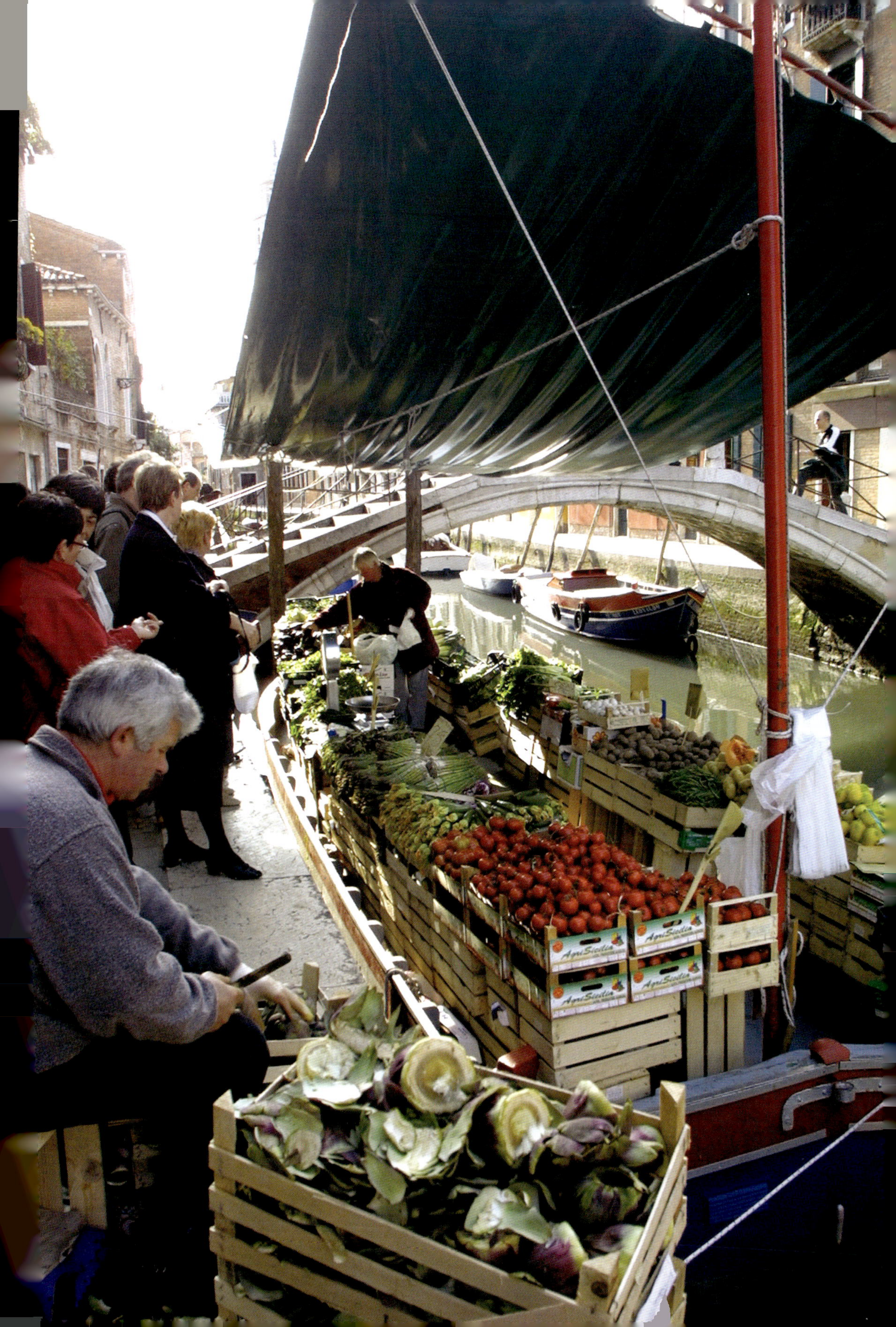
AgriSicilia
AgriSicilia
AgriSicilia
AgriSicilia

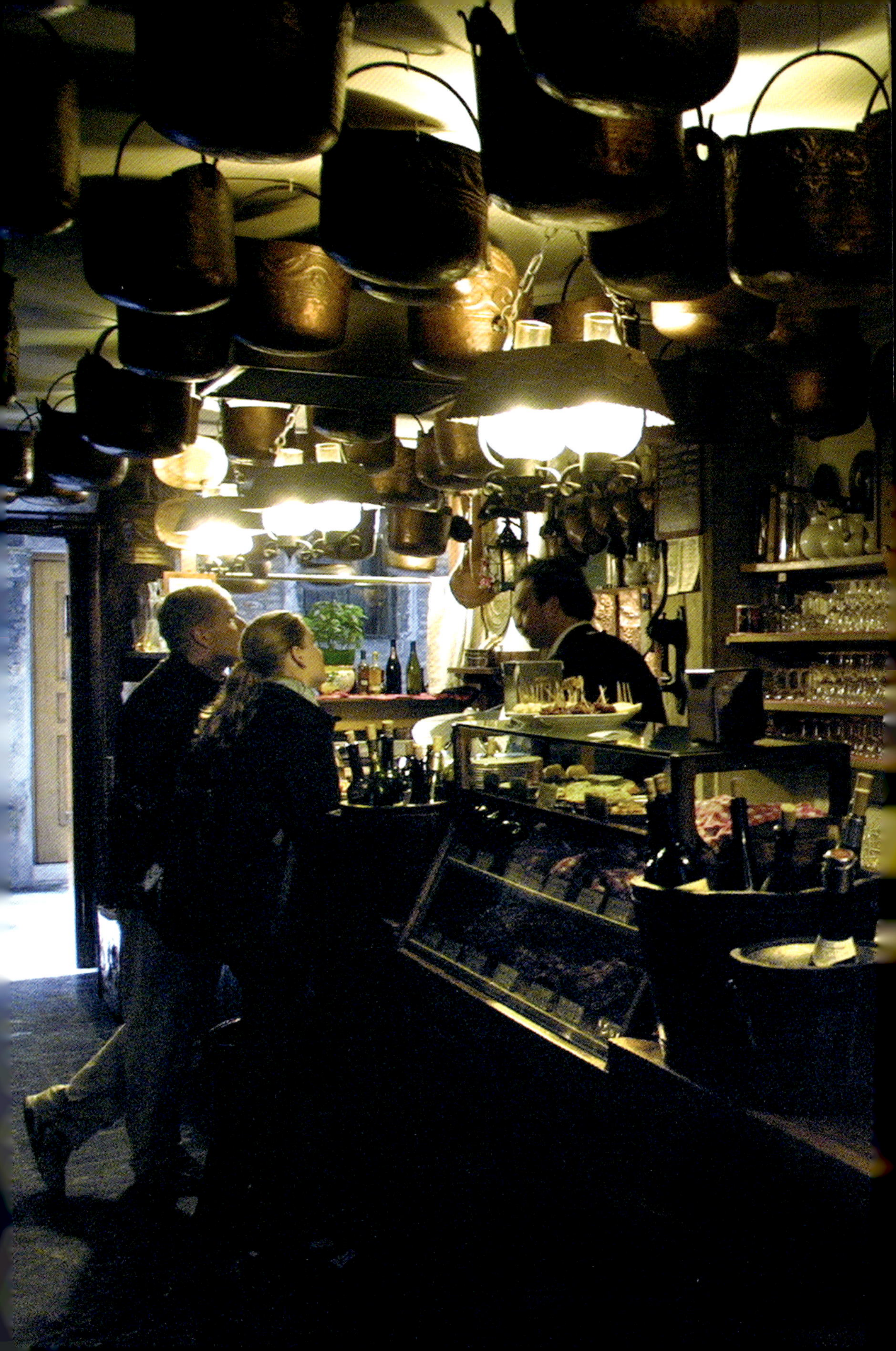

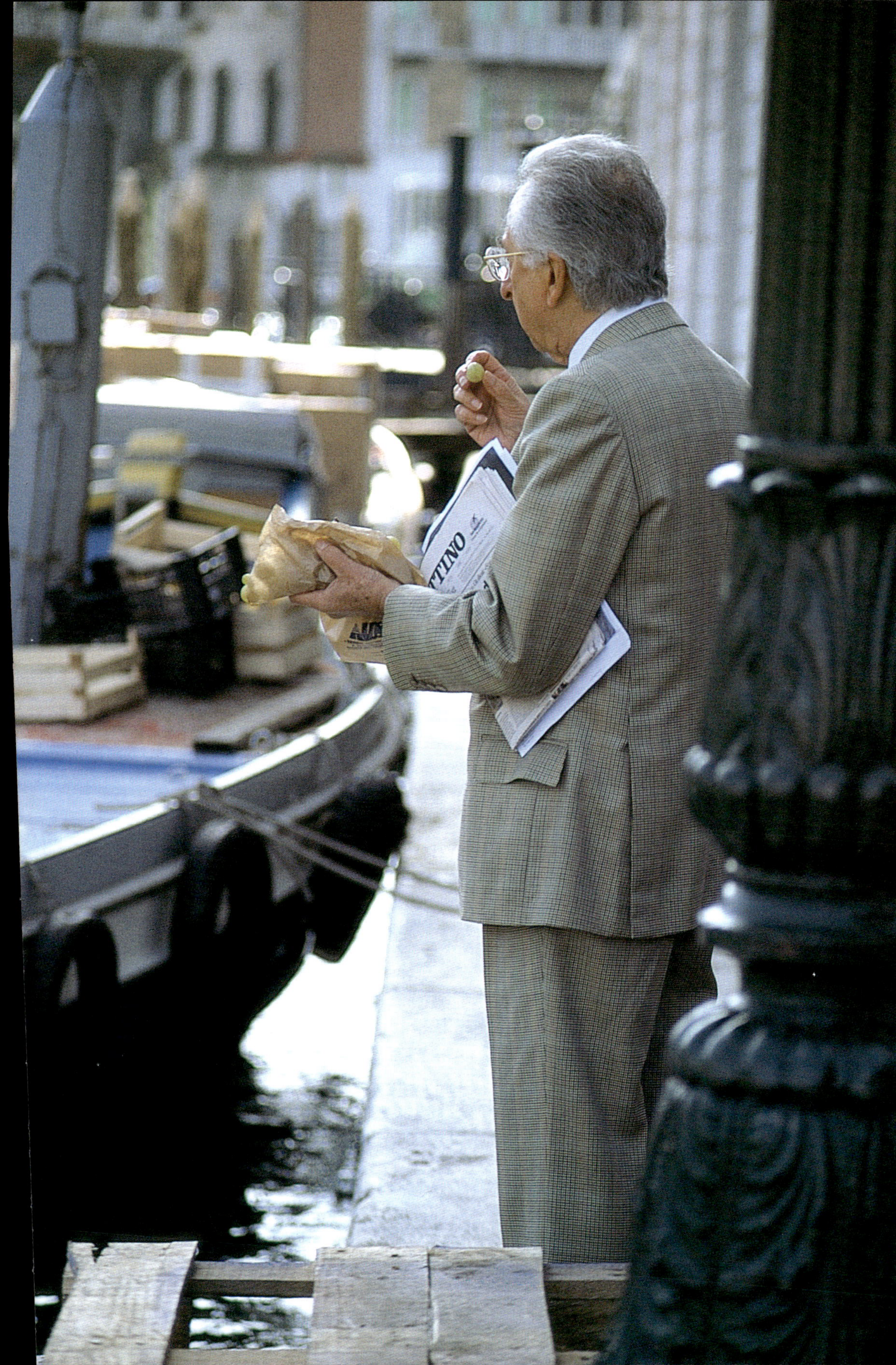
TTINO

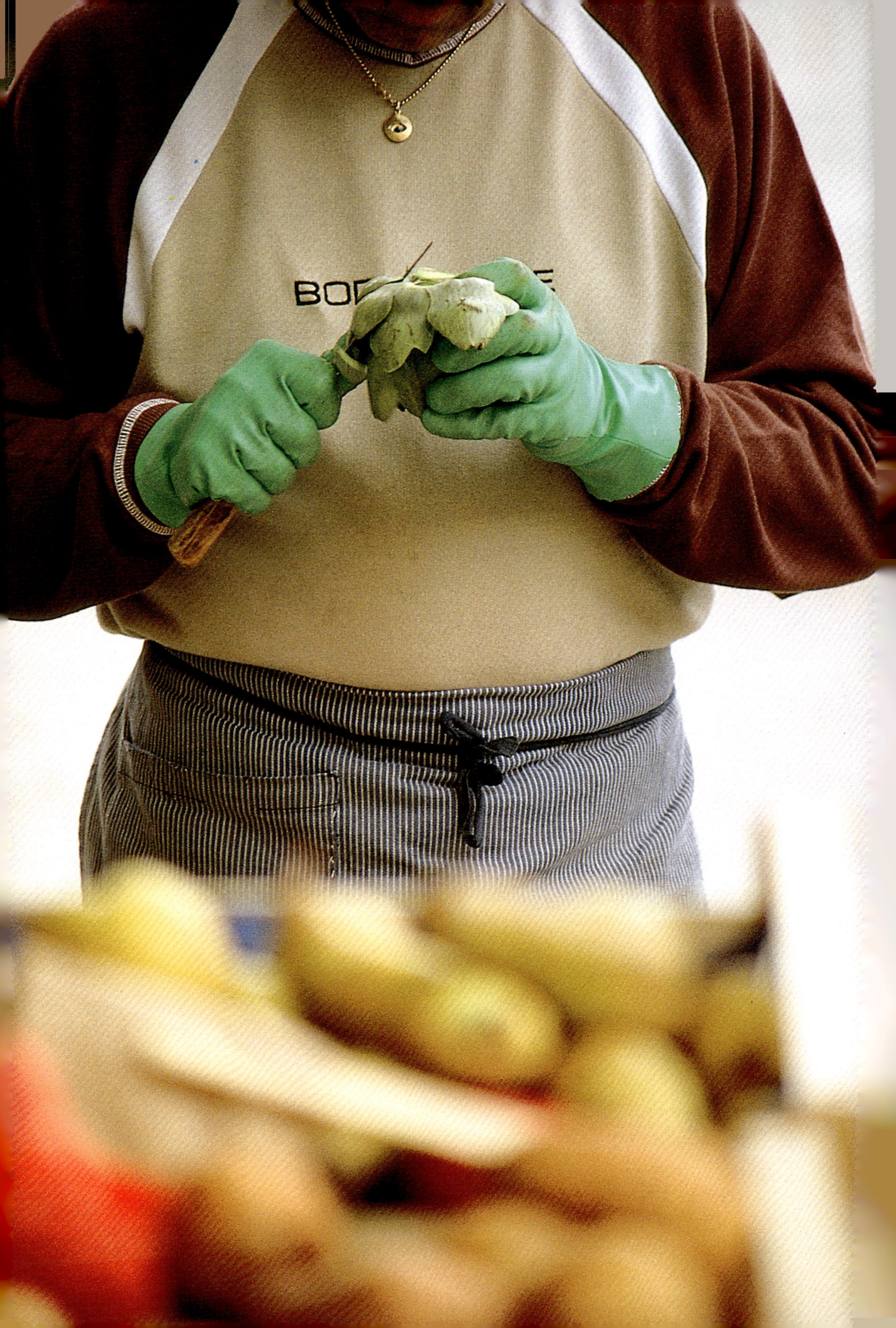

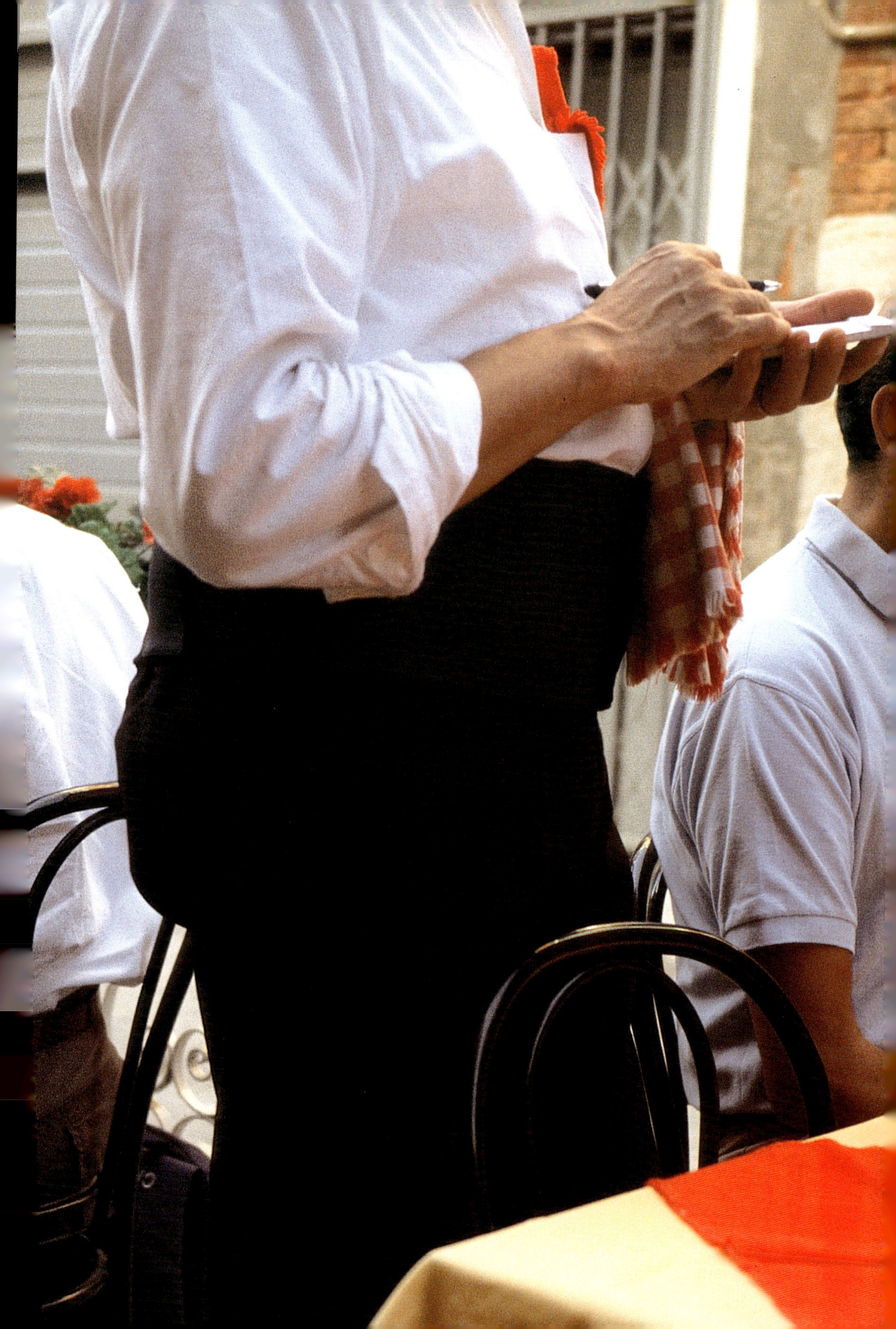

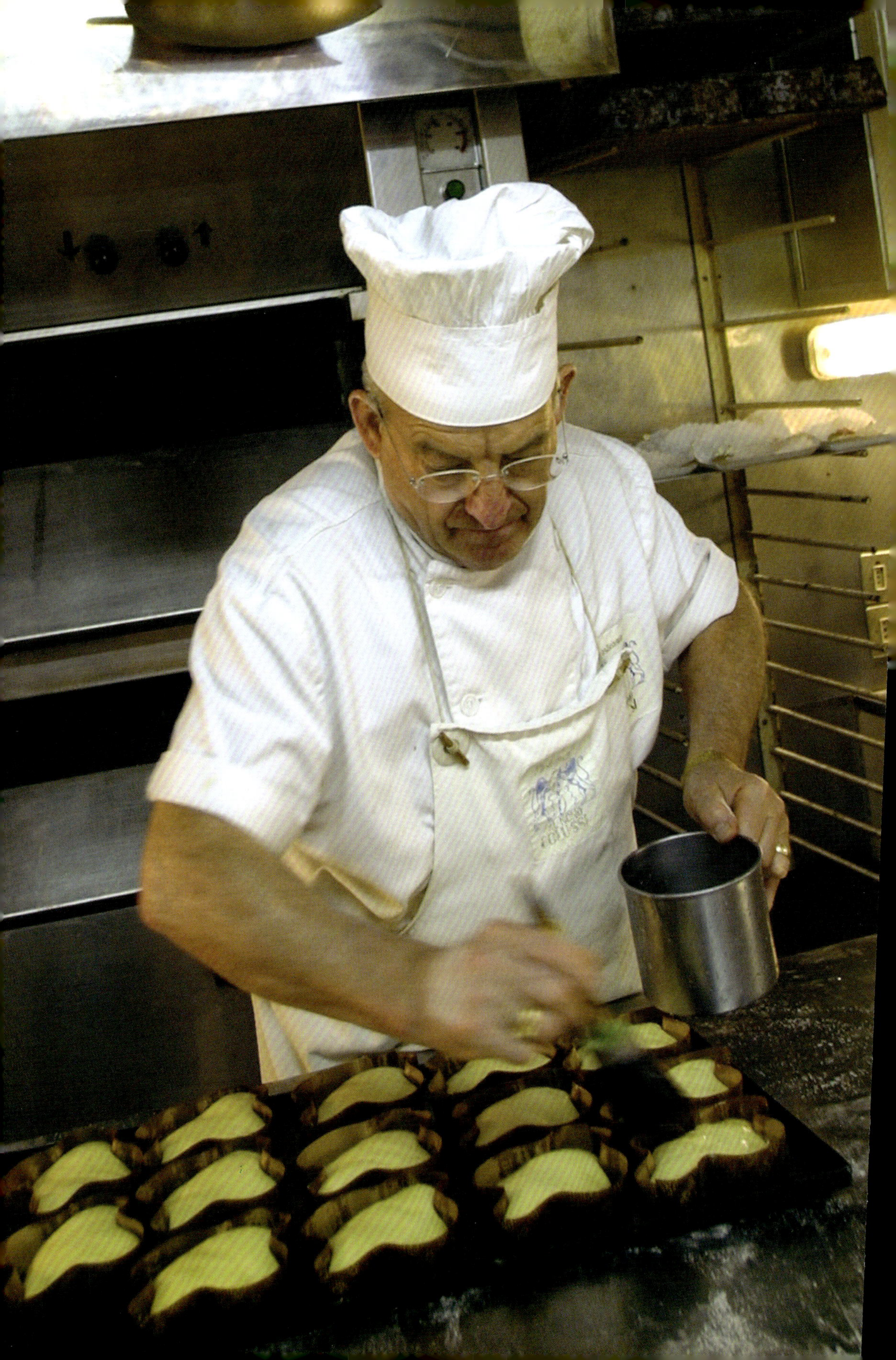

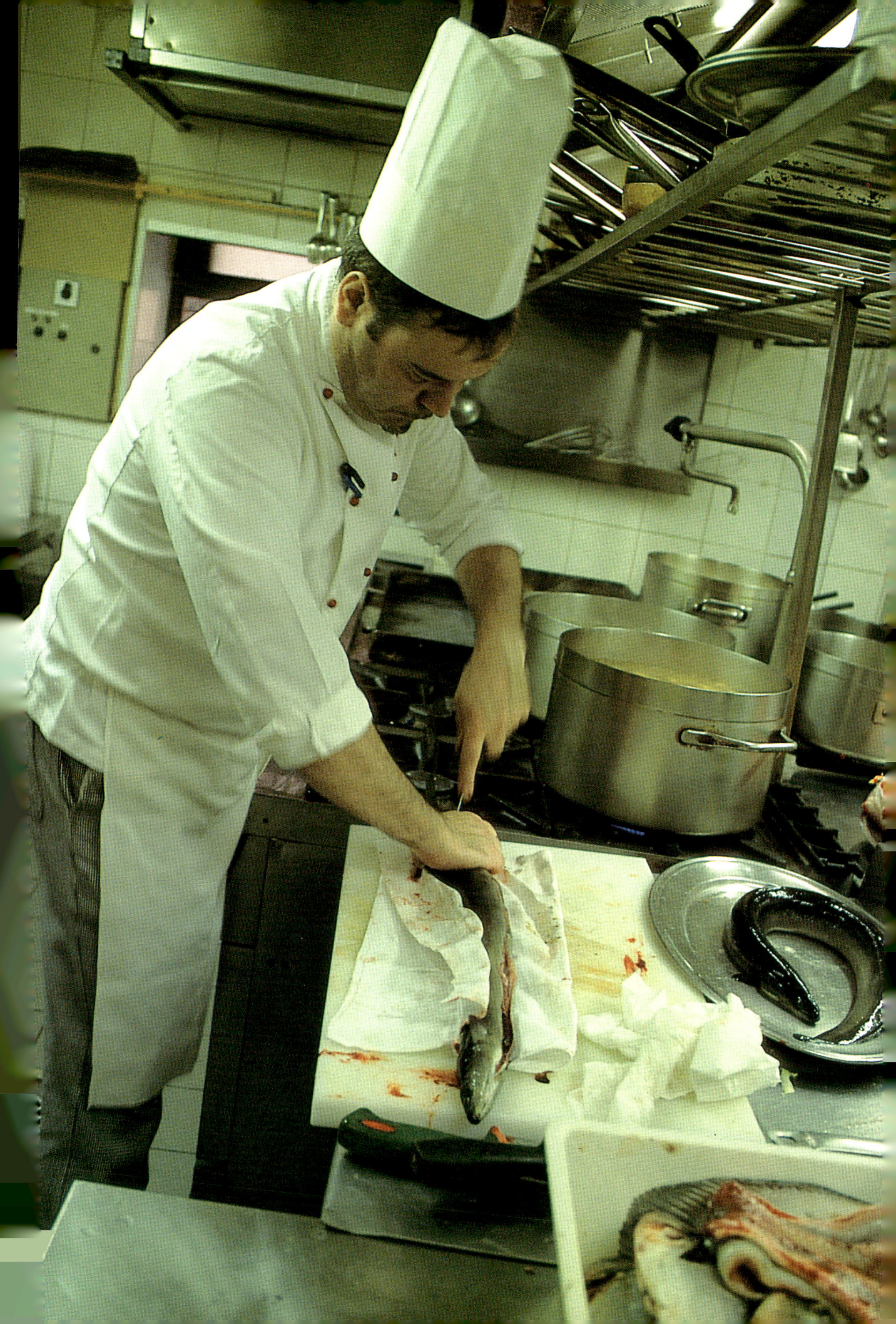

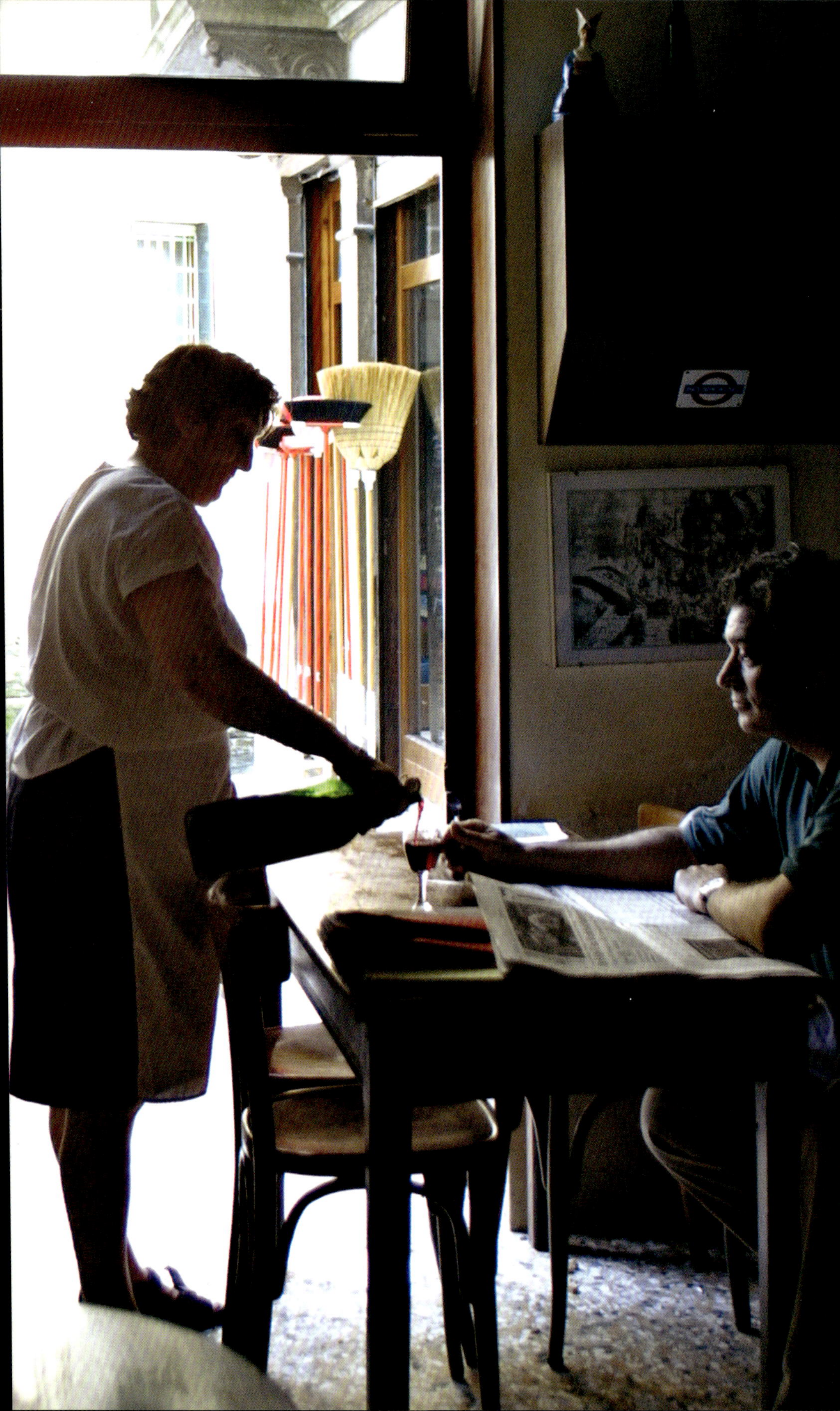

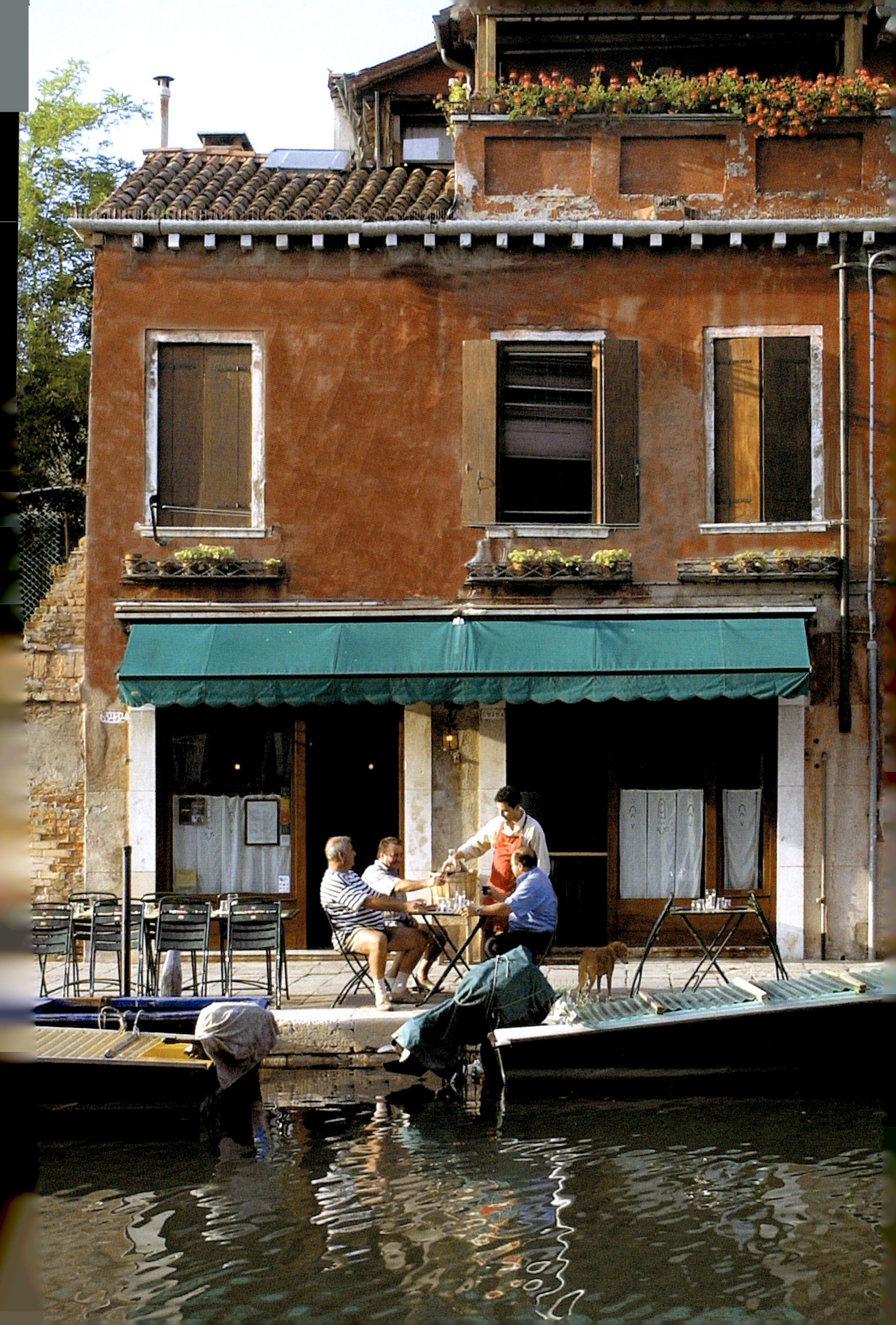

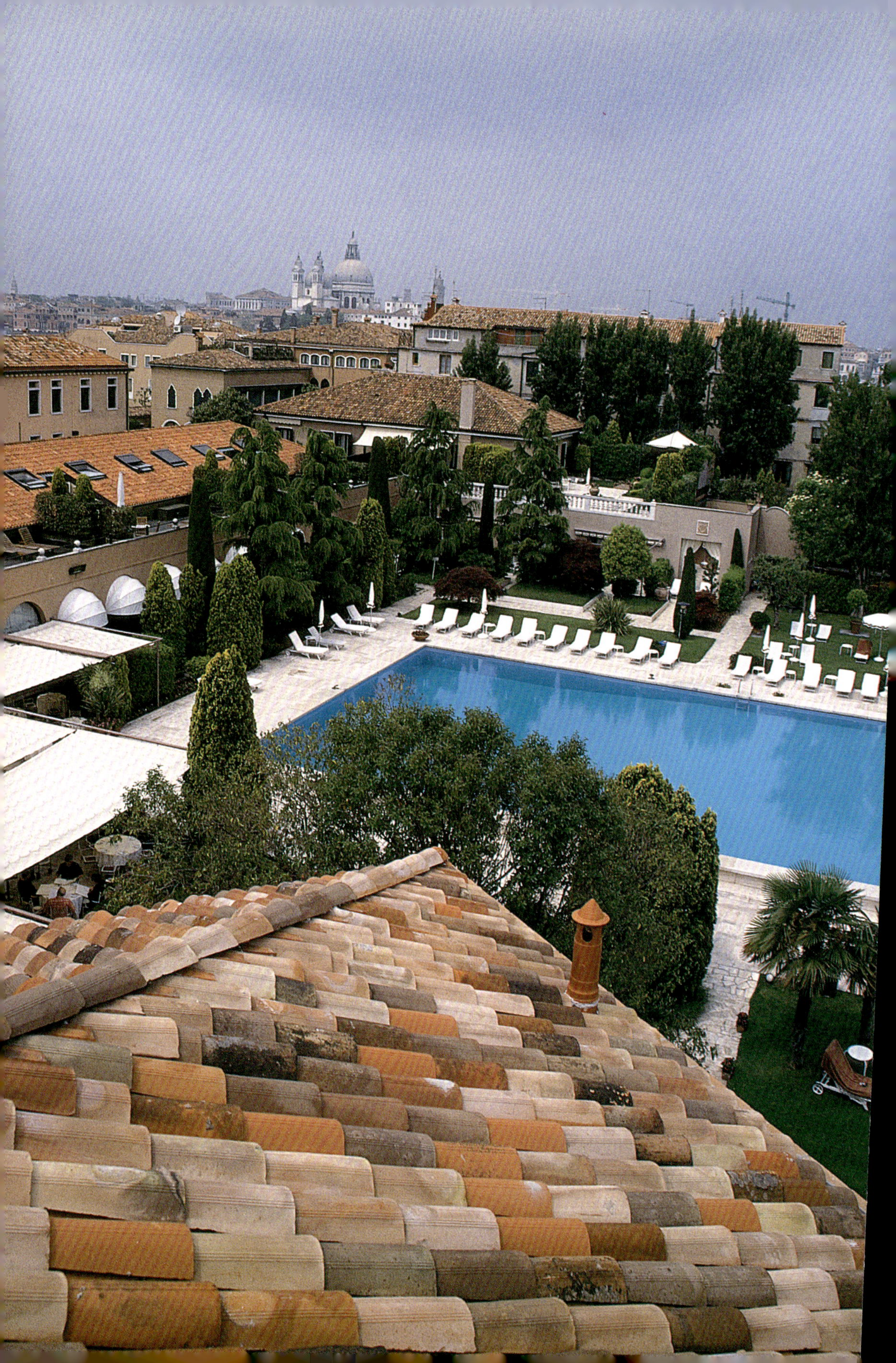

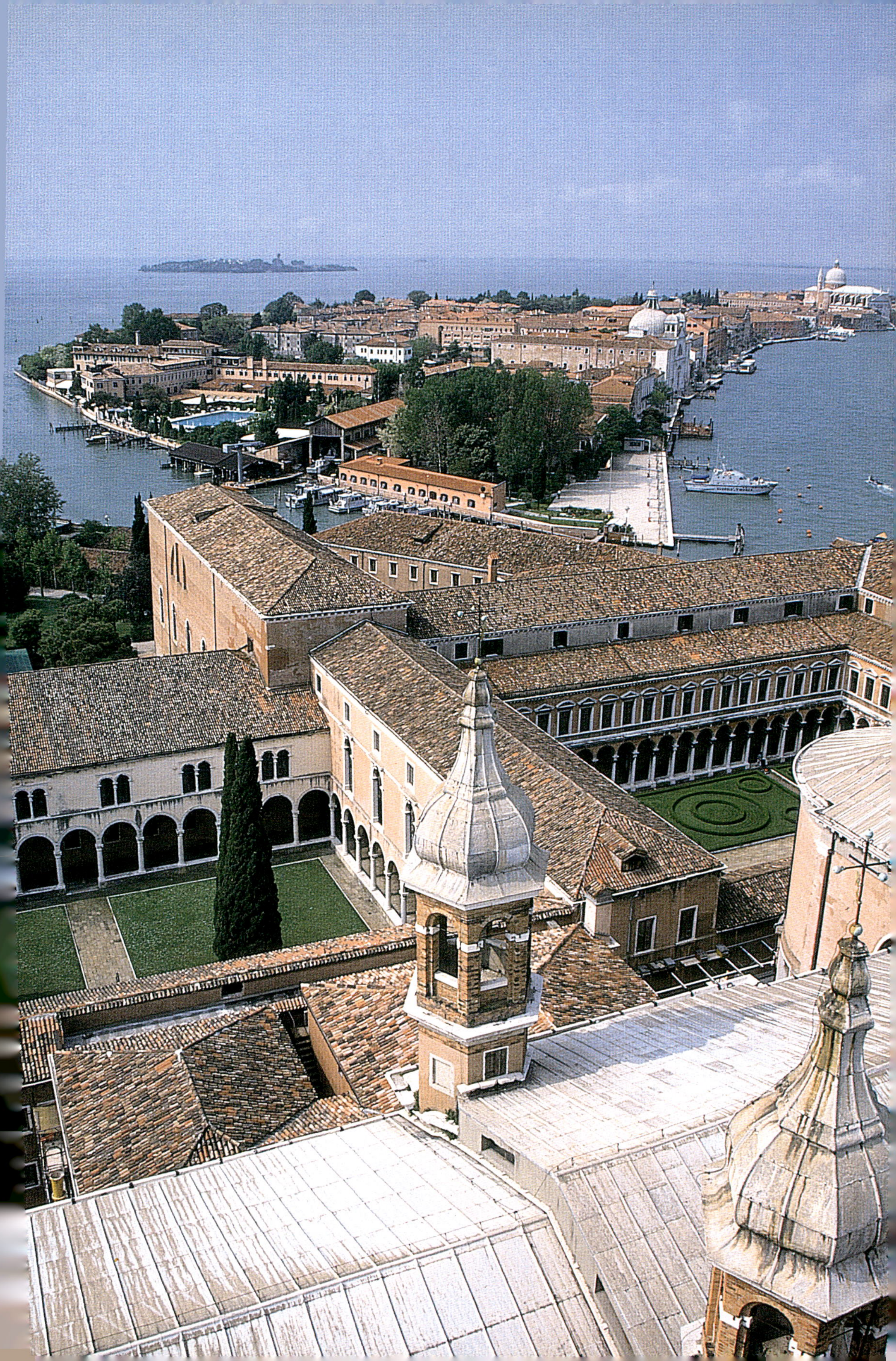

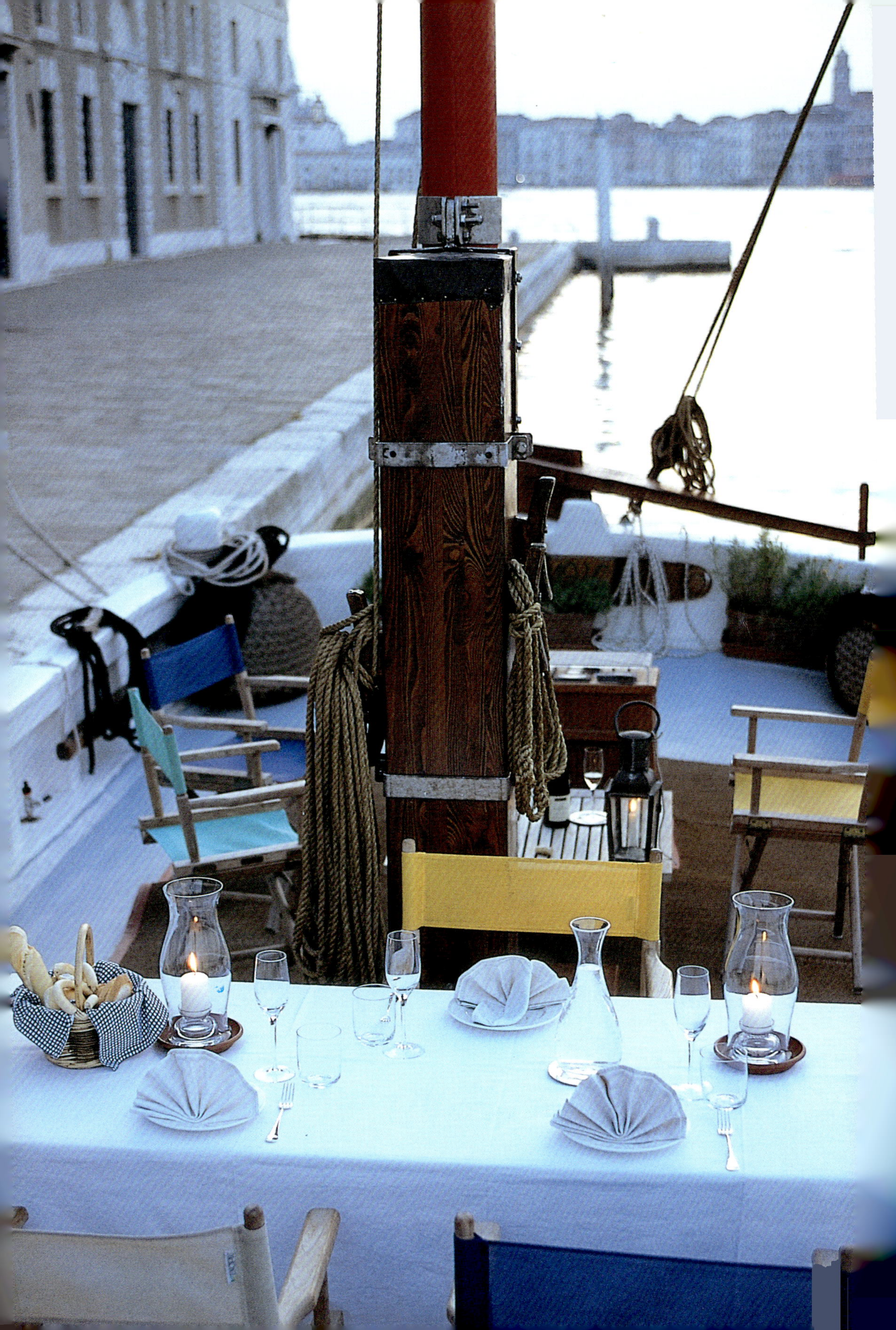

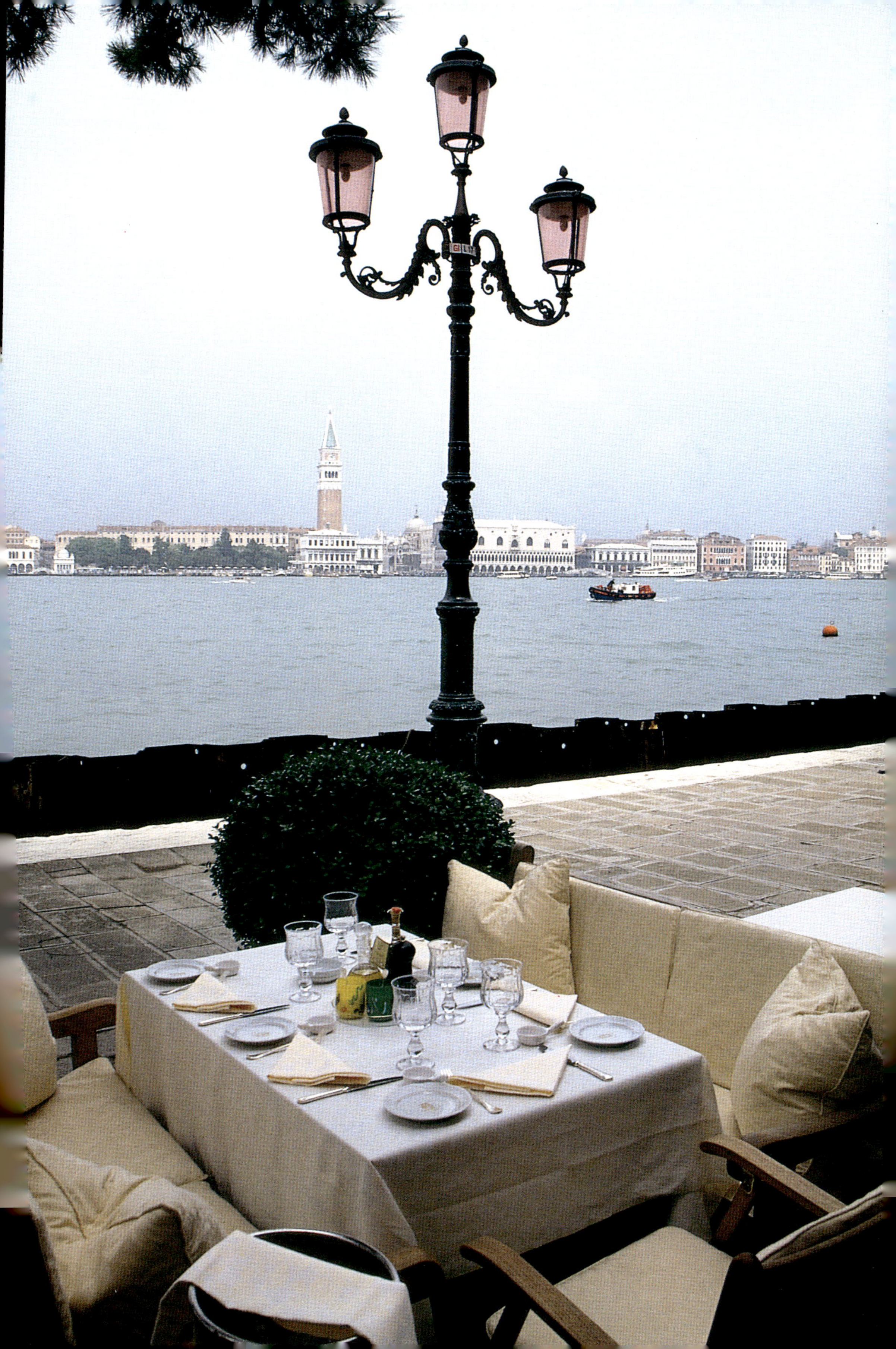

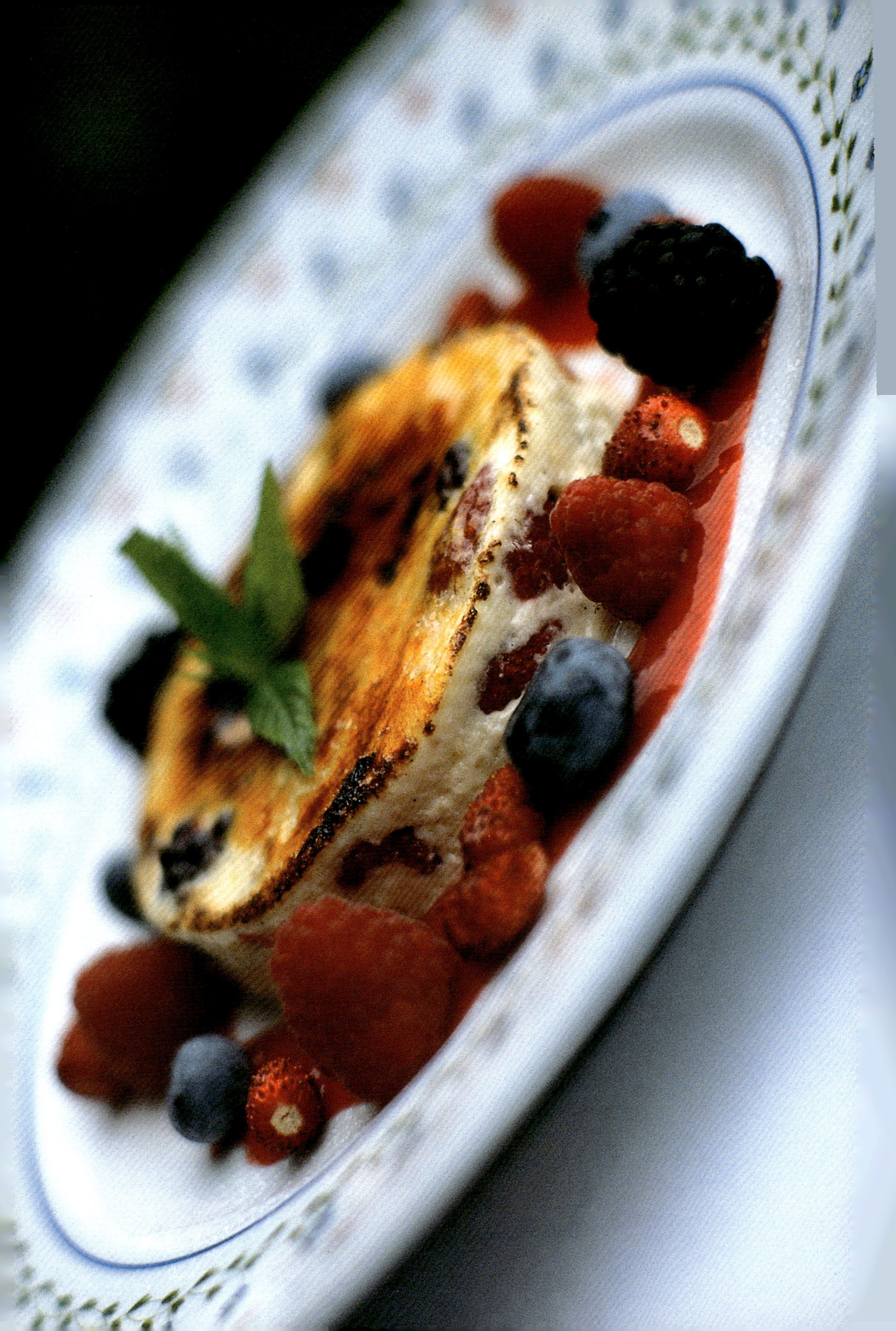

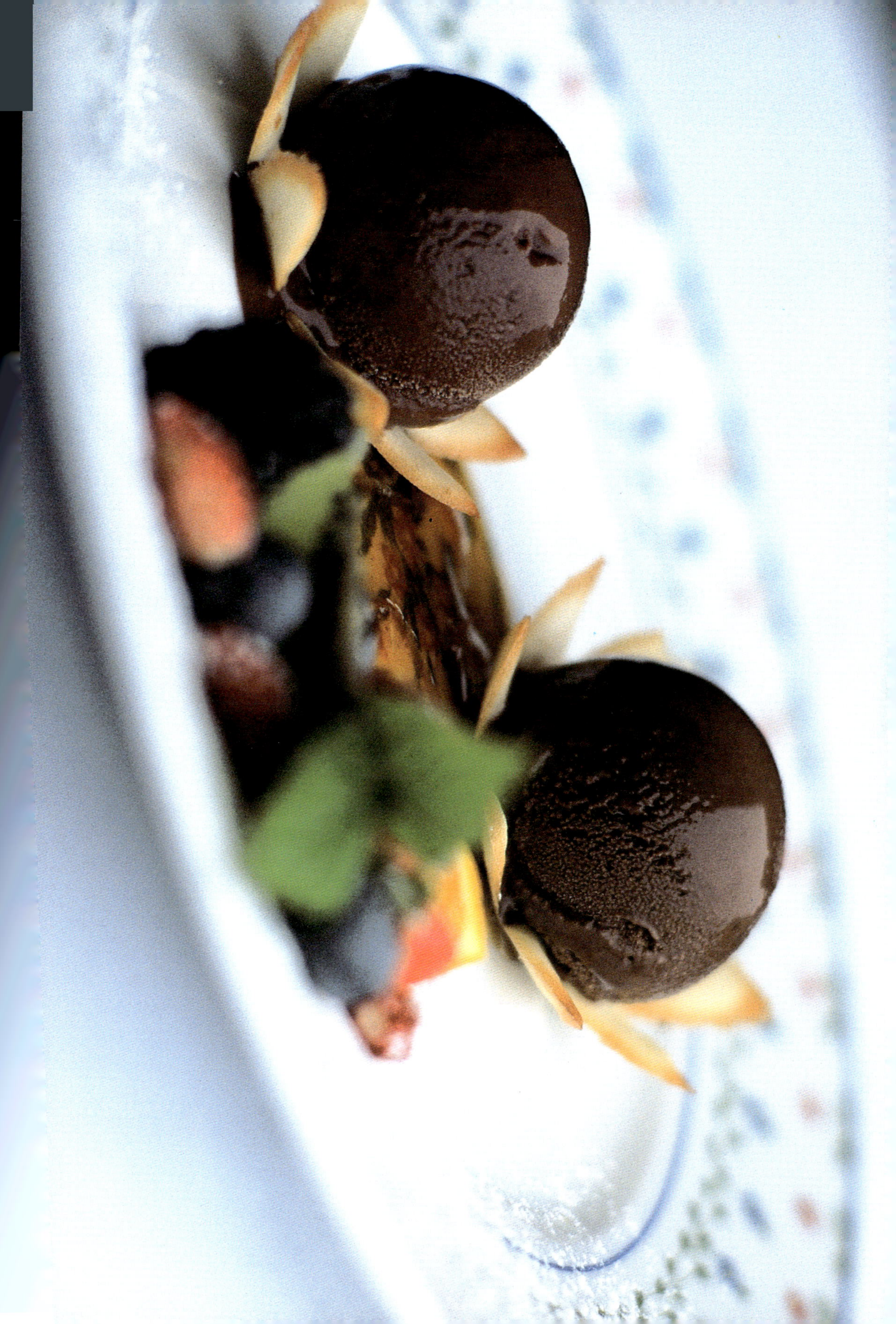

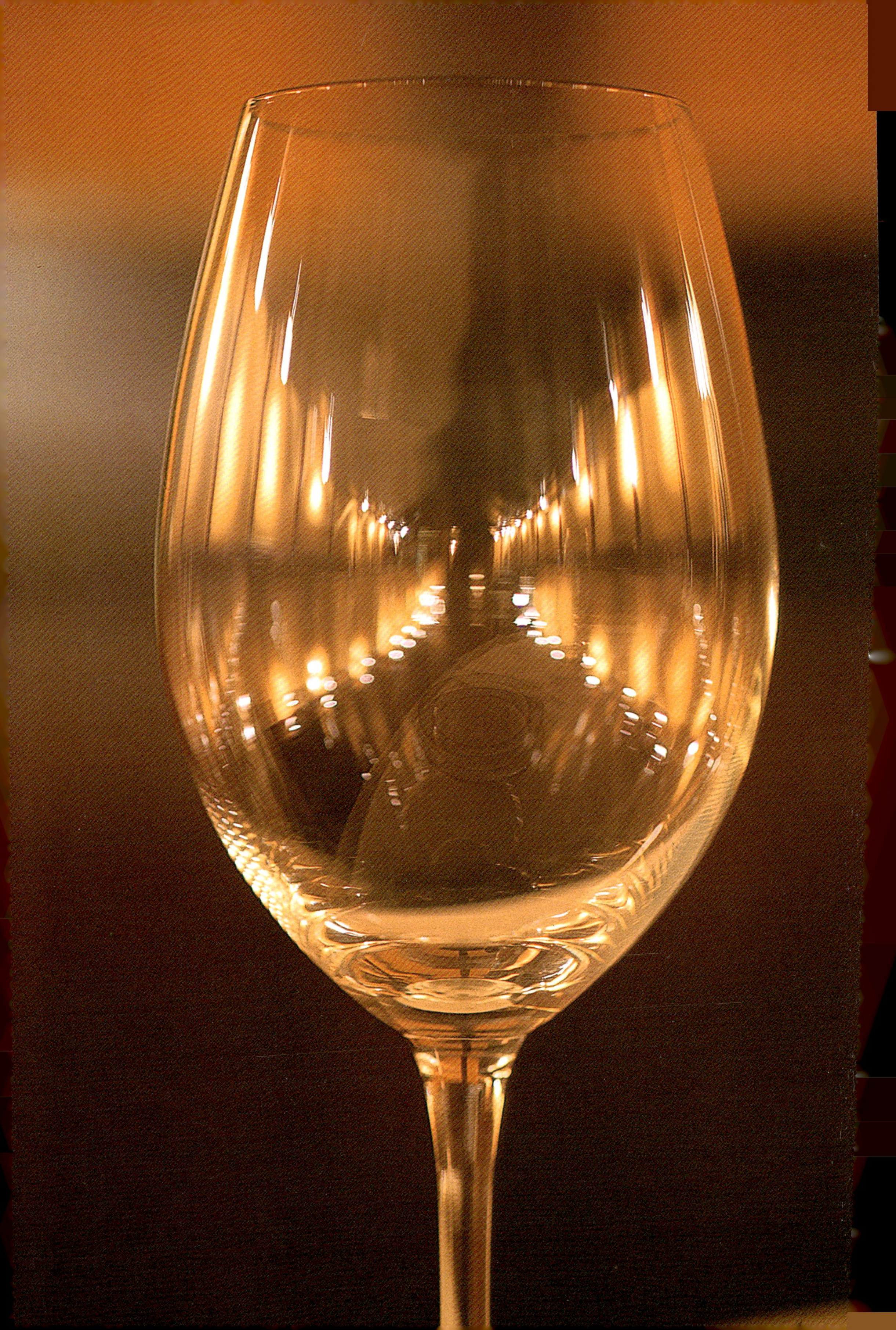

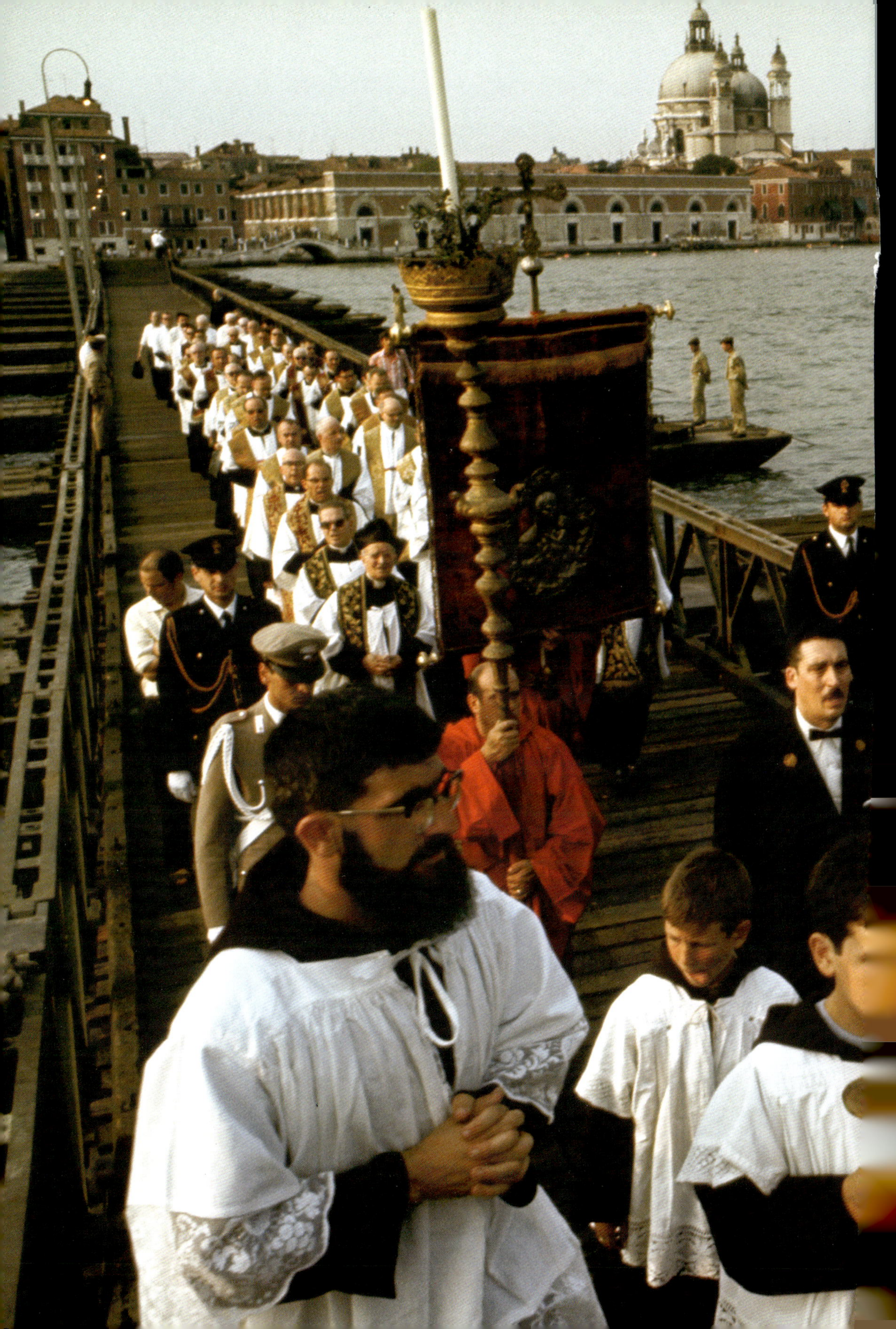

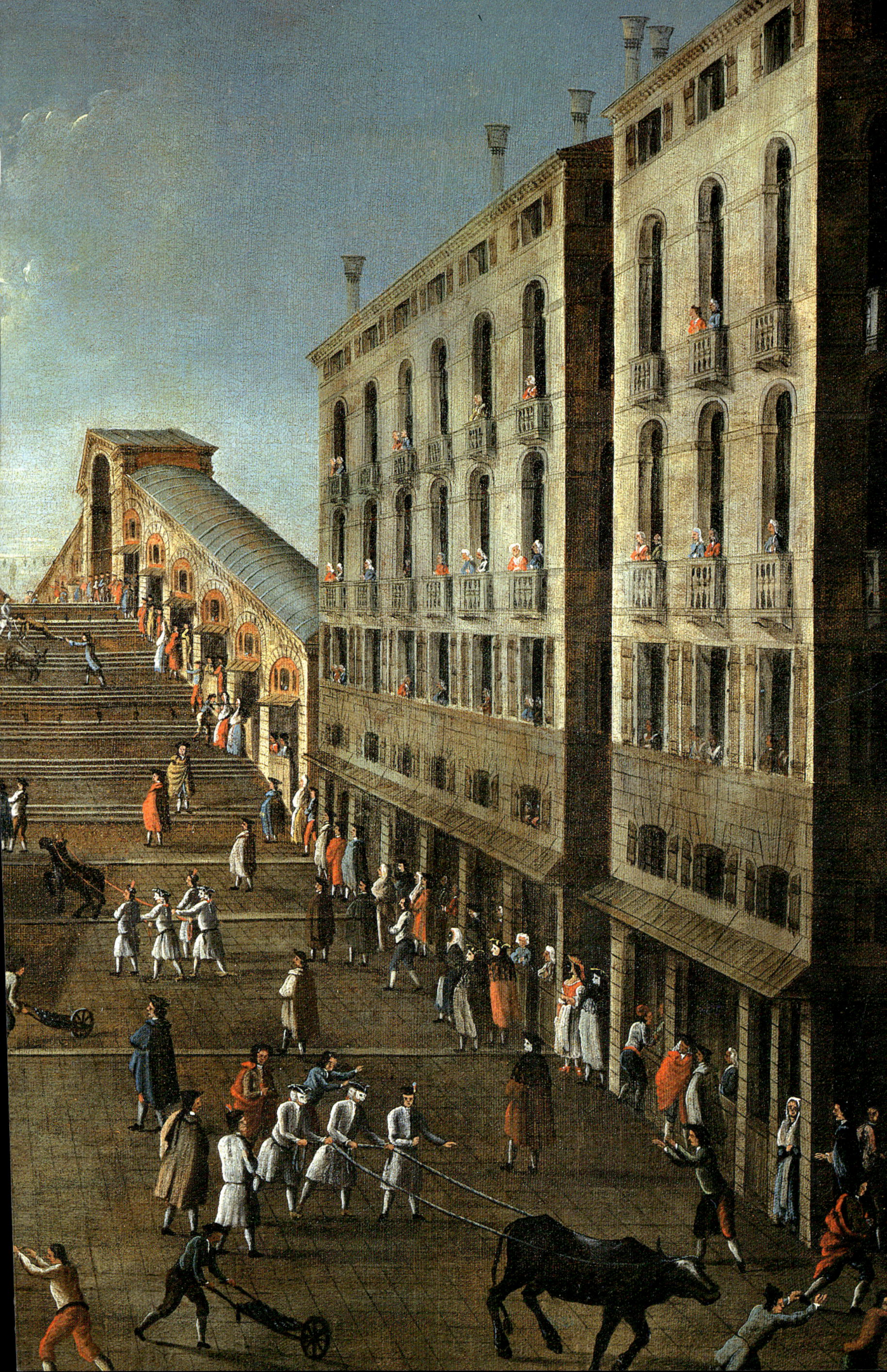

Corso De Tori sopra il
Ponte De Rialto Co La Ca[...]
De Chariolo E' Charn[e]vali

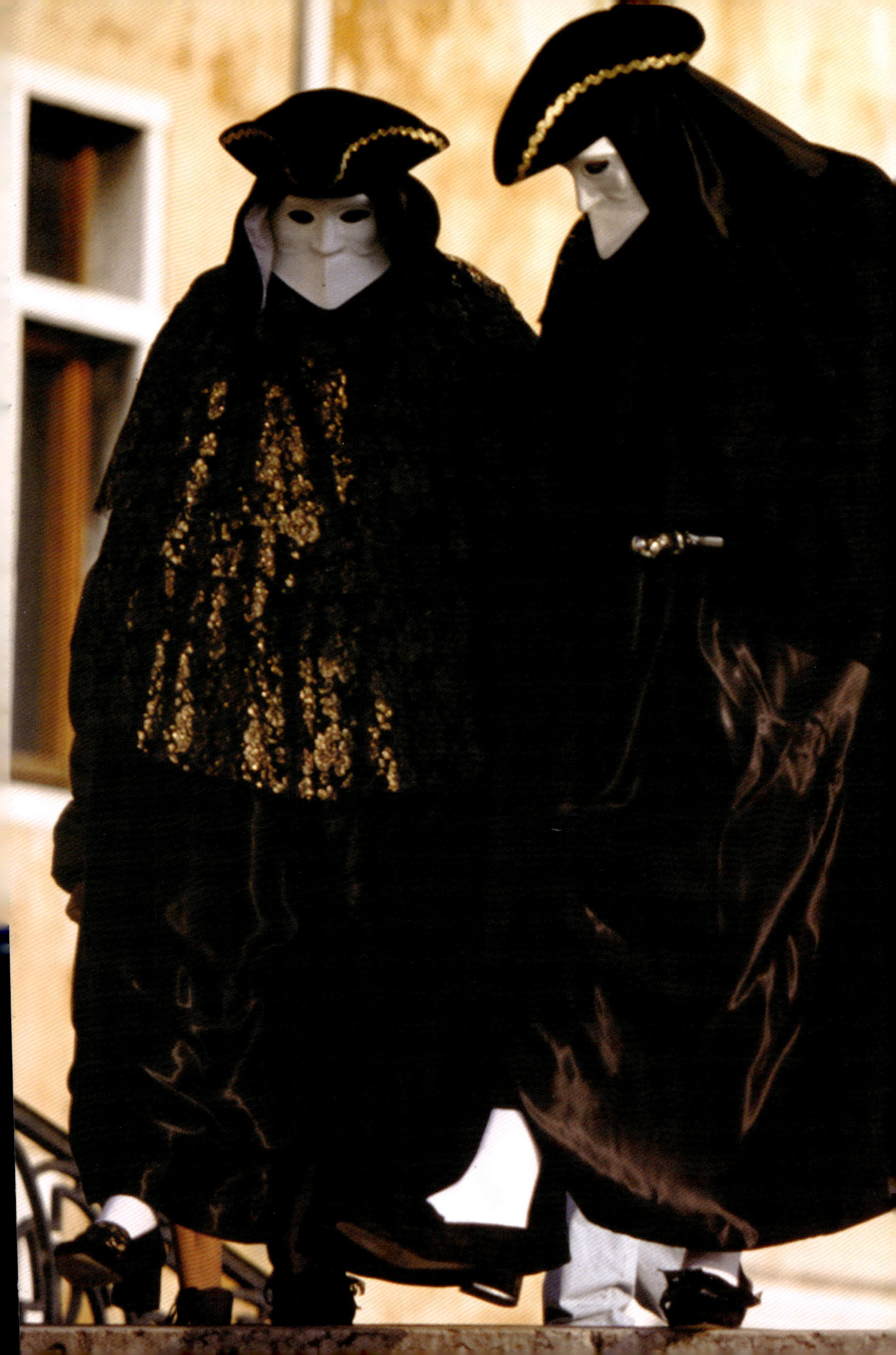

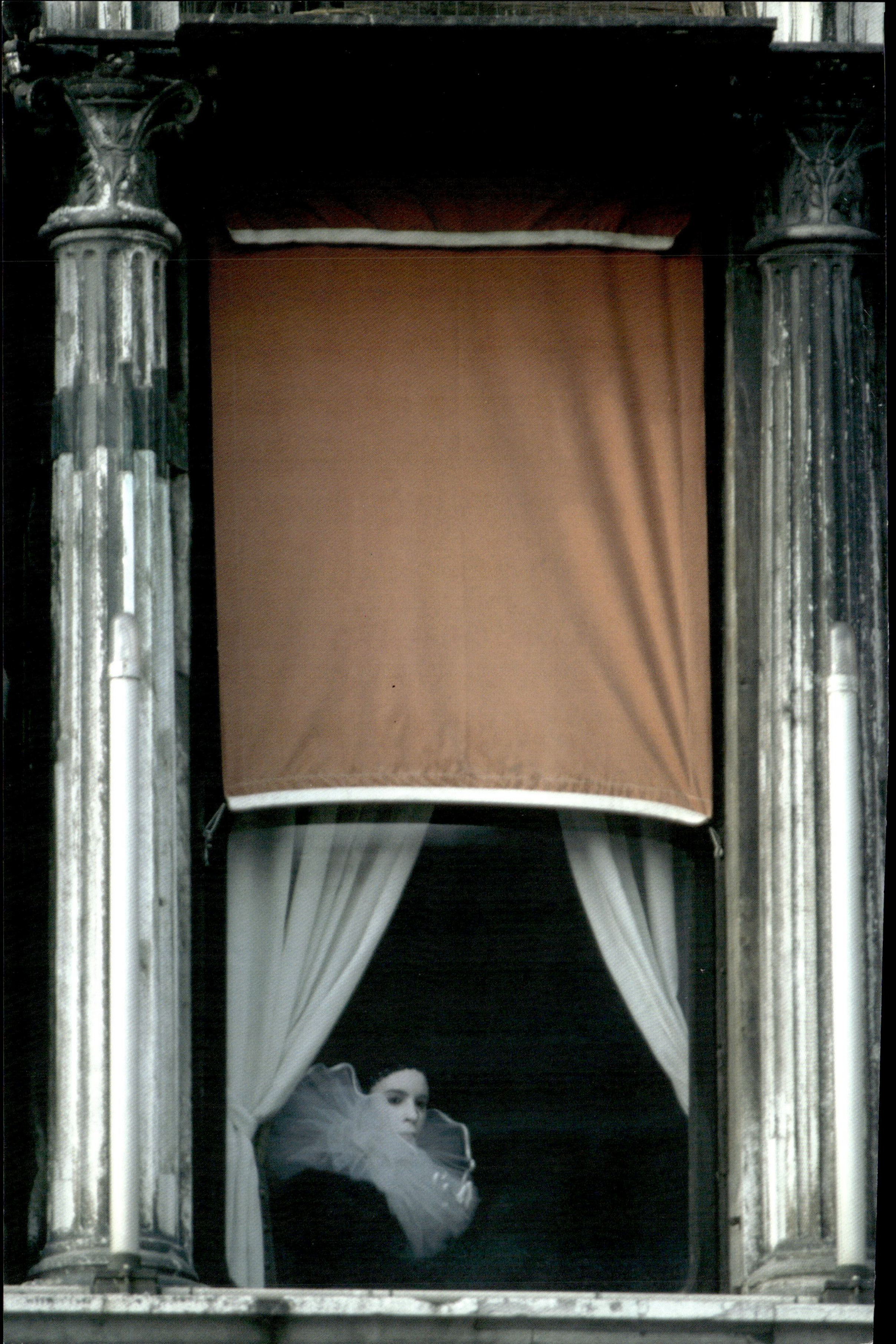

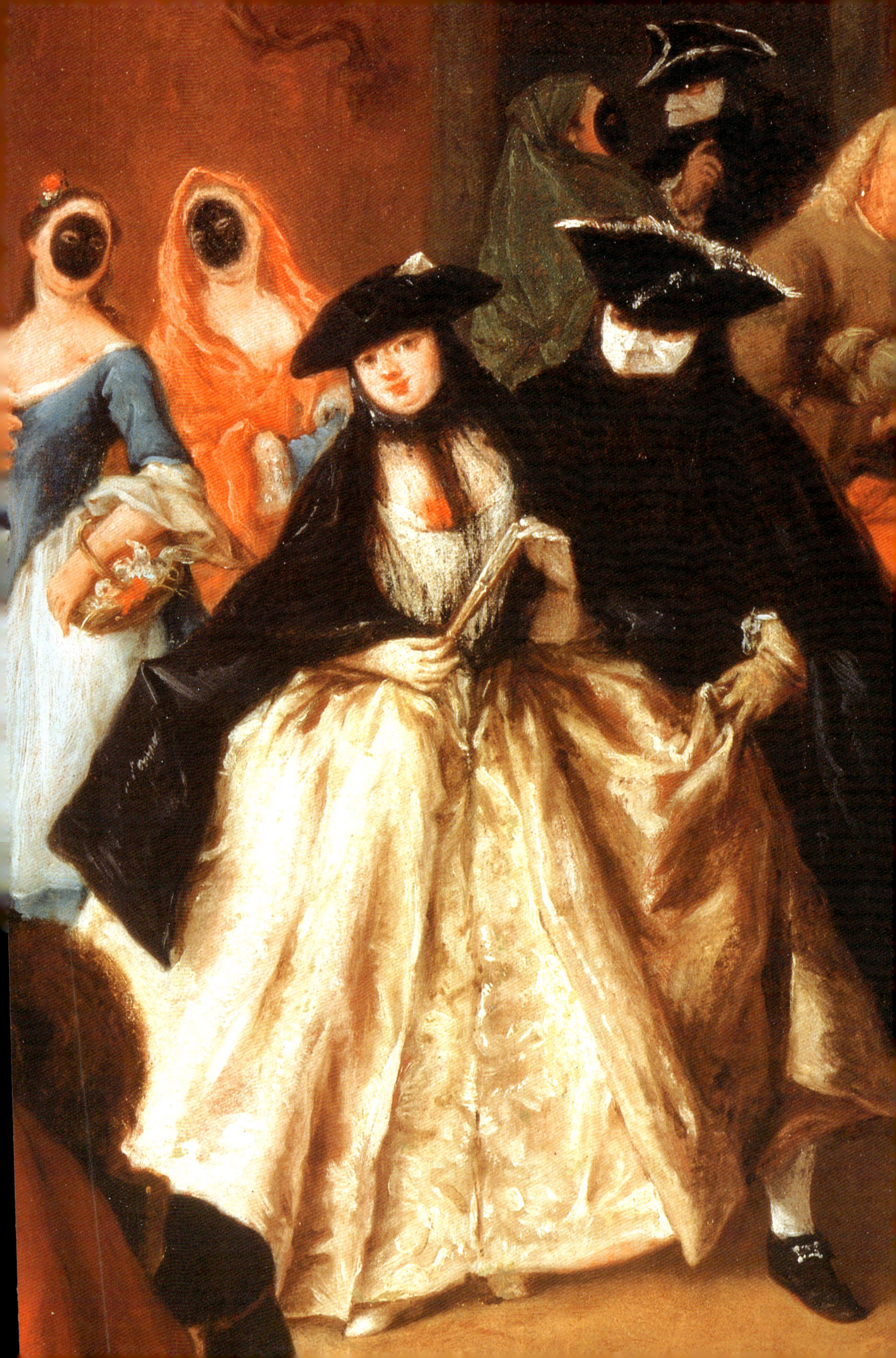

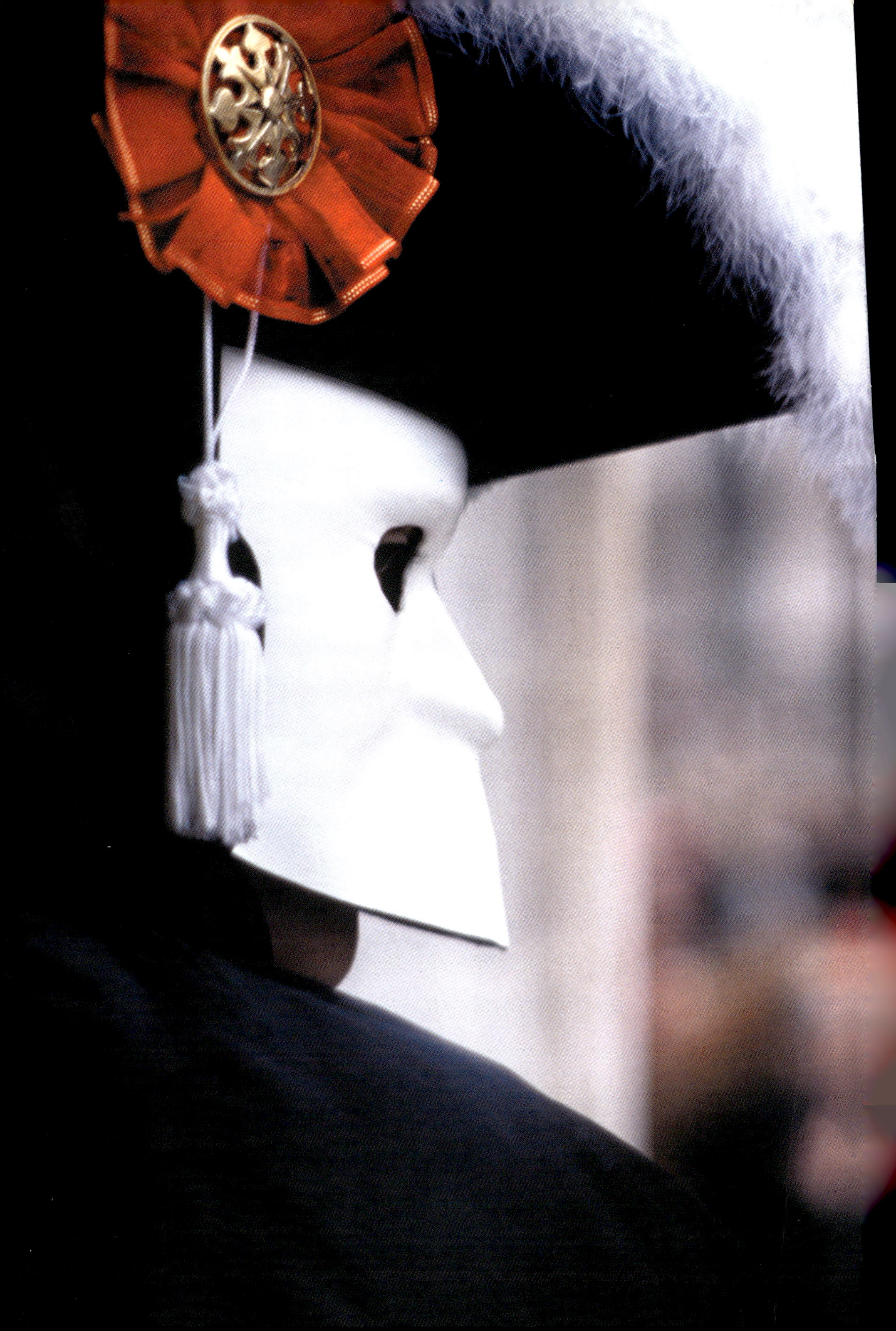

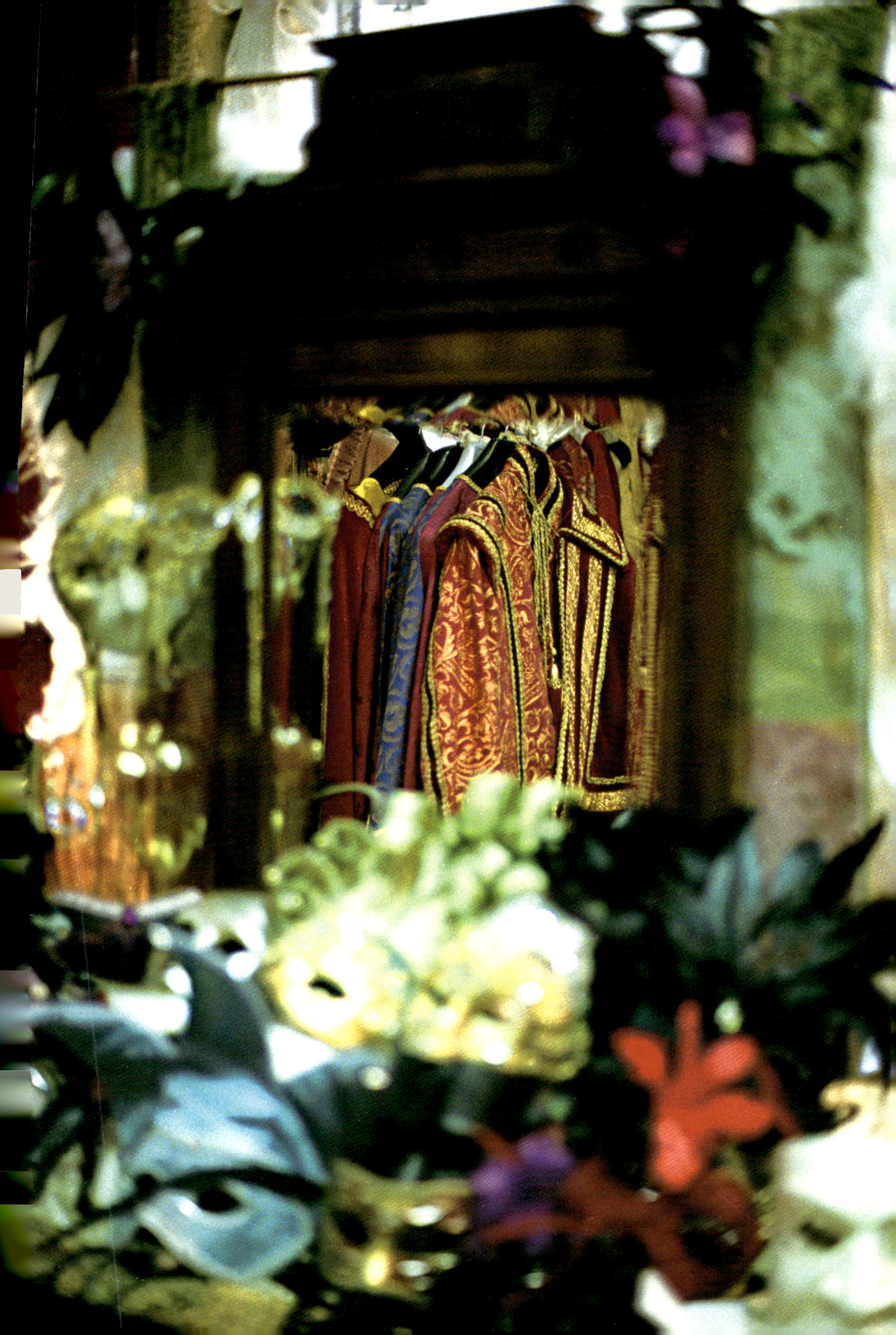

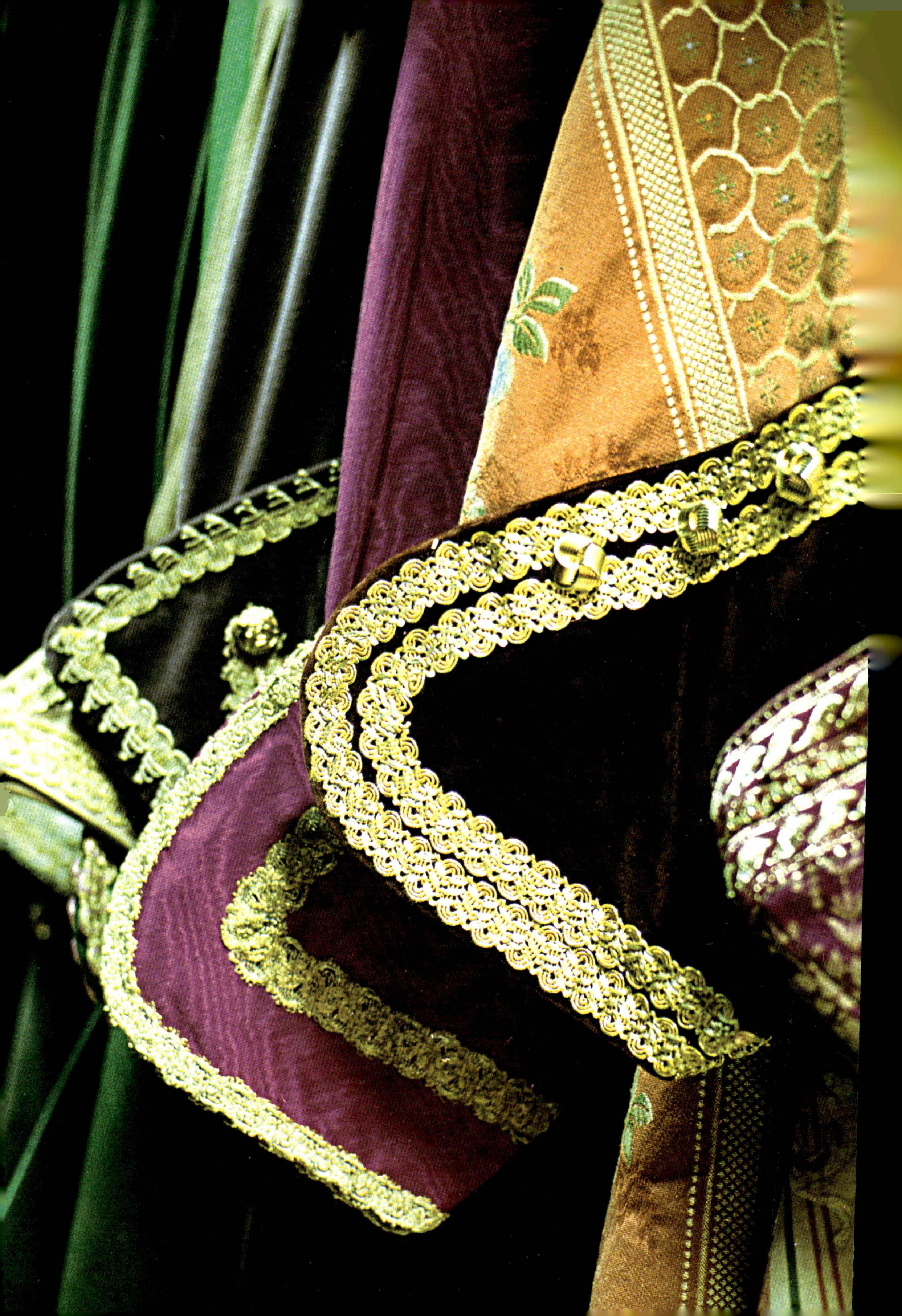

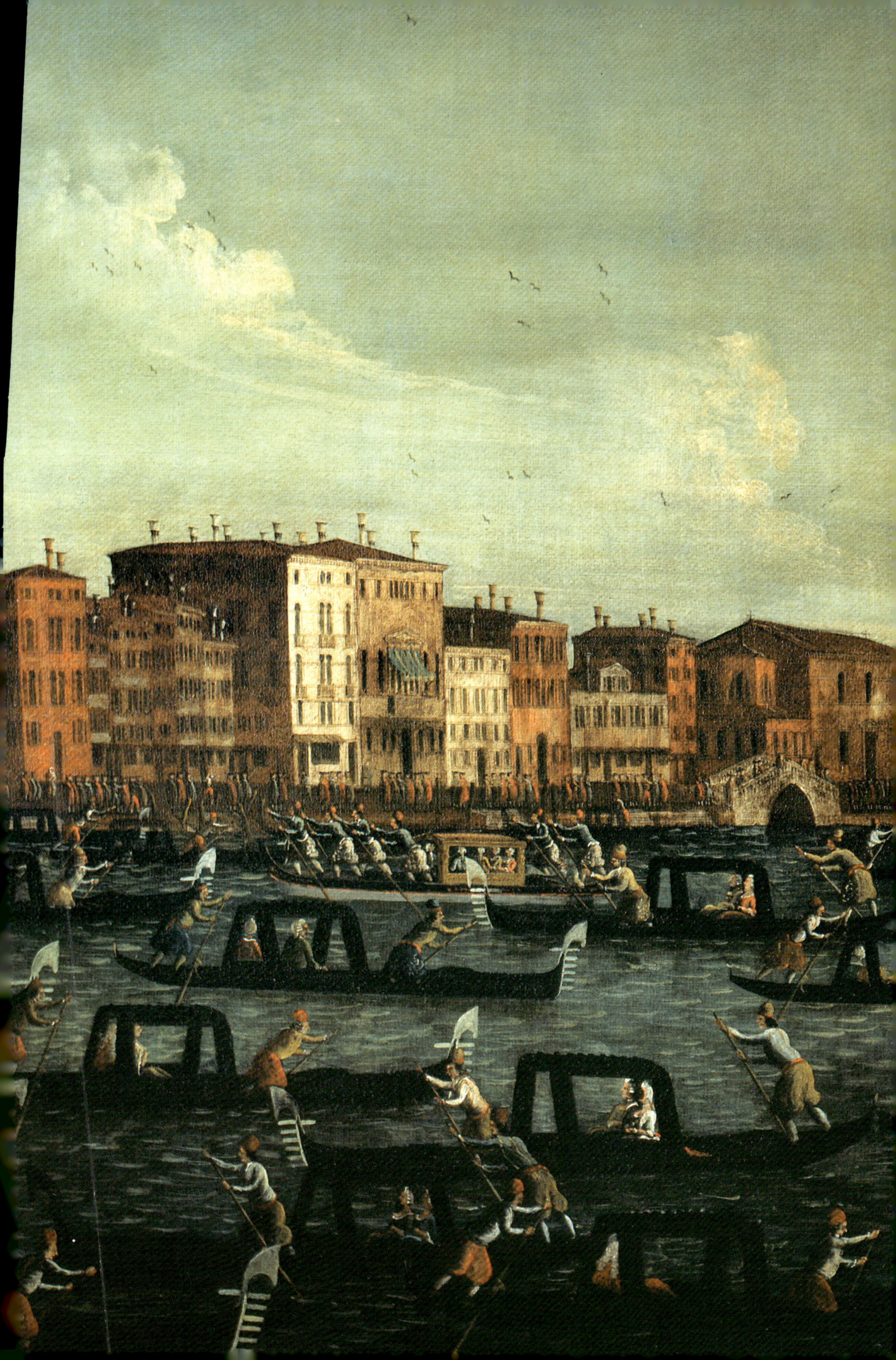

so Nobile Da S:
e Sino Alla Croce

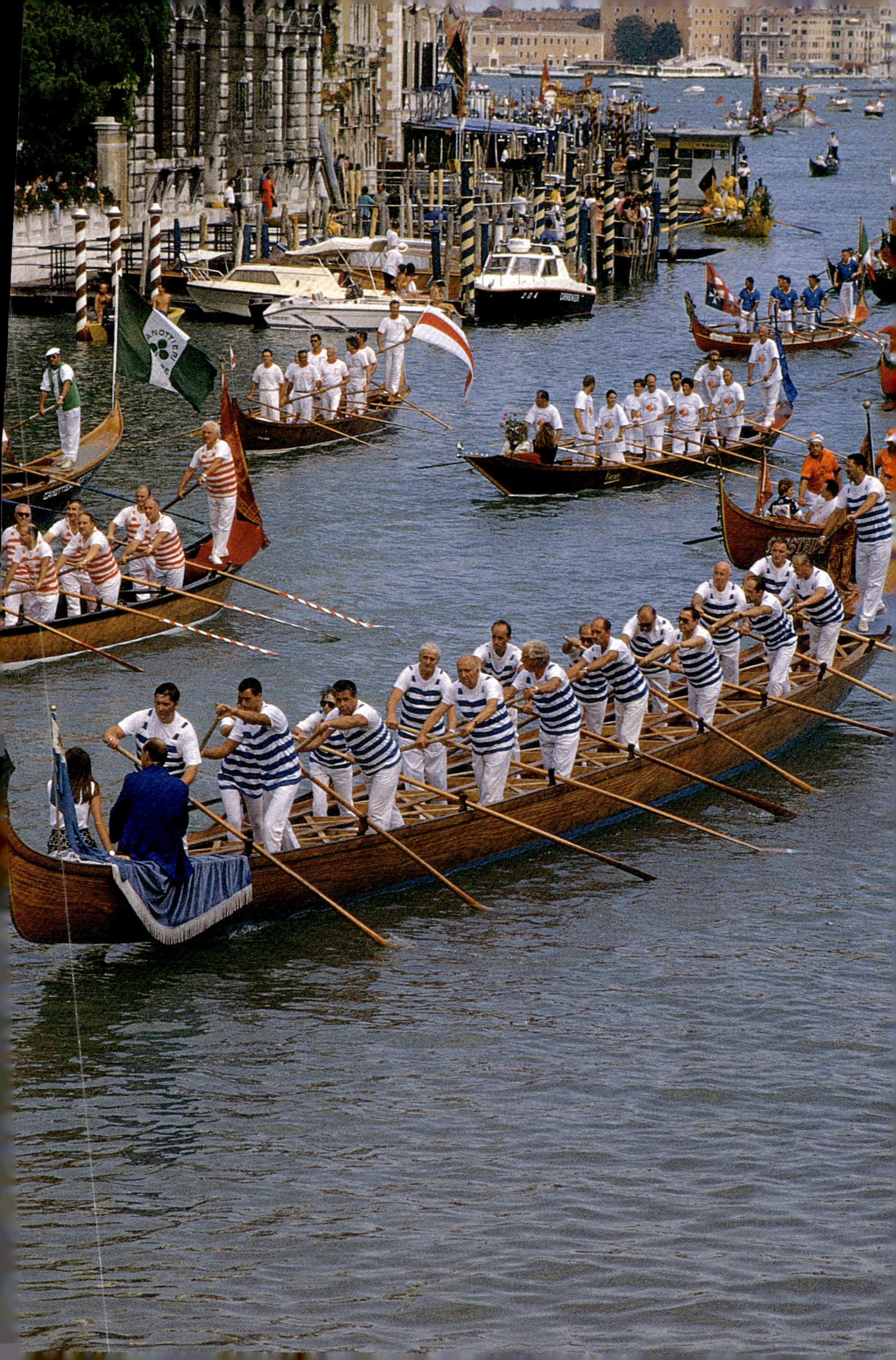

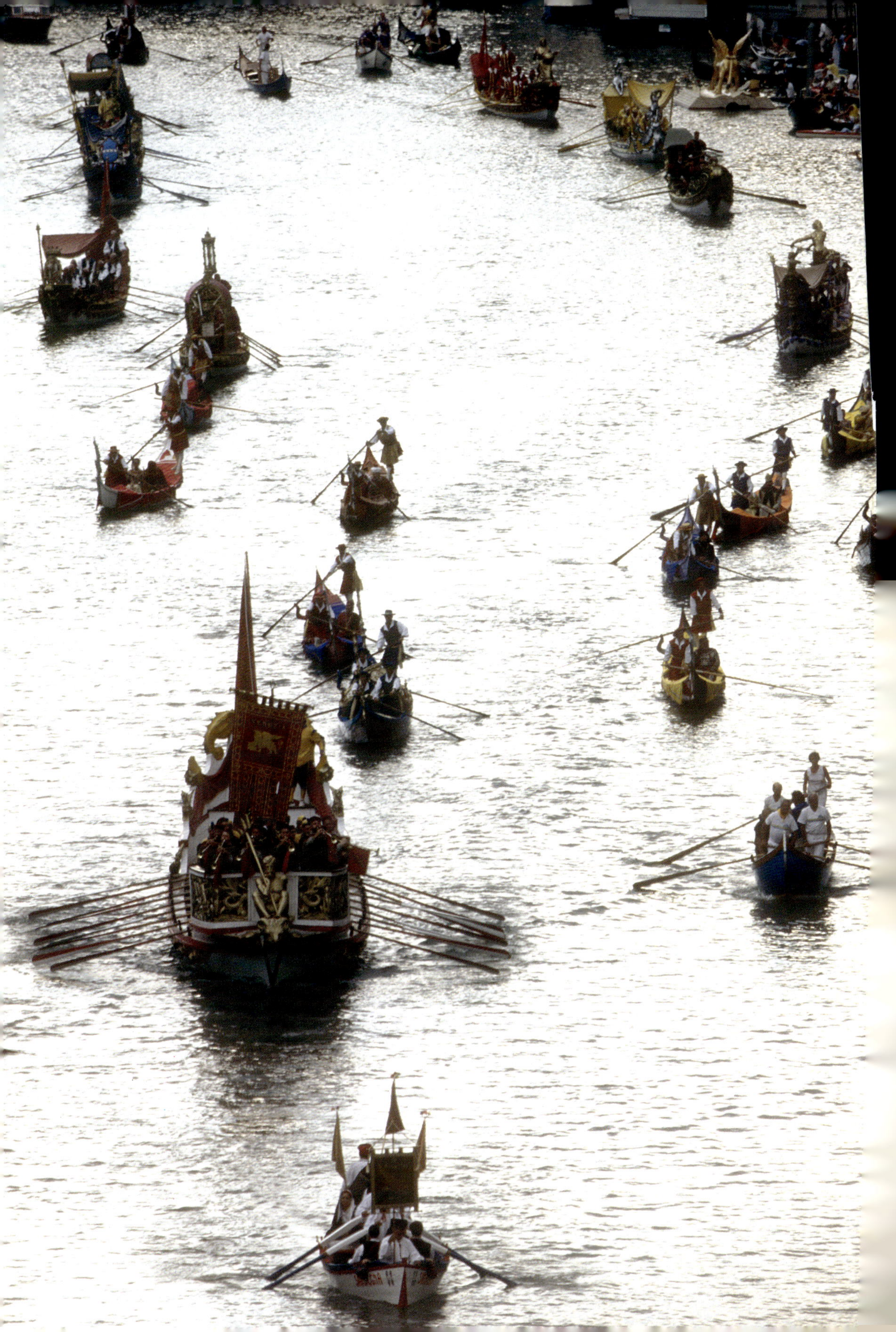

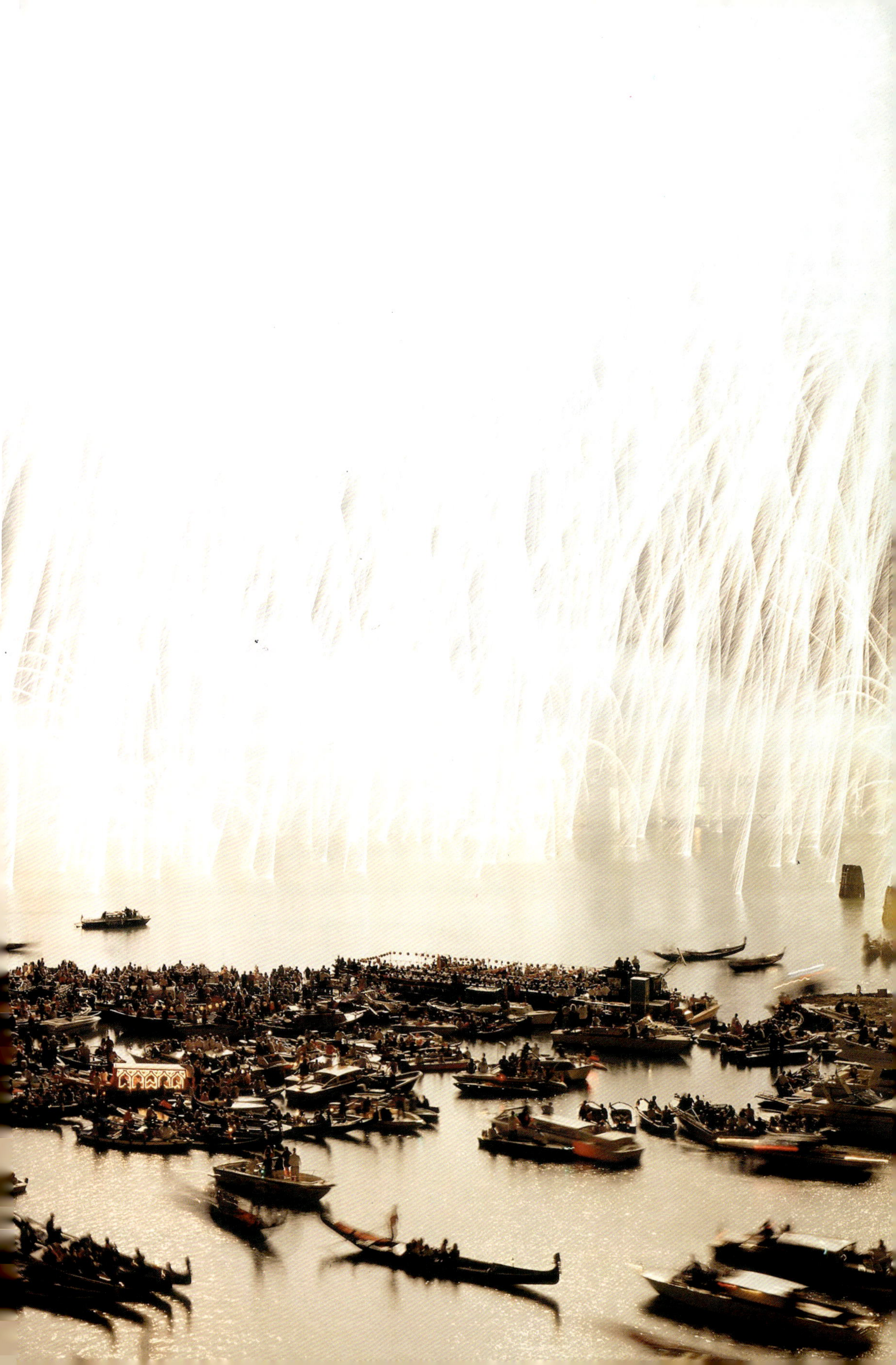

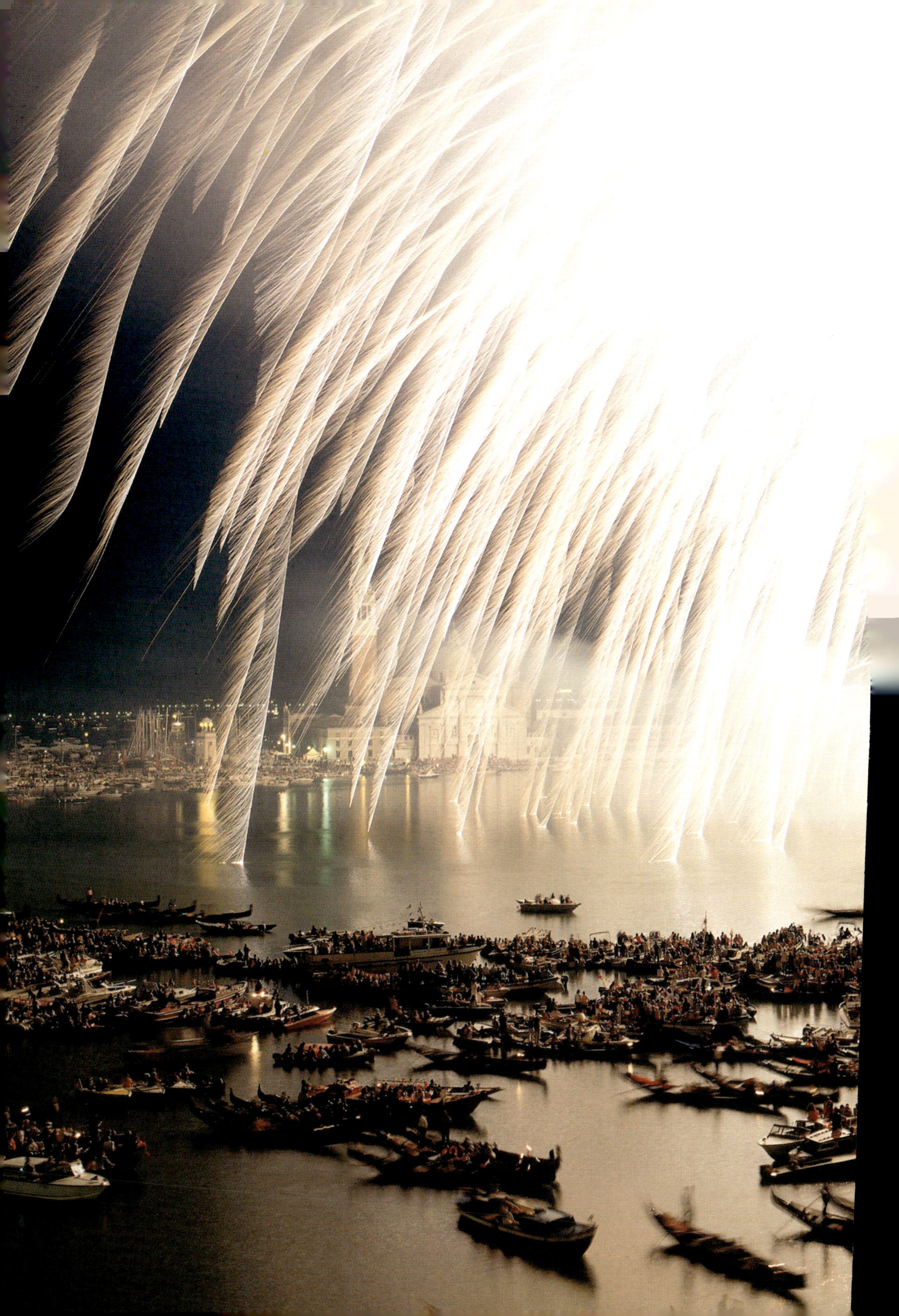

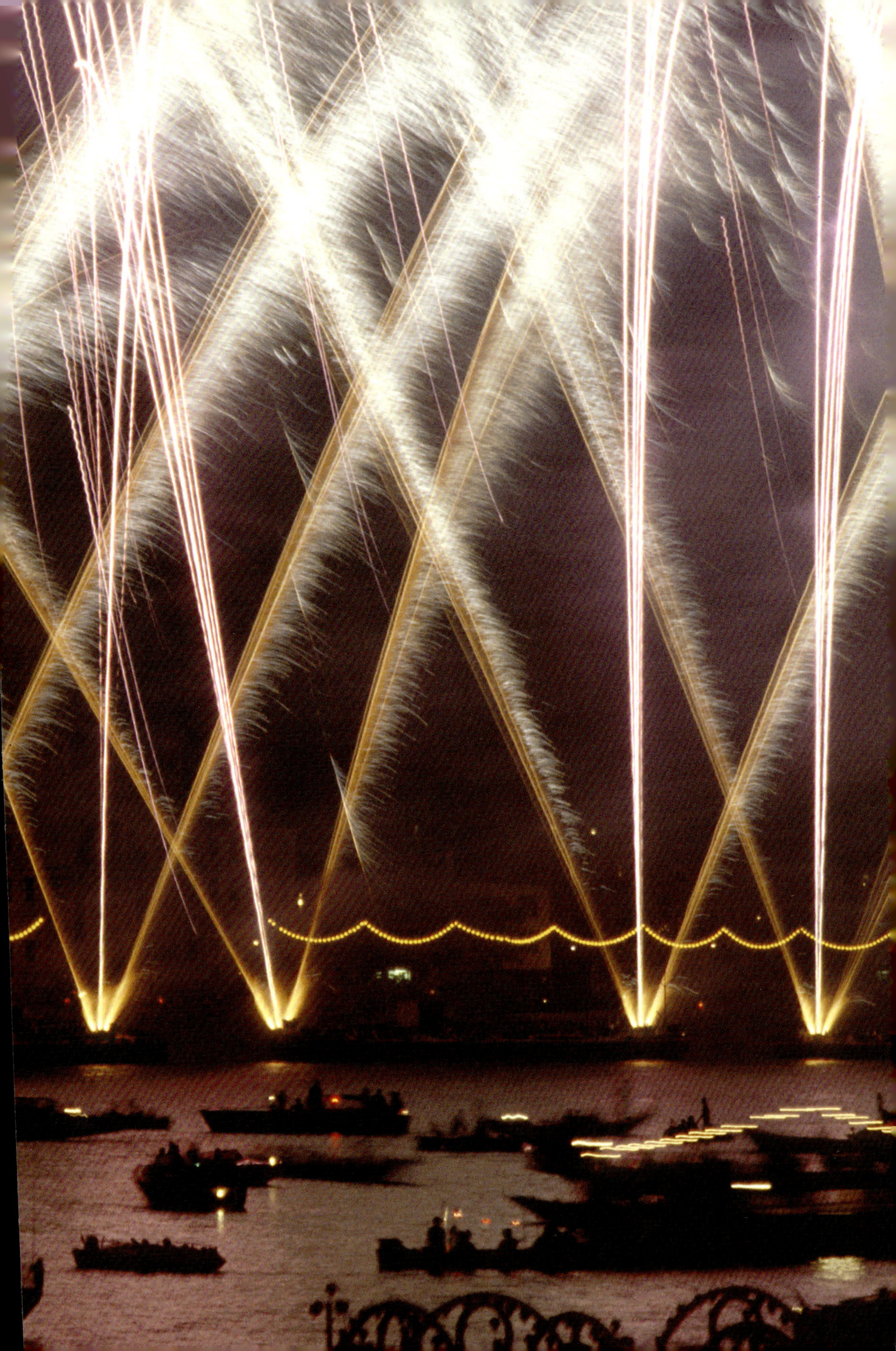

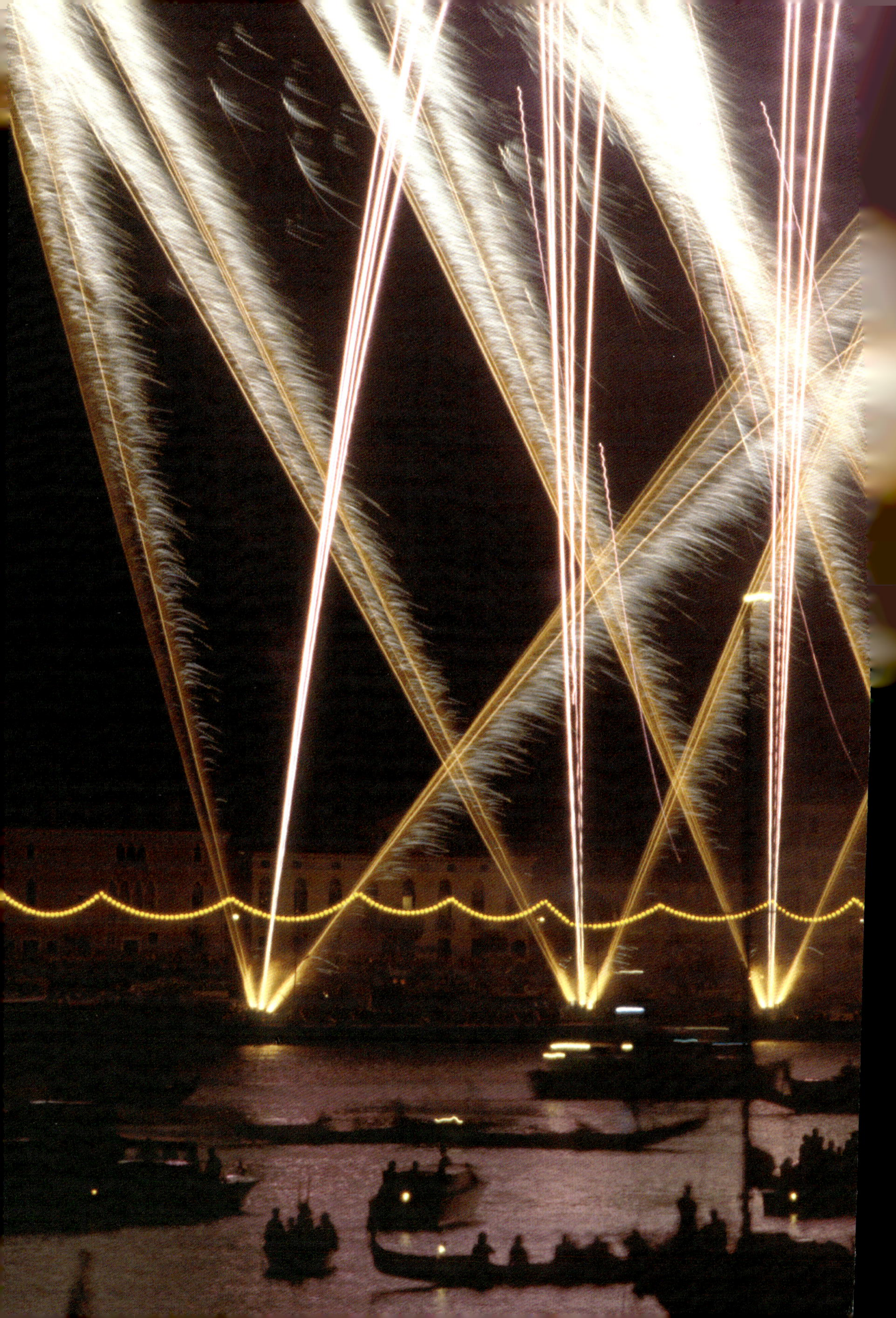

first weekend of October, can either provide the best possible excuse for tasting the first pressing of the new wine or a total washout. Essentially a wine festival, it takes place on the island of Erasmus, not far from Murano, and combines wine-tasting with a "day out in the country", which is how Venetians treat the islands of the lagoon. This is not a festival of spectacle, but a pleasant and undemanding way of watching Venetians and their families at play.

Meanwhile, there is such a thing as the Venice Marathon. Venetians will look a little put out at the suggestion that a Marathon race in Venice seems a little bizarre. "Surely," we ask hesitantly, "don't the canals get in the way?" Not a bit of it. The Venice Marathon is on the last Sunday in October, a 42-kilometre run that begins outside the Villa Pisani, which *Carnevale* revellers will recognize as a great place to have a party, and continues along the banks of the Brenta Canal, finishing up, having crossed a specially built pontoon, in the heart of Venice at the Riva degli Schiavoni. It's all very informal, with a mixture of agile Venetians and visitors taking part.

The festivals of Venice that make our hearts beat faster have colour and spectacle and glowing history attached to them and the best of those outside the summer months is the Festa della Madonna della Salute in November. Remarkably similar to the Festa del Redentore, it too celebrates Venice's delivery from the plague, the later one of 1631. Another pontoon bridge is strung across the Grand Canal, from the Campo Santa Maria del Giglio to La Salute, and a procession, led by the Patriarch of Venice, makes its way from San Marco. There is much chanting and praying, but Venetians always apply a light touch and the processional route is dotted with sweet stalls and vendors who provide candles for the faithful to light once they reach the church. This is a morning affair, so no picnics and no fireworks. Instead everyone goes home to lunch and thank the Lord and the Madonna, one more time, for continuing to look after Venice. As do we all.

fascinating, and unlikely art from all around the modern world. First hints that the Biennale is on its way is usually in March or April, when a barge carrying, as it did one year, a huge polystyrene nude reclining on a giant plastic hamburger, or, the following week, a sculpture made entirely of crumpled Coca Cola cans, may slip guilelessly along the Grand Canal bound for the Giardini where the main events are held.

As a film location Venice is unequalled and has taken a starring role in many films including, of course, Luchino Visconti's Death In Venice, with Dirk Bogarde; Paul Schrader's The Comfort of Strangers, with Christopher Walken and Natasha Richardson; Nicholas Roeg's Don't Look Now, with Julie Christie and Donald Sutherland; Woody Allen's Everyone Says I Love You, with Julia Roberts; and, best of all, the 1950s romantic heart-breaker starring Katherine Hepburn and Rosanno Brazzi, Summer Madness.

Inaugurated in 1895. the Biennale has grabbed headlines ever since. Picasso was rejected in 1910; in 1964 Pop Art from America annoyed French Academicians and recently one pavilion was overrun by a flock of sheep, which had apparently lost their way – an event that had Lord McAlpine, British resident and eccentric, remarking, "That Little Bo Peep really should take more care."

Some see the Biennale as a funfair for adults, a huge play centre that is amusing, attention-grabbing, but here today, gone tomorrow. Others believe that this festival signals that Venice is still alive, still can surprise, entertain and move people with art that is different and new, even in an atmosphere that reveres the old and prefers glory to be faded.

Competing for media attention, and most of the time winning it, is the Venice Film Festival, also a summer occasion starting at the end of August, or the beginning of September. The actual festival, that is the screenings of the movies, traditionally takes place on the Lido in the Palazzo del Cinema or the Palagalileo. The big stars are also inclined to stay on the Lido, which is the nearest Venice can manage to emulating Cannes.

The Excelsior, once the happy hunting ground of Cole Porter, Elsa Maxwell and their Jazz Age friends in the '20s, is still a favoured venue, although wearing a faded, or possibly jaded air. So is the Hotel des Bains. But these days, producers who really want to impress put their big stars into the Cipriani and transport them from screening to party to press launch to photo opportunity in high speed water taxis.

Autumn can either be the most beautiful of seasons in Venice, or the most unreliable. Consequently, Sagra del Mosto, on the wrote of onboard parties with "tables decked out as if for a bridal supper. They had also brought out the costly globe lamps from their drawing-rooms and the lace and silken curtains from the same places, I suppose."

But then, summer is crammed with festivities of one sort or another. There are starlit concerts in the courtyard of the Palazzo Ducale and band performances in the Piazza. Candle-lit processions are hugely popular, winding as they do along the canals and through the *calli*, mostly to finish up at the Basilica di San Marco. And there are regattas, as colourful, as busy, as riotous as anything painted by Canaletto nearly 300 years ago. The most flamboyant is the Regata Storica on the first Sunday in September, which begins with a procession of elaborate boats rowed along the Grand Canal by local youths, in even more elaborate 16th-century costumes. Venetians will shrug their shoulders and say that this part of the *festa* is only for tourists and they are far too busy to stop and stare. But few can resist a show, especially when the star is their own city, and on a beautiful day when the Grand Canal sparkles in the sunlight there is nowhere to be but canalside, enjoying the spectacle.

The real action, however, comes when the races start, and these are serious affairs. Amateur rowers, some barely teenagers, battle it out with experienced *gondolieri*. Women, as expert as any of the men, have their own race; and at the end is the most difficult contest of all when sporting gondolas, requiring two *gondolieri*, compete to be named champions of the day. The finishing line is where the Grand Canal makes one of its snake-like curves between Palazzo Barbi and Ca' Foscari and it is here where the judges sit, on their own ornate craft, ready to hand out the prizes.

The Biennale, or to give it its full title, Esposizione Internazionale d'Arte della Biennale di Venezia, also bursts forth in the summer, albeit only once every two years, opening mid-June and carrying on until early November. This is the huge, startling, awe-inspiring festival dedicated to the most outrageous, the most extraordinary, the most nerve-wracking,

It is getting quite heated in the neighbourhood delicatessen, or *salumeria*, of Campo Santa Margherita. The shop has inadvertently run out of freshly made seafood salad and roasted sweet peppers, and the customers are not amused.

FESTIVAL TIME

This is the third Saturday in July, which, as everybody knows, is the Festa del Redentore, when whole families take to the lagoon in whatever craft they can lay their hands on for a get-together to celebrate the miraculous deliverance of Venice from the Plague in 1576. The Festa del Redentore is the oldest continuously celebrated date in the Venetian calendar, and is much enjoyed by the local population. The church, Il Redentore on the island of Giudecca, designed by their beloved Palladio, rises in great glory and splendour above the flurry of boats and people and merry-making, and the whole occasion turns a sultry afternoon in July into a wonderful excuse for a party. Naturally a party needs a picnic and what is a picnic, irate Venetian housewives are demanding in their local *salumeria*, without their favourite *insalata di mare* and, worse still, without their *peperonata*? The *festa*, they mutter darkly, will be impossible without them.

Somehow, even without quite enough *antipasti* on the Campo Santa Margherita, the *festa* gets into full swing, as it has for over 400 years. Those who are not in boats, from glamorous yachts to fruit barges and gondolas, can make their pilgrimage on foot since a pontoon bridge is thrown across this very wide part of the canal between Giudecca and the Zattere. Those who make the journey see a new and totally different aspect of a familiar view.

As the partying continues and the sky above Il Redentore goes a moody purple the night suddenly erupts and becomes bright and loud with fireworks. Some party-poopers manage to get home before daybreak, but the faithful remain well into Sunday, enjoying just one of the festivals unique to Venice.

Mark Twain, bedazzled by the moonlit festival, described the many lanterns bobbing on the canal as "like a vast garden of many-coloured flowers". As for the elegance of the picnics, he

In 1740, English aristocrat Lady Mary Wortley Montague recorded how the boats of the great families could be decorated for such festivals. The Pisani family boat "bedecked with twenty four statues for the twenty four hours of the day and the moon rising above the stars", while the Doria family went in for a hunting scene with the Goddess Diana to the fore surrounded by stags, peasants, nymphs, "all done naturally".

As for the *palazzo*, already rather special, it was revamped with a lavishness that beggars description. Embellished with cloth of gold, with silk from the orient, velvet and fanciful tapestries, all hand-embroidered for the occasion, anything that wasn't already marble became so and the paintings were not only original Tintorettos, Bellinis, Titians and the like, but were especially commissioned for the occasion. Henry, an admirer of the simple life, was surrounded by over 3,000 guests who ate from silver plates, and after the gargantuan meal finally drew to a close the first opera ever seen in Italy was performed. Henry was never quite the same again. As a party it was something to remember.

Three hundred and fifty years later, in the 1920s and '30s, the Americans discovered Venice. The parties thrown by Cole Porter and Elsa Maxwell were not quite up to the standard set by the 16th-century gala at Ca' Foscari, but the two great revellers had great fun trying. As the New York Times reported at the time, "A wave of entertaining has swept over Venice within recent weeks. One of the most elaborate balls was given this week by Mr and Mrs Cole Porter in the Rezzonico Palace, the residence occupied by the Robert Brownings on the Grand Canal. The guests entered from the canal, ascending the steps between gondoliers attired in red and white costumes instead of the usual liveried footmen. Medieval torches replaced the usual electric lights." It was said that uninvited members of the smartest set left town rather than face the social disgrace.

At another soirée, held at the Hotel Excelsior at the Lido, "the hit of the evening", reported by the New York Times on 29 August 1926, "was furnished by Miss Elsa Maxwell, who, clad in a bathing-suit with a curly blonde wig covering her cropped head, sang, 'Just a Lonely Little Lady on the Lido' with such stupendous effect that she was forced out from behind the scenes again and again and finally repeated it." Those applauding her performance until their palms ached included Prince Frederick Leopold of Prussia, Baroness d'Erlanger, Baroness de Gunzburg, Lady Wimborne, Lady Diana Cooper, Mr Billy Reardon, Contessa Frasso and the Marchesa Sonuni-Picciardo. "The bar", the reporter thoughtfully noted, "did a rushing business." As Mr Cole Porter might have said, "what an elegant, swellegant party it was."

Guardi's painting of the Ridotto, the famous casino, can be seen in the Cole Porters' former residence, Ca' Rezzonico, now the newly restored Museum of The Eighteenth Century.

At another 16th-century banquet, almost as grand, guests discovered to their delight that everything on the table, from knives, forks and glasses to saltcellars, was designed by one of Venice's greatest architects, Jacopo Sansovino and made of sugar.

All the mask shops in Venice sell the traditional bautta *with its cloak and hat, but it is one of the least popular with 20th-century revellers, who prefer the highly decorated,* papier maché *masks that turn them, both men and women, into Titania, Queen of the Fairies or a golden-faced Sun King.*

Should you venture past the glass factories on the island of Murano and follow the Fondamente Sebastiano to its end, you will find the church of Santa Maria degli Angeli, which backed onto a convent where Casanova conducted one of his most bizarre affairs. The lady was a libertine nun, encouraged by her Mother Superior, who was herself the mistress of the French Ambassador. The church, unfortunately, is closed except for High Mass at 11am on Sundays.

While sense of responsibility was never a failing of the 18th-century Venetians, they took their mask-wearing most seriously, understanding that games only work when everyone knows the rules. The masks themselves were not merely coverings for the eyes and nose. They included a cape that enfolded the whole head and shoulders, with a little tricorne hat worn on top, so no one was recognizable. It became a uniform. Everyone danced about Venice in total disguise, from chambermaids to chancellors, from mothers who carried masked babes in their arms to ministers. One lawyer was even known to wear a mask during his summing-up speech in court.

To penetrate a disguise was considered very bad manners. The anonymity, embraced by Venetians for properly anonymous reasons, also had great charm, adding a certain allure to an event or assignation. Men and women from the finest families could wander about town undetected and enjoy incredible adventures. No wonder Goldoni called the mask "the most advantageous thing in the world". This was the era in Venice when Casanova prowled the bedrooms and the ballrooms of the city, enjoying a life of gilded debauchery.

It was in Venice that satirist, Pietro Aretino, a favourite of Casanova, laughed himself to death, and in Venice where even market traders, who had to be at their stalls at break of day, sang for sheer joy. Casanova's Venice is still largely intact. His birthplace was in the romantic quarter of San Samuele: the Ridotto, where the young Casanova perfected his gambling skills, still exists, and so does the Palazzo Soranzo on the Campo San Polo where he found his great patron, Senator Bragadin.

Yet, although the city at this time was dedicated solely to pleasure it couldn't touch the sheer extravagance of ancient Venice when she decided to show off. One of the most splendid parties ever conceived may well have been that to welcome the 23-year-old King Henry III of France in 1574. It took place at Ca' Foscari where Henry was transported under triumphant arches designed by Palladio and decorated by Tintoretto and Veronese. His ship was escorted by 14 galleys, and, just in case he got bored on the journey, glass-blowers from Murano were commissioned to make objects then and there for his amusement.

The truly fantastical images contemporary masks present are relatively new - mostly dating back to the 18th century when the pursuit of pleasure was an acceptable occupation and many among the leisured classes lived it up riotously from morning to night, especially during the months of *Carnevale*.

The balls and parties in Venice today require a costume, a mask and some insider information. Most good costumiers can provide all three, and they make certain that not only their racks of silks, satins and party hose are kept up to standard but also that their contacts are equally reliable. Flavia Zorzo, in Campo S. Lio will first dress her clients in the greatest finery, complete with wig, lace handkerchief and beauty spot. Only then will she reveal the addresses and contacts for the best balls and smartest parties. Anna Sautter at Max Art Shop in the Frezzeria San Marco organizes the most dazzling balls in the equally dazzling Palazzo Pisano Moretta overlooking the Grand Canal. This is a *palazzo* that has seen style. The leading families of Venice considered it enormously flattering to be asked to contribute to the good of the state, and did so with largesse. At a party honouring the Prince of Wurtemberg in 1763, the Pisano family spent 18,700 ducats, a considerable fortune, on a single evening's entertainment, with the basin of the canal turned into a magic garden, filled with music, nymphs and dryads to add to the fairytale atmosphere.

Unlike the revellers of the past, present-day *Carnevale* merrymakers looking to dance the night away in *palazzi* decorated by Tiepolo or Tintoretto, lit by thousands of candles, dining on food prepared by one of the best restaurants in Venice, can book tickets online. It may not be as romantic, but it is certainly practical.

The *palazzo* still belongs to the Pisani family and reeks with atmosphere. For *Carnevale* the ballroom is illuminated entirely by candles, not an electric light to be seen, and the floors, covered in mosaic-like carpets and inlaid with mother-of-pearl, are made for romantics who long to minuet and waltz the night away.

To attend such balls one must be in costume, and, says Anna Sautter darkly, "a tuxedo is not a costume". For those who find the idea of strutting about in frills and furbelows just too embarrassing, the wearing of a mask is a possibility. As Anna explains, "it gives you the chance of being more than you are, something liberated. It will let you be a child again in a life which has so much responsibility."

Venice in the depths of winter: a north wind blowing across the lagoon cutting into your knees like ice; gondoliers, wrapped in anoraks and woolly trousers, rubbing their hands together to keep out the cold, and muttering, *"Phoof, che vento!"* as another gust of wind curls around their ears and makes their eyes water.

MASQUERADE

Out of the mists a couple appears like a pair of pantomime ghosts. Their arms and legs are bare, except for filmy cloaks made from insubstantial stuff that wafts ineffectually around them. They are *Pierrot* and *Pierrette*. Their faces are painted white except for the bright pink splodges on their cheeks and a gash of red where their mouths should be, and the two of them, as carefree as if it were high summer, are having a wonderful time. He may be *Pierrot*, she may be *Pierrette*; it could be the other way around, since nothing is as it seems in this scenario.

This has always been one of the important aspects of *Carnevale*, and reaches back in the dark psyche of Venice to the Republic's days of glory in the 15th and 16th centuries. Then, during *Carnevale*, anyone could be who, or what, they pleased. Laws were upturned and social divisions ceased to exist as the entire populace donned masks and disguises and disported themselves through the streets. Today they do the same - over the first two weeks of February, revellers flow into Venice, ready to whirl to the city's music and become part of the colour and ritual of Venice at carnival time.

"To sit upstairs at a corner table at Caffé Quadri and watch the *carnevale* below in the Piazza San Marco is one of life's great moments". Lord McAlpine, writer and resident.

As always in Venice, there are two distinct faces of *Carnevale*. One is the laughing mask of gaiety, the celebration of spectacle and of showing off. The other is a much more simple disguise with no discernible features. It is the mask of anonymity. Throughout its history *La Serenissma* has demanded total sub-servience from its citizens. The cult of personality never stood a chance. From the *Doge* as an anonymous figurehead to a government run by a series of committees, the only personality tolerated was Venice itself. Hiding behind the mask began when aristocrats wanted to roam through the city, unrecognized and undetected. The decoration of those masks, and the game-playing that went on behind them, came much later.

NITE are the
ENTS of these
SOES, THAT THE
DRAWN MANY TO
HE REMOTEST PARTS
M, TO CONTEMPLATE
UTIES AND ENJOY
ALLIANCES".

THOMAS CORYAT, 'CRUDITES', LONDON, 1611

"SO INFI
ALLUREM
AMOROUS CALYP
FAME OF THEM HATH
VENICE FROM SOME OF T
OF CHRISTENDO
THEIR BEA
THEIR PLEASING D

own who must be honoured in the proper, festive fashion, and even though there are at least a hundred of these saints, Venice finds time for most of them.

The Film Festival, which is concentrated on the Lido, is another excellent excuse for a party, or several, as famous faces mix with café society and hopeful film fans.

But most celebrated of all is the *Carnevale*, a chaotic, colourful masked ball that spins itself out over ten days until it all comes to a shuddering finish on Mardi Gras and the beginning of the Lenten season. Any other city as old and revered as Venice should be wrapping herself up warm and putting her feet up for the winter – not *La Serenissima*. If it's February it must be *Carnevale*, when the city goes slightly mad, dressing in elaborate costume, playing even more elaborate practical jokes and splashing out on balls, parties and high octane revelry.

FE
world is going to bed."

Over there is a Japanese visitor dressed as Marco Polo, complete with red and yellow tights, a crimson cloak and a hat balancing on his ears like a sausage. Crossing the *piazza*, feathers ruffling in the breeze, is a masked conjuror wearing a tall, bejewelled cone on his head like Merlin and a crescent shaped moon painted over one eyebrow. And this is the middle of the day... Where are they off to? A secret party, a private ball, a clandestine assignation? Or, more prosaically, to have coffee with a friend at the Caffè Quadri, only lifting their masks to wipe the cappuccino froth from their lips? Venetians who haven't made the annual migration to the ski slopes or taken the tranquil mountain air of Cortina might also join in the revelries, flirting behind their masks and playing games their 18th-century ancestors perfected hundreds of years ago. *Carnevale*, after all, comes but once a year.

Some dismiss the ten days' celebration and spectacle as yet another commercial device instigated by the tourist office. But as you walk down an empty *calle* in February, as you see the shutters close on windows opposite and imagine Venice has turned its back on *Carnevale* revelry, listen carefully ... behind a door somewhere, people are dancing.

CHAPTER FIVE

THE HIGH LI
"Here they are getting dressed, while the rest of the

So said Ange Goudar, 18th century thief, wit and spy, but Venice does not appear to be a party city. Places close by midnight most of the time, and you could find yourself wandering back to your hotel after dinner, alone in the *piazza* except, possibly, for a stray and rather fat cat and a few, even fatter pigeons.

Yet there is no better setting than Venice for joyful events. Some of the most glamorous weddings in Europe take place in Venice, as great families join with other great families and five hundred of their closest friends fly in from all four corners of the globe to celebrate the occasion. To arrive at your wedding in a gondola, to dine in a magnificent *palazzo*, lit with a thousand candles and with the warmth of friends and family, and to dance through the night in the grandest of ballrooms is something so special that couples happily travel to Venice for the wedding of their dreams. There is even a website – not very romantic but very practical – that will do it all for you: www.venice-weddings.com is the address to look for.

Then there are the festivals, which abound, mostly in the name of this particular saint or that. Every parish has a saint of its

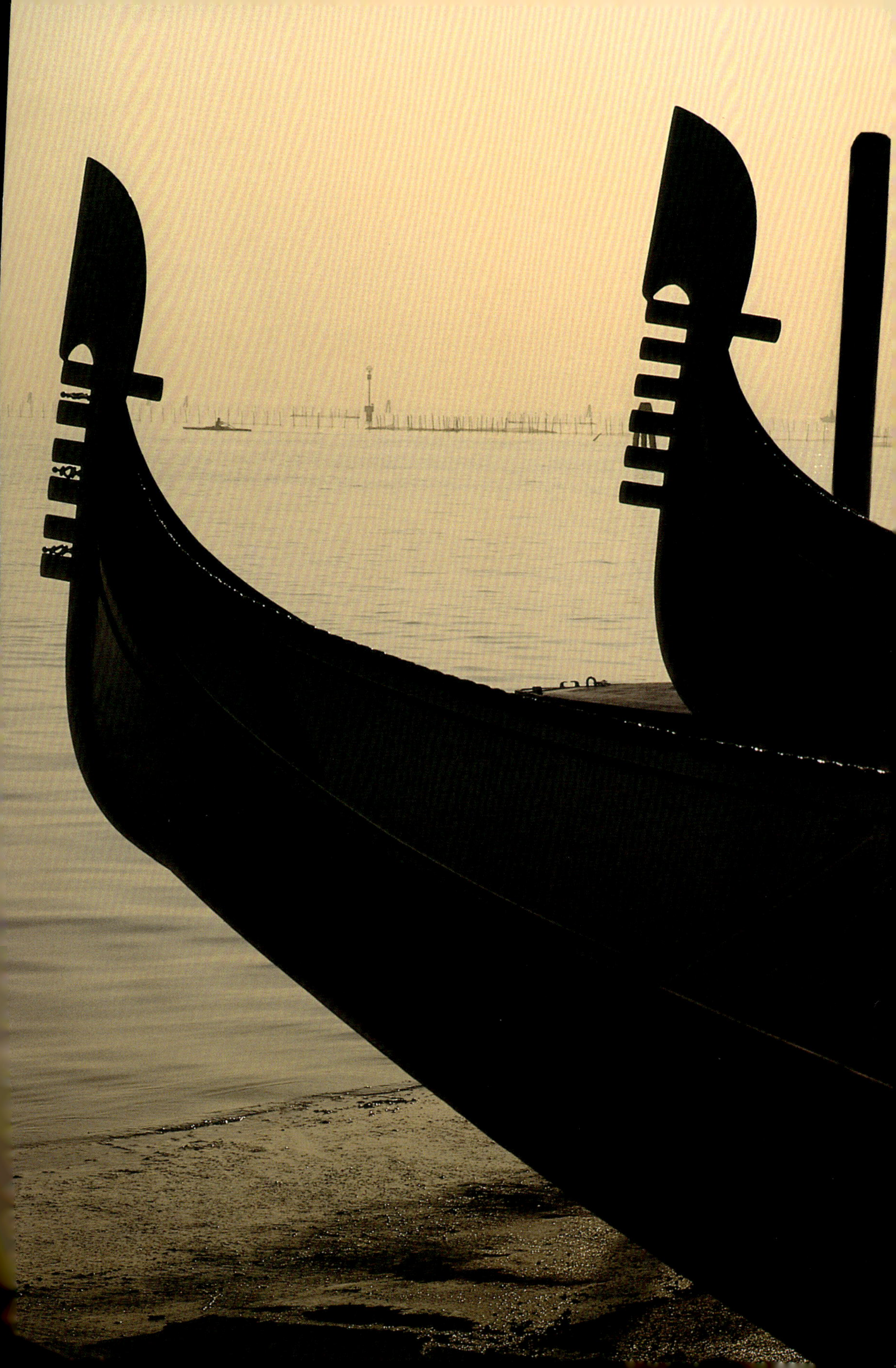

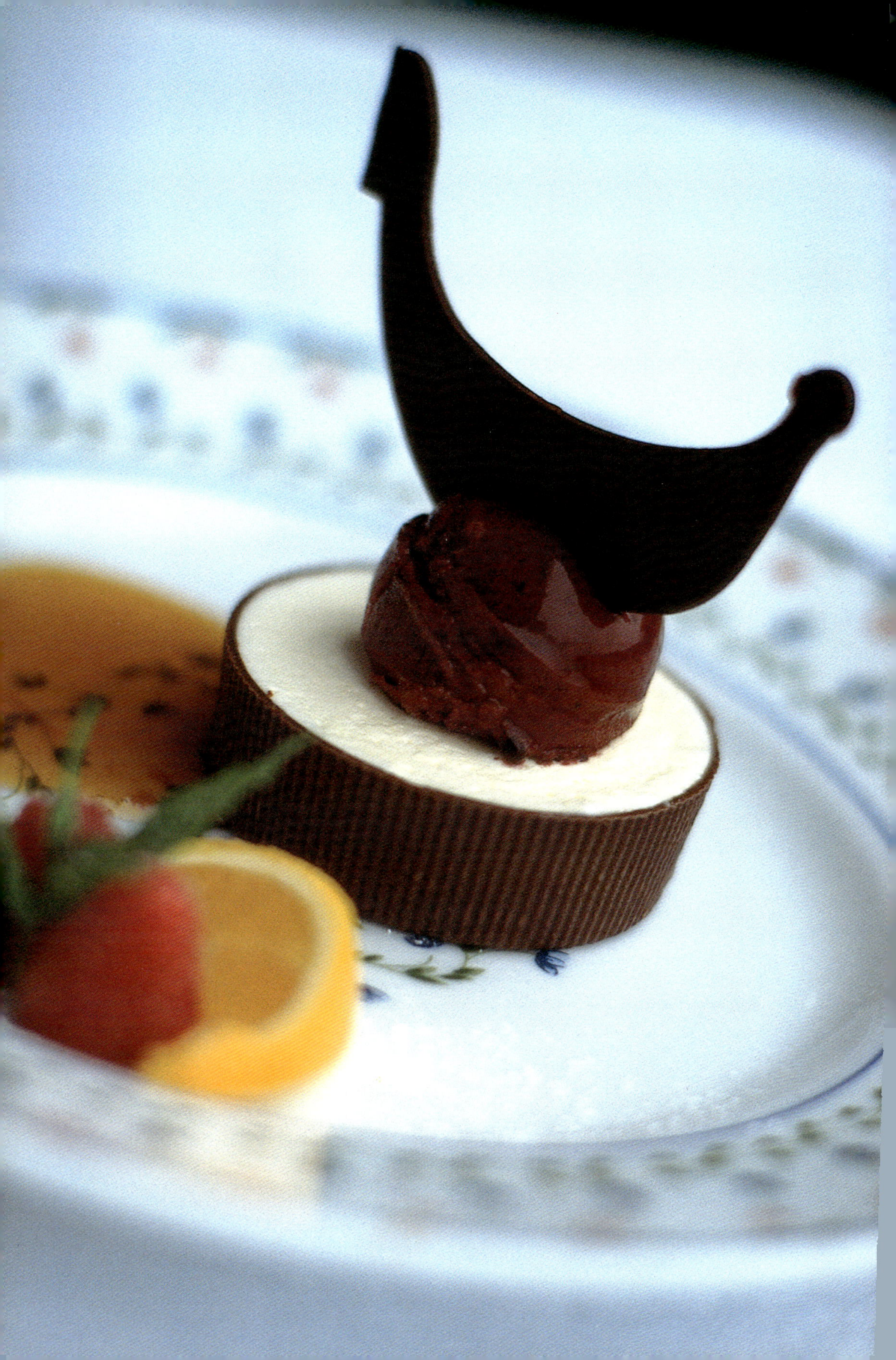

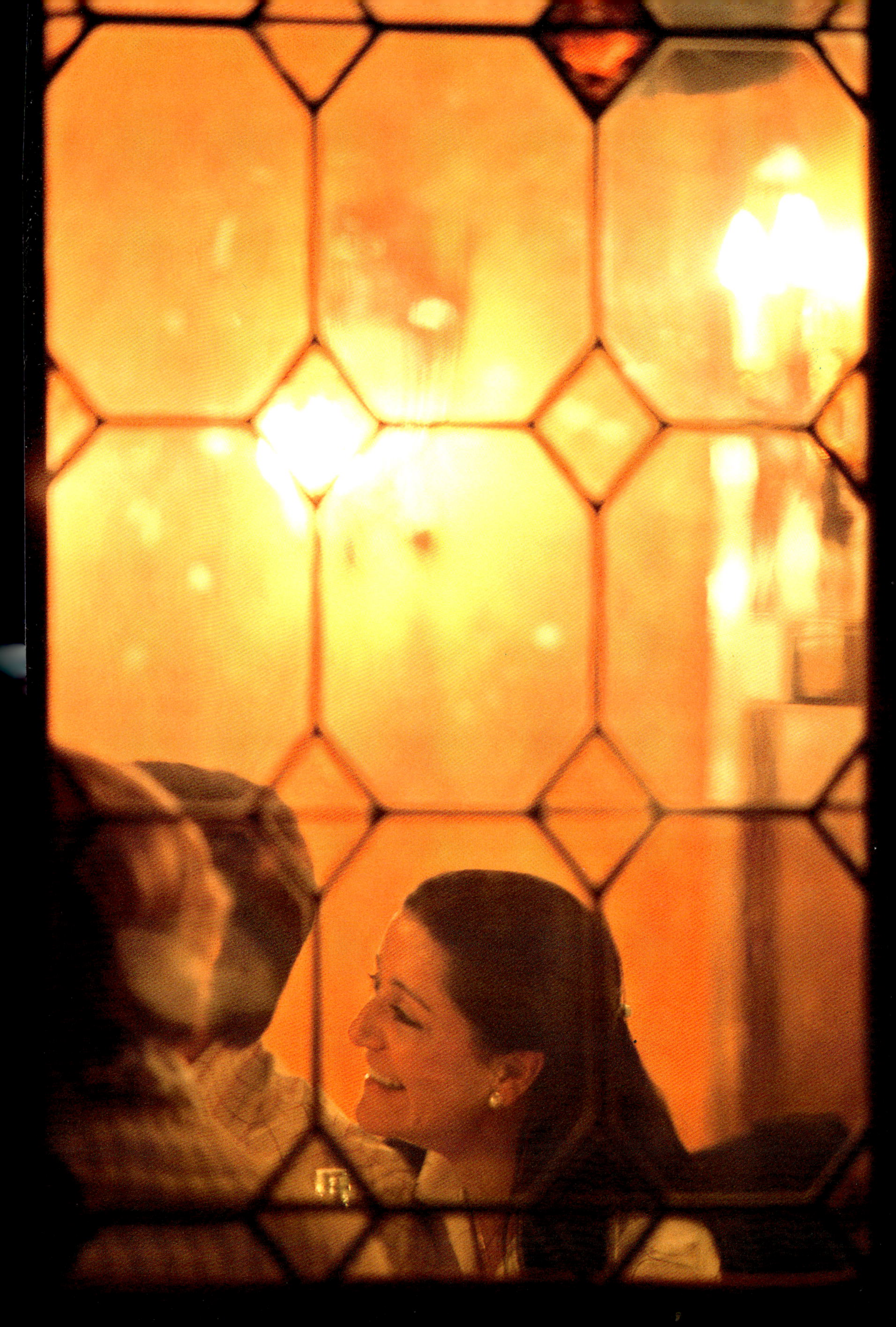

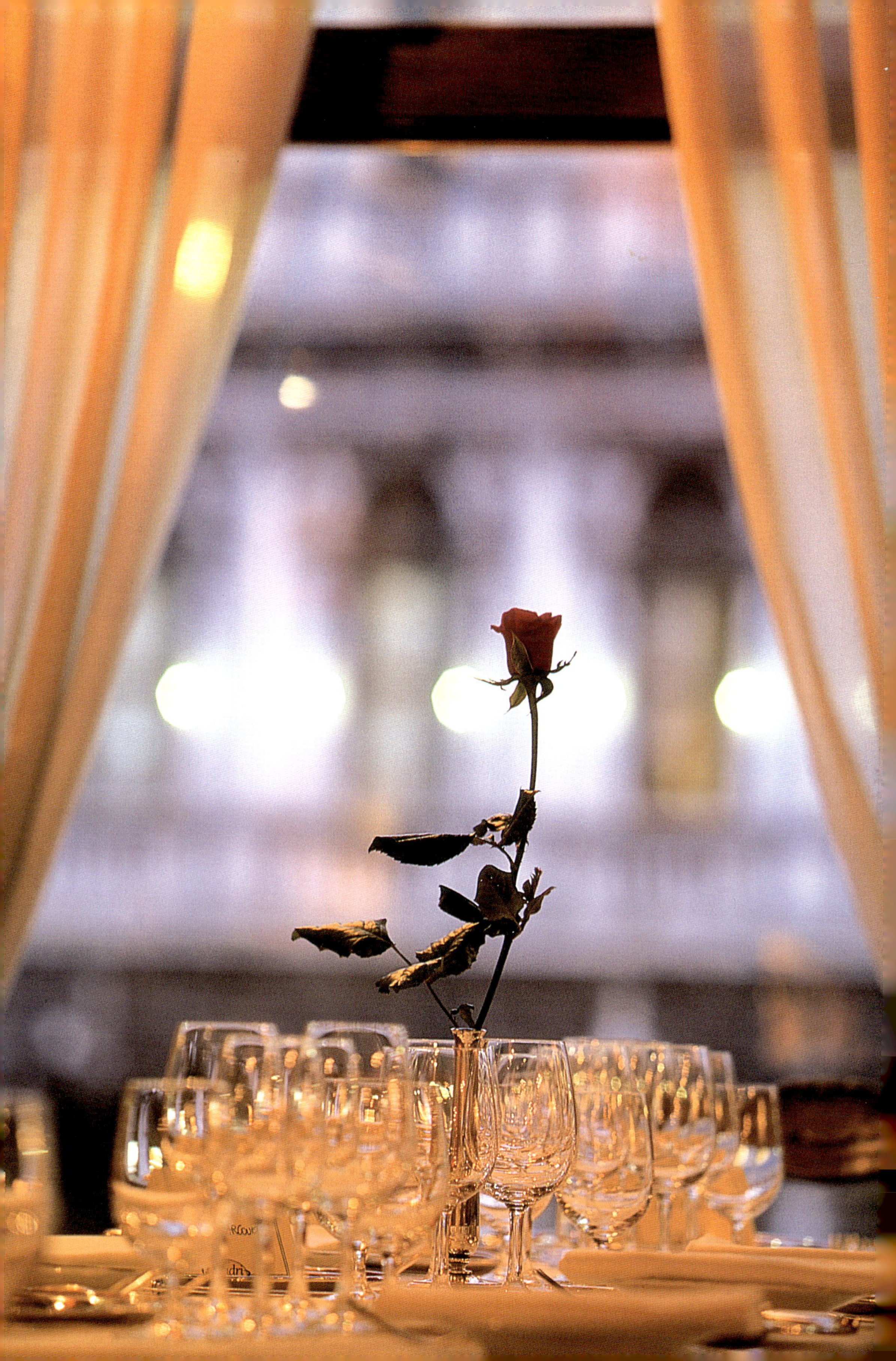

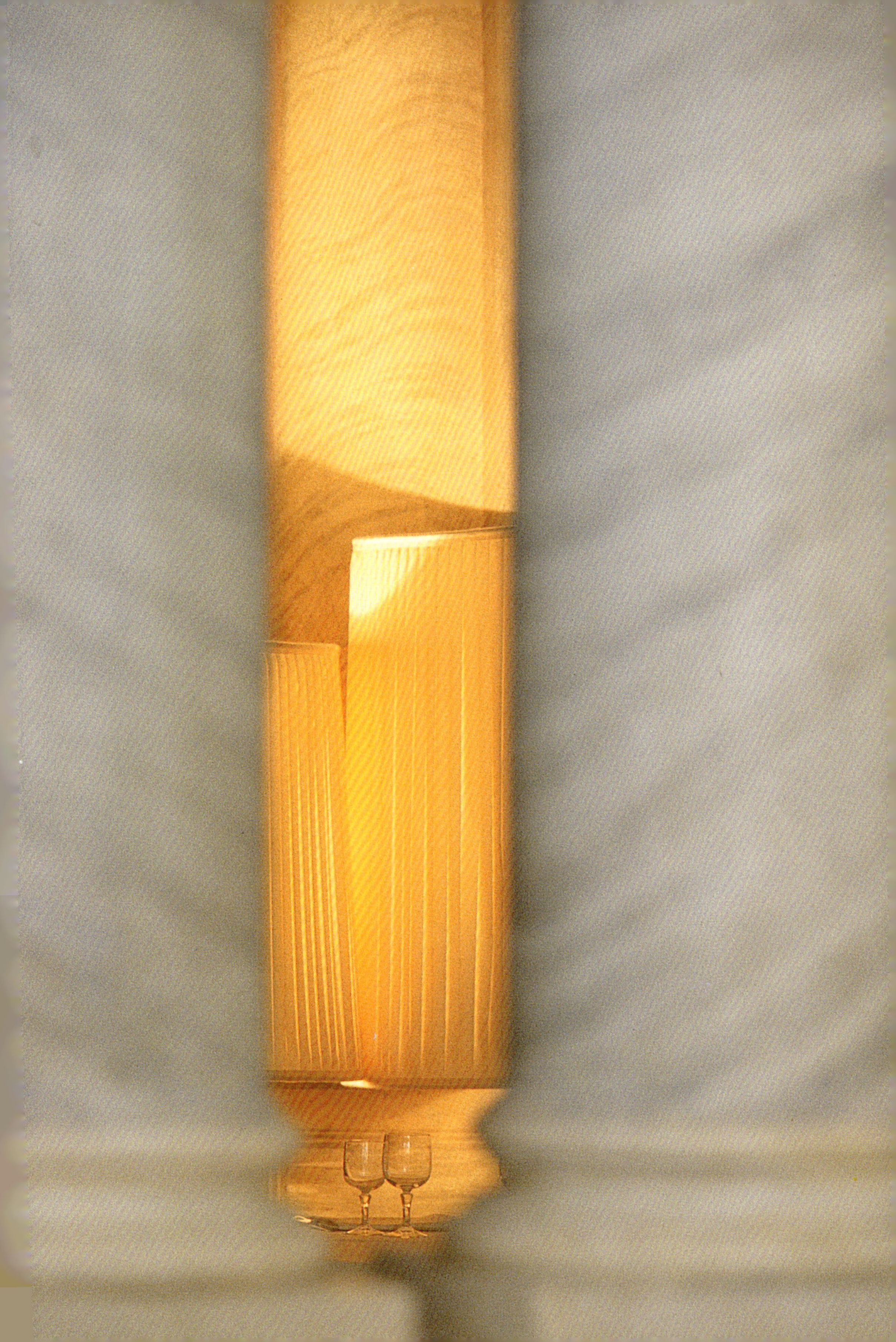

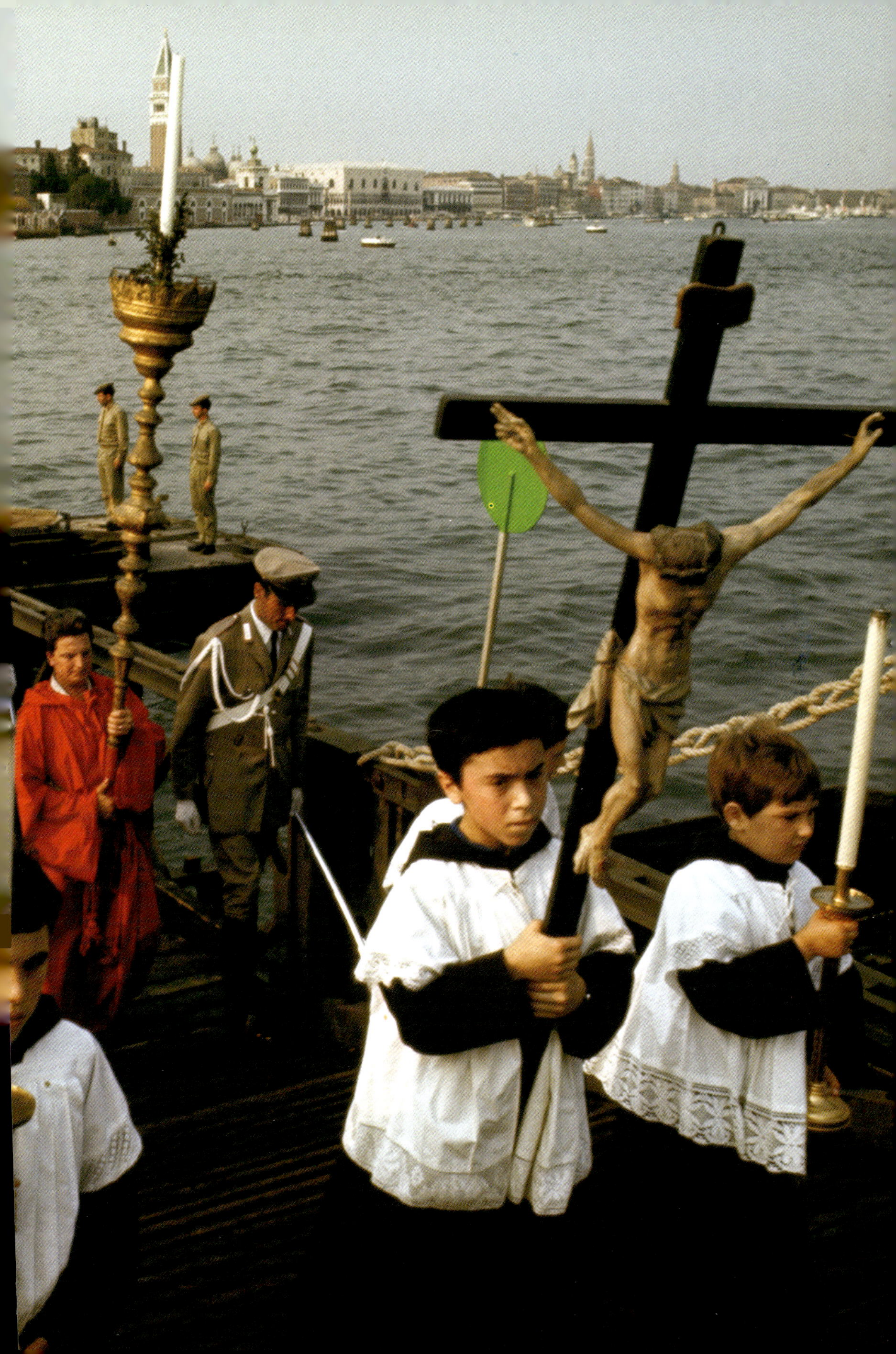

La Noua Pianta
Della Fiera Della Sensa

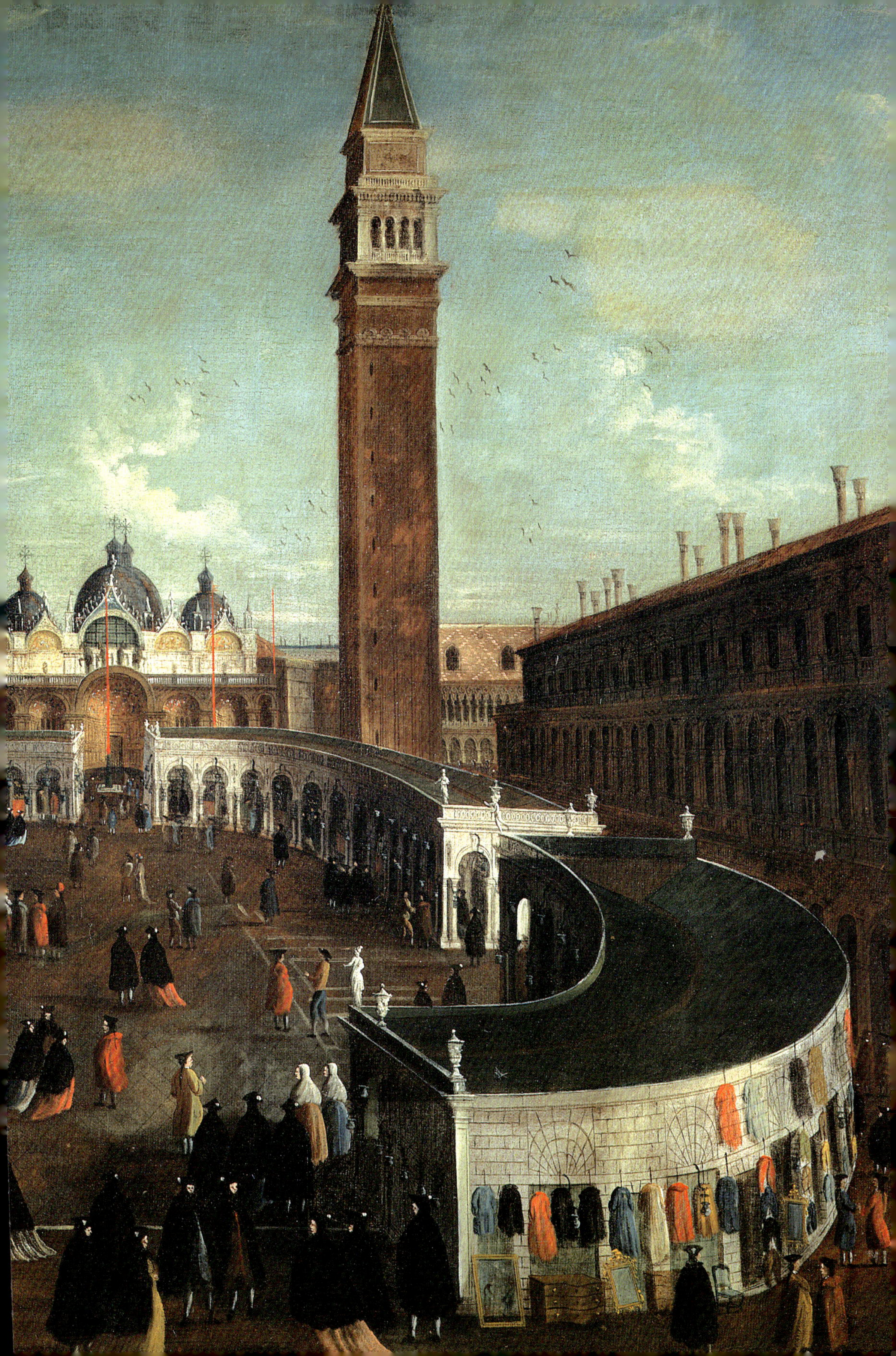

CHAPTER SIX

AFTER DAR

"Like the sun setting over the water, she cast on all

When we speak of "Venice after dark" what do we mean? Early evening in spring, when the sky is starting to turn lilac? Or the end of a sultry summer day, when the light only slips out of the sky after ten o'clock? Then there is that time when the rose-coloured glow of the streetlamps and the sheen of the surrounding sky seem one and the same. It only lasts for a few weeks, until winter moves in bringing all the mists and fogs off the lagoon to shroud the city in an eerie blanket of silver grey.

All of these moments are Venice "after dark" because this is a city that manages its lighting better than any opera house. The darkness, when it falls, only adds defining shadow and emphasis.

K

she was leaving an unforgettable farewell light."
Philippe Monnier, *Venise au XVIIIe Siècle*

But then, perhaps this is not what we mean. After dark also implies nightlife, gaiety and music. It hints at the bars that might have appeared dull and blameless during daylight hours but then miraculously change into buzzy, companionable places filled with life and opportunity as evening falls. Music after dark can either be haunting and classical in a venue filled with history or it can be raw jazz, sweet and soulful in a smoky *bacaro* in Misericordia. Sometimes you chance upon it in the street when a group of musicians with a band and a couple of loudspeakers take over a *campinello* and play their hearts out. Nothing has been planned, certainly not announced in any newspaper or magazine, but the grapevine works here just as anywhere else and once you arrive you'll find another several hundred are there before you.

A city with the heritage of Venice would be a poor place indeed without earnest young poets and philosophers finding a place to express themselves. Of course, such offerings are all in Italian, and possibly even in Venetian dialect, but to get under the skin of Venice and experience a little performance art a trip one evening to Le Bistrot near the Rialto is another adventure.

What "Venice after dark" really means is a touch of magic, of sweet unreality. Everything works: the huddled, dimly lit streets, the deep, black stillness of the canals, the echo of a whisper from over the bridge. Venice after dark has much to offer in pure, unique atmosphere. We should take it while we can.

You are just finishing dinner, at Cip's bistro perhaps, overlooking one of the world's most dazzling views; the lagoon, then the Grand Canal and finally Venice itself with the *campanile* of the Basilica di San Marco reaching up to the sky. Or possibly you're sitting on the terrace of the Cipriani, where you can hear the soft splash of the water readjusting itself after the hotel boat disappears into the night heading for Piazza San Marco.

THE INTIMACY OF SILENCE

Your table might well have been Sophia Loren's table once, or Elizabeth Taylor's or Jack Nicholson's or Franco Zefferelli's. They have all stayed here, all stared at that same view and all watched the sky change colour over the dome of San Giorgio Maggiore as night fell. Douglas Fairbanks Jnr. has written about how twilight over Venice is never quite the same. "I'd dare it," he said, "to be the same pinkish colour as yesterday or the same soft purple of the night before, but it is always different."

As you sip a wickedly strong espresso you might discover that what appeared to be ordinary truffles are in fact bitesized dollops of ice cream, encased in crisp, cold dark chocolate. The heat of the coffee combined with the icy sweetness of the chocolate could almost convince you to stay right where you are and allow your cup to "runneth over".

But Venice is waiting. Douglas Fairbank's changing sky has turned navy blue, and the hotel boat that travels backwards and forwards to Venice and back 24 hours a day eases into its mooring at Piazza San Marco. As the steps are washed by the ripple of the wash, cast your mind back to this sight and the sounds that went with it half a dozen hours ago. Crowds milling together in bunches, some covered head to foot in pigeons, the bobbing umbrellas of the tour guides directing their charges from this important site to that, the cries of the gondoliers competing for business, the whispers of free tickets for a one way ride to Murano and always in the background the click, click, click of the photo opportunity. Could this place, serene and almost empty, with only an occasional straggler pigeon picking some wayward corn from between the flagstones, be somehow the same?

Those who have already been seduced by Venice in the daylight must prepare themselves for another city in another mood once night falls. Other cities turn on their floodlights and spotlight their treasures, but Venice becomes like a *trompe l'oeil* painting, neither real nor imaginary, neither shadow nor substance.

Marguerite, Countess of Blessington-d'Orsay, early in the 19th century wrote: "The silence of Venice constitutes, in my opinion, one of its greatest charms. This absence of noise is peculiarly soothing to the mind and disposes it to contemplation. I looked out from my balcony late one night, when the Grand Canal reflected a thousand brilliant stars on its water, turbid though it be; and the lights streaming from the windows on each side, showed like golden columns on its bosom. Gondola after gondola glided along, from some of which soft music stole on the ear, and sometimes their open windows revealed some youthful couple with their guitars, or some more matured ones, partaking their light repast of fruit and cakes; while not infrequently a solitary male figure was seen reclined on the seat absorbed in the perusal of some book. The scene realised some of the descriptions of Venice read years ago...". The Countess could have been writing of a summer evening in Venice in the 21st century. Besides, that blessed absence of noise she spoke of means so much more to us travellers today who spend much of our time locked in the hurly-burly of modern life.

To wander through Venice at night and experience the extraordinary intimacy of silence awakens a profound sense of peace. There is nothing menacing here, nor unwelcoming; echoing voices, laughter drifting across a canal, the clink of coffee cups, the clatter of high heels on a nearby bridge, all become part of the scene evoking images of a more private Venice than is to be found in the daytime.

Here and there are pockets of a more predictable nightlife. Harry's Bar isn't far away, there is a jazz scene both in Campo Santa Margherita and along the Fondamenta della Misericordia. Earlier on, wine bars have been jam packed. But just before midnight, when much of the city seems empty, there is a wonderful opportunity to slip into the harmony of Venice.

Marguerite, Countess of Blessington-d'Orsay (1789-1868), adventuress, traveller, novelist, fading beauty and continually in debt, was a friend of Byron, Landor and Dickens. Her Venetian sojourn was part of a trip, taken on a whim and in doubtful company, around France, Switzerland and Italy that inspired a three-volume epic called *The Idler in Italy*, published in 1840.

"MOON

IS A GREAT BEAUT

AND ESPECIALLY

TOUCHED WITH TH

FROM A PALACE TO A

IT SOFTENS

RENDERS FAIRER

AND DIS

TENDER ME

IN HARMONY WITH

LIGHT
IFIER,
OF ALL THAT HAS BEEN
E FINGER OF DECAY,
WOMAN.
WHAT IS HARSH,
WHAT IS FAIR,
POSES THE MIND TO THE
LANCHOLY
ALL AROUND."

MARGUERITE, COUNTESS OF BLESSINGTON-D'ORSAY, 1820

It's 11pm in Harry's Bar and the place is buzzing with life. Venetians who stopped-off hours ago for a quick Martini or maybe a Negroni swap insults with chief bartender, Claudio Ponzio, who has been polishing glasses and mixing cocktails behind this bar since the 1960s. New arrivals in town, still bleary-eyed and a bit jet-lagged, sip their first Bellini and wonder at the miracle that is wrought when pure peach purée is mixed with light Italian *prosecco*. Over in the corner an ancient aristocrat – he must be an aristocrat with a face so immaculately carved – sips an Americano and argues in noisy and voluble Italian about baseball. In another, Silvana Mainardis, chic, blonde and one of the city's most important art patrons, discusses how Titian and her favourite abstract artist, Mondrego, are brothers under the skin.

A COCKTAIL LEGEND

To say that Harry's Bar is legendary is an understatement. This is where Hemingway used to stride about, showing off and frightening sensitive women by slinging a brace of pheasants he'd shot that afternoon onto the bar before downing his first Martini. It is where Charlie Chaplin, Bogie and Bacall, Frank Sinatra and a steady stream of dukes and duchesses all headed when they found themselves in Venice. The Windsors, Wallis and David, were *habitués*; so was Orson Welles, who always lurked, it is said, somewhere near the toasted sandwiches. Truman Capote loved Harry's Bar as did Frederico Fellini, Marcello Mastroiani and Rita Hayworth.

> "I had no idea about the water factor, that there were no cars. I know that makes me sound like an idiot and I don't care. I was stunned, just stunned."
> Julia Roberts.

Harry's Bar continues to be the first stop for visiting film stars. Madonna has visited, so has Nicole Kidman. When Julia Roberts first came to Venice to make *Everyone Says I Love You* she perched at the bar and tried her first Bellini – possibly seated on the very same stool used by Robert Benchley when he composed his famous "streets flooded, please advise" telegram. Woody Allen found shades of his beloved Manhattan in the sheltering booths, and Gore Vidal claimed that, since the closure of the US Consulate in the '70s, "Harry's Bar is sometimes the only place for Americans in acute anxiety to go for comfort and advice."

First-time visitors making their way into the place have trouble understanding what the fuss is all about. In appearance the bar is dark brown and understated, rather like the interior of a ship, and not a particularly grand one. There is a lot of smooth wood and comfortable leather, but, despite sitting on the Grand Canal with dazzling viewing possibilities, Harry's Bar turns its back to all that and professes that the most interesting panorama in Venice is provided by its own colourful and diverse customers.

It is a philosophy that has worked spectacularly since the day the bar opened in 1931. The story is that Guiseppe Cipriani, the genius hotelier who also created those other legends the Hotel Cipriani and Locanda Cipriani on the island of Torcello, met Harry Pickering, a Boston financier who was grumbling about bars in Venice and how he couldn't find one that suited him. Guiseppe's ideas appealed and Harry gave him, then and there, the first $40,000 to realize his dream. Harry's Bar, that is a bar for Harry, was the result, and has been delighting new customers ever since.

These days Harry's Bar is run by Guiseppe's son, Arrigo (Harry) Cipriani, who claims that he is the only man in the world named after a bar. Like Claudio Ponzio, who learned the secret of great cocktails from Guiseppe himself, Arrigo is a constant presence, welcoming the famous, indulging the infamous and somehow making the rest of us feel we are part of the scene.

Those who argue that Harry's Bar and its mood and atmosphere is somehow at odds with the rest of Venice, her dignified monuments and the piety of her churches, only have to cast their minds back to that earlier Venice. The great parties and festivities of the Renaissance had the rest of the world on its knees in sheer admiration, while in the 17th and 18th centuries pleasure was pursued with an energy and determination that was almost heroic. In 1789, Lady Thrale, a diligent chronicler, observed, "These dear Venetians have no notion of sleep being necessary to their existence, I believe, as some or other of them seem constantly in motion and there is really no hour of the four and twenty in which the town seems perfectly still and quiet."

Today it is only the dedicated boat for Hotel Cipriani guests that operates a 24-hour service. Even Harry's Bar closes at midnight, but until its customers spill out into the silent streets to creep back home, Venice has been at play the way she always was.

Mrs Thrale, erstwhile friend of Dr Johnson and Fanny Burney, was a wealthy English widow with eleven children when she met and married an Italian musician, Gabriel Piozzi. Dr Johnson disapproved and never spoke to her again. Undismayed she wrote her *Observations and Reflections* made in the course of a journey through France, Italy and Germany, which she published in two volumes.

We are wandering around the Accademia Bridge at twilight during the last few days of summer. It is not dark quite yet, but shop assistants, bank tellers, tourist guides and gallery owners have shut up shop and are scurrying past, looking forward to getting home. But we visitors are still about, still looking for something else to discover about Venice and we are faced with youthful Venetians in a quandary.

SOUND OF MUSIC ~ CLASSICAL

They are the students hired to put on 17th-century costume and persuade us to go to listen to Venetian music in one of the great venues of the city. By the end of a hot day their wigs are looking a little out of control, their panniered dresses, often slung over jeans, have a weariness about them and the enthusiasm of the morning has waned. But there are still tickets to sell and we tourists are still out; the programme is Vivaldi, the city's favourite local composer, and the performers are talented players who need an audience.

Antonio Vivaldi's first calling was as a priest, but so popular was his music that if he felt suddenly inspired with a melody in the middle of Mass and rushed off to the Sacristy to write it down, no one in the congregation minded. Music and love of God went together, hand in hand.

Should we decide to put these earnest music students out of their misery, and buy the last book of tickets for the concert at the Scuola Grande di San Giovanni Evangelista or the Palazzo Zenobio, or for the choir and orchestra at the church of Santo Stefano? We are in for a treat and a very Venetian one at that. The programme will always feature Vivaldi and probably at least one of his *Four Seasons*. There may be a little Boldini, perhaps, or Corelli or Tartini; dancers of the Balletto Ducale may perform graceful gavottes and minuets; and the entire orchestra could well be in period costume, with well-fitted wigs and costumes, and even the occasional beauty spot for authenticity.

Some may hesitate over concerts with such obvious populist appeal, but all these doubts disappear within the first 30 seconds or so. The performers are charming, the music itself has been enchanting audiences for the past two or three hundred years, and the locations are amongst the best Venice has to offer. As night falls and the music starts there is nowhere else to be.

Both the Orchestra di Venezia and Società Veneziana di Concerti organize concerts at the Scuola Grande di San Giovanni

Evangelista, a magnificent 14th-century building decorated with works by Tintoretto, Palma the Younger and Tiepolo. Collegium Ducale perform Venetian baroque in various churches including Santo Stefano, San Samuele and Santa Maria Formosa.

La Pietà, the church most associated with Vivaldi, is used by Centro di Co-ordinamento Culturale who present an all female string quintet, Le Putte di Vivaldi, who play in costume and who are named after the young girls (*putte*) in the city's orphanages of the 17th and 18th centuries who were encouraged to learn an instrument or to sing. They performed regularly and many became musicians of great quality. Writing in 1780, William Beckford, after enjoying one of their concerts noted: "The sight of the orchestra still makes me smile. You know, I suppose, it is entirely of the female gender, and that nothing is more common that to see a delicate white hand journeying across an enormous double bass, or a pair of roseate cheeks puffing with all their efforts at a French-horn. Some of them who are grown old and Amazonian have abandoned their fiddles and their lovers and take vigorously to the kettle drum; and one poor limping lady, who had been crossed in love, now makes an admirable figure on the bassoon." Venice was awash with music at this time. There were four music conservatories; to be in a choir or to be an instrumentalist was an excellent and valued occupation and music-making reverberated throughout the churches and in the grand *palazzi*. Composers and performers, recognized as being amongst the best in Europe, were fêted by the city and its inhabitants who couldn't imagine life without music and burst forth with it on occasion themselves.

Gondoliers were not only known to quote poetry at each other, but would favour passengers with renditions of old Venetian love songs. These days, an evening trip down the Grand Canal in a gondola is more likely to be accompanied by a version of an ancient Frank Sinatra song or something Neopolitan. But every now and again, when the mood is right and the gondolier is young and romantic and possibly in love himself, he may give full voice to a glorious aria just like a young Pavarotti. And somewhere nearby another, who just can't help himself, might join in. After all, this is Venice, where such things can happen.

There is nothing like flash photography to destroy the mood at these evening concerts in Venice. Both the performers and fellow spectators appreciate members of the audience leaving their cameras at home.

For the most comprehensive collection of classical music in Venice and immaculately produced CDs featuring Venetian music, often recorded in the churches and *scuole* of Venice, try the city's most charming music shop, the Vivaldi Store, in San Bartolomeo near the Rialto Bridge. The owner, a talented musician himself, is on hand to discuss what's new, what's exciting, what captures the spirit of Venice most completely.

La Serenissima lives up to her name throughout most of this city. Even the sparky Campo Santa Margherita, which is the Covent Garden or Greenwich Village of Venice, cools down around midnight thanks to the city's stringent noise pollution laws that pull the plug on anything that is amplified after 11pm.

SOUND OF MUSIC - JAZZ

But there is a new and exciting alternative. When the rest of Venice closes its shutters, hip young Venetians head straight for a secret neighbourhood well away from the Piazza San Marco, that has suddenly, finally, begun to sprout a buzzy nightlife that can go on until three or four in the morning. Some arrive in rowing boats on the canal, others zoom up in a speedboat or they might even roller blade – not easy in a city of 450 bridges. Along a dark back street that runs alongside an inky, silent canal, suddenly there is a world of bars open almost till dawn, waterside terraces teeming with cool, young Italians, exotic restaurants whose kitchens are open until the early hours, live bands and interactive cyber cafés. It's hard to believe that you're still in Venice. Aficionados, influenced no doubt by too many American movies, call it "Misericordia Boulevard". To the rest of us it is Fondamenta della Misericordia, and is in the newly trendy *sestiere* of Cannaregio.

A visit to Misericordia is an adventure and not for the faint-hearted. Cafés are noisy and boisterous, the clientele is made up of students, youngsters who have somehow drifted into Venice en route to "finding themselves" somewhere further east and canny locals who enjoy good but unpretentious food accompanied by equally unpretentious prices. The music is jazz or Jamaican. Those who have yet to experience the clang and clatter of West Indian music are in for a unique experience. A Jamaican reggae band echoing across the canals of Venice is not something you hear every day.

As for the food and drink, it's excellent and remarkably varied. Venice may not have a French restaurant, but here there is a Mexican bistro, a Syrian restaurant and the exotically named Le Notti Orientale is a *pizzeria* these days (they are *great* pizzas).

Those looking for music could start at the most famous establishment, Paradiso Perduto, which is packed from the moment the doors open. With its sparse brick walls decorated with exhibitions by local artists, this is the place to meet some locals, as everyone sits along long wooden tables listening to live jazz or reggae. It can get pretty wild late in the night.

The Iguana Café is not only Venice's first and only Mexican restaurant, it serves spicy *tortillas*, *burritos* and killer margaritas to the tune of Brazilian blues. Live music is on the menu on Tuesdays and happy hour, between 7 and 9pm, features *cubinos* (rum and Coca Cola) which must make for one of those experiences you never would have thought you'd find in Venice.

The Camelot Pub is one of the most recent around here. Open until 4am, with a tiny bar but a big terrace, they play a vast selection of music from jazz to funk. Drinks will seem amazingly cheap after more traditional establishments, which means it can get pretty lively when the other bars have stopped serving.

Pub Da Aldo is undoubtedly the most popular spot on the Boulevard, drawing vast crowds, attracted by the cheap drinks, a huge choice of beers, and lack of hassle from the huge figure of Aldo, who lets his customers make as much noise as they want and doesn't care what the rest of Venice says.

At Sahara, eccentric owner Mouffak has persuaded locals to change from pasta and pizza to his native Syrian cuisine. He also mixes a lethal *Spritz al Bitter* cocktail of Campari and white wine. It's even better in the summer when he organizes live concerts on a boat moored by his terrace on the canal.

Osteria Anice Stellato is chic and stylish – all cool marble, subtle lighting and designer décor, which, now that Misericordia has been discovered, will probably be the way forward. Charming owners and excellent cocktails make it well worth a visit.

Part of the real charm of Misericordia Boulevard is not just the music, even though it can include some of the best jazz you'll hear in this part of Italy, it's the locals. Their presence proves that Venetians may no longer make pleasure-seeking a career, but they like letting their hair down just like everyone else. Here, along a back street *fondamenta* that appears less than interesting during daylight hours, life takes on a colourful, chaotic charm as soon as night falls. After dark, Misericordia is worth discovering.

For those of us who still prefer our Venice with its traditional touches the most enjoyable establishment in this trendy string of nightspots is Osteria al Bacco, one of the most beautiful old *osteria* in all Venice, perfectly preserved, complete with a tiny garden at the back. This is the place for a gourmet, romantic meal before hitting the town. It specializes in traditional Venetian cuisine, especially fish from the Adriatic.

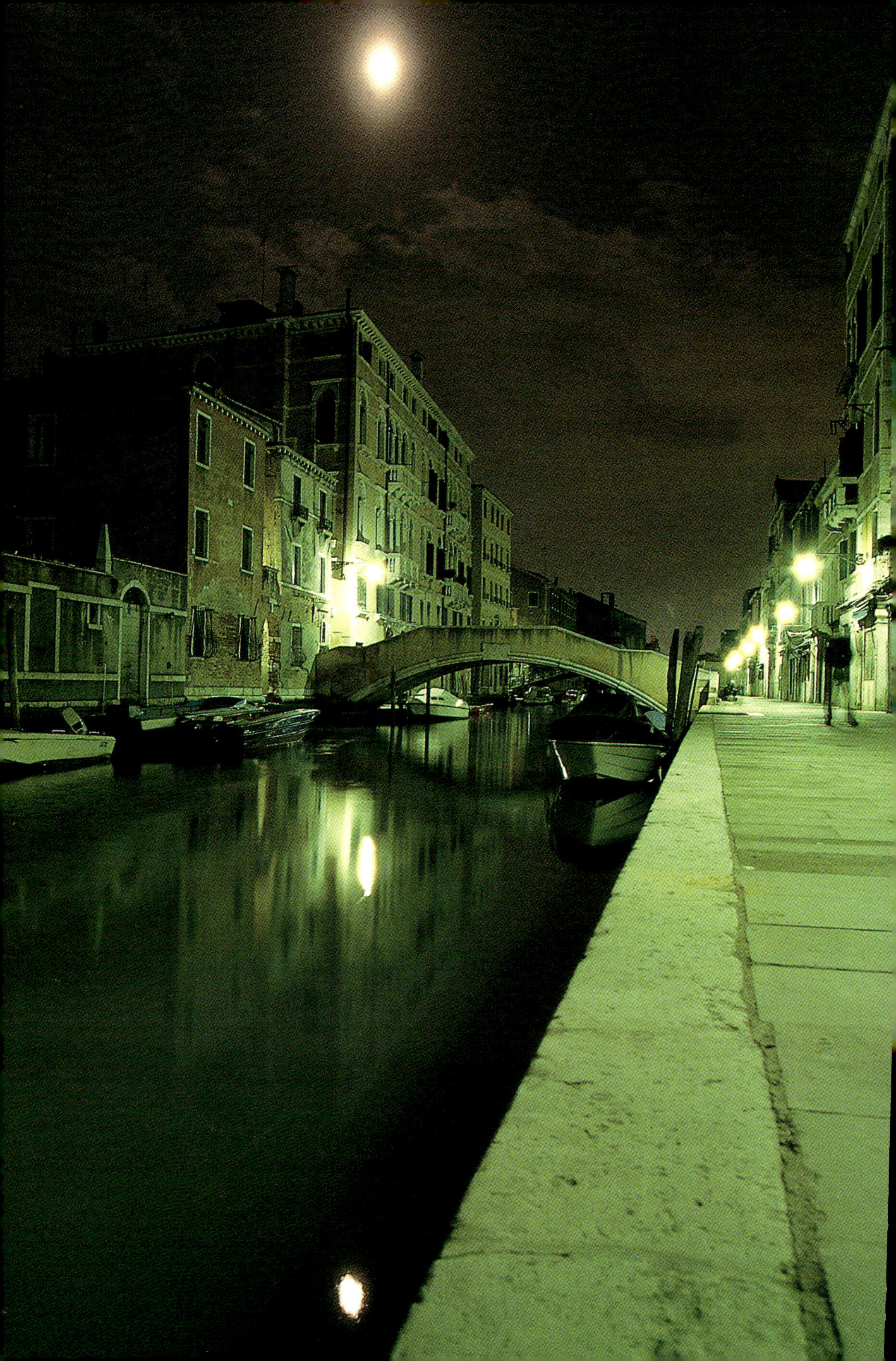

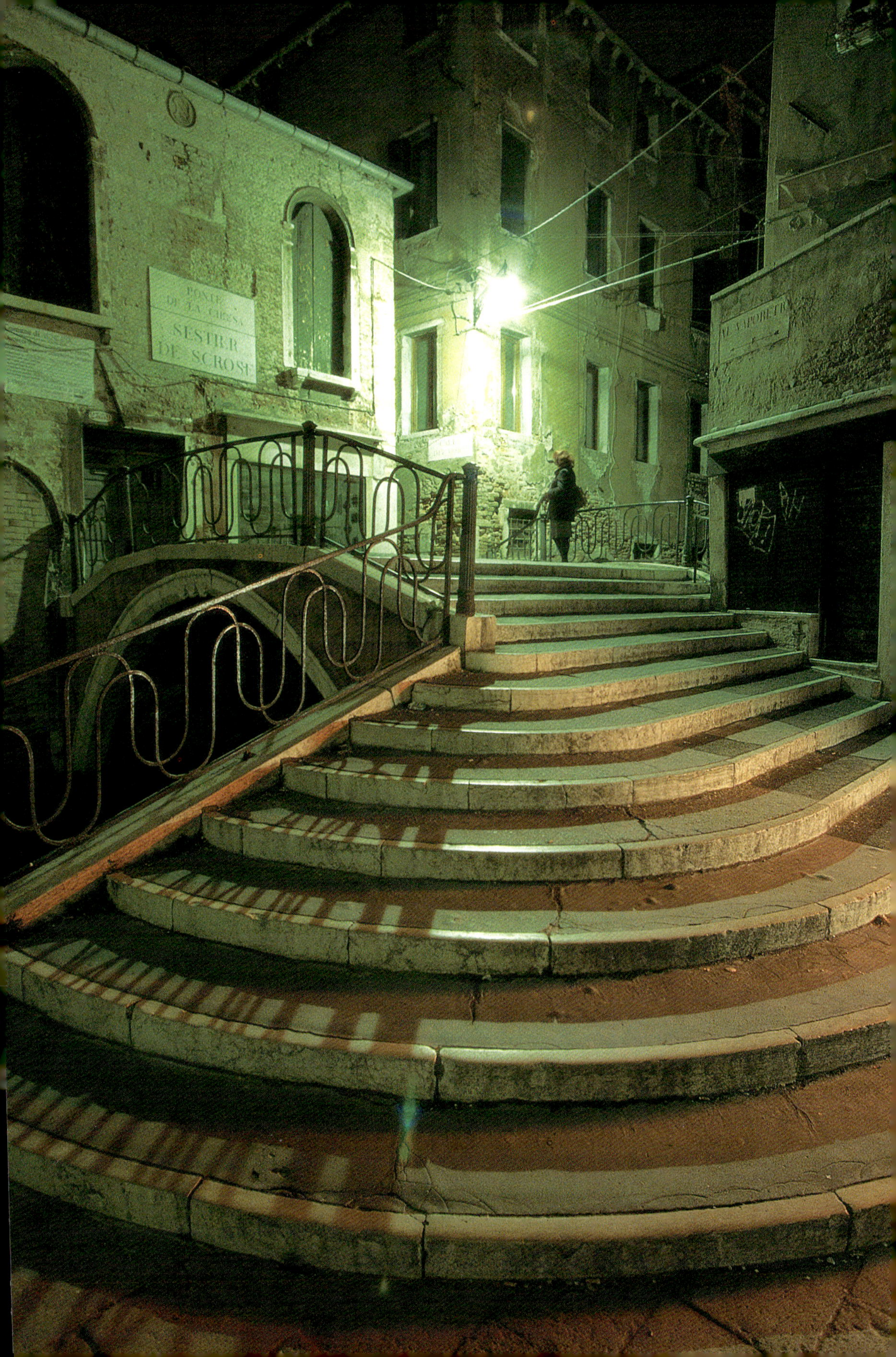
SESTIER
DE SCROSE

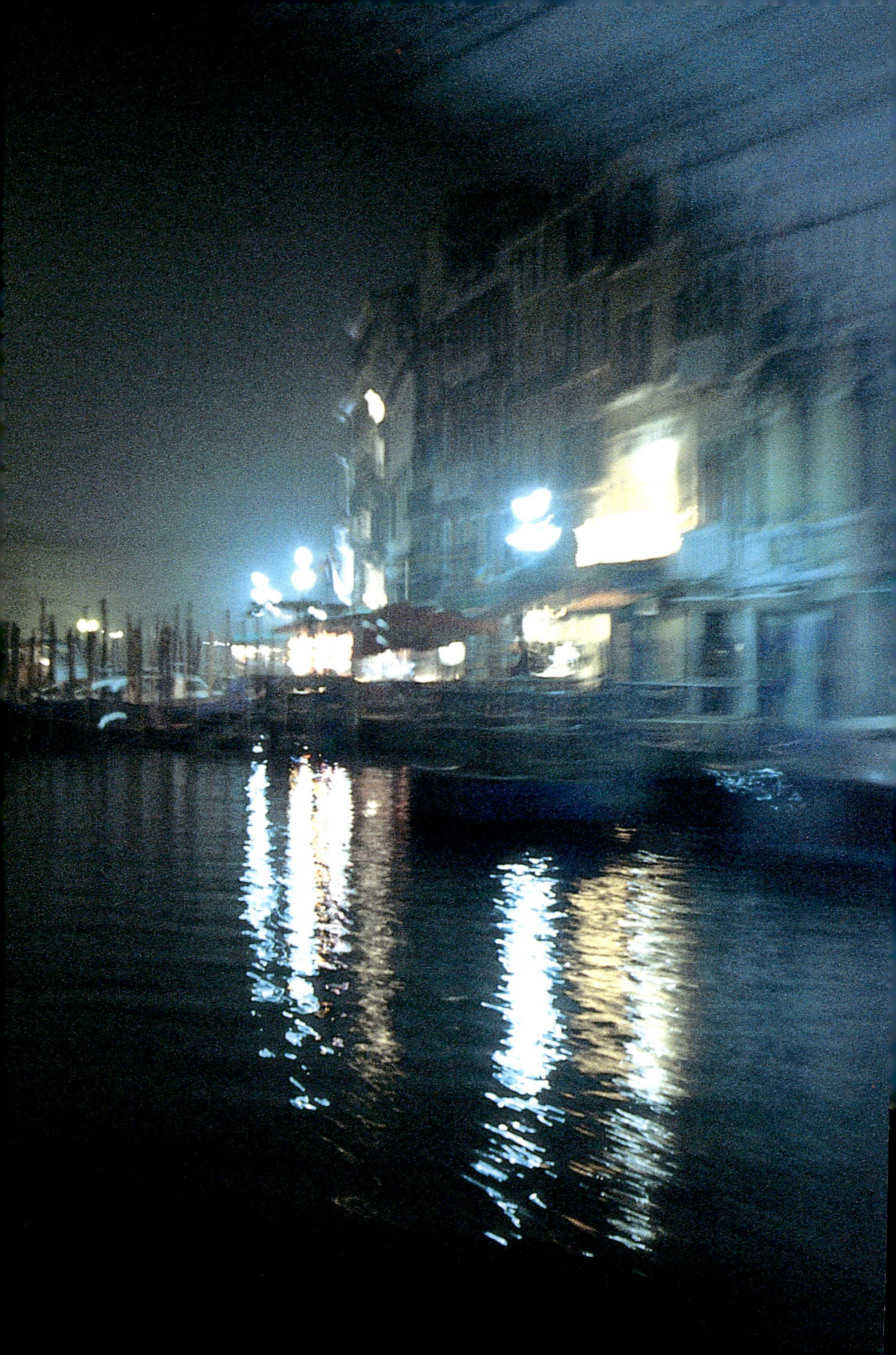

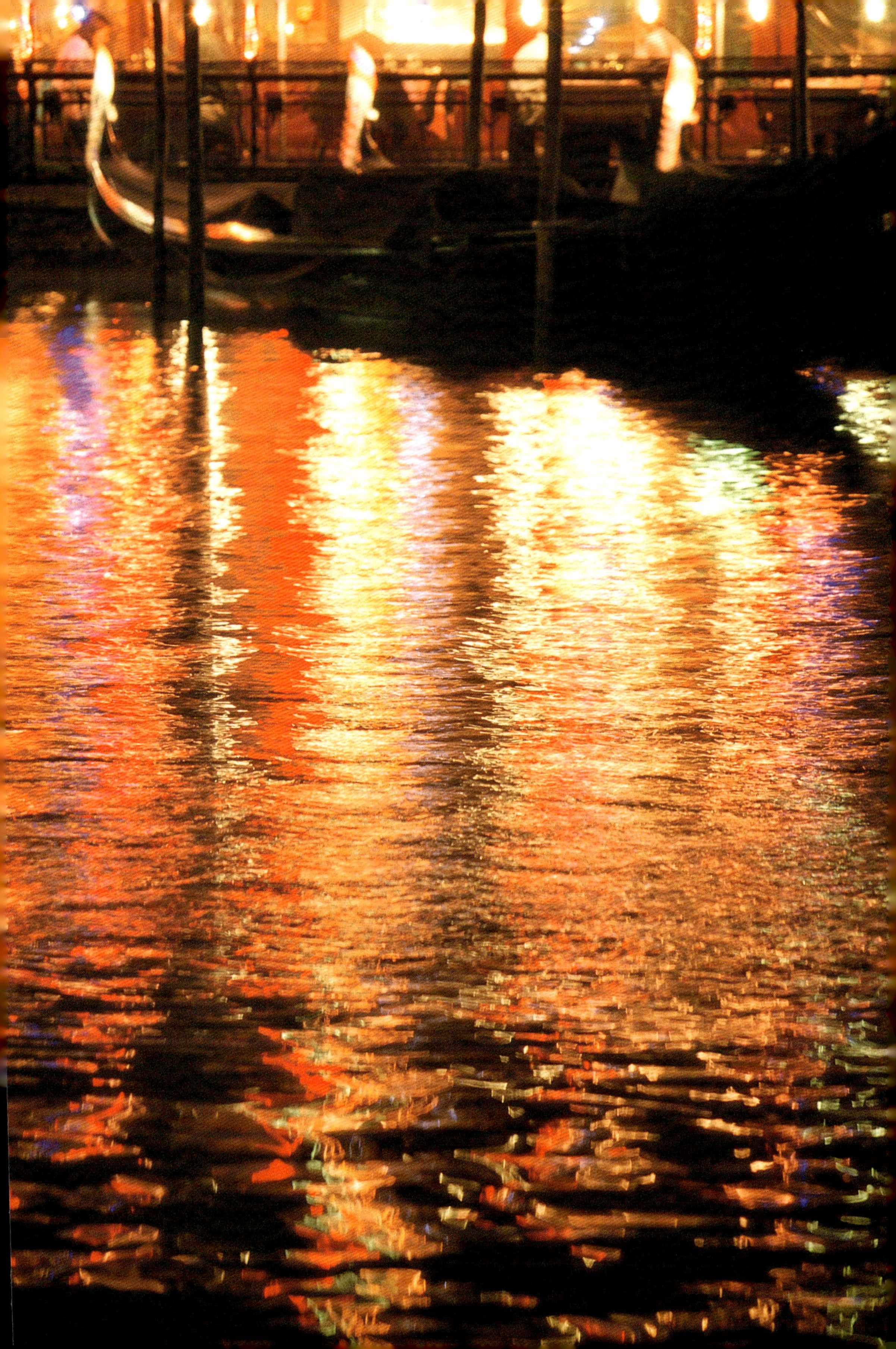

CAFFÈ

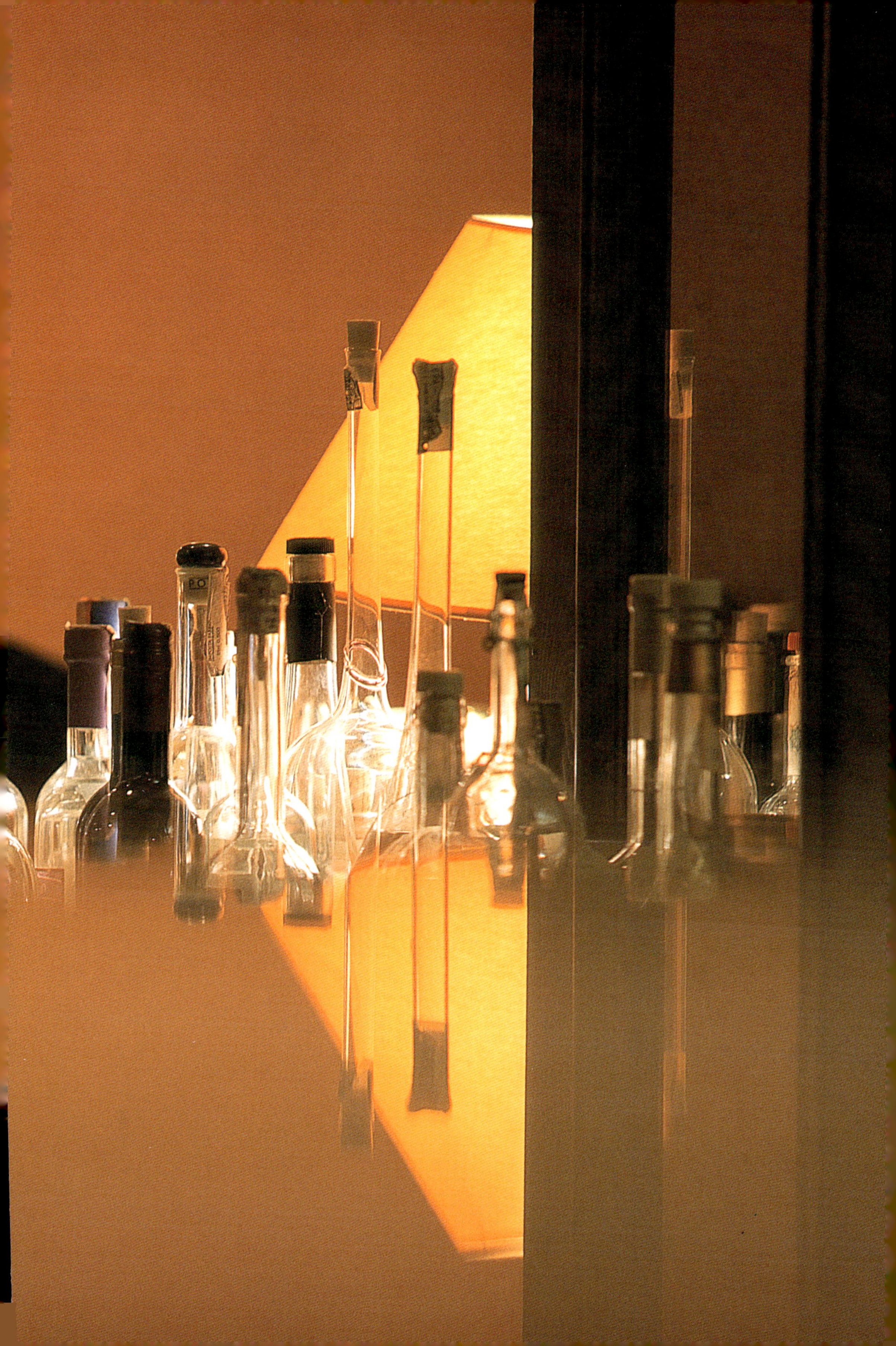

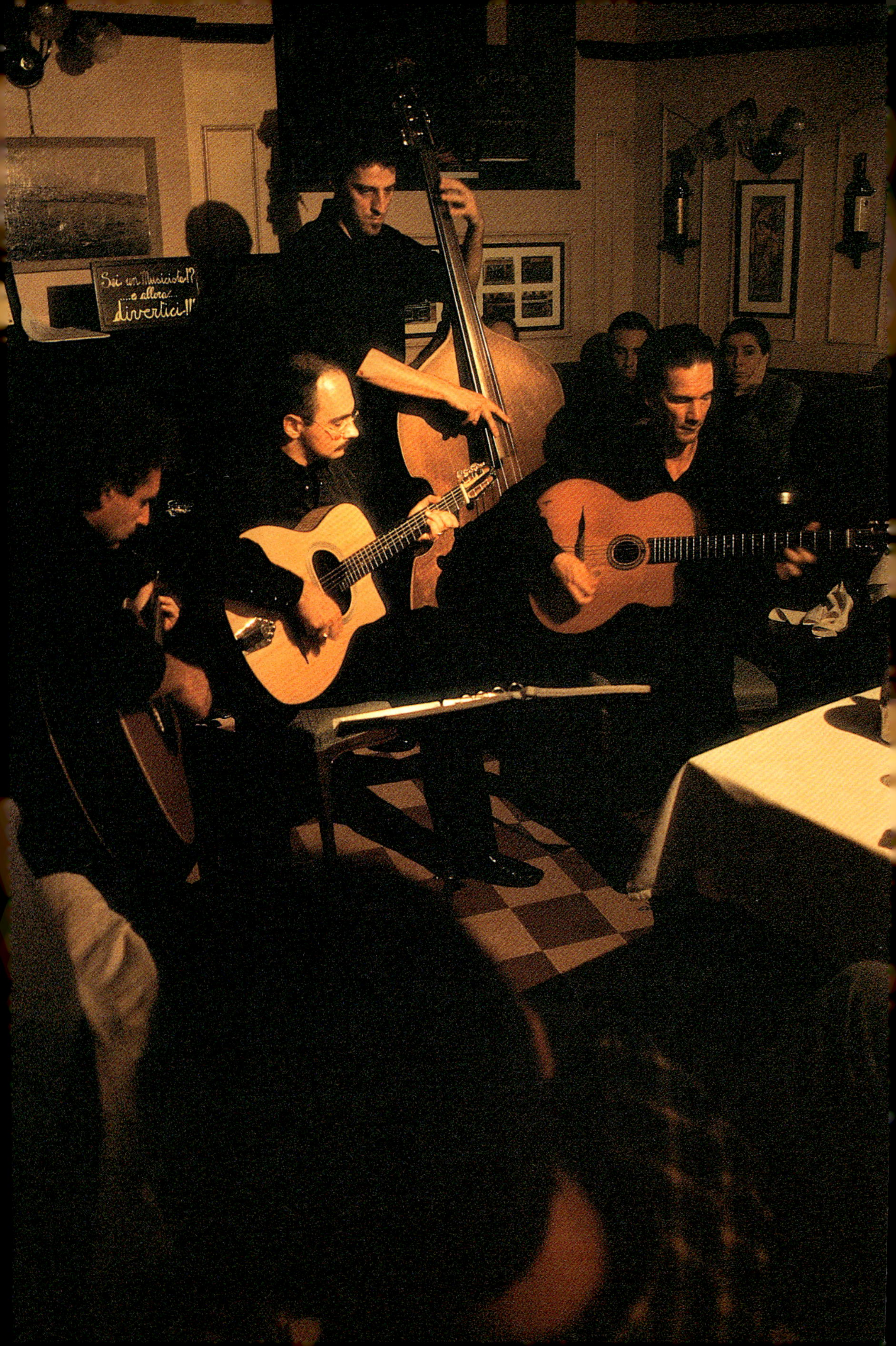
Sei un Musicista!?
....e allora....
divertici!!

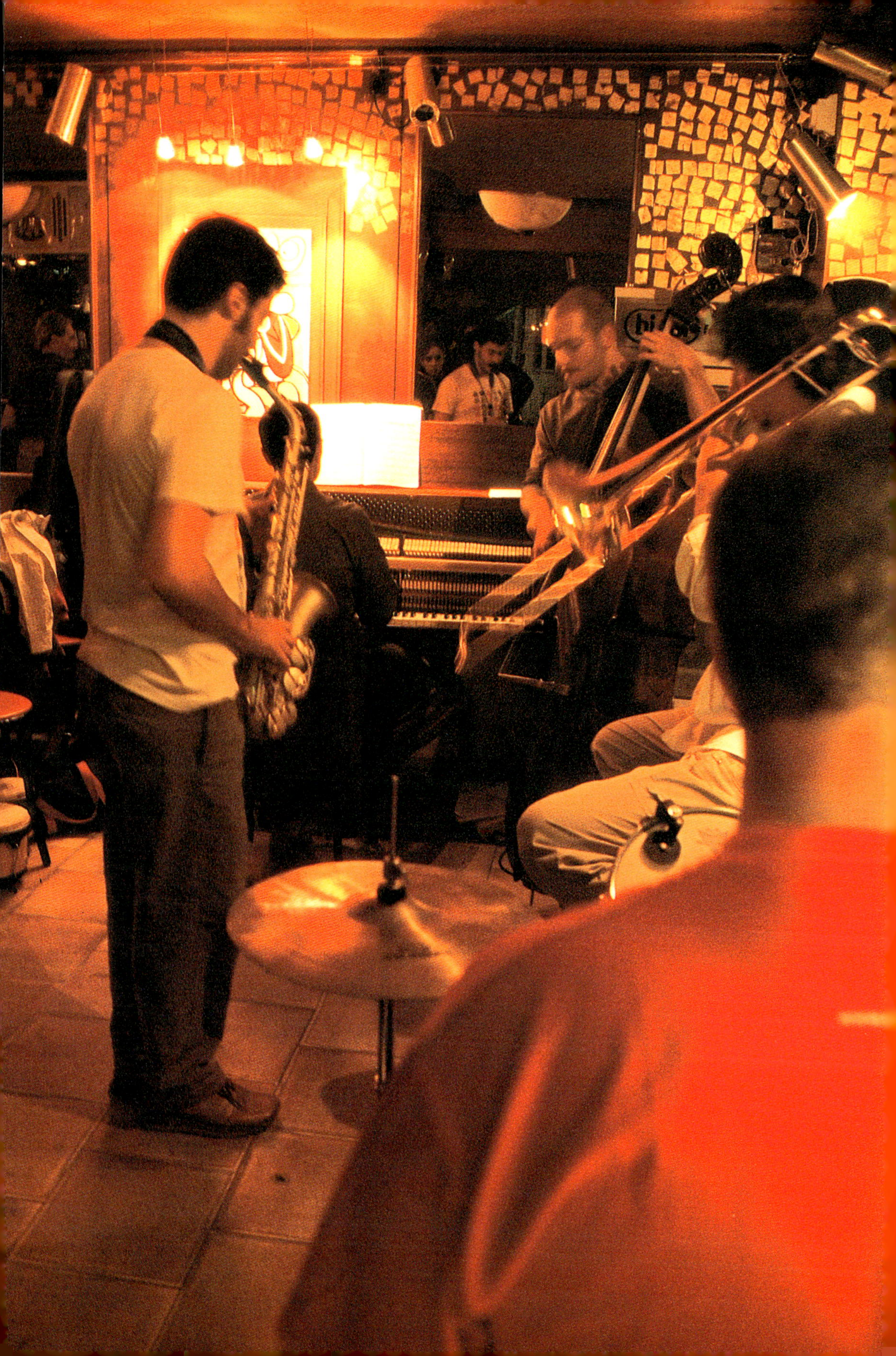

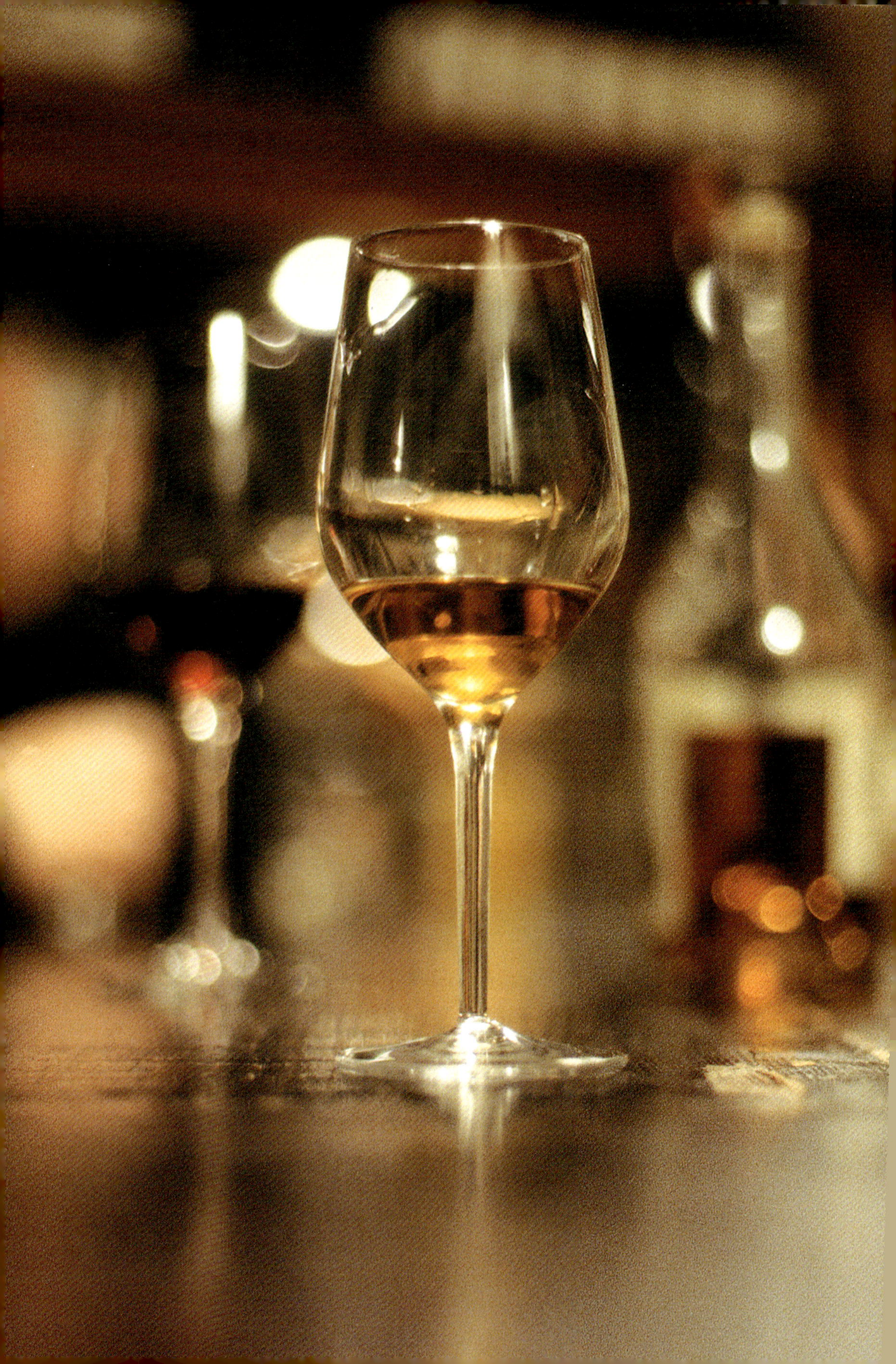

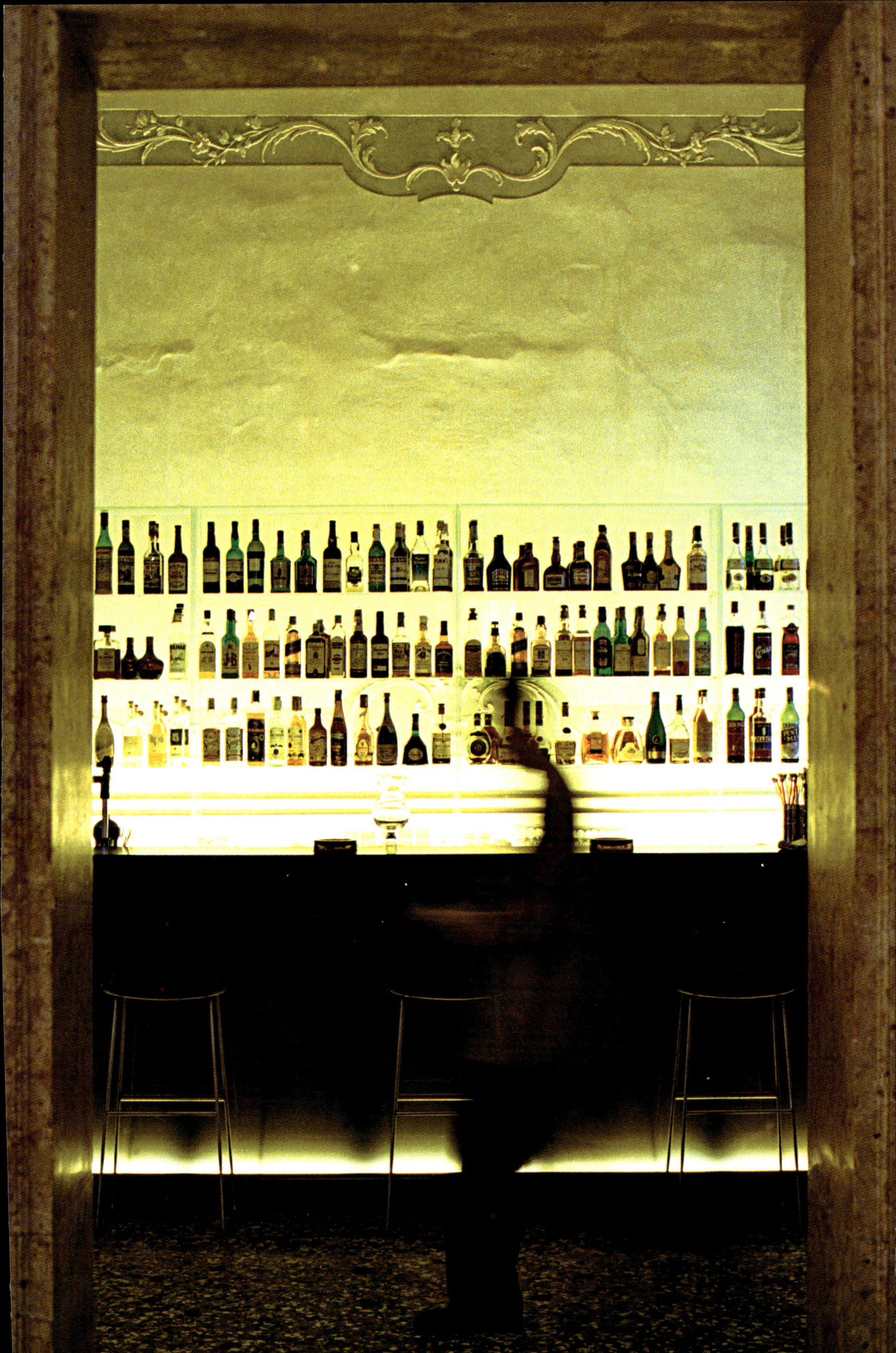

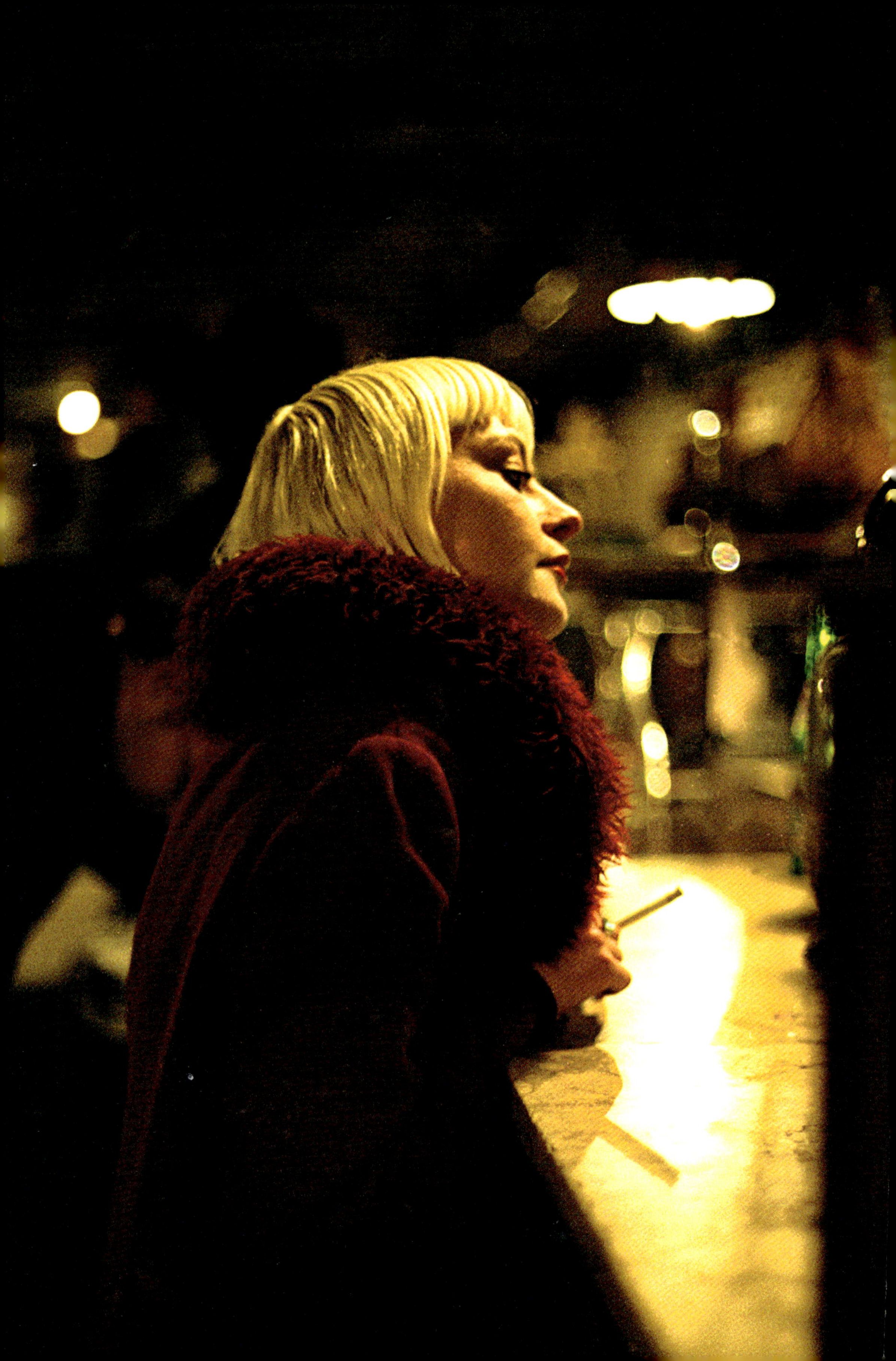

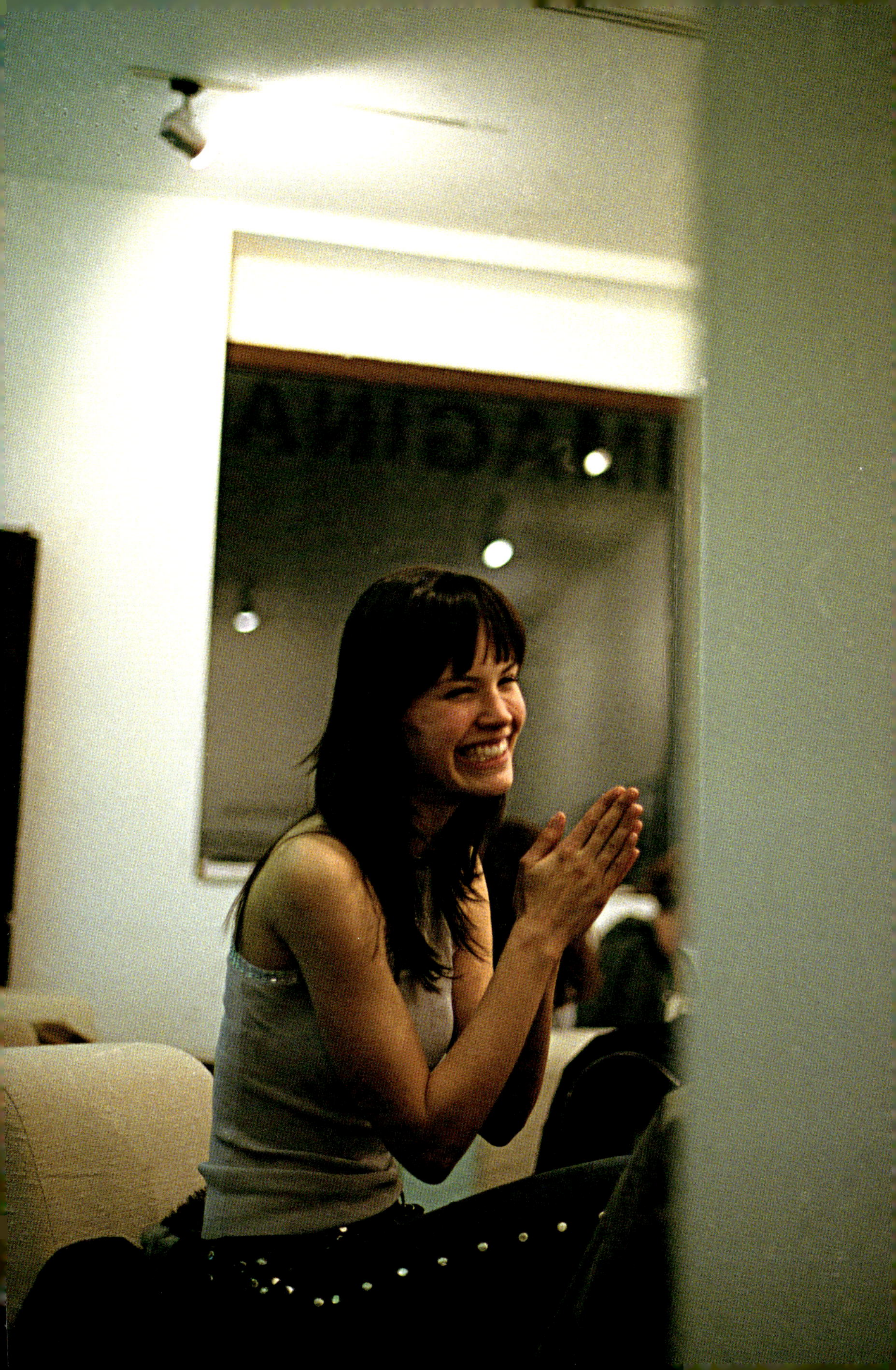

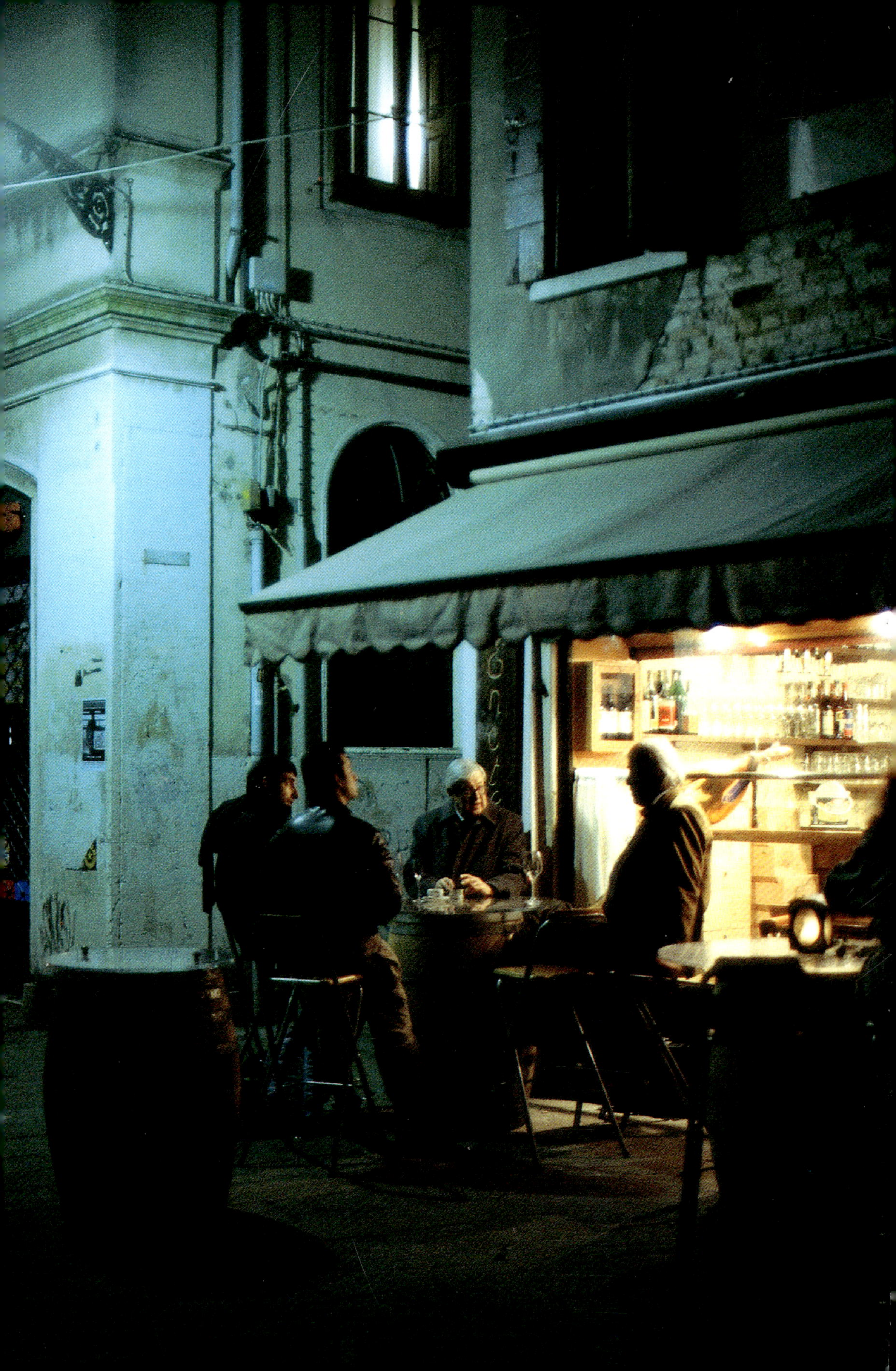

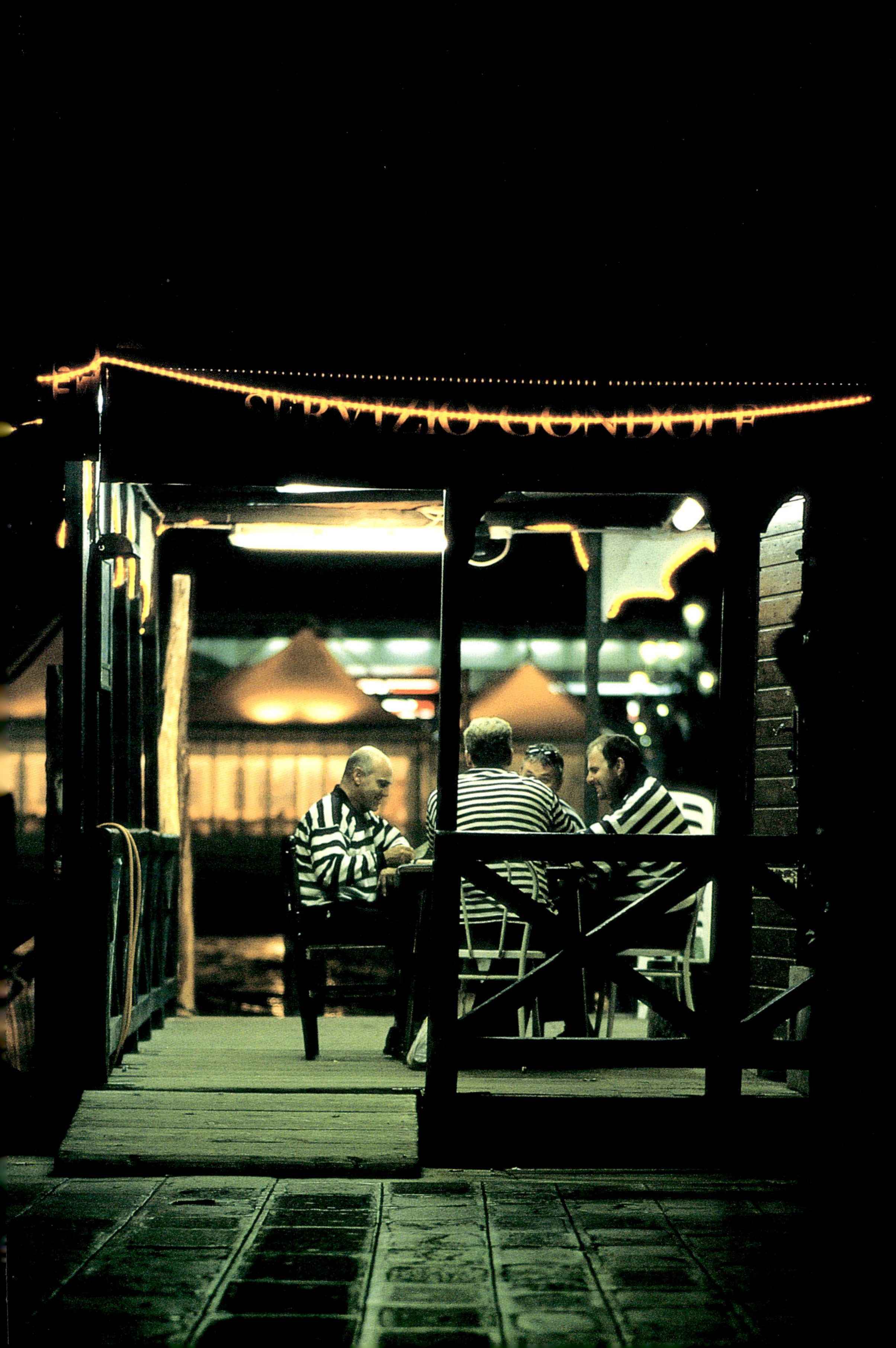
SERVIZIO GONDOLE

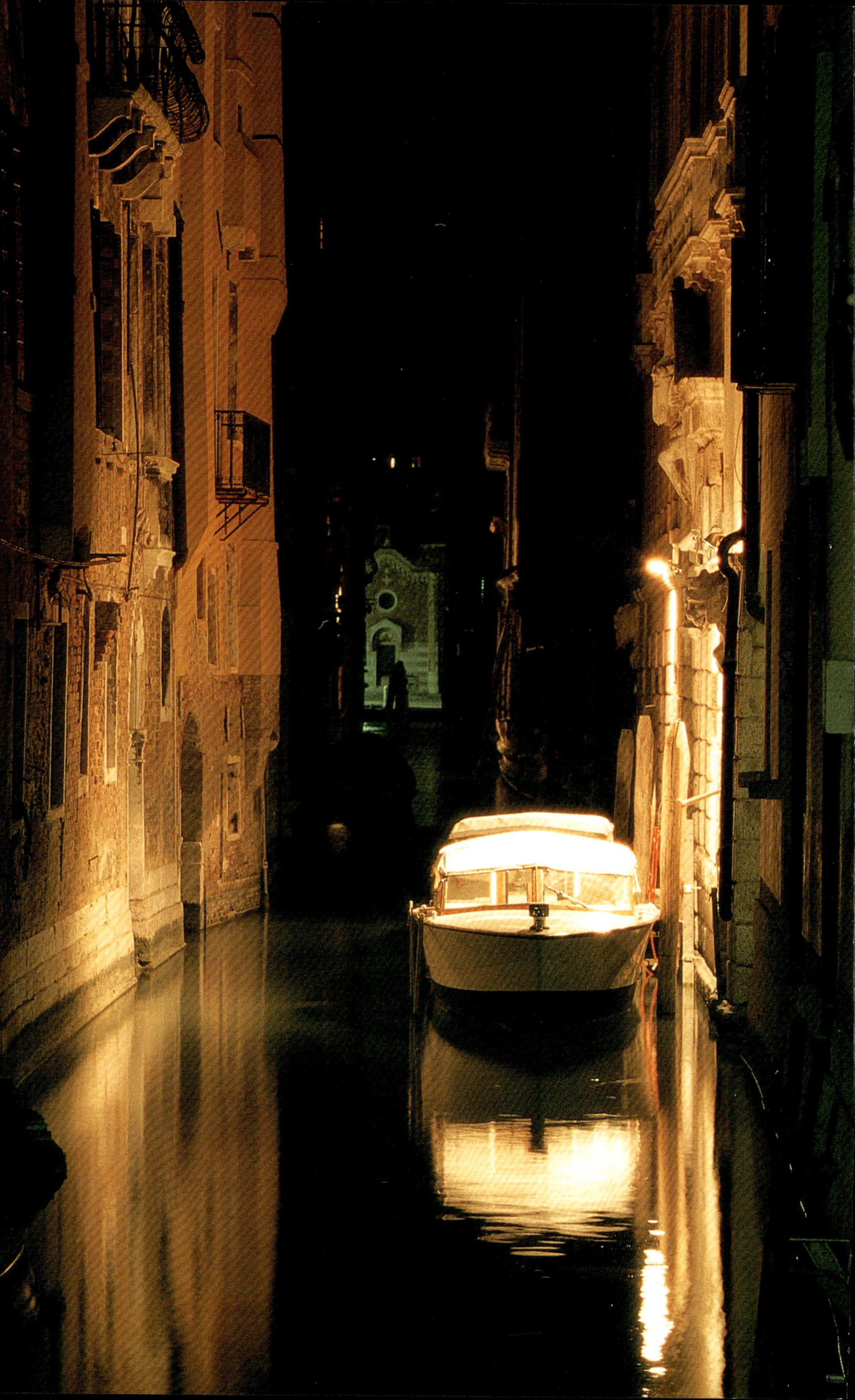

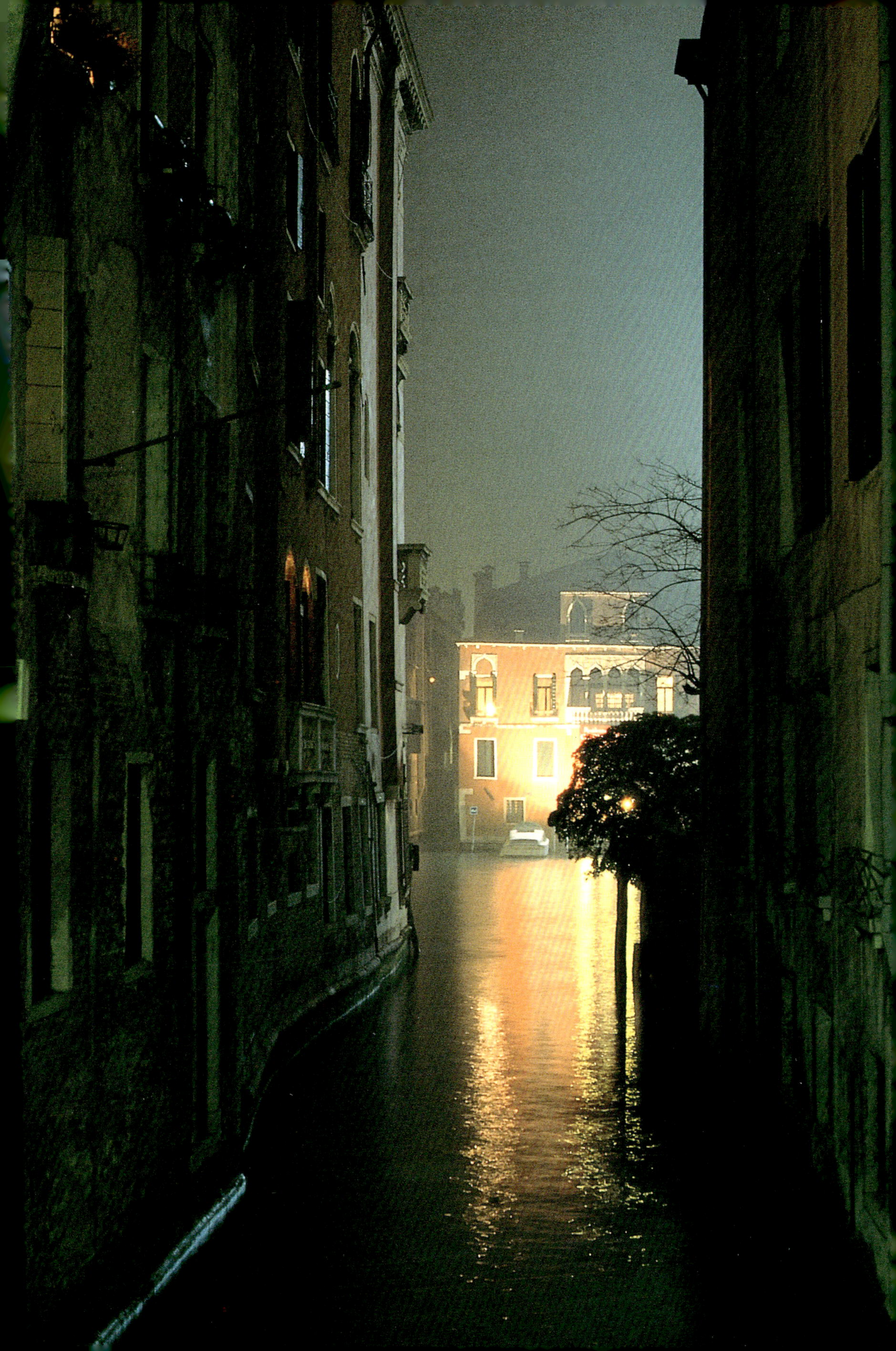

CHAPTER SEVEN

COMING BA

"Time flies when you rest your elbows on the ledges

CK

of Venetian windows," said Henry James.

For those of us who were seduced by Venice years ago and are now hopeless lovers with no possible chance of disentangling ourselves, the day of packing our bags, paying our bills and bidding fond and damp farewells is a black day indeed.

There are sunnier climes, there are more exotic locations, and almost anywhere has a better beach than Venice. But this mistress of a city with her winters of fogs and mists and her summers of sultry heat and perspiring crowds is not easy to put aside with the holiday snapshots as just another vacation. Venice must be revisited. In fact the only way to cope with the good-byes is to think ahead of the hello-agains.

Perhaps your first trip was in the spring, when the sun came in a soft lemon variety and skipped in and out of the clouds at whim. A springtime Venetian sky can look crisply ironed and barely used, whereas in the summer, when there is a heat haze on the Grand Canal, that same sky can look limp and out of sorts until it picks itself up sometime in the afternoon and becomes a colour straight off Canaletto's brush.

Venice in Autumn is one of the best times, when there is no humidity and yet it is still warm enough to sightsee in T-shirts and catch the sun as we lick an ice cream on a canal-side terrace. But winter, when the mists gather over the lagoon, is possibly the most stunning of all. The *campanile* of San Marco can look like an illusion in some lights and the domes of the Salute and Maggiore hover above the city, seemingly detached from everything around them. What is more, most of the other visitors have trundled off home, leaving favourite restaurants and the *calli* around San Marco and Rialto blessedly free.

So, where to go and what to do the second time around? Those who have discovered the pleasures of Venetian cuisine may well want to learn how to concoct some of those delicious recipes themselves; and there can't be a better place to do so than in the kitchens of the Hotel Cipriani.

COURSES IN VENICE

Dottore Natale Rusconi, a *doge* among hoteliers, introduced cooking schools to Italy when he was manager of the Gritti Palace Hotel back in 1972, and the pots and pans have been bubbling ever since. The cuisine is mostly *"haute"* but not always. A morning demonstration may include a hands-on guide to making pizza or pasta, and, as you learn that the difference between the great pizza and the merely ordinary is about chemistry, you may consider that in this elegant hotel, with the lagoon lapping gently at the walls outside, there can be few more inspiring surroundings for self-improvement. Some courses are put together with the help of American food expert, Robert Wilk, whose books, *Roberto's Table*, have become Italian cooking classics. Naturally 'Roberto' will work side-by-side with experts in their field to add to the proceedings. So you could learn how to make the best *gelato* in the world with Chef Picolloto, whose *Gelato Cioccolato* is a taste sensation like no other. Or you could find yourself tutored by Fulvia Sesani, one of Italy's most celebrated chefs and another regular.

The first cookbook celebrating haute cuisine *was not French, but Italian – printed in Latin, Platina's* Health and the Art of Good Living *appeared in 1470.*

Courses at the Cipriani are, naturally, about the finer points of cooking, but they are also about eating. Consequently, there are not only welcoming cocktail parties, but feasts at the hotel, which are conducted like private dinner parties for a group of much loved friends. As there are rarely more than about 20 fellow cooks, many of them couples, real friendships develop. And, just to get an inkling about what life is really like behind the façades of the great *palazzi*, your cooking course could well include invitations to dinner parties in Venetian homes. One local count took his role as host so seriously that he not only did all the cooking himself, but ate, drank and danced with his guests with such enthusiasm he developed gout and had to spend the following weeks with his feet up, recuperating!

Other less energetic diversions can include olive-oil tastings, getting to know the Rialto markets, a wine excursion to one of the little-known villas in the Veneto countryside, grappa tastings in revered distilleries, or visits to the homes of some noble and charming families who all have at least one Tiepolo painting of their own, if not on the wall then possibly on the ceiling.

Another possibility is to combine the course and the trip in one glamorous package and investigate a culinary or cultural holiday. There are worse ways to visit Venice than under the guidance of an experienced and sophisticated host who gently points you in all the right directions. Robert Wilk has also branched out into this area and, as most of his customers have returned again and again, he must be doing something right.

Another gourmet who offers excellent 'foodie' tours is Bev Gruber, a celebrated professional chef and culinary tour guide. Bev organizes tours around *Carnevale*, which includes the balls, the parties and the costumes with some delicious cooking thrown in.

Then there are the boat trips. We are not talking of the best ever gondola trips here, or even rattling up and down the Grand Canal in the practical, although very noisy, *vaporetti*. These are essentials that must be experienced on a first trip to Venice. Instead, consider gliding around the lagoon for a few days aboard a beautiful old craft, restored to all her shining beauty, equipped with everything you could possibly want, including a five-star chef.

Eolo, Venice's only restaurant boat, was once a true *bragasso*, a traditional fishing boat whose design dates back to the days of the *Doges*. Now in the hands of Mauro Stoppa, one-time agronomist and full-time Venice romantic, Eola offers trips that could be for one day or as many as you like, gliding around the lagoon, stopping at this island or that, occasionally partaking from the menu of some highly recommended restaurant, but, more often than not, eating on board some of the best and most interesting cuisine to be found in the area. Mauro, who does everything from the heart, is an innovative chef and, occasionally helped by his sisters Lucia and Julia, he and his

Cole Porter once tried to launch a restaurant boat in Venice, sadly unsuccessfully, despite the addition of an onboard jazz band. Prime complainer was the legendary Diaghilev of the Ballet Russes, who was not only a party-pooper but, by today's standards, a racist. "The whole of Venice," he cried in 1926, "is up in arms against Cole Porter because of his jazz and his Negroes... They are teaching the Charleston on the Lido Beach! It's dreadful!"

beautiful boat provide an experience unique to Venice. What makes his food, particularly his fish, so good is that he buys direct from the fishermen of the lagoon. "Fish of this quality," he says, "even the best restaurants cannot get. There just isn't enough caught every day. Sometimes when we're sailing out in the evening, the fisherman is coming back and sees our boat and he stops then and there to sell us something." But spending two or three days drifting about the lagoon would take too large a bite out of a first Venice itinerary, which is what makes planning for your return to *La Serenissima* so exciting.

Tourists in Venice may happily speak English and expect that the locals will not only understand them but speak excellent English right back. But once we start coming back to *La Serenissima*, immersing ourselves in the atmosphere and playing at being Venetian, not speaking Italian becomes simply unacceptable. It is not a matter of simple communication; a language is a remarkably accurate guide to a culture and a people. Knowledge has always been power, and knowing Italian, getting to grips with its grammar, with its impatient short-cuts, the way it rolls off the tongue like lyrics of an opera, opens a whole new level understanding, not only of Italy and the Italians but of Venice and the Venetians. Of course the people are volatile, vibrant, expressive – listen to their language!

Useful websites for learning Italian in Venice include: www.istitutovenezia.com, www.it-schools.com and www.eurolinga.com/italian

Exciting as all this is, actual learning is still required, but how much more inspiring to take on an Italian course in Venice. There are plenty of opportunities, most particularly from Istituto Venezia in Dorsoduro near the Accademia Bridge to Centro Studi Era 2000 which is in nearby Mestre. Each offers both Italian culture and language courses with tuition either individually or in groups. There are also possibilities of staying in your tutor's home, learning not only language and culture but life-style first hand.

A painting course is another Venice natural. Even those of us who have never picked up a paint-brush can't help wishing we had the talent and the knowledge to translate that special, secret view into a watercolour or an oil painting. There are excellent painting courses organized in Venice by La Scuola Internazionle di Grafica which offers lessons not only in drawing and painting, but also in printing, lithography, photography and graphics. Either you can get in touch with the school direct or perhaps go through a programme put together by Boston University which is highly recommended. Many of the courses also include language lessons, trips to relevant museums and *scuole*, and lectures on Venetian art history. There is also a series of courses organized by Pratt Education. Expertise and experience are not vital – the talent required is between you and your Maker, but the knowledge can be learned with a good teacher and a bit of enthusiasm. The Hotel Cipriani also organizes painting courses every year, so it is worth checking. As the teachers are always renowned artists, even the most novice painter has the chance of turning out an original worth taking home – with or without a little help!

But the best and most rewarding way to come back to Venice again and again is to put the guidebook away, including even this one, and make like a local. Take an apartment. Views on Venice, set up and run by youthful Venetian entrepreneur, Filippo Gaggia, has some wonderful properties, many in converted *palazzi*, and there are other companies offering the same facility which are included in the listings at the back of this book. Hurrying to the Rialto market around 8am, when all the freshest produce is still wet with early morning dew (when they're carrots) or even still trying to scurry off the slab (when they're spider crabs), is the only time the locals consider shopping. Preparing a meal in your own little Venetian hideaway, even doing the washing up afterwards, has a touch of charm when the Grand Canal is just outside. Striding firmly past the designer stores, except during the sales, and concentrating on small, out of the way antique shops where you might still pick up a charming little dresser or an embroidered footstool can fill an entire day. Dropping into Ceramiche di Bassano, San Angelo for a perfect tureen crowned with ceramic lemons, reminiscent of Venice without being too obvious; crossing the Bridge, saluting the man who paints all his views of Venice with his back firmly to the Grand Canal, and browsing in Cornici Trevisanello for the perfect frame for one of your better watercolours. Experiences like these are unique and make us all feel as if we are locals – true Venetians

Orient-Express run botanical and flower painting masterclasses at the Hotel Cipriani. For more information, contact the hotel directly or email: christine.martyn@orient-express.com

Websites for painting courses include: www.scuolagrafica.it, www.bu.edu/abroad/cities/venice *and* www.pratt.edu/abroad/venice/courses

For those who long for their own unique mementos of Venice, commissioning an artisanal masterpiece is an essential activity. To this end, getting to know American Leslie Genninger of Genninger Studio is rewarding. Her selection of Murano glass is amongst the best in the city, and commissioning something individual and special from Leslie or one of her fellow artists in glass is an entirely satisfying and joyful experience.

A PERSONAL MASTERPIECE

Another imaginative jeweller is Swedish Katarina Rothfjell, whose home-based company, Pianeta Perla, is a truly 'insider' discovery. Katarina's Nordic 'cool' mixed with Venetian passion makes for unique, innovative jewellery which can be made to order using contemporary or antique beads. Prices are affordable.

Ignoring the big showrooms along Fondamenta Vetrai at Murano, another way to spend a productive time in Venice is to seek out a glass factory where you can order your own chandelier and watch it come together. Fornasier Luigi is a good place to start. The gorgeous silken Fortuny lamps you first saw at the Cipriani or in the windows of Venetia Studium can also be found in glass. The only shop licensed to copy the originals is Bottega d'Angolo in Calle Fiubera behind San Marco.

The artisans of Venice are not few and far between, nor are they ancient, grizzled old men whose skills will die with them. Venice, as we have noted throughout this book, is giving youth a chance. Two of the finest young boat-builders operating in one of the old shipyards outside the city are Marco Ceccato and Denis Fornasiero, both thirtyish, both highly skilled and talented enough to work for themselves, creating boats of the quality and finish that Venice was famous for when she ruled the Adriatic. Today, young entrepreneur Giovanni Giol is attempting to recreate that heritage of boat-building into a new and thriving business, GiolMarine. His boats, built by hand by Marco and Denis, and fitted with all the modern machinery and technical efficiency of the 21st century, are elegant, all-purpose powerboats, not for Venice itself, where the motorboat is rattling the city's foundations, but for the south of France, for the costas, for Florida, Palm Beach and the Bay of Salerno. To come to Venice, home of the greatest boat-builders in the world, expressly to find the boat of your dreams must come close to topping the ultimate wish list.

If a boat of your own is not your style, the creative juices in the Giol family do not begin and end with Giovanni. The glamorous sandals and evening bags designed by his French wife, Servane, are already a Venice sensation, available in the Cipriani boutique and in Vogini, near Harry's Bar. But how Venetian to commission a set for yourself. These young designers have exciting ideas, but they are also immersed in the history and tradition of Venice and manage to combine the two with a personal touch that makes a commissioned piece utterly unique.

When Patrizia Fiorenza creates a piece of *haute couture* for a client from her tiny shop tucked away in a corner of Campo San Lucca, she takes every detail into consideration, not just size, colouring and occasion, but mood, style and the changing nature of the waistline. Customers have been known to drop into Godi Fiorenza for a preliminary discussion and fitting and then flit off around the rest of Italy only to come back a few weeks later for the finished article. This is not tourists' stuff, it is the style of a sophisticated traveller who understands that behind the fairy-tale of Venice is a city buzzing with life, ideas and new discoveries.

Might you have time to sit for a portrait? Why not? Especially when the studio is that of Geoffrey Humphries whose portraits of celebrated visitors could fill several galleries on their own. Mr Humphries, an English artist, came to Venice in 1966, "washed up," he says, "by the floods." He came for six months and decided that he couldn't afford to go back to London. "Venice, in those days, was a poor man's Paris", filled with art and artists but affordable. His studio, near Harry's Dolci, on the opposite end of Guidecca Island from the Cipriani, is drenched with natural light and filled with comfortable places to sit and watch and gossip the hours away. It also acts like a magnet to the cognoscenti of Venice, who rave as much about his legendary parties as his pictures. Geoffrey will always welcome browsing customers, but should the idea of the "painted in Venice by Geoffrey Humphries" label appeal, his order-book gets crammed very quickly. Planning that new and exciting aspect of your return to Venice is vital.

It is on a return trip that you can take time to explore the lagoon properly. Murano and the lace island of Burano may be the most popular day trips, but there are so many other islands to discover, starting with the most far-flung, Torcello. All the ghosts of Venice-past haunt this island, where the first settlement was founded in the fifth century. Torcello's supremecy did not last long. Too many mosquitos for one thing – gone now, but their memory lingers on. Even the Bishop of Torcello decamped to the island of Murano, leaving behind two fine churches. Yet those who choose to come here today and spend a few days fall in love with what Jan Morris calls the island's "exquisite melancholia".

THE LAGOON

There is only one place to stay, Locanda Cipriani, which is, in itself, something of a legend. A charming house, with just six rooms to let, simply but elegantly furnished with no television, no distractions and only the sunset to watch in the evening. And yet everyone, from Ernest Hemingway to Kim Novak to H.M. Queen Elizabeth II to Bette Davis has fallen in love with it. The restaurant is supreme, especially in the warmer months. In fact it is tempting to sit all afternoon under the pergola and allow the flower petals to drift into your salad. But it would be a mistake to come to Torcello and not visit the cathedral of Santa Maria Assunta, the oldest church on the lagoon, dating back to AD638. Do have lunch first, because the mosaic Madonna in the church, still vivid, still glowing, has the saddest eyes in Christendom.

There are 34 islands in the lagoon, some totally deserted, others with small, close-knit communities. They are considered to be the countryside for Venetians, who come for picnics, to go fishing (for shrimp at low tide) and to enjoy the sweet wildness of the islands that was somehow left behind in the building of the great republic. When Katherine Hepburn and Rossano Brazzi fell in love in the definitive "Venice" film *Summer Madness* they came out to these islands, lay in the long grass and felt a million miles away from the hustle and bustle of Rialto.

As for newly proficient artists and photographers, fresh from their courses, these islands of the lagoon reveal a whole other side to the Venice experience. The wetlands have a fresh, untamed feel to them that contrasts dramatically with the *trompe l'oeil* city that exists across the water.

'It is reasonably easy to plan a trip. *Vaporetti* make long, laborious journeys, stopping at the better-known islands. Or the daring can hire a boat for the day and have an adventure on Sant' Erasmo, perhaps, where the best and freshest of Venice's salads and vegetables come from; San Lazzaro degli Armeni, a former leper colony and now a world centre of Armenian culture with a museum containing priceless manuscripts; or San Francesco del Deserto, a world away from the crowds and the commerce of the Piazza San Marco.

While people-watching in Venice is fascinating, people-spotting is the game to play while visiting the islands of the lagoon. There are 4000 cypresses on the aptly named San Francesco del Deserto and just eight people, all monks. In the 14th century Torcello, the mother island of Venice, could boast over 20,000 inhabitants. Today only 20 people live there.

Such explorations will, of course, only make a Venice obsessive more addicted, and eventually the black day will come around and there you are, saying good-bye again. If by the remotest chance you are not already determining to come back, let me share my most evocative image of Venice...

Should you take a water taxi towards the airport on a misty morning when all the buildings are blurred and fading in the half-light, look back when San Giorgio Maggiore seems far behind you. There is a moment when the two *campanili* of San Marco and San Giorgio seem to be placed one behind the other, with San Marco providing a shadow, an *ombra*, if you like of San Giorgio. Perhaps it works even better in the sunshine, when the sky is Canaletto-blue and the buildings of Venice are etched clearly on the skyline. I don't know: I have only seen the hazy version, and for me it is the vision of Venice that I have taken to my heart.

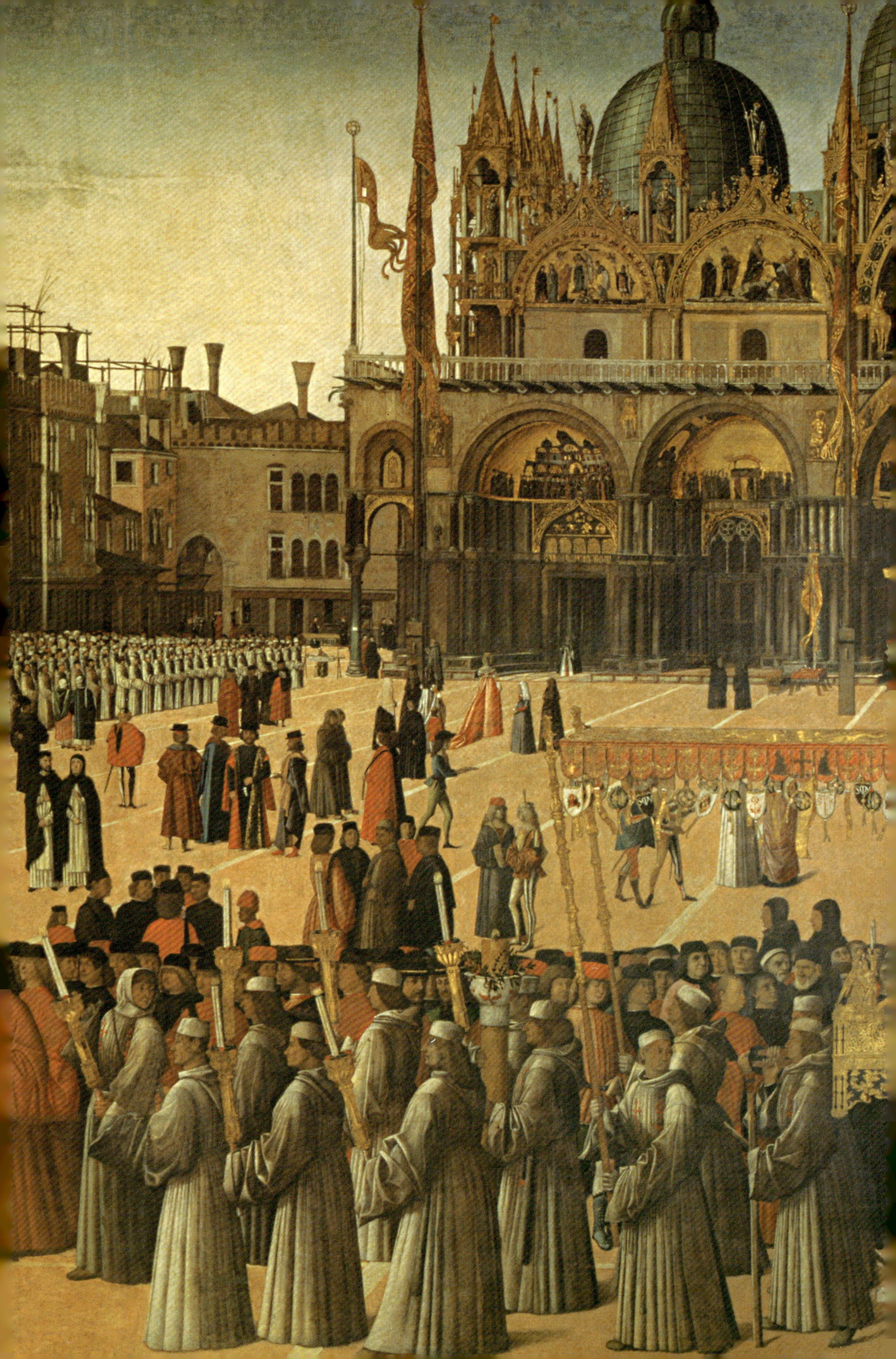

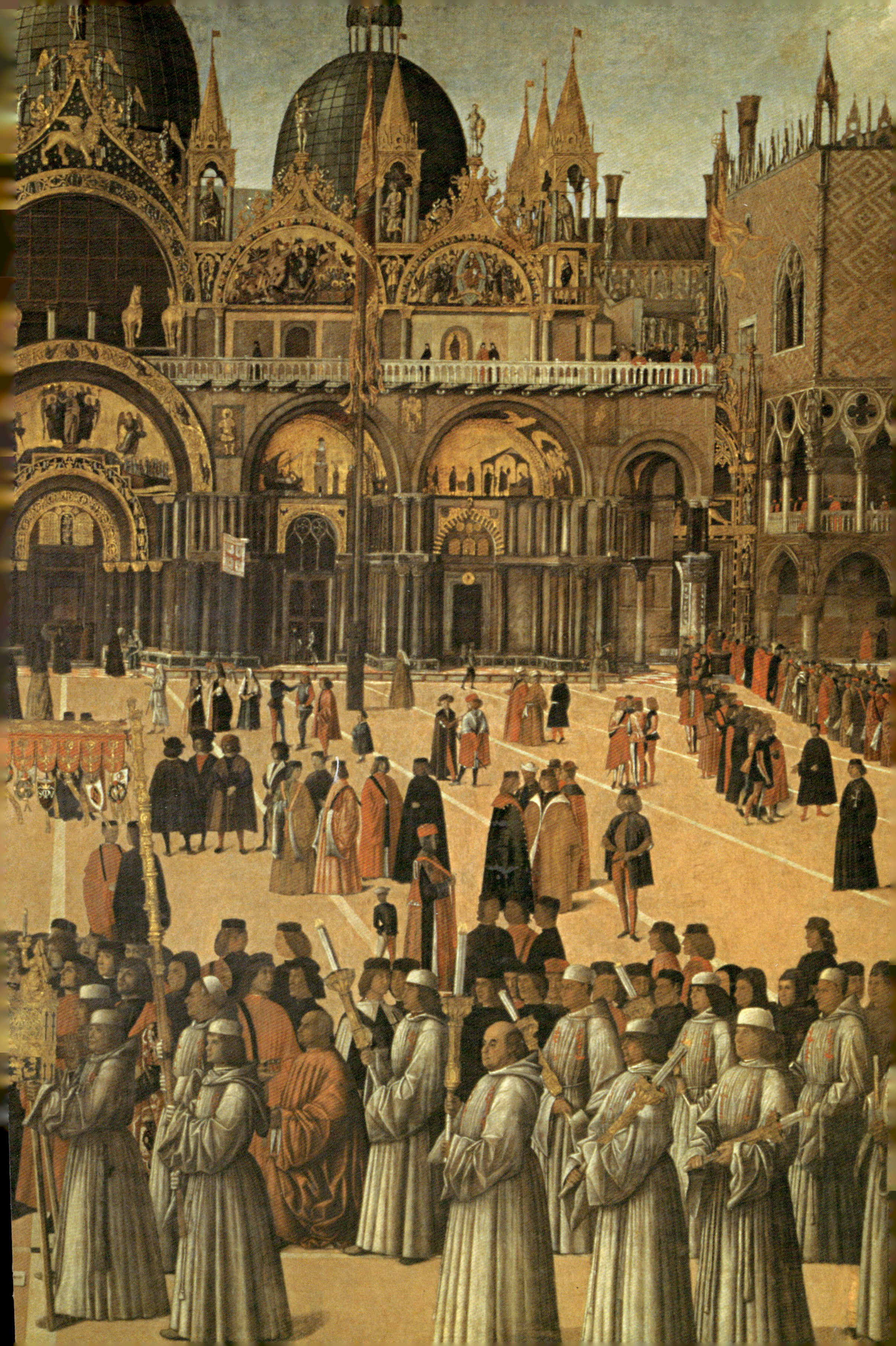

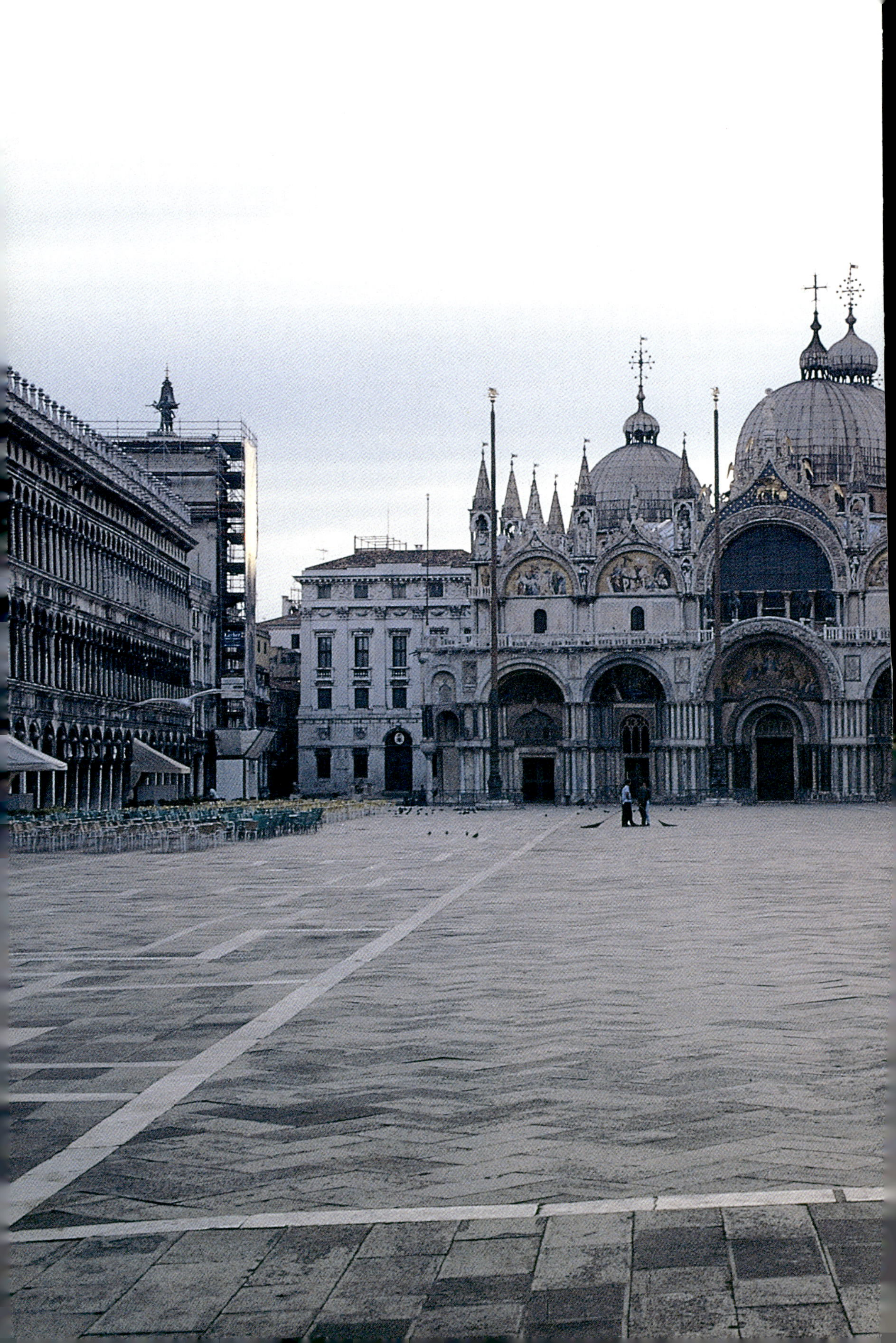

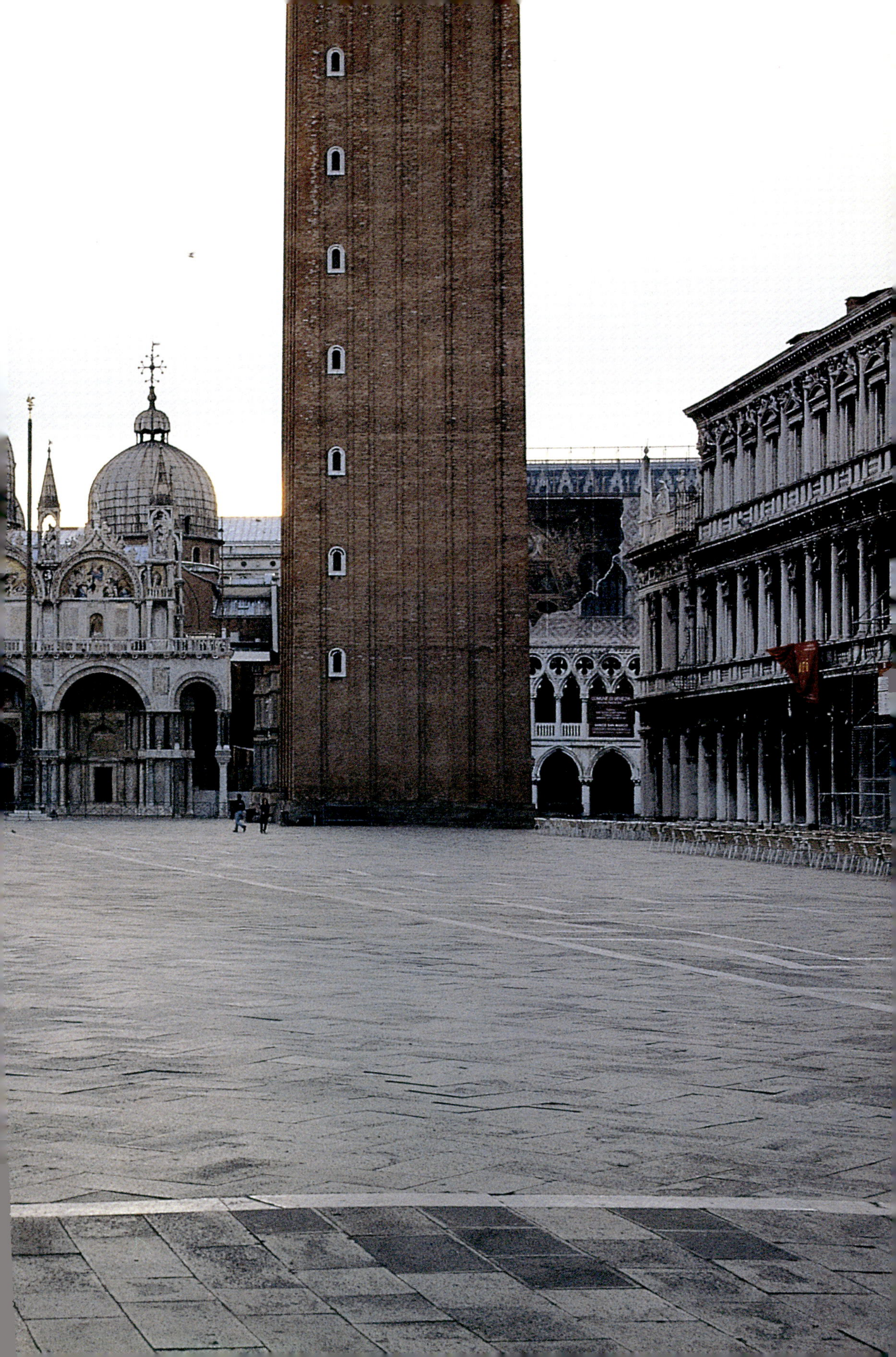

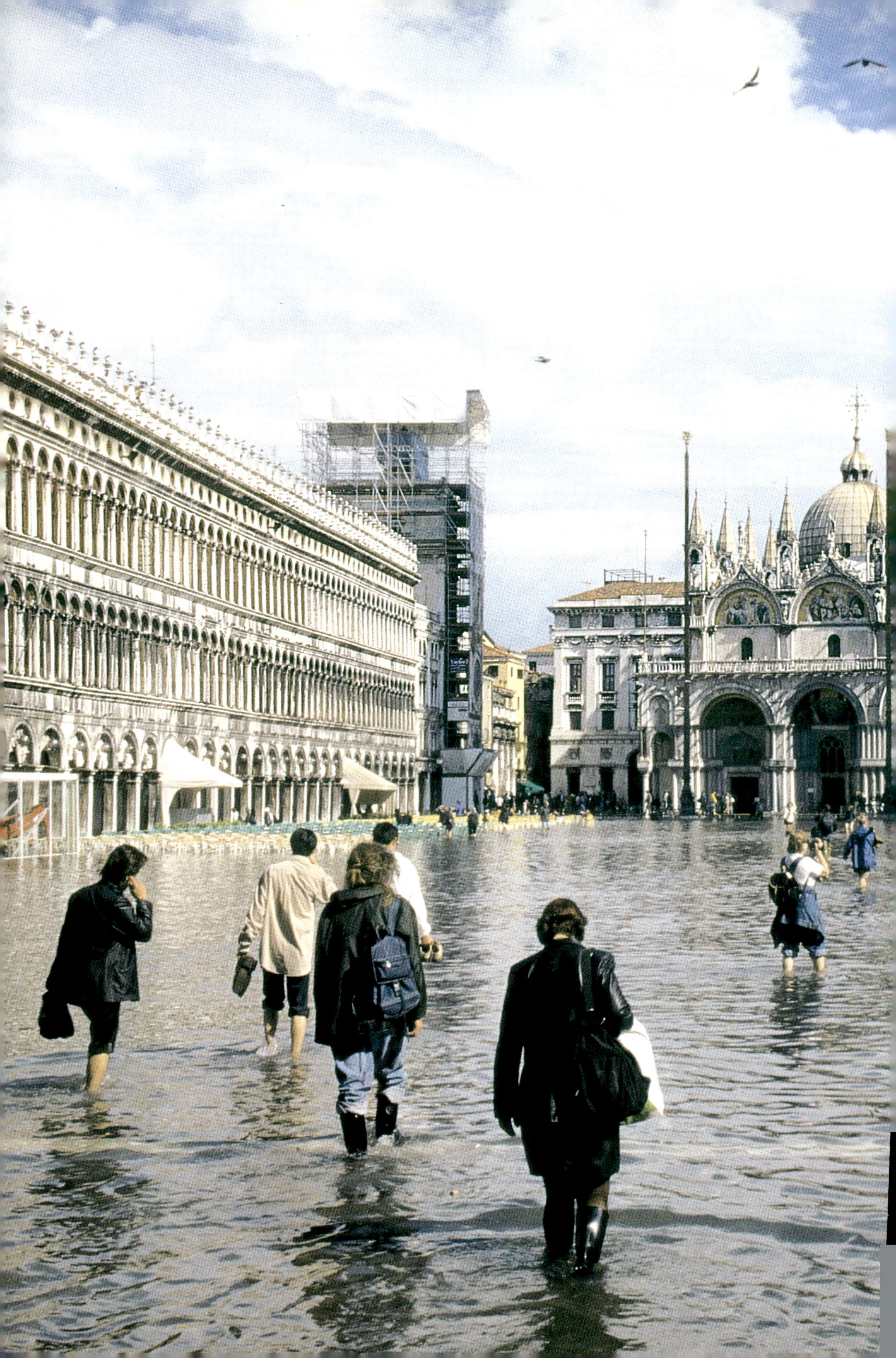

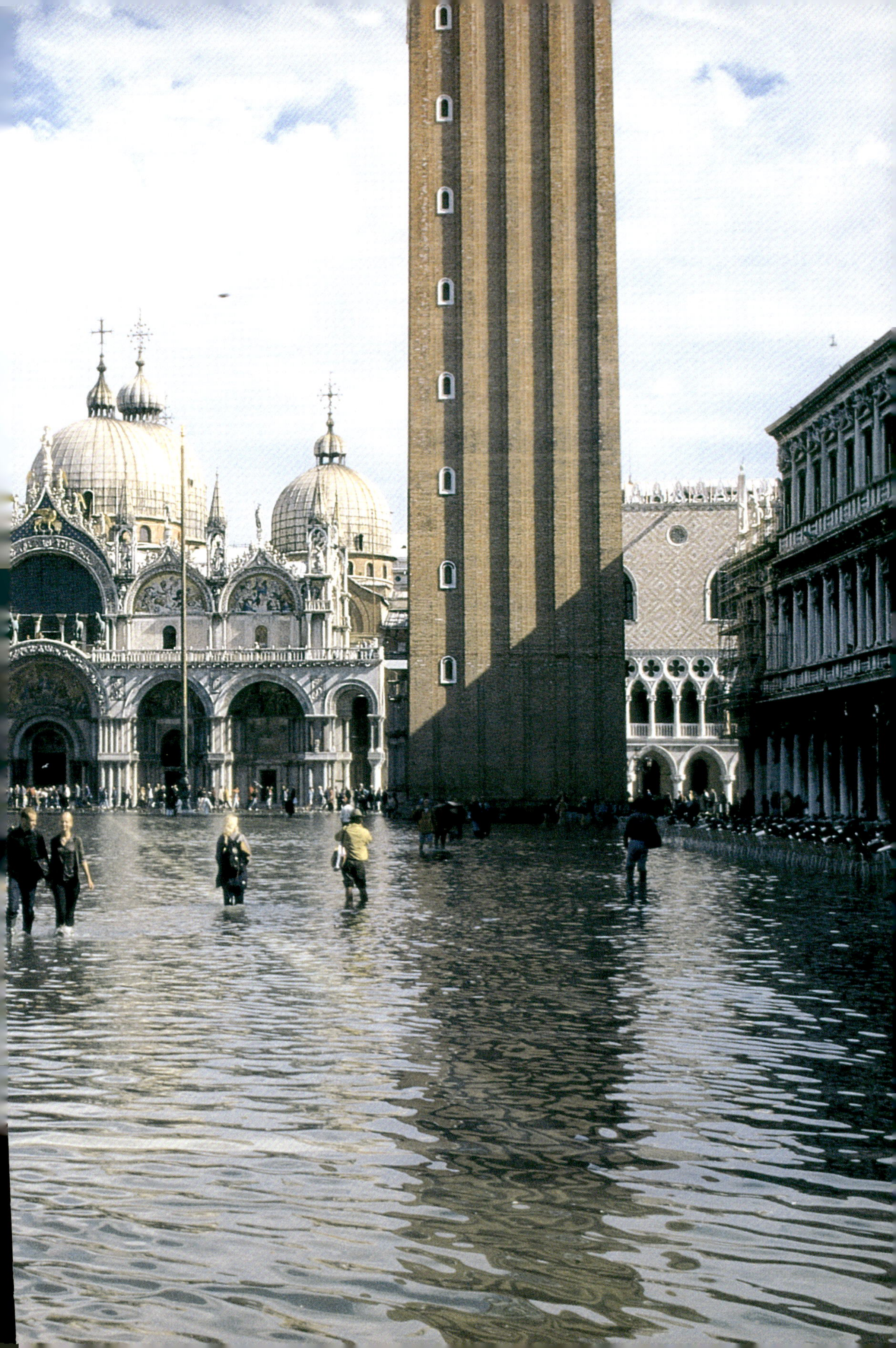

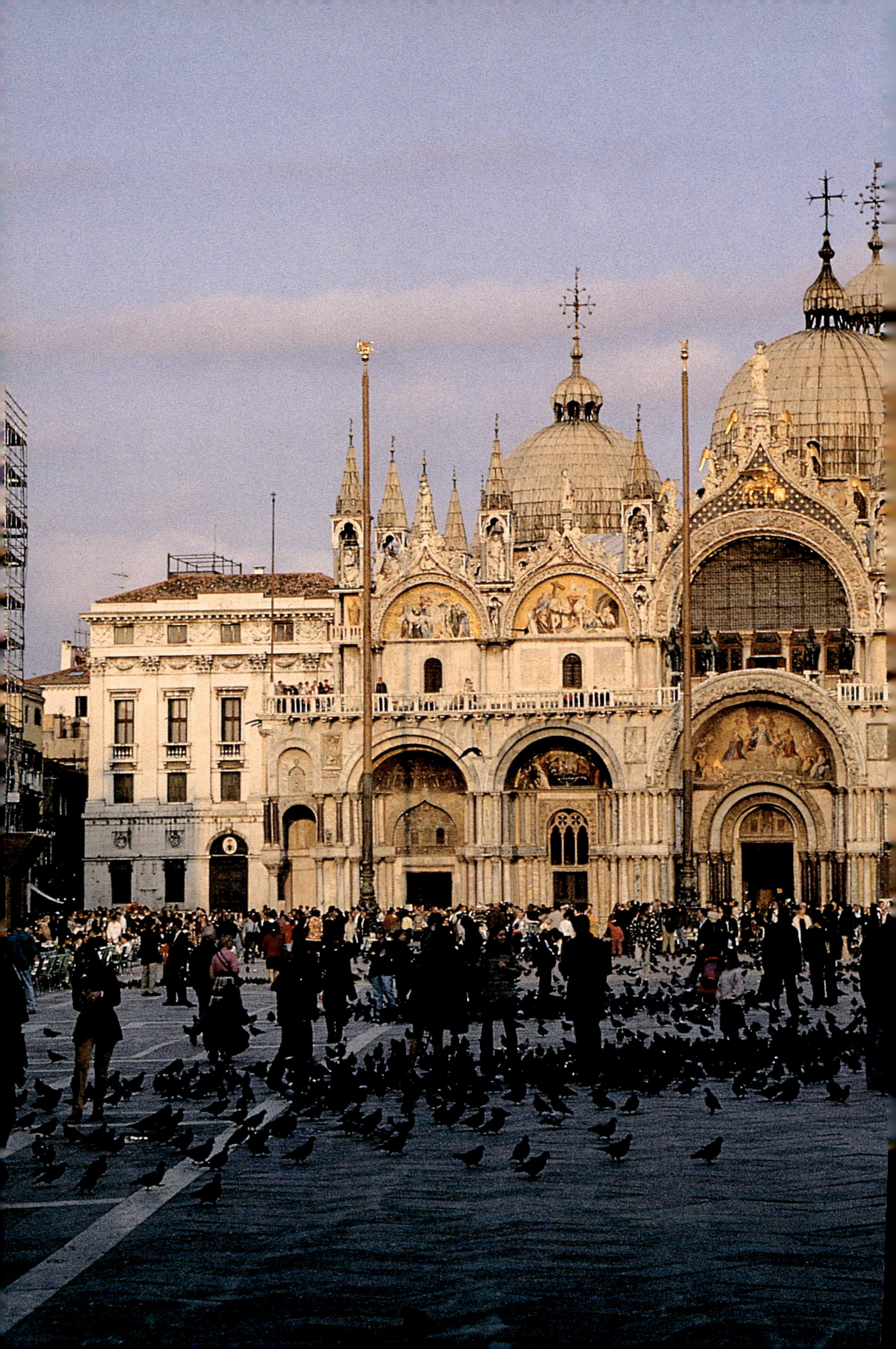

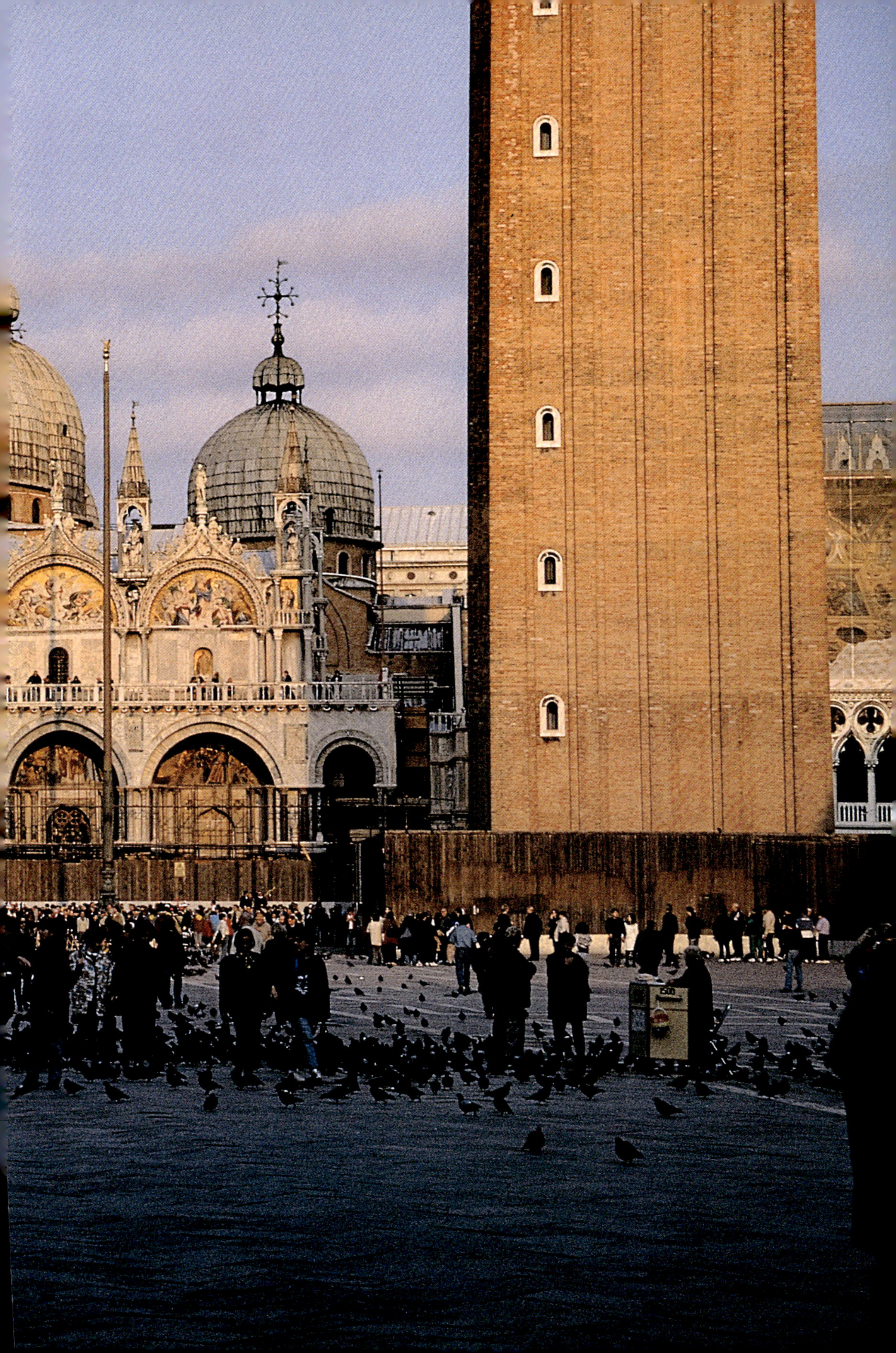

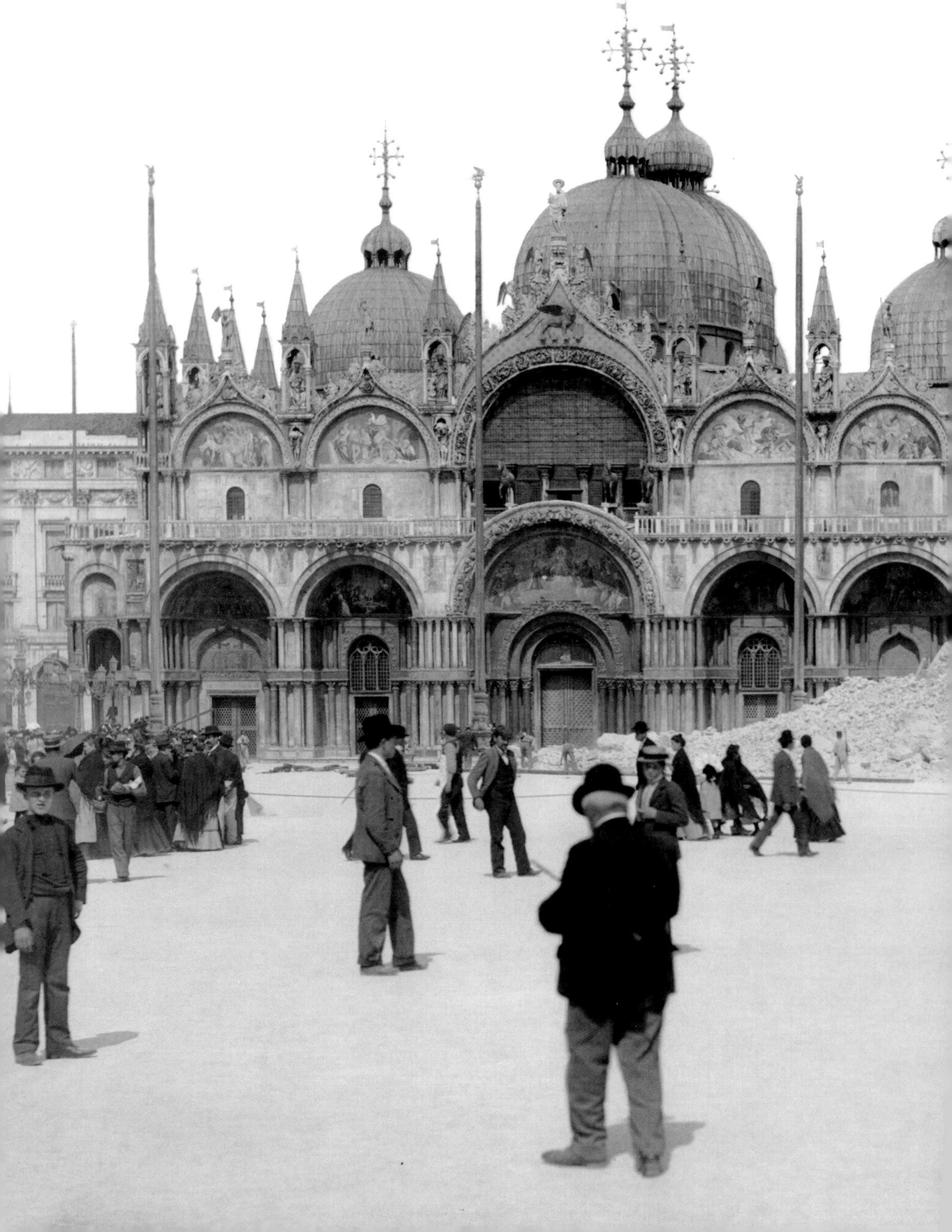

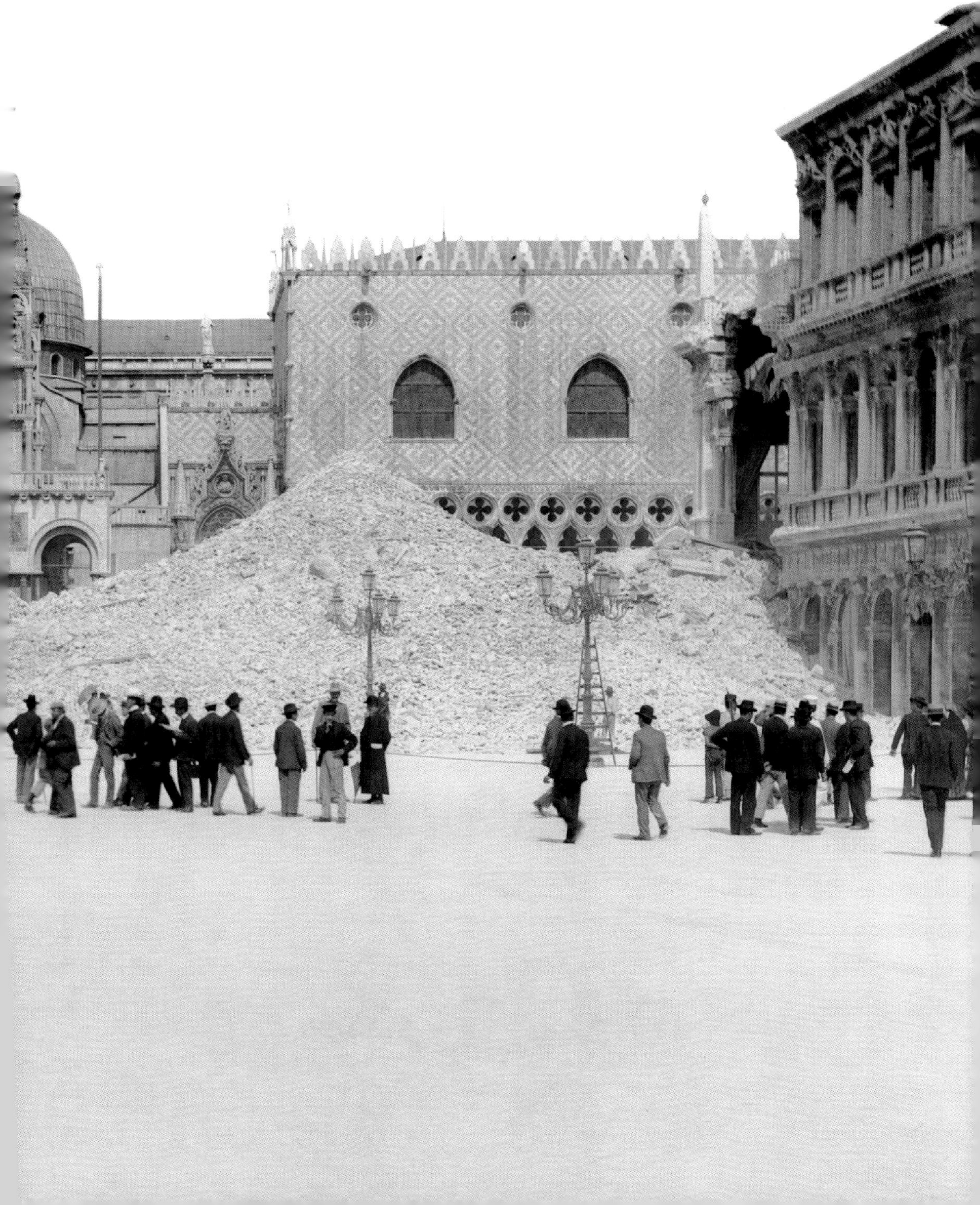

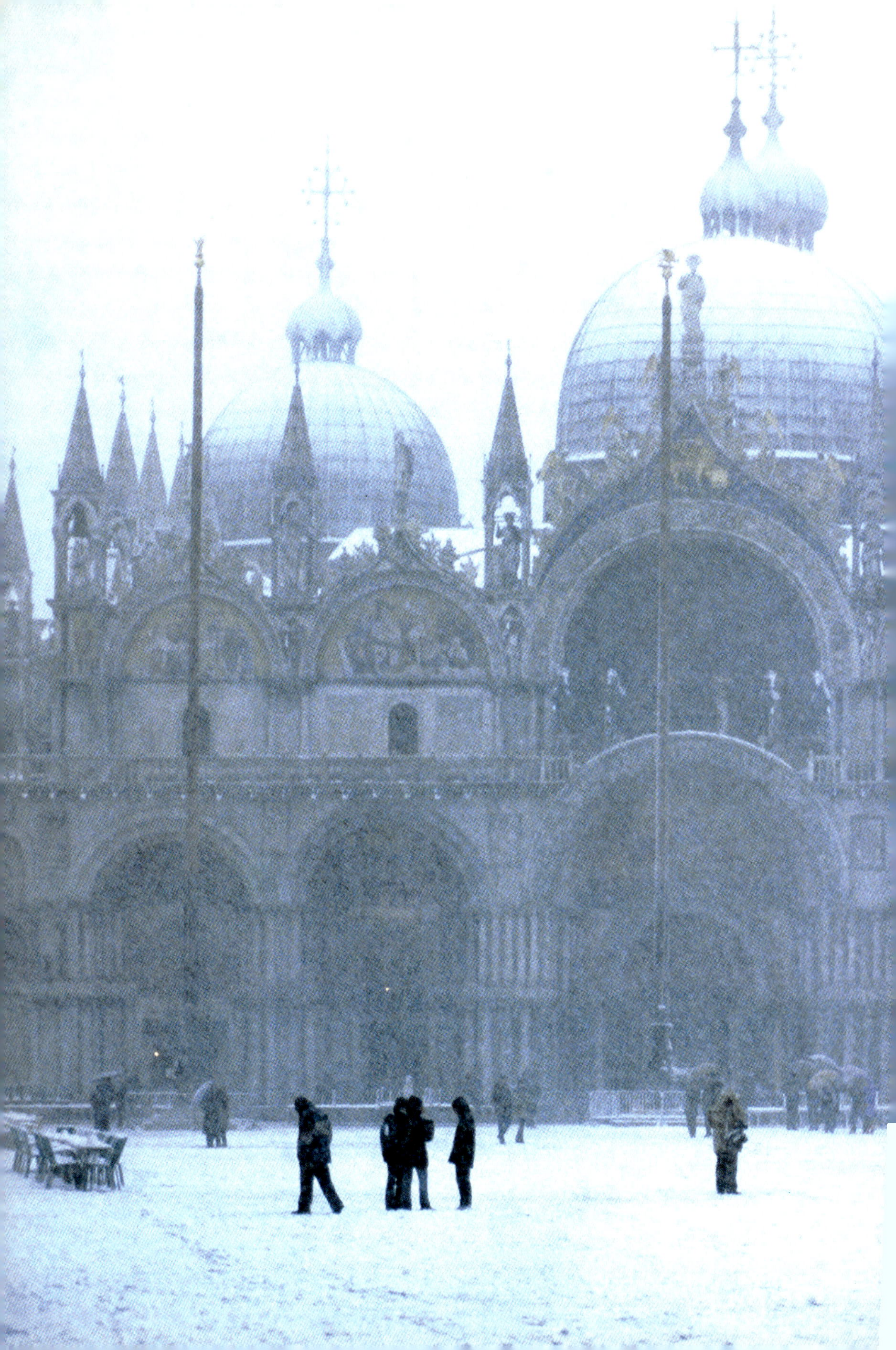

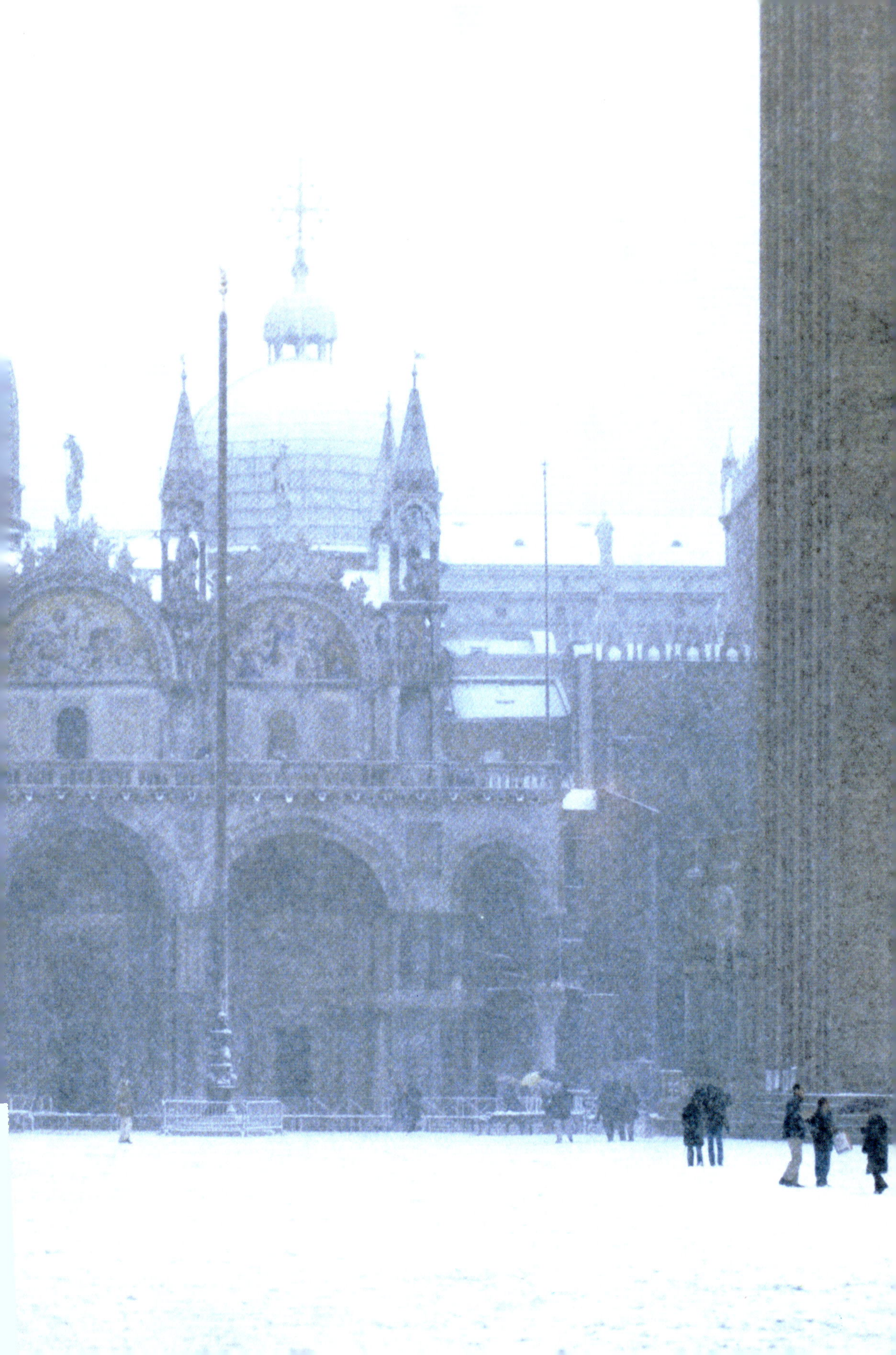

DIRECTORY

ONE: ARCHITECTURAL TREASURES

INTRODUCTION

BASILICA DI SAN MARCO
Piazza San Marco
Tel: 041 522 5205
Opening hours:
Apr-Sep, Mon-Sat: 9:30am-5:30pm, Sun: 2-5:30pm;
Oct-Mar, Mon-Sat: 10am-4:30pm, Sun: 2-4:30pm
and
CAMPANILE DI SAN MARCO
Tel: 041 522 4064
Opening hours:
Oct-Feb daily: 9:30am-4pm;
Mar-June, daily: 9am-7pm;
July-Sept, daily: 9am-9pm
Closed: Jan 7-31

BIBLIOTECA MARCIANA
(LIBRERIA SANSOVINIANA)
Piazzetta San Marco
Tel: 041 520 8788
Library opening hours:
Mon-Fri: 9am-7pm;
Sat: 9am-1.30pm

CA' DARIO
Just beyond Vaparetto
Salute, on the left bank
(from San Marco)

CA' REZZONICO
(MUSEUM OF
18TH CENTURY ART)
Dorsoduro 3136,
Fondamenta Rezzonico
Tel: 041 241 8506
Opening hours:
May-Sep, daily: 10am-5pm;
Oct-Apr, daily: 10am-4pm
Closed: Fridays

IL REDENTORE
Campo del Redentore,
Giudecca Island
Opening hours:
Daily: 3pm-6pm
Closed: Sundays

LA ZECCA
Piazzetta San Marco
Tel: 041 520 8788
Library opening hours:
Mon-Fri: 9am-7pm;
Sat: 9am-1.30pm

PALAZZO DUCALE
(DOGES' PALACE)
Piazza San Marco 1
Tel: 041 522 4951
Opening hours:
Apr-Oct, daily: 9am-7pm
(ticket office closes 5.30pm)
Nov-Mar, daily: 9am-5pm
(ticket office closes 3.30pm)

PALAZZO GRASSI
San Samuele 3231,
Campo San Samuele
Tel: 041 523 1680
Opening hours:
During exhibitions, daily:
10am-7pm

SAN GIORGIO MAGGIORE
Isola di San Giorgio Maggiore
Tel: 041 522 7827
Opening hours:
Apr-Oct daily: 9:30am-12:30pm and 2:30-6pm;
Nov-Mar daily: 10am-12:30pm and 2:30-4:30pm

SANTA MARIA DEI MIRACOLI
Campo Santa Maria Nova
Opening hours:
Mon-Sat: 10am-5.30pm;
Sun 3-5pm

IN PRAISE OF GOD AND BEAUTY

BASILICA DI SAN MARCO
(*see under*
ARCHITECTURAL
TREASURES; Introduction)

I GESUATI
(MARIA DI ROSARIO)
Fondamenta Zattere
ai Gesuati
Opening hours:
daily: 8am-12pm, 5pm-7pm

IL REDENTORE
(see under
ARCHITECTURAL
TREASURES; Introduction)

MADONNA DELL'ORTO
(TINTORETTO CHURCH)
Campo Madonna dell'Orto
Tel: 041 719 933
Opening hours:
mon-Sat: 10am-5pm;
Sun: 3pm-5pm

SAN GIORGIO DEI GRECI
Fondamenta dei Greci
Opening hours:
Tues-Sat: 9am-12.30pm,
2-4.30pm;
Sun: 10.30am service only

SAN PIETRO DI CASTELLO
Campo San Pietro
Tel: 041 523 8950

SAN SEBASTIANO
Fondamenta di San
Sebastiano
Tel: 041 275 0462
Opening hours:
Daily: 2.30pm-5.30pm
Closed: Saturdays

SAN TROVASO
Campo San Trovaso
Tel: 041 522 2133
Opening hours:
Mon-Fri: 8am-11am,
3pm-6pm;
Sat: 8am-11am, 3pm-7pm;
Sun: 8.30am-1pm

SANTA MARIA
DI ROSARIO
Fondamenta Zattere,
Dorsoduro

SANTO STEFANO CHURCH
Campo Santo Stefano
Tel: 041 522 5061
Opening hours:
Mon-Sat: 10am-5pm;
Sun: 1pm-5pm

BEHIND THE FAÇADES

CA' REZZONICO
(MUSEUM OF
18TH CENTURY ART)
(see under
ARCHITECTURAL
TREASURES; Introduction)

PALAZZO ALBRIZZI
Fondamenta San Andrea
Tel: 041 5232544

PALAZZO DONÀ
DELLE ROSA/
DONATUS VENETIAN
FABRICS
Palazzo Donà
5101 Fondamenta Nove
Tel: 041 1241 5424
Fax: 041 1241 0674
Email: mail@Donatus.com
www.donatus.com

PALAZZO DUCALE
(see under
ARCHITECTURAL
TREASURES; Introduction)

PALAZZO GRASSI
(see under
ARCHITECTURAL
TREASURES; Introduction)

PALAZZO LOREDAN
Campo San Stefano 2945

PALAZZO MOCENIGO/
CHIARASTELLA CATTANA
Santa Croce 1992,
Salazzada San Stae
Tel: 041 721 798
Opening hours:
During exhibitions, daily:
10am-7pm
For a private appointment
with Chiarastella, contact:
San Marco 3357
Tel: 041 522 4369
Email:
chiarastella.cattana@tin.it

PALAZZO PAPAFAVA
Cannaregio, Calle Priuli,
Racchetta 3764
Tel: 041 5235260

PALAZZO PISANI-GRITTI
(GRITTI PALACE HOTEL)
Campo Santa Maria del
Giglio 2467
Tel: 041 794 611

PALAZZO PISANO MORETTA
Grand Canal,
San Polo 2766
Tel: 041 520 5226

BRIDGES TO SIGH OVER

PALAZZO TIEPOLO
San Marco 2159

PONTE CARMINI
Dorsoduro,
near Scuole Carmini

PONTE DEI PUGNI
(Bridge of Fists)
Links Campo Santa
Margherita to the Accademia

PONTE DEI SOSPIRI
(Bridge of Sighs)
Links the Palazzo Ducale
to the prisons

PONTE DELL' ACCADEMIA
(Accademia Bridge)
Vaporetto stop: Accademia

PONTE DELLA GUERRA
Near San Giuliano

PONTE DI RIALTO
Vaporetto stop: San Silvestro

PONTE DI SACCA
near Palazzo Donà
delle Rosa,
Fondamenta Nove

PONTE FOSCA
Near San Sebastiano

PONTE SAN MARZIAL
Near San Sebastiano

PONTE SCALZI
Near Santa Lucia train station

CRUMBLING MAGNIFICENCE

CA' D'ORO
(GALLERIA FRANCHETTI)
Cannaregio 3932,
Calle Ca' d'Oro
Tel: 041 523 8790
Guided tours in Italian:
041 520 0345
Opening hours:
Daily: 9am-2pm

CHURCH OF MADONNA
DELLA SALUTE
Fondamente Salute,
Dorsoduro 1
Tel: 041 522 5558

TWO: CULTURAL DELIGHTS

INTRODUCTION

PALAZZO DUCALE
(see under
ARCHITECTURAL
TREASURES; Introduction)

SANTA MARIA DEI
MIRACOLI
(see under ARCHITECTURAL
TREASURES; Introduction)

SAVOURING THE SUPERLATIVES

BASILICA DI SANTA MARIA
GLORIOSA DEI FRARI
Campo dei Frari
Tel: 041 522 2637
Opening hours:
Daily: 9.30am-12pm,
2.30pm-6pm
Closed: Sundays

CHURCH OF MADONNA
DELL' ORTO
(see under
ARCHITECTURAL
TREASURES; In Praise of
God and Beauty)

CHURCH OF SAN
PANTALON
Campo San Pantalon
Tel: 041 523 5893
Opening hours:
Mon-Fri, Sun: 3pm-5pm

CHURCH OF SAN
SEBASTIANO
(see under
ARCHITECTURAL
TREASURES; In Praise of
God and Beauty)

GALLERIA DELL'
ACCADEMIA
Dorsoduro 1050,
Campo Carità
Tel: 041 522 2247
Email: Accademia.artive@
arti.beniculturali.it
Opening hours:
Mon: 8.15am-2pm;
Tues-Sun: 8.15am-7pm

I GESUATI
(see under
ARCHITECTURAL
TREASURES; In Praise of
God and Beauty)

SCUOLA DI SAN GIORGIO
DEGLI SCHIAVONI
Castello 3259,
Calle dei Furlani
Tel: 041 522 8828
Opening hours:
Apr-Oct, Tues-Sat: 9.30am-
12.30pm, 3.30pm-6.30pm;
Sun: 9.30am-12.30pm;
Nov-Mar, Tues-Sat:
10am-12.30pm, 3pm-6pm;
Sun: 10am-12.30pm

SCUOLA DI SAN ROCCO
Campo San Rocco
Tel: 041 523 4864
Opening hours:
Apr-Oct, daily: 8am-
12.30pm, 2pm-4pm
Nov-Mar, daily: 8am-
12.30pm, 2pm-4pm

**LIVING ARTISTS,
LIVING ART**

GEOFFREY HUMPHRIES'
STUDIO
Contact Holly Snapp Gallery
for details (see below)

GUGGENHEIM MUSEUM
(PALAZZO VENIER
DEI LEONI)
Fondamenta Venier dei
Leoni, Dorsoduro 701
Tel: 041 520 6288
www.guggenheim-venice.it
Opening hours:
April-Oct: Mon, Wed, Fri,
Sun: 11am-6pm;
Sat: 11am-10pm
Nov-Mar: Mon, Wed-Sun:
11am-6pm
Closed: Tuesdays

HOLLY SNAPP GALLERY
Calle delle Botteghe
(near Palazzo Grassi at
Campo Santa Stefano),
San Marco 3133 3217

VENICE DESIGN
ART GALLERY –
SAN SAMUELE
3146 San Marco
Tel: 041.520 7915
Fax: 041.520 5276
Email:
venicedesignartgallery1@
tin.it
Opening hours:
Mon-Sat: 10am-1pm,
3pm-7pm
and
VENICE DESIGN –
CALLE VALLARESSO
1310 San Marco
Tel: 041.523 9082
Fax: 041.523 8530
Email:
venicedesignartgallery2@
tin.it
Opening hours:
Mon-Sat: 10am-1pm,
3pm-7.30pm

THE PERFORMING ARTS

BASILICA DI SANTA MARIA
GLORIOSA DEI FRARI
(see under
CULTURAL DELIGHTS;
Savouring the Superlatives)

GOLDONI THEATRE
San Marco 4650
Tel: 041 240 2011

GRAN TEATRO LA FENICE
Campo San Fantin
www.teatrolafenice.it

I GESUATI
(see under
ARCHITECTURAL
TREASURES; In Praise of
God and Beauty)

LA PIÈTA CHURCH
Riva degli Schiavoni,
Vaporetto San Zaccaria
Tel: 041 523 1096

MALIBRAN THEATRE
Corte delle Ostreghe,
San Marco 2359
Tel: 041 523 2162

PALAFENICE
Tronchetto island
Tel: 041 786 511

SANTO STEFANO
(see under
ARCHITECTURAL
TREASURES; In Praise of
God and Beauty)

SCUOLA GRANDE DI
SAN ROCCO
Campo San Rocco,
San Polo 3052
Tel: 041 523 4864
Email: sanrocco@libero.it
www.sanrocco.it
Opening hours:
Mon, Fri: 10am-1pm;
Sat-Sun: 10am-4pm:

EASTERN MYSTIQUE

PALAZZO DUCALE
(see under
ARCHITECTURAL
TREASURES; Introduction)

GONDOLA GARAGE
Canal di San Trovaso

THREE: RETAIL INDULGENCE

FAMOUS LABELS

ARMANI, BULGARI,
CARTIER, DOLCE E
GABBANA, FENDI, FERRE,
GUCCI, MAGLI, MISSONI,
PRADA, LOUIS VUITTON,
VALENTINO, VERSACE,
ERMENEGILDO ZEGNA
These and more can all
be found in four streets
in the vicinity of San Marco:
Calle Vallaresso;

Salizzada San Moisè
which leads into
Calle Larga XXII Marzo;
Calle Goldoni;
and The Mercerie

MALO
Calle delle Ostreghe,
San Marco 2359
Tel: 041 523 2162

**THE ART OF
VENETIAN GLASS**

BAROVIA & TOSO
Fondamenta Vetrai,
Murano 28
Tel: 041 739 049

BERENGO FINE ARTS
Fondamenta dei Vetrai,
Murano 109/A
and
Fondamenta Manin,
Murano 1
and
Calle Larga,
San Marco 412/3
Tel: 041 739 453

ELITE MURANO
Calle del Cinitero 6,
Murano
Tel: 041 736 168

FRATELLI BARBINI
Calle Bertolini 36, Murano
Tel: 041 739 777

GALLERIA ROSELLA JUNCK
Calle delle Botteghe,
San Marco 3463
Tel: 041 528 6537

GALLERIA MARINA
BAROVIER
Salizzada San Samuele,
San Marco 3216
Tel: 041 522 6102

GENNINGER STUDIO
Calle del Traghetto,
Dorsoduro 2793/A
Tel: 041 522 5565

GLASS MUSEUM
Fondamenta Giustinian,
Murano
Tel: 041 739 586

VENINI
Fondamenta Vetrai,
Murano 50
Tel: 041 739 955
and
Piazzetta dei Leoncini,
San Marco 314
Tel: 041 522 4045

**SILKS, SATINS,
BUTTONS, BOWS**

ANNELIE
Dorsoduro 2748,
Calle Lunga San Barnaba

GAGGIO
Calle dell Botteghe,
San Marco 3451
Tel: 041 522 8574

HOTEL CIPRIANI
Giudecca 10, off
Fondamenta San Giovanni
Tel: 041 520 7744
www.hotelcipriani.it
www.cipriani.com

JESURUM
San Marco 60-1,
Piazza San Marco

LA FENICE ATELIER
San Marco 3537,
Campo Sant' Angelo

MARTINUZZI
San Marco 67/A,
Piazza San Marco

PALAZZO DUCALE
(*see under*
ARCHITECTURAL
TREASURES; Introduction)

RUBELLI
Campo San Gallo,
San Marco 1089

TROIS
Campo San Maurizio,
San Marco 2666
Tel: 041 522 2905

VENETIA STUDIUM
Calle Larga XXII Marzo,
San Marco 2403
Tel: 041 522 9281

**DISCOVERING THE
UNUSUAL**

CA' MACANA
Dorsoduro 3172,
Calle delle Botteghe
Tel: 041 520 3229

CODOGNATO
San Marco 1295, Calle Dell'
Ascensione, 30124
Tel: 041 522 5042

CORNICI TREVISANELLO
Dorsoduro 662
Tel: 041 520 7779

DORADOR
Campo San Barnaba,
2808 Dorsoduro

EL SOLE E LA LUNA
Frezzeria,
San Marco 1503

GILBERTO PENZO
San Polo 2702,
Calle Il dei Saoneri
Tel: 041 719 372

GODI FIORENZA
San Marco 4261,
Rio Tera San Paternian
Tel: 041 241 0866

GUALTI
Dorsoduro 3111,
Rio Tera Canal
Tel: 041 520 1731

HOTEL CIPRIANI BOUTIQUE
Giudecca 10, off
Fondamenta San Giovanni
Tel: 041 520 7744
www.hotelcipriani.it
www.cipriani.com

IL CANOVACCIO
Castello 5369-70
Tel: 041 521 0393
Email:
ilcanovaccio@inwind.it
www.ilcanovaccio.com

LA BOTTEGA DEI SOGNI
Calle Fiubera 818,
San Marco 30124
and
San Polo 601, Rialto
(behind Campo
San Bartolomeo)

LA BOTTEGA DELL' ARTE
Campo San Barnaba,
Dorsoduro

LA RICERCA
Ponte delle Ostreghe
(near Campo Santa
Maria del Giglio),
2431 San Marco
Tel: 041 521 2606

LA VENEXIANA ATELIER
Ponte Canonica,
Castello 43228
and
Frezzeria,
San Marco 1135

LIBRERIA EDITRICE FILIPPI
Castello 5284,
Calle Casselleria
Tel: 041 522 5042

LINDA MARIA GONZALEZ
San Marco 1854
Tel: 041 528 5563

LORIS MARAZZI SCULTORE
S. Margherita, 2903
Tel. 041 523 9001

MONDO NOVO
Rio Terà Canal,
Dorsoduro 3063
Tel: 041 528 7344

NORELENE
Calle della Chiesa,
727 Dorsoduro
Tel: 041 523 7605

**VE'NINA SANDALS/
PALAZZO FALIER**
For private appointment,
tel: 041 522 4217
Email: Servanegiol@tin.it

VENETIA STUDIUM
(see under
RETAIL INDUGENCE;
Silks, Satins, Buttons, Bows)

VOGINI BOUTIQUE
Salizzada San Moisé,
San Marco 1257/a
Tel: 041 5222 573

FOUR: GOURMET PLEASURES

INTRODUCTION

HARRY'S DOLCI
Fondamenta San Biagio,
Giudecca 773
Tel: 041 522 4844
Email:
harrysdolci@cipriani.com
www.cipriani.com

HOTEL CIPRIANI
Giudecca 10, off
Fondamenta San Giovanni
Tel: 041 520 7744
www.hotelcipriani.it
www.cipriani.com
Restaurant open daily

LE BISTROT
San Marco 4685,
Calle dei Fabbri
Tel: 041 523 6651
Opening hours:
Daily until 1am

L'INCONTRO
Dorsoduro 3062,
Rio Tera Canal
Tel: 041 522 2404
Closed: Mondays

**OF MARKETS
AND MANNERS**

BAR ROSSI
Cannareggio 1409,
Rio Tera San Leonardo
Tel: 041 718 245
Opening hours:
Mon-Sat: 9am-9.30pm

BISTROT AI DO DRAGHI
Campo Santa Margherita,
Dorsoduro 3665
Tel: 041 528 9731

ERBERIA
(FRUIT AND
VEGETABLE MARKET)
Begins at the foot of the
Rialto Bridge

HOTEL CIPRIANI
Giudecca 10, off
Fondamenta San Giovanni
Tel: 041 520 7744
www.hotelcipriani.it
www.cipriani.com

PESCHERIA
(FISH MARKET)
Set in a neo-Gothic hall by
the quayside at the foot
of the Rialto Bridge
Closed: Mondays

CLASSIC RESTAURANTS

HOTEL CIPRIANI
Giudecca 10, off
Fondamenta San Giovanni
Tel: 041 520 7744
www.hotelcipriani.it
www.cipriani.com

DA FIORE
Calle del Scaleter,
San Polo 2202
Tel: 041 721 308
Closed: Sundays
and Mondays

DO FORNI
Calle dei Speccherieri,
San Marco 468
Tel: 041 523 2148

FIASCHETTERIA TOSCANA
San Giovanni Crisostomo,
Cannaregio 5719
Tel: 041 528 5281
Closed: Tuesdays and
Monday lunchtimes

LA CUSINA
Calle Larga XXII Marzo,
San Marco 2161
Tel: 041 521 3785

QUADRI
Piazza San Marco,
San Marco 120
Tel: 041 528 9299
Closed: Mondays and
Tuesday lunchtimes

OFF THE BEATEN TRACK

AL MASCARON
Calle Lunga Santa Maria
Formosa, Castello 5225
Tel: 041 522 5995
Closed: Sundays and
mid-December–January

IL NUOVO GALEON
Castello 1308-1309,
Via Garibaldi
Tel: 041 520 4656
Closed: Tuesdays

IL SOLE SULLA
VECHIA CAVANA
Rio Terà,
SS. Apostoli, 4624
Closed: Mondays

OSTERIA DI SANTA
MARINA
Castello 5911,
Campo Santa Marina
Closed: Sundays and
Monday lunchtimes

OSTERIA ENOTECA
SAN MARCO
Frezzeria, San Marco 1610
Tel: 041 528 5242

TAVERNA LA FENICE
San Marco 1939
Tel: 041 522 3856

ON THE BACARO TRAIL

BANCOGIRO
Campo San Giacometto,
San Polo, 122
Tel: 041 523 2061
Closed: Mondays and
Sunday evenings

CANTINA DO MORI
Calle dei Do Mori,
429 San Polo
Tel: 041 522 5401

ENOTECA DO COLONNE
Cannaregio 1814
Tel: 041 524 0453

HARRY'S BAR
(see under
AFTER DARK;
A Cocktail Legend)

HOTEL CIPRIANI
Giudecca 10, off
Fondamenta San Giovanni
Tel: 041 520 7744
www.hotelcipriani.it
www.cipriani.com

LA CANTINA
Campo San Felice,
Cannaregio 3689
Tel: 041 522 8258

LA COLUMBINA
Corte del Pegoloto,
Cannaregio 1828
Tel: 041 275 0622

LE BISTROT
(see under GOURMET
PLEASURES; Introduction)

OSTERIA ALLA BOTTE
Calle della Bissa,
San Marco 5482
Tel: 041 520 9775

SACRO E PROFANO
Under Rialto bridge

VINI DA GIGIO
Fondamenta della Chiesa,
Cannaregio 3628/a
Tel: 041 528 5140

SWEET TEMPTATIONS

ANTICO CAFFE ROSA
SALVA
Campo San Lucca,
San Marco 4589
Tel: 041 522 5385

DA NICO
Zattere, Dorsoduro 922
Tel: 041 522 5293

FLORIAN'S
Piazza San Marco
Tel: 041 520 5641
www.caffeflorian.com

GRAN CAFFE QUADRI
Piazza San Marco 120
Tel: 041 522 2105

HARRY'S DOLCI
(see under GOURMET
PLEASURES; Introduction)

HOTEL CIPRIANI
Giudecca 10, off
Fondamenta San Giovanni
Tel: 041 520 7744
www.hotelcipriani.it
www.cipriani.com

IL DOGE
Dorsoduro, 3059
Tel: 041 523 4607

PASTICCERIA BALARIN
Calle dell'Oca,
Cannaregio 4323
Tel: 041 522 1009

FIVE: THE HIGH LIFE

INTRODUCTION

GRAN CAFFE QUADRI
(*see under*
GOURMET PLEASURES;
Sweet Temptations)

To arrange a marriage and honeymoon in Venice try: www.venice-weddings.com

MASQUERADE

CA' FOSCARI
On Grand Canal,
near S. Tomà

CA' REZZONICO
(*see under*
ARCHITECTURAL
TREASURES; Introduction)

FLAVIA ZORZO
Campo S. Lio, 30122
Email:
info@venetiancostumes.com

GRAN CAFFE QUADRI
(*see under*
GOURMET PLEASURES;
Sweet Temptations)

HOTEL EXCELSIOR
Lungomare Marconi, 41,
Lido di Venezia
Tel: 041 526 0201

MAX ART SHOP
Frezzaria,
San Marco 1232
www.Ballodeldoge.com

PALAZZO PISANO
MORETTA
San Polo 2766
Tel: 041 520 5226

PALAZZO SORANZO
Campo San Polo 2171

SANTA MARIA DEGLI
ANGELI
Fondamenta Sebastiano,
Murano

FESTIVAL TIME

BASILICA DI SAN MARCO
(*see under*
ARCHITECTURAL
TREASURES; Introduction)

THE BIENNALE
For further information,
tel: 041 272 8397
Email:
infogruppi@labiennale.org
www.labiennale.org

CA' FOSCARI
(*see under* THE HIGH LIFE;
Masquerade)

HOTEL EXCELSIOR
(*see under* THE HIGH LIFE;
Masquerade)

HOTEL CIPRIANI
Giudecca 10, off
Fondamenta San Giovanni
Tel: 041 520 7744
www.hotelcipriani.it
www.cipriani.com

HOTEL DES BAINS
Lungomare Marconi, 17/A,
Lido di Venezia
Tel: 041 526 5921

IL REDENTORE
(*see under*
ARCHITECTURAL
TREASURES; Introduction)

PALAZZO DUCALE
(*see under*
ARCHITECTURAL
TREASURES; Introduction)

VENICE FILM FESTIVAL
For further information,
tel: 041 521 8711
www.labiennale.org
Film Festival venues:
PALAZZO DEL CINEMA
and PALAGALILEO
Both: Lido di Venezia

VILLA PISANI
(see under PALAZZO
PISANO MORETTA; THE
HIGH LIFE; Masquerade)

SIX: AFTER DARK

INTRODUCTION

LE BISTROT
(see under
GOURMET PLEASURES;
Introduction)

THE INTIMACY OF SILENCE

CIP'S BISTRO,
HOTEL CIPRIANI
Giudecca 10, off
Fondamenta San Giovanni
Tel: 041 520 7744
www.hotelcipriani.it
www.cipriani.com

HARRY'S BAR
(see under
AFTER DARK;
A Cocktail Legend)

A COCKTAIL LEGEND

HARRY'S BAR
Calle Vallaresso,
San Marco 1323
Tel: 041 528 5777
Email:
harrysbar@cipriani.com
www.cipriani.com

HOTEL CIPRIANI
Giudecca 10, off
Fondamenta San Giovanni
Tel: 041 520 7744
www.hotelcipriani.it
www.cipriani.com

LOCANDA CIPRIANI
Torcello,
Piazza Santa Fosca 29
Tel: 041 730 150
Closed: Tuesdays and the
whole of January

SOUND OF MUSIC – CLASSICAL

LA PIETÀ CHURCH
(see under
CULTURAL DELIGHTS;
The Performing Arts)

PALAZZO ZENOBIO
Fondamenta del Soccorso,
Dorsoduro 2596
Tel: 041 522 8770

SAN SAMUELE CHURCH
Campo San Samuele

SAN STEFANO CHURCH
Campo San Stefano
Tel: 041 522 2362

SANTA MARIA FORMOSA
CHURCH
Castello, Campo Santa
Maria Formosa
Tel: 041 523 4645

SCUOLA GRANDE DI SAN
GIOVANNI EVANGELISTA
San Polo 2454
Tel: 041 718 234
Opening hours:
Monday only: 4pm-6pm

VIVALDI STORE
Rialto, San Bartolomeo,
Fontego dei Tedeschi,
5537/40
Tel: 041 522 1343
www.vivaldistore.com

SOUND OF MUSIC – JAZZ

CAMELOT PUB
Cannaregio 2754
Tel: 033 9443 0617
Closed: Mondays

IGUANA CAFÉ
Cannaregio 2515
Tel: 041 713 561
Closed: Mondays

LE NOTTI ORIENTALE
Cannaregio 2578
Tel: 041 717 315
Closed: Tuesdays

OSTERIA AL BACCO
Cannaregio 3054
Tel: 041 717 493
Closed: Mondays

OSTERIA ANICE STELLATO
Cannaregio 3272,
Fondamenta della Sensa
Tel: 041 720 744
Closed: Mondays

PARADISO PERDUTO
Cannaregio 2540
Tel: 041 720 581
Closed: Wednesdays

PUB DA ALDO
Cannaregio 2710
Tel: 041 715 834
Closed: Sundays

SAHARA
Cannaregio 2519
Tel: 041 721 077
Closed: Mondays

SEVEN: COMING BACK

COURSES IN VENICE

BEV GRUBER/EVERYDAY
GOURMET TRAVELER
5053 NE 178th St., Seattle,
Washington 98155
USA
Tel: 206-363-1602,
888-636-1602
E-mail:
gourmetravel@aol.com

BOSTON UNIVERSITY
International Programs
232 Bay State Road,
5th Floor
Boston,
Massachusetts 02215
Tel: 617 353 9888
Email: abroad@bu.edu
www.bu.edu/abroad/cities/venice

CENTRO STUDI ERA 2000
Via Ospedale, 9, Mestre
Email:
info@centrostudiera2000.com

CERAMICHE DI BASSANO
San Angelo

HOTEL CIPRIANI/
CIPRIANI COOKING AND
WINE TASTING SCHOOL/
CIPRIANI PAINTING
COURSES
Giudecca 10, off
Fondamenta San Giovanni
Tel: 041 520 7744
Email:
info@hotelcipriani.com
www.hotelcipriani.it
www.cipriani.com

CORNICI TREVISANELLO
(see under
RETAIL INDULGENCE;
Discovering the Unusual)

EOLO
Restaurant Boat Cruises
Mauro Stoppa
Tel: 041 241 0301
Fax: 041 241 0664
Email: infoberto@tin.it
www.cruisingvenice.com

GRITTI PALACE HOTEL
Campo Santa Maria del
Giglio, 2467,
San Marco
Tel: 041 794 611
Fax: 041 520 0942

INSTITUTO VENEZIA
Dorsoduro 3116/A
www.institutovenezia.com

LA SCUOLA
INTERNAZIONALE
DI GRAFICA
San Marcuola, Cannaregio
Calle Seconda del
Cristo, 1798
Tel: 041 721 950
www.scuolagrafica.it

ORIENT-EXPRESS
BOTANICAL AND FLOWER
PAINTING MASTERCLASSES
For more information,
contact the Hotel Cipriani
(see above for contact
details) or email:
christine.martyn@orient-express.com

PRATT EDUCATION
For more information,
contact School of
Professional Studies
Tel: 718 636 3453
Venice coordinator: Diana
Gisolfi, tel: 718 636 3598
Email: prostudy@pratt.edu
or dgisolfi@pratt.edu
www.pratt.edu/abroad/venice/courses

ROBERT WILK
Roberto's Italian Table,
Dorsoduro 3441
Fax: 041 714 571
Email:
roberto@italiantable.com
www.italiantable.com

VIEWS ON VENICE
San Marco 4267/A
Tel: 041 241 1149
Fax: 041 241 5821
Email:
info@viewsonvenice.com
www.viewsonvenice.com

A PERSONAL MASTERPIECE

BOTTEGA D'ANGOLO
Calle Fiubera,
San Marco 803
Tel: 041 523 5237
Email: gipereno@tin.it
www.veneziart.com

FORNASIER LUIGI
Calle del Paradiso 70,
Murano
Tel: 041 736 176

GEOFFREY HUMPHRIES'
STUDIO
(see under
CULTURAL DELIGHTS;
Living Artist, Living Art)

GENNINGER STUDIO
Calle del Traghetto,
Dorsoduro 2793/A
Tel: 041 522 5565

GIOLMARINE
Dott. Giovanni Giol
Tel: 041 926 409
Email: giolmarine@yahoo.it

GODI FIORENZA
(see under RETAIL
INDULGENCE; Discovering
the Unusual)

HOTEL CIPRIANI
Giudecca 10, off
Fondamenta San Giovanni
Tel: 041 520 7744
www.hotelcipriani.it
www.cipriani.com

PIANETA PERLA
Katarina Rothfjell
Campo Marco Stringari 23,
S. Elena
Tel: 041 277 8553

VENETIA STUDIUM
(see under
RETAIL INDULGENCE;
Silks, Satins, Buttons, Bows)

VOGINI BOUTIQUE
(see under
RETAIL INDULGENCE;
Discovering the Unusual)

THE LAGOON

ISLAND OF SAN
FRANCESCO DEL
DESERTO
Tel: 041 528 6863

LOCANDA CIPRIANI
Torcello,
Piazza Santa Fosca 29
Tel: 041 730 150
Closed: Tuesdays and the whole of January

MEKISTARIST MONASTERY
Island of San Lazzaro degli Armeni
Tel: 041 526 0104

MUSEUM OF THE LAGOON
Torcello
Tel: 041 730 7761

SANTA MARIA ASSUNTA
Torcello, 30100
Tel: 041 730 084

TORCELLO CATHEDRAL
Torcello
Tel: 041 730 084

PICTURE CAPTIONS

Places pictured only and not featured in main text:

CHAPTER ONE

SCALZI CHURCH
Cannaregio

CHAPTER THREE

ROLANDO SEGALIN COBBLER
Calle dei Fuseri

CHAPTER FOUR

RIVETTA
Calle Sechera
Santa Croce 637a
Opening hours:
Daily: 8.30am-9.30pm
Closed Sundays

CHAPTER FIVE

HOTEL MONACO BAR
San Marco 1325

CHAPTER SIX

ATELIER PIETRO LONGHI
San Polo 2604b
Tel: 041 714 478
www.pietrolonghi.com

CAFFE CITTÀ DI TORINO
Campo San Luca

LA CANTINA STRADA NOVA
Cannaregio 3689
Campo San Felice
Tel: 041 522 8258
Opening hours:
Daily: 10am-10pm
Closed: Sundays

CHAPTER SEVEN

IMAGINA
Rio Terà Canal 3126
nr Campo Santa Margherita
Dorsoduro
Tel: 041 241 0625
Closed: Sundays

MONACO BAR
(see under PICTURE CAPTIONS; CHAPTER FIVE, Hotel Monaco)

INTRODUCTION

Striped poles for glamorous moorings on the Grand Canal.

Too cold for gondola rides: Santa Maria della Salute on a snowy afternoon.

Fluted chimney pots on Ca'Dario.

Those same chimney pots captured by Vittore Carpaccio (c. 1460-1526) in his painting at the Accademia, *Miracle of the Relic of the Holy Cross*.

Dappled sunlight and dancing reflections in Bacino Orseolo.

Reflections in an ornate gilt mirror on a *palazzo* wall.

Children by a well in Piazza S. Giovanni e Paolo, captured by the photographer Naya, late 19th/early 20th century.

A deserted well opposite Ponte Storto ('the crooked bridge') in Campiello Calagheri, near La Fenice.

Detail of the Basilica San Marco, showing characteristic stilted Byzantine arches.

Washing lines are the banners of Venice. This one is in a *calle* off Campo Santa Margherita.

More washing lines strung across Calle del Prete Zoto, with the campanile of the church of San Guiseppe in the background.

Not even canals deter Venetian laundresses. Life in the back streets of Cannaregio.

Rio della Fornace, Dorsoduro.

Aqua bassa (low water) in the canals of Venice, revealing the silt of yesteryear.

Tiny alleyways, too narrow to walk two abreast, make up the criss-cross jumble of Venetian back streets.

Early morning preparations in S. Giovanni e Paolo.

A scrunch of Fortuny fabric in Venetian old gold.

One of the proud bronze horses of San Marco. No one is quite sure whether they are Greek or Roman or even precisely how old they are but they are great trophies of war and icons of Venetian pride.

Stone figure in Campo dei Mori of Antonio Rioba, an eastern merchant.

'The Moor', at the house of Tintoretto in Cannaregio.

280

CHAPTER ONE

A unique view of Venice: the domes of the Basilica and the rooftops of San Marco in the snow.

Detail of stone tracery on the charming neighbourhood church of Santo Stefano.

Similar intricate tracery on the church of Madonna Dell'Orto.

The perfect symmetry of Ca'Dario at high tide.

Venice old and new. Lady Isabella Hervey at at Ca'Pesaro Papafava wears fashion by Godi Fiorenza.

Doorways (from top left, clockwise): portal of church of Madonna dell'Orto; St. Michael killing the dragon, church of San Michele in Isola; Palazzo Soranzo Van Axel; Sotoportego dei Todeschini; Palazza Donà delle Rosa; The Accademia; private doorway in Dorsoduro; on the Grand Canal; Ca' Dolfin, Dorsoduro.

The windows of The Procuracy (c. 1517) reflected in *aqua alta* (high water).

Façade of the Palazzo Salviati on the Grand Canal.

Detail from *Scenes From The Life of St. Ursula: Return Home of the Ambassadors*, by Vittore Carpaccio, in the Accademia (Academy of Fine Arts).

A private view inside the Palazzo Barbaro.

Not content with merely inventing the mirror, the Venetians embellished them into works of art.

Respecting historical continuity while introducing a contemporary feel, architect Michael Carpetian's highly acclaimed renovation of the 16th century Palazzo Zen.

Once a brewery on the island of Giudecca, the Hans Wagner loft, another of Michael Carpetian's projects, successfully combines today's designs with a turn of the century setting.

The imposing Church of San Rocco, built by Bartolomeo Bon from 1489-1508 but considerably altered by Giovanni Scalfarotto in 1725.

The exuberant Scalzi Church, named after the order of Carmelitani Scalzi ('barefoot Carmelites'). The façade is by Giuseppe Sardi.

A shrine near Santa Maria del Giglio traghetto.

Inside the Frari looking towards Titian's gigantic masterpiece, *Assumption of the Virgin*.

The mosaic floor of the church of Il Redentore, designed by Antonio Palladio and built from 1577 to 1592. The bronze sculpture of the crucifixion is by F. Terilli, 1610.

The circular nave of the church of Santa Maria della Salute, considered to be the greatest baroque edifice outside of Rome. Built in 1631 to commemorate the end of the plague in 1630 and designed by Venetian Baldassare Longhena.

Countess Servane Dufau de la Border on the way to her wedding to Venetian entrepreneur, Sig. Giovanni Giol.

Detail from *Miracle of the Relic of the True Cross* by Gentile Bellini (1429-1507), elder of the two great Bellini brothers whose paintings can be found in the Accademia and in the Museo Correr.

The ubiquitous mobile phone, in the *palazzi* ...

A private bridge behind the Guggenheim Museum in Dorsoduro, with the windows of Ca'Dario in the background.

No matter how much you have seen in Venice, there is always one more tour ... and one more tour-seller.

Painting of an urn near Taverna La Fenice.

CHAPTER TWO

If ever music was the food of love it is so, and always was, in Venice. Detail from *Il Concertino*, a concert at the Palazzo Goldoni, by Pietro Longhi (1702-1785).

The bicentenary of Venice's most prolific playwright, Carlo Goldini, makes a wonderful excuse for an outdoor concert.

The great Spanish guitarist, Andres Segovia, playing on stage at the old Teatro Malibran.

The great warehouses of the Arsenale take on a new role every two years when they become art galleries for the Biennale art festival.

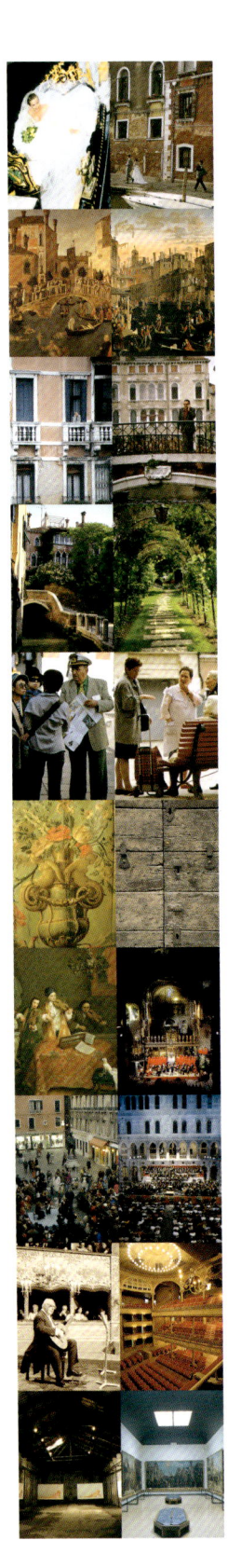

Weddings and Venice are made for each other.

Vittore Carpaccio (1465-1525) was another great painter of religious subjects and his *Miracle of the Relic of the Holy Cross* can be seen at the Accademia.

...and on the *ponti* of Venice.

In the gardens of the Hotel Cipriani looking towards the vineyards of Casanova which now produce an exclusive 'Casanova' vintage for hotel guests.

The gossipy, friendly neighbourhood of Campo Santa Margherita.

A doorway near Campo San Pantalon.

In modern times a concert of old Venetian music still thrills the senses in the Basilica of San Marco.

Napoleon's 'great drawing room of Europe', Piazza San Marco is an ideal venue for a concert under the stars.

The newly restored Malibran theatre, opened in 2001.

The Accademia, calm, serene and designed by Carlo Scarpa. This room, XXI, features Carpaccio's *St Ursula* sequence.

282

'The Drunkenness of Noah', near the Ducal Palace, probably dates from around the late 14th century.

Venice in the snow has its own magic, especially for school children determined to make their own snowman...

The detail on a Venetian gondola is as lovingly crafted today as it ever was.

Tired and a little past their prime, these carved lions were brought to Venice as trophies and placed at the Gate of the Arsenale, after the triumphant victories of Admiral, later Doge, Francesco Morosini in the Peleponnese in 1682...

CHAPTER THREE
The discreet charm of Lady Isabella Hervey at Ca'Pesaro Papafava wearing a gown designed by Godi Fiorenza.

A modern jewellery shop to discover and enjoy is Gualti on Rio terà near Campo Santa Margherita.

Venice past meets Venice present and the two go together very well indeed. Innovative Murano glass on display.

They should be the softest suede shoes you ever wore, except that they are carved in wood by sculptor, Loris Marazzi in Campo Santa Margherita.

Pietro Longhi's *The Apothecary's Shop* which can be seen at the Accademia.

That most Venetian craft, the gondola, is still made from 280 different woods in a shipyard on the island of Giudecca.

The famous 'Four Porphry Tetrarchs', Treasury of San Marco.

...Who did they use as their snowman model? Surely not Woody Allen, in town to make his film, *Everyone Says I Love You* with Julia Roberts.

Fortuny found much to inspire his unique fabric designs in Venice, including perhaps the tracery on a gondola.

...They once guarded the harbour at Piraeus.

Venice was famous for its prostitutes or *donne del buon tempo* (good time girls) as they were sometimes known. Visitors commented on their professionalism. Carpaccio captured their mood and demeanour perfectly in *The Courtesans*, which can be seen in Museo Correr.

Malo, for label shopping at its best.

These you can actually wear. 'The cobbler of Venice' Rolando Segalin has been making shoes in his tiny shop in calle dei Fuseri for over 50 years.

Mirrors, frames, gilding, carving, all to be found in shops like Cornici Trevisanello in Dorsoduro.

Detail of a gondola's *forcola*, or 'fork', where the gondolier places his pole.

283

Making marbled paper by hand in the old tried and true Venetian way, in the shop with no name near the Fenice Theatre, overlooking Campo San Fantin.

That beautiful marbling effect in close-up.

Delicate, exotic, mysterious, enigmatic, the masks of Venice can disguise or embellish...

... Some of the best are made by Franco at Bottega dei Sogni in Calle Fiubera, San Marco.

Bolts of Fortuny fabric at Trois in Campo San Maurizio.

The finest hand-beading is part of the service at Godi Fiorenza.

CHAPTER FOUR

Gulls with an eastern slant to their eyes perch on fishermen's canes as dusk settles over the lagoon.

Silvery, slippery, shiny, sleek, the freshest fish are to be found in the Rialto market.

Fruit delivery comes by boat in this part of the world.

The greengrocer and his wares at Rialto market.

Clockwise from top left: radicchio; borlotti beans; radicchio di Treviso; beefsteak tomatoes.

Venice's favourite floating market, on the canal near Campo San Barnaba.

Do Mori, one of the oldest and most picturesque *bacari* in the Rialto market. Sip an *ombra* and become a local.

Breakfast is fresh produce from the market.

Artichokes are in season, peeled of course.

A busy waiter at Il Nuovo Galeon in far away Via Garibaldi, where the fish is as fresh as if the market was next door.

A most important person in Venice, the pastry cook.

Chef Ivano Frezza at Le Bistrot de Venise.

Rivetta, a genuine local *bacaro*, away from the usual tourist haunts in Calle Sechera, Santa Croce.

Anice Stellato in Fondamenta della Sensa, Cannaregio, an out of the way bistro/bar. Great for an *ombra* or *cicheti* or a full course meal.

284

Views of the Hotel Cipriani...

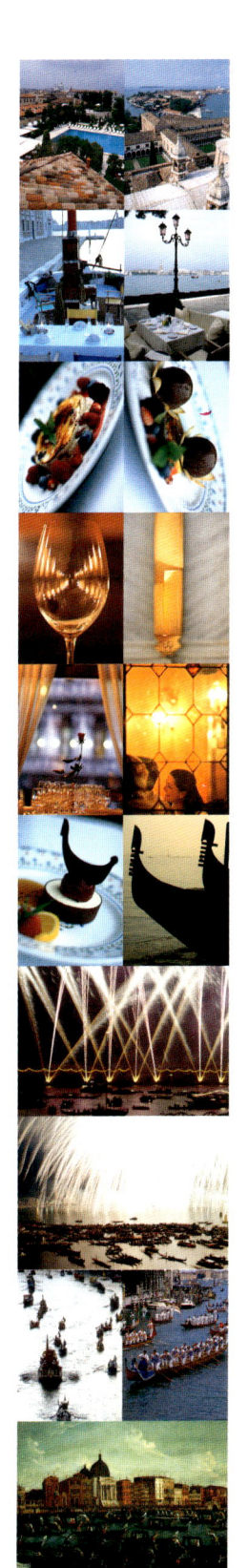

... and the island of Giudecca.

On board the Eolo, Venice's most stylish floating restaurant.

One of the best views in Venice, looking out from Cip's Restaurant on Giudecca.

Sweet concoctions from the dessert chef of the Hotel Cipriani.

Sip wine in glamorous surroundings in one of the best restaurants in Venice, Da Fiore.

Classic elegance at the Hotel Monaco restaurant.

Sumptuous luxury at Caffè Quadri in Piazza San Marco.

A glimpse through the distinctive windows of the Taverna La Fenice.

Nowhere but at the Hotel Cipriani is a dessert so distinctly Venetian.

Classic gondola silhouettes.

CHAPTER FIVE

Fireworks fill the Venetian skies for the Festa della Redentore, the oldest, continuously celebrated festival in Venice which takes place on the third Sunday of July.

Hundreds of gondola and richly decorated boats fill the waters of the lagoon to witness the breathtaking displays.

The immensely popular Regata Storica, featuring magnificent craft and a water procession of ornate boats rowed by locals in 16th century costume. The procession is for the visitors...

... the races that follow are for the locals.

Noble Race from San Stae to the Croce, by Gabriel Bella (c. 18th century) who was famous for painting festivals, events and public holidays. He painted 67 in all.

Richly decorated sleeves of 18th century *Carnevale* costumes.

The *'bauta'* mask, one of the least favourites today, but one that was worn by everyone in the 17th and 18th century.

A clown at the window, waiting for a partner, or maybe for enough courage to parade through the streets of Venice.

Gabriel Bella's *Bull and Wheelbarrow Races at the Rialto*, 18th century.

Gabriel Bella, *New Fair of the Sensa–San Marco*.

CHAPTER SIX

It may appear as just a long, dark back street that runs alongside an inky, silent canal, but this is Fondamenta Misericordia, a world of bars and bistros open until the early hours.

The Grand Canal: dark, silky, ...

Campo Santa Margherita, a haunt for the hungry where the pizzerias stay open longer.

Tony Green at Le Bistrot de Venise, a traditional venue for music, poetry and readings.

The Atelier Pietro Longhi, near the Frari in San Polo, outfit novice *Carnevale* revellers and artistes from the Comedia del' arte.

Detail from *Il Ridotto* by Pietro Longhi.

Revellers or locals dressed to thrill on the Riva degli Schiavoni. They could be either, or both, during *Carnevale*.

A procession of Roman Catholic priests and acolytes in full vestments cross the temporary pontoon bridge across the Giudecca Canal for the opening of the Festa della Redentore.

Calle dei Morti, appropriately dead quiet at this time of night.

... and always filled with shimmering reflections.

One of the newest restaurants in town, Il Sole sulla Vecia Cavana.

Music at the Caffe Città di Torino, Campo San Luca.

Glasses rarely stay empty at Do Forni restaurant.

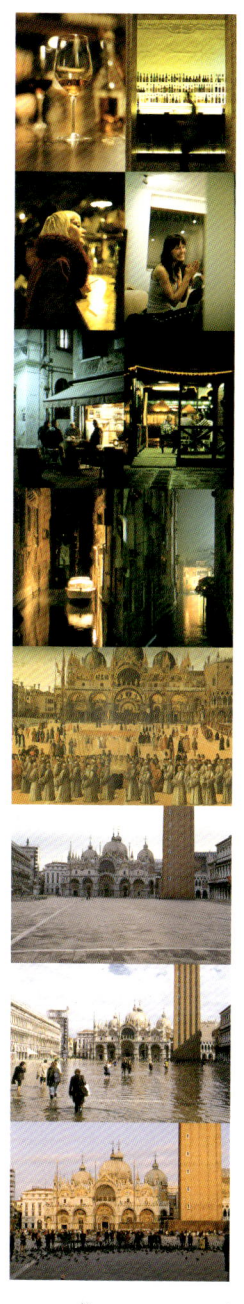

Casual elegance at the Monaco Bar.

An evening at Paradiso Perduto, where the wine, the *cicheti* and the music can continue until the small hours.

Imagina, the first photography gallery in Venice with a coffee shop attached, Rio Terà Nova near Campo Santa Margherita.

Popular with locals and visitors alike, La Cantina Strada Nova.

Gondoliers keeping up their strength opposite the Scalzi Church.

Calle del Spezier near Campo Santo Stefano.

Looking across the Grand Canal from Strada Nova.

CHAPTER SEVEN

One of the great panoramic paintings of Gentile Bellini, the elder of the Bellini brothers, *Procession In The Piazza San Marco* (1496) which can be seen in the Accademia.

As early as the 15th century locals complained of 'too many tourists' in Piazza San Marco. They should have come at dawn, when, 600 years later, barely a pigeon smudges the tranquil scene.

Nowhere does Aqua Alta make such an impact as in Piazza San Marco, designed to stand triumphantly, ruling the waves. Except, of course, at 'high water'.

There is no light, no season, no weather, no moment when the Piazza San Marco is ordinary. But when the setting sun catches the mosaics in the façade and sets them aglow, the Basilica di San Marco is breathtaking.

What's missing? The most famous *campanile* in Venice, San Marco, when, on a summer's morning, July 17th in 1902, it collapsed in a heap of rubble. By 1912 it was triumphantly rebuilt and, in another of those moments of perfect timing, made the inauguration on 25 April 1912 precisely 1,000 years after its original foundation.

Suddenly looking more eastern and Russian than ever, the Basilica under a mantle of snow.

287

ACKNOWLEDGEMENTS

AUTHOR'S ACKNOWLEDGEMENTS
Many thanks to Keith Kyle, John Julius Norwich, Gudrun Kosmos, Servane Giol, Manuela Rampada, Deborah King, Patrizia and Samanta Fiorenza, Filippo Gaggia and Michael Carpetian.

PUBLISHERS' ACKNOWLEDGEMENTS
The publishers would like to thank all contributors to this title on "the most photographed city in the world", not only for their published material but for all their background efforts in trying to capture the elusive qualities of Venice on paper: as many will agree, before and after them, an almost impossible task.

PHOTOGRAPHIC CREDITS: ABBREVIATIONS
AKG   Archiv fur Kunst und Geschichte, Berlin and London
MA   Mark Andreani, London, www.markandreani.com
GA   Graziano Arici, Venice
FTB   Studio Bohm, Venice
MJ   Michael Jenner, London
JP   Jonathan Perugia, London, achildseye@yahoo.com
SQ   Sarah Quill/Venice Picture Library/Bridgeman Art Library, London
DR   Daniele Resini, Venice

FRONTMATTER
Endpapers, pages 2-3, 12-13: © SQ
1: © Image Bank/Grant V. Faint
6-7: DR/© FTB
8-9: © Corbis/Jonathan Blair

INTRODUCTION
22, 23, 24, 26, 27, 29, 30, 32, 33, 34, 35, 37, 40, 41: © SQ
25: Accademia, Venice/DR/© FTB
28: DR/© FTB
31, 36: MA
38: © Tessa Traeger, London
39: © AKG/Erich Lessing

CHAPTER ONE
54-55, 56, 57, 60 (all), 61, 62, 64, 68, 69, 80, 81: © SQ
58, 70, 71, 75, 78, 79, 82, 83, 84, 85: MA
59: Godi Fiorenza/Tim Griffiths
63, 76, 77: Accademia, Venice/DR/© FTB
65: © Interior Archive /Nicolas Bruant
66, 67: JP
72, 73: © AKG/Erich Lessing
74: Sandra Harris

CHAPTER TWO
98, 105: Accademia,Venice/DR/© FTB
99, 100, 101, 102, 103, 109: DR/© GA
104, 110: MA
106, 107,111, 112, 113: © SQ
108: © DR

CHAPTER THREE
128: Godi Fiorenza/Tim Griffiths
129: Museo Correr, Venice/DR/© FTB
130, 131, 134, 135, 140, 141, 142, 143, 144, 145: JP
132-133: © Interior Archive/Fritz von der Schulenburg
136: Accademia, Venice/DR/© FTB
137, 139: © DR
138: MA

CHAPTER FOUR
158, 159, 165, 166, 167, 169, 176, 177, 182, 183: MA
160, 162 (all): © SQ
161, 172, 173, 175: © MJ
163, 164, 168, 170, 171: © DR
174: © Gilles de Chabaneix
178, 179, 180, 181: JP

CHAPTER FIVE
196-197: DR/© GA
198-199: © Katz/Simeone/Figaro
200: © DR
201: © SQ
202-203, 210-211, 214-215: © Biblioteca Querini Stampalia, Venice/Scala, Florence
204, 205: JP
206: © Luciano Testi, Modena
207: Fondazione Scientifica Querini Stampalia, Venice/DR/© FTB
208: © Corbis/Yann Arthus-Bertrand
209: © Corbis/Marco Cristofori
212-213: © Corbis/Ted Spiegel

CHAPTER SIX
228, 229, 230, 231, 232, 233, 236, 237, 238, 239, 240, 242, 243: JP
234, 235, 241: MA

CHAPTER SEVEN
254-255: Accademia Venice/DR/© FTB
256-257, 258-259, 260-261: © SQ
262-263: DR/© GA
264-265: © DR

COVER
Front cover: © SQ

For more information on Orient-Express services, visit www.orient-express.com

First published in Great Britain in 2003 by
PAVILION BOOKS LTD
An imprint of Chrysalis Books Group plc

The Chrysalis Building
Bramley Road
London W10 6SP
www.chrysalisbooks.co.uk

ISBN 1 86205 502 5

Design/layout © Pavilion Books, 2003
Text © Pavilion Books, 2003
Photographs © Pavilion Books, 2003, except where credited otherwise

All rights reserved. No part of this publication may be reproduced, stored in a retrieval system, or transmitted in any form or by any means, electronic, mechanical, photocopying, recording, or otherwise, without the prior written permission of the copyright owner.

Series concept: Sandra Harris
Designer: Stafford Cliff
Editor: Emily Preece-Morrison
Commissioned photographers:
Mark Andreani and Jonathan Perugia
Picture research: Jenny de Gex
Production artwork: Ian Hammond
Publisher: Vivien James

Printed by: Leefung-Asco Printers Holdings Ltd., China